World Economic Development

Bassim Hamadeh, CEO and Publisher
Carrie Montoya, Manager, Revisions and Author Care
Kaela Martin, Project Editor, Revisions
Jeanine Rees, Production Editor
Jess Estrella, Senior Graphic Designer
Alexa Lucido, Licensing Supervisor
Eric Butow, Interior Designer
Natalie Piccotti, Director of Marketing
Kassie Graves, Vice President of Editorial
Jamie Giganti, Director of Academic Publishing

Printed in the United States of America.

ISBN: 978-1-5165-4610-7 (pbk) / 978-1-5165-4611-4 (br) / 978-1-5165-4612-1 (sb)

cognella® | ACADEMIC PUBLISHING

World Economic Development

Second Edition

Edited by Molly Malloy Cooper

cognella® | ACADEMIC PUBLISHING

Contents

Preface

The admittedly ambitious goal of this text is to explore economic development around the world since the beginning of time. The reading in the first section provides an overview in examining "Why Isn't the Whole World Developed?" In this paper, Richard Easterlin provides a review of the economic history literature that points to institutional evolutions such as private property rights and other mechanisms for increasing economic incentives, mass education, and secularization as being critical for economic development and to explain the remaining disparities. The second section explores the formation of civilization, which was a consequence of settled agriculture, referred to as the "Neolithic Revolution," a term coined by archeologist V. Gordon Childe. Economist and Nobel Laureate Douglass North refers to this development as the "First Economic Revolution" because the conversion from nomadic hunter gatherer tribes to more complex agrarian civilizations required fundamental institutional change as well as technological advancement.

Topic Three explores economic development in the Greek and Roman Empires. At one time, the conventional wisdom was that an abundance of slave labor explained the relative lack of technologic innovation during an era that added so much to the stock of general knowledge. The chapter by Helmuth Schnider, entitled "Technology" in *The Cambridge Economic History of the Greco-Roman World*, demonstrates that there were many technological improvements indeed. This section concludes with a discussion of the conditions at the conclusion of the Roman Empire that led to the emergence of the manorial system in Western Europe. An economic reason for the rise and fall of the manorial system throughout Europe is provided in Topic Four.

Topic Five looks at the premodern era, the centuries between the devolution of the manorial system in Europe and the First Industrial Revolution in Britain. The first reading examines the rise of trade, including overseas exploration by Europeans, and the associated increasing complexity of economic transactions. In the second reading, Andre Frank looks at the reasons for the decline of Asia and subsequent rise of Europe.

The First Industrial Revolution is the topic of the next section. The readings describe the important innovations in the textile, metalworking, ceramics, and food processing industries. This section provides an analysis of the positive and negative consequences of industrialization as well as an examination of why the industrialization first took place in Britain and in the nineteenth century. Topic Seven looks at the transportation revolution, the free trade era, and further technological changes and economic development spurred throughout the world in the century after the First Industrial Revolution during the Transition Period and the Second Industrial Revolution.

Finally, the readings in Topic Eight analyze the 1929 stock market crash and the Great Depression. The first reading looks at the role of fundamentals in the boom market and analyzes why a bubble likely occurred. The second reading on the Great Depression compares the US experience with that of the rest of the world.

Topic One

Overview of Difference in Economic Development

CHAPTER ONE

Why Isn't the Whole World Developed?

Richard A. Easterlin

The worldwide spread of modern economic growth has depended chiefly on the diffusion of a body of knowledge concerning new production techniques. The acquisition and application of this knowledge by different countries has been governed largely by whether their populations have acquired traits and motivations associated with formal schooling. To judge from the historical experience of the world's twenty-five largest nations, the establishment and expansion of formal schooling has depended in large part on political conditions and ideological influences. The limited spread of modern economic growth before World War II has thus been due, at bottom, to important political and ideological differences throughout the world that affected the timing of the establishment and expansion of mass schooling. Since World War II there has been growing uniformity among the nations of the world, modern education systems have been established almost everywhere, and the spread of modern economic growth has noticeably accelerated.

> *With the coming of the modern age formal education assumed a significance far in excess of anything that the world had yet seen. The school, which had been a minor social agency in most of the societies of the past, directly affecting the lives of but a small fraction of the population, expanded horizontally and vertically until it took its place along with the state, the church, the family and property as one of society's most powerful institutions.*
>
> George S. Counts[1]

It is now a full two centuries since the coming of the modern technological age was signalled by James Watt's invention of the single acting steam engine. In this period output per capita and per unit of labor input have risen at long-term rates never before seen in human history—first in northern and western Europe and Northern America, subsequently

1 *Encyclopedia of the Social Sciences* (New York, 1931), vol. V, p. 410.

Richard A. Easterlin, "Why Isn't the Whole World Developed?" *The Journal of Economic History*, vol. 41, no. 1, pp. 1–19.

in Japan, southern and eastern Europe, and parts of Latin America and Oceania.[2] So great is the contrast with prior experience that it has led Simon Kuznets to designate this period as a new epoch in world history, the epoch of modern economic growth.[3] Yet, after two centuries, the great majority of the world's population continues to live in conditions not much different from those at the start of this epoch.

Given the startling contrasts in national experience, an objective look at the history of the past two centuries would not, I think, place in the foreground the questions that now dominate the study of economic history. The current preoccupation of Western scholars with American and European—largely northwestern European—economic history can only seem provincial, for the striking feature about these areas is the fundamental similarity in their experience. Rather, the foremost question of modern economic history, the one that challenges explanation, is why the spread of economic growth has been so limited: why isn't the whole world developed? Beyond this, there is the question of the future: *will* the whole world become developed? If so, how soon? What is the outlook for the "epoch of modern economic growth"?

No one can pretend to know the answers to these questions—but it is worth talking about them, if only to build a case for redirection of research in economic history. Let us begin with the question about the past: why has the spread of economic growth been so limited?

I

> The heart of the whole process of industrialization and economic development is intellectual: it consists in the acquisition and application of a corpus of knowledge concerning technique, that is, ways of doing things.
>
> David Landes[4]

In thinking about the past, let us imagine, to start with, a world not unlike that of the late eighteenth century—a world of low and roughly equal levels of economic productivity everywhere, and with fairly limited international contacts through trade, migration, and investment. Suppose now that in one nation economic productivity starts rising rapidly and steadily, because of an unprecedented rate of technological progress. Before long, a second nation sets off on a similar course as technological change also accelerates dramatically, and, then, a third. After a century or so, the total number of nations so embarked remains—on a worldwide scale—small, though increasing.

---

2 Richard A. Easterlin, "Economic Growth: Overview," *International Encyclopedia of the Social Sciences* (New York, 1969), vol. IV, pp. 395–408.

3 *Modern Economic Growth: Rate, Structure and Spread* (New Haven, 1966), chap. 1.

4 "The Creation of Knowledge and Technique: Today's Task and Yesterday's Experience," *Daedalus*, 109 (Winter 1980), 111.

Consider now a few implications of this development. In the course of time, large and growing disparities would emerge between income levels in those nations enjoying the fruits of rapid technological progress and those that are not. International trade and investment would expand greatly as a result of sharp shifts in comparative advantage caused by differential technological progress, and also because international transfer costs would fall substantially if, as seems likely, those nations benefiting from new technology apply it to problems of international as well as domestic transport. The resulting increased flow of goods and resources internationally would have some beneficial effect on income levels generally, but such effects would be relatively small compared with the dominating effect on income levels of major differences in the rate of technological change.

This, I suggest, is the essence of what has occurred in the past two centuries.[5] During this period international income differences have grown at unprecedented rates, as have foreign trade and investment. The prime mover in this drama has been the sharp acceleration in the rate of technological change in a relatively small number of nations.

If this view is correct, then it follows that explaining why modern economic growth has spread so slowly becomes a question of explaining why rapid technological change has been limited to so few nations. To answer this, one must first consider whether rapid technological change, when it occurred, was based on a new technology in each country that was indigenous or borrowed. On this, the view that a common technology diffused from one country to the next is certainly the more realistic one. This is evidenced by the classic studies of W. O. Henderson and David Landes of the spread of industrial technology in Europe; in the accounts of the modernization of Japan by scholars such as Tuge and Saxonhouse; and in Strassman's studies of contemporary experience.[6] It is evidenced as well by the striking likeness of modern industrial technology among the various high productivity nations themselves. Only in regard to agriculture, where local environmental conditions play an important part in production, might one hesitate to stress the borrowed over indigenous elements in modern technological change. But even in agriculture, one finds that many of the principles of modern technology, such as irrigation, seed selection, livestock breeding,

5 For similar views see Kuznets, *Growth*; Rondo Cameron, "The Diffusion of Technology as a Problem in Economic History," *Economic Geography*, 51 (July 1975), 217–30; William N. Parker, "Economic Development in Historical Perspective," *Economic Development and Cultural Change*, 10 (Oct. 1961), 1–7; William Woodruff, *Impact of Western Man* (New York, 1967); Paul Bairoch, *The Economic Development of the Third World since 1900* (Berkeley and Los Angeles, 1975); John Robert Hanson, *Trade in Transition: Exports from the Third World, 1840–1900* (New York, 1980); William Ashworth, *A Short History of the International Economy, 1850–1950* (London, 1952). A valuable framework for the study of international political development is presented in Stein Rokkan, "Dimensions of State Formation and Nation Building: A Paradigm for Research on Variations within Europe," in Charles Tilly, ed., *The Formation of National States in Western Europe* (Princeton, 1975), pp. 562–600.

6 William O. Henderson, *Britain and Industrial Europe*, 3d ed. (Leicester, 1972); David S. Landes, *The Unbound Prometheus: Technological Change and Industrial Development in Western Europe from 1750 to the Present* (Cambridge, 1969); Hideomi Tuge, ed., *Historical Development of Science and Technology in Japan* (Tokyo, 1961); Gary Saxonhouse, "A Tale of Japanese Technological Diffusion in the Meiji Period," this Journal, 34 (March 1974), 149–65; W. Paul Strassman, *Risk and Technological Innovation* (Ithaca, 1959).

fertilizer, and, more recently, development of hybrids and use of pesticides, exhibit quite similar features among nations. Thus it seems reasonable to conclude that the question of explaining differential technological change among nations in the modern period is a matter chiefly of explaining the limited diffusion of a common technology.

Much of the research on technological diffusion has been admirably synthesized and critiqued by Nathan Rosenberg.[7] One strong impression that emerges from reading this literature is the extent to which the transfer of technology is a person-to-person process. As Rosenberg points out, "the notion of a production function as a 'set of blueprints' comes off very badly … if it is taken to mean a body of techniques which is available *independently* of the human inputs who utilize it."[8] According to Svennilson, "much of the detailed knowledge that is born in the course of industrial operations, can more easily and in part exclusively be transferred by demonstration and training in actual operations."[9] Similarly, to Arrow, "it seems to be personal contact that is most relevant in leading to … adoption [of an innovation]."[10]

This emphasis on the personal element in the transfer of technology suggests that understanding of it might usefully be approached by analogy with a situation in which most of us here have some relevant experience, namely, as an educational process, in which a new and difficult subject—"modern" technology—must be taught and learned. From this point of view, explanation of the limited spread of modern economic growth turns into a question of identifying the factors that have constrained the dissemination of a new type of knowledge—that of modern technology.

II

> Education produces large, pervasive, and enduring effects on knowledge and receptivity to knowledge.
>
> Herbert H. Hyman et al.[11]

---

7 Nathan Rosenberg, "Factors Affecting the Payoff to Technological Innovation," unpublished document prepared for the National Science Foundation (1974). See also David J. Teece, *The Multinational Corporation and the Resource Cost of International Technology Transfer* (Cambridge, MA, 1976).

8 Nathan Rosenberg, "Economic Development and the Transfer of Technology: Some Historical Perspectives," *Technology and Culture*, 11 (Oct. 1970), 555, emphasis added.

9 Ingvar Svennilson, "Technical Assistance: The Transfer of Industrial Know-how to Non-Industrialized Countries," in Kenneth Berill, ed., *Economic Development with Special Reference to East Asia* (New York, 1964), p. 408, emphasis in original.

10 Kenneth J. Arrow, "Classification Notes on the Production and Transmission of Technological Knowledge," *American Economic Review: Papers and Proceedings*, 52 (May 1969), 33; see also Daniel Lloyd Spencer, The *Technological Gap in Perspective* (New York, 1970).

11 Herbert H. Hyman, Charles R. Wright, and John Shelton Reed, *The Enduring Effects of Education* (Chicago, 1975), p. 109.

Viewing the transfer of technology as an educational process leads naturally to questions about teachers and students. If new technological knowledge spread slowly, did the fault lie on the teachers' side or the students'?

One reason for minimizing the teachers' responsibility is that when entrepreneurs or governments in low productivity nations wanted teachers, they seem to have been able to beg, borrow, buy, or steal them, as well as send their nationals to the high productivity nations for instruction. After the Meiji Restoration, for example, Japan imported numerous foreign scholars and technological experts and sent students to the West.[12]

The more important question lies on the side of the students. What is it that makes for effective learning? Learning is, as we all know, partly a matter of inherent intelligence; partly of aptitudes; and partly of incentives. What we all seek are bright, well-trained, and highly motivated students.

I think we can safely dismiss the view that the failure of modern technological knowledge to spread rapidly was due to significant differences among nations in the native intelligence of their populations. To my knowledge there are no studies that definitively establish differences, say, in basic IQ among the peoples of the world.

A more persuasive case might be made with regard to incentives for learning; institutional differences among countries undoubtedly created variations in the incentives for mastering the new technology. In their studies of the historical development of property and other institutions, Jonathan Hughes, Douglass North, Robert Thomas, and others are, in this respect, filling an important gap in knowledge about incentive structures.[13] But it is important to recognize that the new technology itself created incentives for learning via the competitive pressures exerted through international trade. Thus the rapid response by producers in parts of Continental Europe and the United States to the British industrial revolution was partly induced by the growing flood of imported British manufactures in their markets. The new technology also created pressures for its more widespread adoption by endowing its possessors with superior military capability. The threat to political sovereignty thus posed was a strong incentive for governments in low productivity countries to initiate and promote programs of technological modernization, as in Japan. In the course of time such economic and political pressures were felt in many nations throughout the world; yet often the new technology failed to be taken up. The question is, why?

The answer, I suggest, has to do in important part with differences among countries in the extent of their population's formal schooling: the more schooling of appropriate content that a nation's population had, the easier it was to master the new technological knowledge becoming available. Moreover, as I shall note subsequently, substantial increases in formal schooling tend to be accompanied by significant improvement in the incentive

12 Tuge, *Science*; for early data on Japanese students studying abroad, see Reinhold Schairer, *Die Studenten im internationalen Kulturleben: Beitrage zur Frage des Studiums in fremdem Lande* (Munster in Westfalen, 1927), chap. 1. See also Henderson, Europe.

13 Douglass C. North and Robert Paul Thomas, *The Rise of the Western World: A New Economic History* (Cambridge, 1973); Jonathan R. T. Hughes, *Social Control in the Colonial Economy* (Charlottesville, 1976).

structure. Hence increased motivation often accompanied increased aptitudes for learning the new technology.

The notion that learning potential depends on prior education should come as no surprise here, for it is a guiding principle in most schools and colleges. Given intelligence and motivation, one prefers students with better academic records from better schools, and with more training in relevant subjects. If one's concern is to explain why some nations were rapid learners and others slow, it seems only reasonable to ask what sort of differences there were in the educational systems that prepared their populations for acquiring new knowledge.

As a first step toward establishing the facts, Figure 1.1 presents historical data for twenty-five of the largest countries of the world—in 1960 they accounted for over three-fourths of the world's population—on a very crude indicator of educational development, the primary school enrollment rate. These countries, I believe, are reasonably illustrative of experience more generally.[14] The primary school enrollment rate at any date is simply the number enrolled in primary school per 10,000 total population. It is subject to both conceptual and measurement biases, most notably to variations in the proportion of school age population to the total.[15] It can, however, reasonably be taken as an index of differences among nations and trends over time in their population's exposure to formal schooling. Roughly speaking, values less than 400 signify relatively little exposure of a nation's population to formal schooling; values in the 400–800 range, a moderate exposure; and values greater than 800, substantial. To facilitate comparisons among countries in the figure, the section of each graph bracketed by an enrollment rate of zero to 400 in the period through 1940 has been shaded. Differences among countries in peak values and the trend in these values are of little analytical significance because they reflect chiefly variations in the proportion of school age population. For this reason, and to reduce confusion in the figure, a country's curve was not plotted after it reached a fairly high level.[16]

The first impression that emerges from the graph is the very limited extent of formal schooling in most nations throughout most of the period covered in the graph. In 1850, only a little more than a century ago, virtually the entire population of the world outside of

14 The countries chosen were those with 1960 populations greater than 18 million. Because of insufficient historical data, Poland, Pakistan, and Viet Nam are omitted.

15 Among other comparability problems are the occasional use of attendance rather than enrollment data, variations in the time of year for which enrollment is reported, differences in the length of the school day and school year, and differences in schools included in the "primary" category (e.g., kindergartens).

16 For other studies of enrollment rates see UNESCO, *World Survey of Education*, vol. 2 (New York, 1958), pp. 42–60; Alexander L. Peaslee, "Education's Role in Development," *Economic Development and Cultural Change*, 17 (April 1969), 293–318. Although enrollment is used here in preference to literacy because it is a more reliable indicator of the expansion of formal mass schooling, valuable work has been done to develop historical literacy data. See Peter Flora, "Historical Processes of Social Mobilization: Urbanization and Literacy, 1850–1965," in Shmuel N. Eisenstadt and Stein Rokkan, eds., *Building States and Nations*, vol. I (Beverly Hills, 1973), pp. 213–58; Carlo M. Cipolla, *Literacy and Development in the West* (Baltimore, 1969); UNESCO, *Progress of Literacy in Various Countries* (Paris, 1953); UNESCO, *World Illiteracy at Mid-Century* (Paris, 1957); James F. Abel and Norman J. Bond, "Illiteracy in the Several Countries of the World," *Department of the Interior Bureau of Education Bulletin* No. 4 (1929), pp. 1–68.

northwestern Europe and Northern America had little or no exposure to formal schooling. Even by 1940 this was still largely the case in Africa, most of Asia, and a substantial part of Latin America.

Does the graph offer any support for the idea that spread of the technology of modern economic growth depended on learning potentials and motivations that were linked to the development of formal schooling? The answer, I believe, is generally yes. Within Europe the most advanced nations educationally, those in northern and western Europe, were the ones that developed first. Not until the end of the nineteenth century did most of southern and eastern Europe start to approach educational levels comparable to the initial levels in the north and west, and it was around this time that these nations began to develop. With regard to the overseas descendants of Europe the picture is the same: the leader in schooling is the leader in development, the United States. Within Latin America, Argentina, the most developed nation there today, took the lead in educational growth in the last half of the nineteenth century. In Asia, Japan's nineteenth-century educational attainment is clearly distinctive, and this was true even before the Meiji Restoration, though important reforms were introduced in 1872.[17] In contrast, note the persistently low educational levels until very recently in Turkey, a nation subject in many ways to external economic and political pressures similar to those experienced by Japan, but failing until recently to show substantial technological modernization.

There is, of course, the matter of cause and effect: are we looking here at the effect of education on economic growth, or vice-versa? Is the growth of schooling merely induced by the process of economic growth itself? In theory, economic growth is a cause of educational growth, but it is only one factor and not clearly the dominant one. Some empirical evidence suggesting that the growth of formal schooling often occurred largely independently of economic development is offered by Figure 1.1 itself. Note that in the United States and Germany development of widespread formal schooling clearly preceded the onset of modern economic growth. Note, too, that for a number of countries the schooling curves show abrupt upswings that are not matched by concurrent surges in economic development—examples are Rumania between 1880 and 1910; the Philippines between 1900 and 1920; and Mexico and Thailand between 1920 and 1940.

Even if one were to agree that in a general way theory and evidence are consistent with the notion that formal schooling fosters attributes in a population that are conducive to the acquisition of modern technology, there remain important questions about the type of schooling and attributes. Is it true, for example, that "the spread of technological knowledge, narrowly considered, is not a matter of mass education, but of the training of a small

17 Ronald P. Dore, *Education in Tokugawa Japan* (Berkeley and Los Angeles, 1965); Herbert Passin, *Society and Education in Japan* (New York, 1965). A number of writers stress the role of education in Japanese economic growth. See, for example, Kazushi Ohkawa and Henry Rosovsky, "A Century of Japanese Economic Growth," in William W. Lockwood, ed., *The State and Economic Enterprise in Japan* (Princeton, 1965), pp. 58–59, and Yasukichi Yasuba, "Another Look at the Tokugawa Heritage with Special Reference to Social Conditions," unpublished paper, The Center for Southeast Asia Studies, Kyoto University, October 1979.

elite"?[18] If mass education is important, does it have its effect via training in functional skills such as "the three R's," through "screening," or via political socialization, either of a broad sort, or more narrowly, in instilling a discipline appropriate to factory work?[19] Or is the function of education, as some sociological studies suggest, one chiefly of creating a basic change in human personality—a "modern man" who acquires aspirations and attitudes especially favorable to the adoption of new technology?[20] According to these studies even a small amount of formal schooling has an effect of this sort, although the greater the amount of schooling the greater the effect.[21]

The present state of knowledge does not, I think, provide satisfactory answers to what types of education have what specific effects on economic growth, and clearly the answers need not be mutually exclusive. It seems likely, however, that a substantial primary education system is essential for sustained economic growth. The reason for this is clear if one contrasts the process of achieving higher income levels with that of raising life expectancy. Thanks to modern public health and medical technology, it has proven possible to improve life expectancy markedly even among large populations through measures such as use of pesticides, water purification, and establishment of sewage, systems that require knowledge and action by only a relatively few technologists. In contrast, raising productivity levels involves active participation in new production methods by large numbers of the

18 William N. Parker, "Perspective," p. 1. For valuable discussions of some of the issues in this paragraph see C. Arnold Anderson and Mary Jean Bowman, eds., *Education and Economic Development* (Chicago, 1965); C. Arnold Anderson and Mary Jean Bowman, "Education and Economic Modernization in Historical Perspective" and Lawrence Stone, "Introduction," both in Lawrence Stone, ed., *Schooling and Society* (Baltimore, 1976), pp. xi–xvii, 3–19; Mary Jean Bowman and C. Arnold Anderson, "Concerning the Role of Education in Development," and Martin Carnoy, "Education and Economic Development: The First Generation," *Economic Development and Cultural Change: Essays in Honor of Bert F. Hoselitz*, 25 (Supplement, 1977), 428–48; Frederick Harbison and Charles A. Meyers, *Education, Manpower, and Economic Growth* (New York, 1964); Cameron, "Diffusion"; The World Bank, *World Development Report* (Washington, D. C., 1980), chap. 5.

19 James S. Coleman, ed., *Education and Political Development* (Princeton, 1965); Samuel Bowles and Herbert Gintis, *Schooling in Capitalist America* (New York, 1976); Martin Carnoy, *Education as Cultural Imperialism* (New York, 1974); Robert Dreeben, *On What Is Learned in School* (Reading, MA, 1968); Philip Foster, *Education and Social Change in Ghana* (Chicago, 1965); Harvey J. Graff, *The Literacy Myth* (New York, 1979); Michael B. Katz, *Class, Bureaucracy, and Schools* (New York, 1971).

20 Alex Inkeles and David H. Smith, *Becoming Modern* (Cambridge, 1974); Alex Inkeles, "The School as a Context for Modernization," *International Journal of Comparative Sociology*, 14, no. 3–4 (Sept.–Dec. 1973), 163–79; David C. McClelland, "Does Education Accelerate Economic Growth?" *Economic Development and Cultural Change*, 14 (April 1966), 257–78; William Form, "Comparative Industrial Sociology and the Convergence Hypothesis," *Annual Review of Sociology*, 5 (1979), 1–25.

21 Inkeles and Smith, *Becoming Modern*, chap. 9. Formal education is, to be sure, not the only institution to create modern men; some of the new economic institutions accompanying modern economic growth—most notably, the factory—also work in this way. Thus, there is the possibility of growth "by pulling up on one's own bootstraps"—factories once established create personality changes conducive to further economic growth. But the population exposed to factory experience is much more limited than that potentially reached by a formal school system. Moreover, the evidence indicates that the impact of formal schooling in creating the personality traits of "modern man" is much greater than that of any other institution—more than twice as great, for example, as that of the next most important institution, the factory.

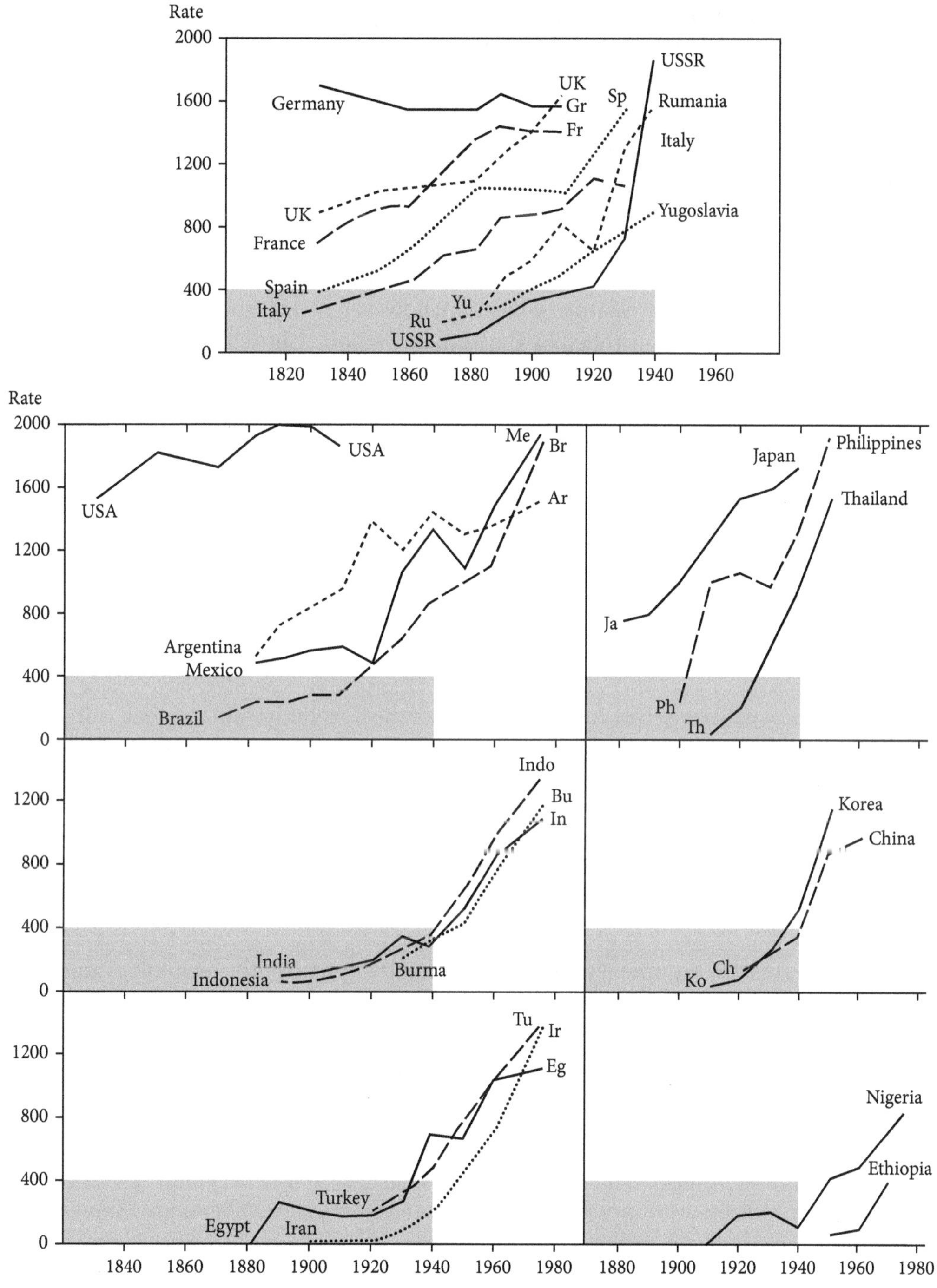

FIGURE 1.1 **Primary School Enrollment Rate, By Country, 1830–1975 (per 10,000 population)**

Source: Appendix Table 1.1.

population—by workers in agriculture, industry, transportation, and so on. This is not to say that secondary and higher education can be ignored; clearly one needs technologists as well as mass education. But increases at higher levels of education typically go together with the expansion of primary education.[22] On the other hand, education of the elite without mass education is unlikely to foster economic growth.[23]

It also seems that the content of education conducive to economic growth is that of a secular and rationalistic type. While such content has usually characterized an expansion in mass education, this has not always been true. Among the countries in Figure 1.1, Spain stands out as a country whose rate of educational development seemingly exceeded its economic growth. A closer look at Spanish education, however, reveals that until the twentieth century it remained closely controlled by the Roman Catholic Church: "the children of the masses received only oral instruction in the Creed, the catechism, and a few simple manual skills. … [S]cience, mathematics, political economy, and secular history were considered too controversial for anyone but trained theologians."[24] One consequence of this is that literacy in Spain fails to show an increase commensurate with what one might expect from the data on primary school enrollment; even by 1900 almost two thirds of the population remained illiterate.

III

> It is necessary that we enter into a new phase of the Revolution which I shall call the psychological revolutionary period; we must enter into and take possession of the minds of children, the consciences of the young, because they do belong and should belong to the Revolution. … It is absolutely necessary to drive the enemy out of that entrenchment where the clergy has been, where the Conservatives have been—I refer to Education.
>
> Mexican General and ex-President Plutarco Calles, 1934[25]

In simplest terms, the argument to this point is that the spread of the technology underlying modern economic growth depended in large part on the extent to which the populations in different countries had acquired appropriate traits and motivation through formal schooling. But even if the plausibility of this view be tentatively granted, it only leads to

22 For example, for 90 countries in the period 1970–74, the adjusted R^2 between primary and secondary enrollment rates is .51; between primary and higher, .41. Data are from UNESCO, *Statistical Yearbook, 1976* (Paris, 1977).

23 In the nineteenth century, educational modernization in the Ottoman Empire, to the extent it occurred, stressed education of the elite; see Andreas M. Kazamias, *Education and the Quest for Modernity in Turkey* (Chicago, 1966). The 1950s data for India presented by Harbison and Meyers suggest a disproportion of secondary and higher education relative to primary *(Manpower,* p. 47).

24 I. N. Thut and Don Adams, *Educational Patterns in Contemporary Societies* (New York, 1964), p. 62.

25 As quoted in J. Lloyd Mecham, *Church and State in Latin America* (Durham, NC, 1934), p. 406.

a more fundamental question: how can one explain the immense differences among the countries of the world in the timing and growth of formal education?

If, to answer this question, one follows the approach of the new economic history, then the appropriate guidelines are those currently offered by economic theory. This theory centers on decision-making in one social institution, the family, and sees the expansion of schooling as a voluntary response to growing payoffs to education generated by economic growth. Government, if it comes into the picture at all, is seen largely as implementing or ratifying private household decisions through public action.

There can be no question that serious research on economic incentives should form a part of research into the causes of expansion of mass education.[26] But the seemingly sizable payoffs to child labor that prevailed in many developed countries in certain phases of their modern economic history should caution against expecting too much from it. Research is needed also on motives and decisions affecting education by social institutions other than those relating to the family. Education is, as we are all aware, a powerful instrument for influencing the minds of individuals in their formative years; indeed, if we did not believe this, I doubt that most of us would be doing as professionals what we are now doing. This elementary fact has hardly escaped the attention of those in society interested in obtaining or maintaining political, social, and economic power.[27] The result has been that the establishment and growth of mass education has often been the product chiefly not of market forces but of political conflict in which major groups in a culture—groups that frequently vary from one society to the next—are ranged against each other. At the risk of oversimplification, let me try to illustrate this point in terms of Figure 1.1.

The most obvious shift in political power with which growth of mass education has been linked is the establishment of independence from a former colonial power. This is suggested by the histories of a number of countries in southeastern Europe in the period prior to World War I (exemplified in Figure 1.1 by Rumania and Yugoslavia), in the mid-East in the 1920s and 30s (as illustrated by Egypt), and in Asia and Africa after World War II (see India, Indonesia, Burma, and Nigeria).[28] This observation implies that colonialism was a major deterrent to the growth of mass education, and thus lends support to the "imperialism" explanation for underdevelopment. Detailed empirical studies of colonial policy such as that currently in progress for the United Kingdom by Lance E. Davis and Robert Huttenback are needed to pursue this issue.[29] But the data in Figure 1.1 suggest reasons against a too hasty generalization of this sort. First, there are cases—though not

26 See, for example, David Mitch, "The Impact of a Growing Demand of Literate Workers on the Spread of Literacy in Nineteenth Century England," presented at the Workshop in Economic History, University of Chicago, no. 7980-2 (Oct. 1979).

27 This has been explicitly recognized in recent economic history research. See, e.g., Alexander James Field, "Economic and Demographic Determinants of Educational Commitment: Massachusetts, 1855," this Journal, 39 (June 1979), 439–57.

28 Flora notes the close association in a number of countries between the date of independence and the date when compulsory education was established. See Flora, "Mobilization," pp. 230–37.

29 Lance E. Davis and Robert A. Huttenback, "Public Expenditures and Private Profit: Budgetary Decisions in the British Empire, 1860–1912," *American Economic Review,* 67 (Feb. 1977), 282–88.

many—where colonial governments promoted mass education. The clearest illustration is the American takeover of the Philippines from Spain; perhaps another example is Japanese policy in Korea.[30] Second, in Latin America decolonization in the nineteenth century was not followed by a great upsurge in mass education; hence colonialism cannot be the scapegoat there. Third, there is the counterfactual issue: in the absence of colonial rule would mass education have been promoted vigorously by independent governments? It is noteworthy that the historical record for Iran and Turkey in Figure 1.1 does not differ clearly from that for Egypt; and that the same is true of the record for China compared with India, and of Ethopia vis-à-vis Nigeria. Even a casual glance at historical experience makes clear the need to consider other factors that have impeded mass education besides colonialism.

One factor that comes quickly to mind is absolute monarchy. The independent countries I have just mentioned—Turkey, Iran, China, and Ethiopia—were all absolute monarchies, and in none of these did a substantial trend toward mass education set in until after autocratic rule was terminated. To judge from Figure 1.1 the same is true of Russia and Thailand. Absolute monarchs seem usually to have regarded mass education as potentially subversive of their power; in contrast, communist governments have vigorously promoted mass education as an instrument of political socialization.[31]

Another deterrent to mass education appears to have been a situation in which the Roman Catholic Church exercised substantial secular power. This has already been touched on in the case of Spain; in Latin America, it is perhaps the dominant factor. The rapid rise in mass education in Argentina after 1880 and in Mexico after 1920 both occurred in conjunction with a substantial shift in power from church to state.[32] In the Middle East, Islam frequently appears to have been a negative influence in the development of formal schooling.[33]

For the countries where mass education was already fairly well established by the early nineteenth century—represented in Figure 1.1 by Germany, England, France, and the United States—sufficient data are not available for analyzing the historical patterns of growth. One can ask, however, what set these countries apart from the rest of the world so early and contributed to their relatively high levels of schooling? Three influences stand out in the literature—Protestantism, humanism, and central government efforts at national integration. One of the main tenets of early Protestant thought, as shaped by leaders like Calvin and

30 Carl H. Landé, "The Philippines," in James S. Coleman, ed., *Political Development*, pp. 313–52; Shinkichi Etō, "Asianism and the Duality of Japanese Colonialism, 1879-1945," in L. Blussé, H. L. Wesseling, and G. D. Winius, eds., *History and Underdevelopment* (Paris, 1980); Andrew J. Grajdanzev, *Modern Korea* (New York, 1944).

31 On Russia and the USSR, see Nicholas Hans, *History of Russian Educational Policy, 1701-1917* (New York, 1964), p. 65, and Jeremy R. Azrael, "Soviet Union," in Coleman, ed., *Political Development*, pp. 233–71.

32 Mecham, *Church*, pp. 245–47, 376–77, 388–93. In Brazil, however, the church does not seem to have played as critical a role in the growth of mass education; there a shift in political control from conservatives to liberals appears to have been more important. See E. Bradford Burns, *A History of Brazil* (New York, 1970), pp. 290, 302–03.

33 On Turkey, see Kazamias, *Turkey*, pp. 73–74; Iran, Hafez Farman Farmayan, "The Forces of Modernization in Nineteenth Century Iran: A Historical Survey," in William R. Polk and Richard L. Chambers, eds., *Beginnings of Modernization in the Middle East* (Chicago, 1968), p. 123. In Egypt, Islam seems to have been less of an obstacle to educational change; see P. J. Vatikiotis, *The Modern History of Egypt* (New York, 1969), pp. 69–70.

Luther, was that "the eternal welfare of every individual depends upon the application of his own reason to the revelation contained in the Scriptures"; in practice, this led to advocacy of formal schooling in the vernacular language so that each individual would have personal access to the Bible.[34] Humanism, which reached fullest expression with the philosophers of the eighteenth-century Enlightenment, preached the ultimate perfectibility of humanity and thus also fostered a view favorable to mass education.[35] Finally, some governments saw in mass education a means of securing allegiance to the central government at the expense of local authorities or the church.

The weight of these influences differed from country to country and not all operated in each. The role of Protestantism was strongest in Germany and the United States, weaker in England where the established Protestant religion was an Anglican version of Roman Catholicism and the vigorous proponents of education were the non-conformists; and weakest of all in France, which was predominantly Roman Catholic, although the separation of church and state was achieved fairly early. Humanism was strongest in France[36] and the United States, perhaps somewhat less so in England, and least influential in Germany. Nationalism and national integration was a potent force in Germany and perhaps France, but largely absent in England and the United States. Occasionally England's laissez-faire philosophy is used to explain its lag in educational growth relative to other countries in northwestern Europe such as Germany, but the United States, which also lacked a national education policy, clearly calls this view into question. The factor that sets the English off most clearly from both Germany and the United States is the differential nature of Protestantism—the much larger representation in the latter countries of what in England would be called non-conformist religions, religions in the tradition of Calvin and Luther.[37]

Earlier, in touching on the question of incentives for learning, I suggested that the expansion of formal schooling often signalled a positive shift in the incentive structure. The reasoning underlying this should now be clear. A major commitment to mass education is frequently symptomatic of a major shift in political power and associated ideology in a direction conducive to greater upward mobility for a wider segment of the population.

34 Paul Monroe, *A Text-Book in the History of Education* (London, 1907), p. 407. Japan seems to have had its own version of the "Protestant ethic"; see Robert N. Bellah, *Tokugawa Religion* (New York, 1957).

35 Carl L. Becker, *The Heavenly City of the Eighteenth-Century Philosophers* (New Haven, 1932).

36 Cf. Thut and Adams, *Educational Patterns*, p. 113: "In the end, Frenchmen committed themselves to the ideas derived from humanism, rather than from Roman Catholic or Protestant theologies, a development which had profound educational consequences."

37 The leading role of non-conformists in the British industrial revolution is emphasized in Everett E. Hagen, *On the Theory of Social Change* (Homewood, Ill., 1962), chap. 13. Valuable discussions of early American education growth are Lawrence A. Cremin, *American Education: The Colonial Experience, 1607–1783* (New York, 1970); Bernard Bailyn, *Education in the Forming of American Society* (New York, 1960); Albert Fishlow, "The American Common School Revival: Fact or Fancy?" in Henry Rosovsky, ed., *Industrialization in Two Systems: Essays in Honor of Alexander Gerschenkron* (New York, 1966). On England, see Marius B. Jansen and Lawrence Stone, "Education and Modernization in Japan and England," *Comparative Studies in Society and History*, 9 (Jan. 1967), 208–32; Stanley J. Curtis and M.E.A. Boultwood, *An Introductory History of English Education since 1800* (London, 1977); Roger S. Schofield, "Dimensions of Illiteracy, 1750–1850," *Explorations in Economic History*, 10 (Summer 1973), 437–54; E. G. West, "Literacy and the Industrial Revolution," *Economic History Review*, 2nd ser., 24 (Aug. 1978), 369–83.

This is not to imply that it signals complete democratization of opportunity, but it often represents a sizable break with conditions of the past. From this point of view the absence of mass education systems for so long in so many countries of the world is indicative of a double impediment to the spread of the technology underlying modern economic growth: limited incentives as well as limited aptitudes in the population generally.

Major advances in mass education are thus likely to signal sizable changes both in incentive structures and aptitudes favorable to modern economic growth. At the same time they are symptomatic of powerful new political and ideological forces at work in the cultures of the various countries. The educational system is therefore a key link between modern economic growth, on the one hand, and a society's culture, on the other; study of the evolution of mass education provides an important clue as to when the net balance of the principal cultural forces in a society shifts in a direction favorable to economic growth.

Some may object that the study of educational systems and the forces that shape them leads away from the traditional concerns of *economic* history.[38] To this, one may reply that if this is what the problem demands, then traditional orientations have to go. In a broader sense, however, it can be argued that such study is, in fact, a return to traditional economic history, to economic history in the spirit of scholars like Marx, Sombart, Weber, and Tawney.

IV

> The intention of the government is within the shortest possible time to uplift the social conditions of the [Sakuddei], But of course without shocks, this you can know for sure, without shocks, and bit by bit bringing them into contact with the general development of the Indonesian society. We want to bring them up in the state that they can understand us you know. … that what is health for, [*sic*] what hygiene for, what is a school for … just the elementary conditions that I think is standard for every normal society in this modern world.
>
> Harun Zain, Governor of West Sumatra"[39]

> Peking Paper Says Getting Rich Is Now an Accepted Socialist Goal.
>
> *International Herald Tribune,* Jan. 2, 1980, p. 3

38 Note, however, the numerous references above to recent economic history research on education. Gallman's recent presidential address also argues for a merger of the new social and economic history; Davis's, of the new political and economic history; see Robert E. Gallman, "Some Notes on the New Social History," this JOURNAL, 37 (March 1977), 3–12; and Lance E. Davis, "It's a Long, Long Road to Tipperary, or Reflections on Organized Violence, Protection Rates, and Related Topics: The New Political History," this JOURNAL, 40 (March 1980), 1–16.

39 From *The Sakuddei* television program as it appeared in the Odyssey series, produced and copyrighted by Public Broadcasting Associates, Inc., 1980. The original *Sakuddei* program was produced and copyrighted by Granada Television. The Sakuddei is a tribal clan living on an island off the west coast of Sumatra.

So far I have speculated about the spread of modern economic growth in the past. But what of the future? Will modern economic growth and its underlying technology continue to spread? Will the majority of the world's population in Asia, Africa, and Latin America be joining before long the minority? The answer suggested by my reasoning and by contemporary experience is yes. Since World War II growth of mass education has become a widespread phenomenon in the Third World, as is demonstrated by Figure 1.1. And in this period rates of economic growth have surged sharply upward in many Third World countries.[40] The diffusion of modern economic growth throughout the remainder of the world is already well under way. My guess is that once the developing countries have completed their demographic transitions—in many cases, probably by the end of this century—their long-term per capita growth rates will be at least as high as those that the developed countries have so far experienced, and that another century, in addition to the two so far experienced, will largely complete the transition to modern economic technology and organization throughout the world, though sizable international income differences may persist. This reasoning assumes, of course, that the international political structure will be able to withstand the new strains caused by the shifts in political power arising from the further spread of economic development.

If this comes to pass, what will the world be like when the triumph of this new epoch of economic history is complete? Will "the economic problem" have been put to rest and humanity turn to more important pursuits, as John Stuart Mill once contemplated? Will humanity have made the great leap into freedom that Marx envisaged?

To answer this requires, at a minimum, a projection of both human wants and economic technology. Will material wants continue to grow, and, if so, will they be supported by an ever-expanding technology? Or will we wind down into a stationary state of comfortable satisfaction with material need banished from the earth?

The answers to these questions are, I believe, already at hand. The evidence is that there is no satiation of human wants; rather, that the mechanism of economic growth causes the luxuries of one generation to become the necessities of the next, and thus leads to ever higher material aspirations.[41] Nor is there reason to expect a declining rate of technical progress, because the march of science, on which technology ultimately rests, is steadily onward.[42] While it would be pleasant to envisage a world free from the pressure of material want, a more realistic projection based on current evidence for the now developed countries is of a world caught on a "hedonic treadmill," a world in which generation after generation thinks it

---

40 David Morawetz, *Twenty-Five Years of Economic Development, 1950 to 1975* (Washington, D.C., 1977); Robert Summers, Irving B. Kravis, and Alan Heston, "International Comparison of Real Product and Its Composition: 1950–77," *The Review of Income and Wealth,* Series 26, No. 1 (March 1980); Everett E. Hagen and Oli Hawrylyshyn, "Analysis of World Income and Growth, 1955–1965," *Economic Development and Cultural Change,* 18, no. 1, part II (Oct. 1969).

41 Richard A. Easterlin, "Does Economic Growth Improve the Human Lot? Some Empirical Evidence," *Nations and Households in Economic Growth: Essays in Honor of Moses Abramovitz* (New York, 1974); Richard A. Easterlin, "Does Money Buy Happiness?" *The Public Interest,* no. 30 (Winter 1973).

42 Derek J. de Solla Price, *Science since Babylon* (New Haven, 1961), chap. 5.

needs only another 10 or 20 percent more income to be perfectly happy. This will be, moreover, a monocultural world, East and West, capitalist and communist, for the personality traits that are formed in the process of modern economic growth ultimately prevail over cultural and ideological differences—in short, the hedonic treadmill becomes universal.

Evidence of growing cultural homogeneity in other respects is clearly apparent in recent research. I quote a summary of recent findings in sociology:

> Western scientific-technical concepts of reality have penetrated almost everywhere. Rapidly expanding education systems universally promote science, technology, and mathematics, implicitly advancing a conception of natural reality as law-like, strictly causally ordered, and manipulable. This conception is also built into institutions of scientific research, national planning, and national industrialization.
>
> Descriptions of transcendental authority also become more uniform. Universalistic and unitary conceptions of God (or equivalently, of history) prevail. Indigenous, localized religious systems applying only to particular groups die out or are transformed to resemble more widespread systems.
>
> Finally, descriptions of the nature of man and society converge. Individuals are seen as both malleable and as possessing many economic and social rights that are remarkably similar, in the abstract, from country to country. Obligations to maintain economic progress and social justice are defined in uniform terms. To a remarkable degree, every sort of state defines for itself uniform long-run economic and social goals.[43]

This, then, is the future to which the epoch of modern economic growth is leading us: a world in which ever-growing abundance is always outpaced by material aspirations, a world of increasing cultural uniformity.

At some point, we may look back and ask what produced this world—how we got where we are. Such inquiry will show, I believe, that the proximate roots of the epoch of modern economic growth lie in the growth of science and diffusion of modern education. In a more fundamental sense, however, it will show that the source of this epoch is the secular, rationalistic, and materialistic trend of intellectual thought that evolved from the Renaissance and Reformation—that in rejecting the authority of the medieval Church, humanity ultimately took up a new "religion of knowledge," whose churches are the schools and universities of the world, whose priests are its teachers, and whose creed is belief in science and the power of rational inquiry, and in the ultimate capacity of humanity to shape its own destiny. The irony is that in this last respect the lesson of history is otherwise: that there is no choice. The epoch of modern economic growth—a world of nations blindly developing—is itself the proof of this.

43 John W. Meyer, John Boli-Bennett, and Christopher Chase-Dunn, "Convergence and Divergence in Development," in Alex Inkeles, ed., *Annual Review of Sociology*, 1 (Palo Alto, 1975), p. 228.

APPENDIX TABLE 1.1 **Estimated Primary School Enrollment Rate by Country, 1830–1975 (Per 10,000 Population)**

Country						Year					
	1830	**1840**	**1850**	**1860**	**1870**	**1882**	**1890**	**1900**	**1910**		
USA	1,500		1,800		1,702	1,908	1,985	1,969	1,828		
UK	900		1,045			1,107	1,261	1,407	1,648		
France	700	846	930	930	1125	1,382	1,450	1,412	1,414		
Germany	1,700		1,600	1,559		1,547	1,642	1,576	1,570		
	1830	**1850**	**1860**	**1870**	**1882**	**1890**	**1900**	**1910**	**1920**	**1930**	**1939**
Italy	300		463	611	681	874	881	927	1,113	1056	1313
Spain	400	537	663	851	1,049	1,058	1,038	1,026	1,232	1,535	
	1870	**1882**	**1890**	**1900**	**1910**	**1920**	**1930**	**1939**			
Rumania	214	261	467	617	839	642	1,307	1,581			
Yugoslavia		303	300	420	512	674	772	888			
USSR	98	133	231	348	395	417	734	1,873			
	1870	**1882**	**1890**	**1900**	**1910**	**1920**	**1930**	**1939**	**1950**	**1960**	**1975**
Argentina		511	709	808	944	1,356	1,172	1,417	1,286	1,339	1,399
Mexico		457	487	544	563	456	1,074	1,314	1,072	1,460	1,905
Brazil	119	207	218	258	271	455	618	854	979	1,087	1,866
Burma							206	316	427	731	1,127
India			94	107	147	192	343	279	513	854	1,082
Indonesia			57	62	96	161	267	338	613	964	1,345
		1882	**1890**	**1900**	**1910**	**1920**	**1930**	**1939**	**1950**	**1960**	**1975**
Japan		722	772	984	1,240	1,508	1,550	1,695			
Philippines				188	970	1,038	936	1,267	1,891		
Thailand					9	179	552	939	1,490		
Egypt		4	264	215	171	171	269	687	662	1,038	1,107
Iran				3	6	10	82	213	457	701	1,353
Turkey						201	318	464	776	1,026	1,376
					1910	**1920**	**1930**	**1939**	**1950**	**1960**	**1975**
China						115	222	329	861	948	
Korea					27	72	246	501	1151		
Nigeria					12	176	191	103	399	479	820
Ethiopia									49	81	366

Source: A: Arthur S. Banks, *Cross-Polity Time Series Data* (Cambridge, 1971); B: *The Statesman's Yearbook 1883–1960* (London, 1883–1960); C: E. Levasseur, *L'Enseignement primaire dans les pays civilisés* (Paris, 1897); D: Richard A. Easterlin, "A Note on the Evidence of History," in C. Arnold Anderson and Mary Jean Bowman, eds., *Education and Economic Development* (Chicago, 1965), pp. 422–29; E: Andrew J. Grajdanzev, *Modern Korea* (New York, 1944); F: UNESCO, *Statistical Yearbook 1977* (Paris, 1978) and United Nations, *Demographic Yearbook 1977* (New York, 1978). Source of data for 1975 is F; for all other dates A, except as follows: USA 1830, 1850–D; UK 1830, 1850–D; France 1830–D, 1840–1860–C; Germany 1930, 1850–D, 1860–C; Italy 1830–D, 1860, 1870–C; Spain 1830–D, 1850–C; Rumania 1870, 1890–C; USSR 1890–C; Argentina 1882–C; Burma 1930–1950–B; India 1890–1930–B; Indonesia 1890–1939–B; Philippines 1900–1939–B; Thailand 1910–1939–B; Egypt 1882–1939–B; Iran 1900–1939–B; Korea 1910–1939–E; Nigeria 1910–1950–B.

Topic One Suggested Supplemental Reading

United Nations Department of Economic and Social Affairs. 2006. "Growth and Development Trends, 1960–2005." In *World Economic and Social Survey 2006: Diverging Growth and Development*. New York: United Nations.

Topic One Questions

1 Discuss the link between education and economic development found by Easterlin. In what ways is basic education of the masses important? In what ways is higher education for the elites important? Which is more important according to Easterlin?

2 Using specific examples throughout global history, explain Easterlin's findings about the importance of secularization on development.

Topic Two

Prehistoric Economics and the Neolithic Transformation

CHAPTER TWO

The Origins of the Civilizations of Egypt and Mesopotamia

L. de Blois and R. J. van der Spek

On the banks of the rivers Euphrates and Tigris in Mesopotamia (largely what is now Iraq) and the Nile in Egypt emerged civilizations that were to have a profound influence on the history of the eastern half of the Mediterranean. The rise of these civilizations, just before 3000 BC, was characterized by increasing urbanization, the birth of states, and the invention of writing. These civilizations did not appear out of the blue, of course; their foundations had been laid over a period that spanned several hundreds of thousands of years. Archaeologists have divided this long period, which is called the Stone Age, into an Old, Middle, and New Stone Age on the basis of changes in the stone implements that were produced during that period. In the Old and Middle Stone Ages people lived off what they happened to come across, off the animals they hunted, and the plants they gathered. They followed their prey into new areas and were hence constantly on the move. By the end of the Middle Stone Age (*c.* 10,000 BC), man had improved his tools to such an extent that he was able to make more efficient use of the natural resources. That meant that some groups of people could remain in one area for a longer period of time, sheltered from the elements in primitive huts or caves. The next step in man's development was the transition to an entirely new way of life characterized by a greater control of nature: man started to cultivate the cereals which he had until then always gathered as wild plants, and domesticated the animals which he had hunted in the past. This transition took place at different times in different parts of the world, but it is believed that it occurred in the Near East first. The process really got under way around the beginning of the New Stone Age, or Neolithic, as this period, characterized by the use of ground stone tools, is also called. Being of such tremendous importance for the further development of civilization, this transformation is often referred to as the "Neolithic revolution," although the whole process actually took thousands of years and the first signs of the fundamental changes that were to take place had already appeared long before the Neolithic.

Two different kinds of agriculture are distinguished: rainfall agriculture and irrigation agriculture. A prerequisite for rainfall agriculture is an annual precipitation of at least 250 mm. So this form of agriculture could be practiced only in Iran, northern Iraq, northern

Syria, and the coastal Mediterranean. Egypt and southern Mesopotamia had to rely on irrigation agriculture. Areas that are dependent on rainfall agriculture are very vulnerable. A slight decrease in rainfall will immediately lead to a food crisis and a more protracted change in climate will have major social and political consequences.

"Irrigation" is understood to include both natural and artificial irrigation. The best conditions for agriculture based on natural irrigation were to be found in Egypt. Every year, the Nile flooded the land before the sowing season (between July and September). The Egyptians could then sow their crops in the damp soil when the river receded. In Mesopotamia the land was less regularly flooded, the floods moreover occurring earlier in the year—from February until April, i.e., just before harvesting time. This meant that the occupants of that region had to practice artificial irrigation. Irrigation agriculture was far more productive than rainfall agriculture, enabling crop yield ratios of at least 15:1, often indeed a lot higher. We get a good impression of how high such ratios are when we compare them with later figures for Greece, Italy, and medieval Europe, where the average ratio was about 4/5:1 and a good ratio was 7/10:1 (e.g., in Campania in Italy). Another reason why crop yields were higher in Mesopotamia is that people in that area used a sowing plow (see Figure 2.1).

The development of agriculture was of fundamental importance for the further history of mankind. It meant that more people could remain settled in one particular area for a longer period of time and that more people could concentrate their attention on activities other than food production. People consequently started to specialize in all kinds of crafts and became carpenters, tanners, scribes (at least after the invention of the art of writing, around 3400 BC) and metalworkers (after around 3000 BC, when man discovered how to exploit and smelt copper ore and produce bronze, an alloy of copper and tin). A civil service and a priesthood emerged (and the associated institutions: the state and the temple). Some of the villages that had originated at the beginning of the Neolithic began to resemble fortified cities; Jericho, for example, had already evolved into a city by around 7000 BC and

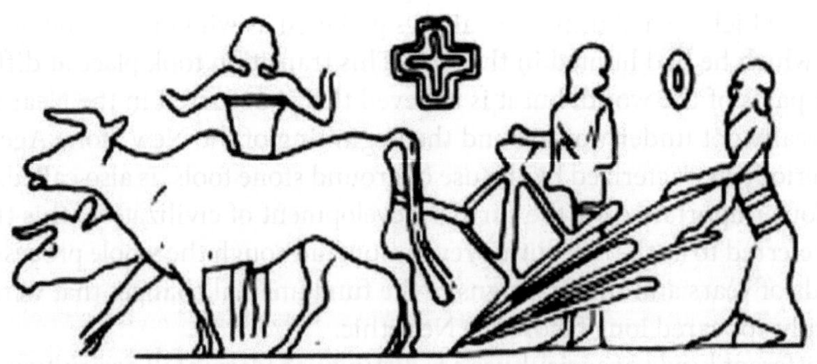

FIGURE 2.1 Sowing plow; impression of a cylinder seal (2nd millennium BC)

Notes. With this instrument plowing and sowing could be combined. The central figure is pouring seed into a chute, which guides it directly into the furrow. This minimized the loss of seed, enabling a prolific harvest.

there were several cities in Asia Minor and Syria. The largest and most influential cities, however, were those that arose on the banks of the major rivers of Egypt and Mesopotamia in the fourth millennium BC. It was there, along those rivers, that the largest quantities of food could be produced and the largest numbers of people could live together.

The core of a Mesopotamian city was the temple, the abode of the state deity, whose needs had to be provided for by the community. Those temples grew into powerful organizations that owned vast estates; they engaged in a wide range of activities, including agriculture, stock breeding, and various crafts, for which they employed a large staff.

It was the requirements of this temple economy that led to the invention of writing, some time between 3400 and 3200 BC. The Mesopotamian script is known as the "cuneiform" script—so called after the wedge-shaped appearance of the impressions of which the later characters of that script were composed. The hieroglyphic script of the Egyptians was developed around the same time as the cuneiform script.

At first, the cuneiform and hieroglyphic scripts were both partly pictographic (with each word being represented by a picture) and partly ideographic (with each word being represented by a symbol). Later on, the signs came to stand for sounds (syllables), too. The Egyptian script only rendered consonants, vowels being ignored. Both the Mesopotamian and the Egyptian script remained highly complex forms of writing and were used only by small groups of specially trained professional scribes.

In antiquity, the presence of cities did not lead to contrasts between the urban and rural populations of the kind known to us from later times. In most of the cities the majority of the inhabitants were peasants, who left the city to work on their land every morning and returned in the evening. In the ancient Near East, a far greater and far more important contrast than that between city dwellers and country folk was that between the sedentary and the nomadic way of life. This contrast was closely associated with a major difference in subsistence patterns. Agriculturalists led a sedentary life; they remained settled in one area because they had to till their land and look after their crops. Herders were nomads; they constantly moved around from one place to another in search of fresh pastures for their animals. However, there was not always such a clear-cut difference between the two. Primitive agriculturalists sometimes remained in one area for only a short period of time, to then move on again a few years later, when they had exhausted the soil. Some herders moved around within a relatively small area, for example from summer pastures to winter pastures. This seasonal migration is called "transhumance." The transhumant nomads liked to remain in the vicinity of the settlements of the agriculturalists, with whom they could then exchange products. Occasionally a group of (semi)nomads would adopt a partly or entirely sedentary way of life and take control of a city. There were also wealthy landowners who owned herds besides land and employed herders to pasture their animals, sometimes at considerable distances from their dwellings. Throughout the entire history of the ancient Near East the representatives of these two opposed ways of life were constantly flung between feelings of hatred and friendship towards one another—hatred because the sedentary peoples were afraid of being plundered by the (semi)nomads, and friendship because the two groups were dependent on one another for the exchange of products. The contrast between the two different ways of life became a popular theme in the literature of this area. It forms the basis of the Biblical story of the shepherd Abel who was murdered by the agriculturalist Cain.

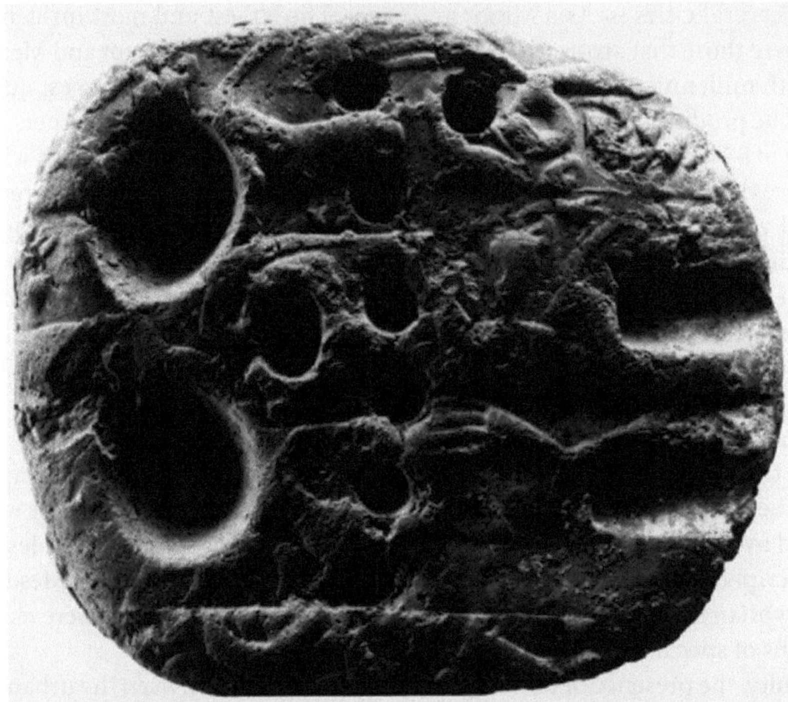

FIGURE 2.2 **Clay tablet from Jebel Aruda, Syria, length 9.2 cm, *c.* 3400–3200 BC.**

Notes. The tablet shows a number (372?) and impressions made by a cylinder seal. A cylinder seal was made of some hard material in which a design was carved in mirror image. When the seal was rolled over soft clay, the design was impressed in the clay. The impressed clay tablets served to identify the owner (private person, temple, palace) of the objects to which they were attached. Clay tablets developed from the custom of keeping records of goods (or cattle) by enclosing clay tokens in a sealed clay envelope. The clay envelope had to be broken when the quantities of the goods were to be checked. Later the number of tokens, representing the quantity of goods, was indicated on the outside of the envelope. In a following stage, the tokens were altogether omitted: the envelope became a solid clay tablet indicating a number. Later clay tablets show numbers and marks representing the goods. This is how the first script originated. At an even later stage, the marks were also used to indicate a sound or a syllable. The same system of numbers encountered on this tablet, which came to light in an excavation conducted by a team of archaeologists from Leiden (the Netherlands) in Syria, is also known from Mesopotamia and southwest Iran (Elam). This points to the existence of intensive trade contacts that embraced the whole of Western Asia by the fourth millennium BC already. This is confirmed by the recurrent motifs that are observable on earthenware all over this region.

The geographical conditions of Egypt and Mesopotamia were very similar in some respects: both areas were dependent on river water due to the almost total absence of rain, and both were poor in various important resources, such as metals and timber. In other respects, however, they were totally different. Conditions for agriculture, for example, were more favourable in Egypt than in Mesopotamia. As already mentioned above, the Nile flooded the land before the sowing season, the Euphrates and Tigris not until later in the year. Whereas the Egyptians could sow their crops in the fertile deposits left behind by the receding river, the Mesopotamians had to go to great efforts to conduct the water to their fields via canals. The water of the Nile was, moreover, of a better quality; that of the Euphrates and the Tigris contained harmful salts, which became mixed with the groundwater. The

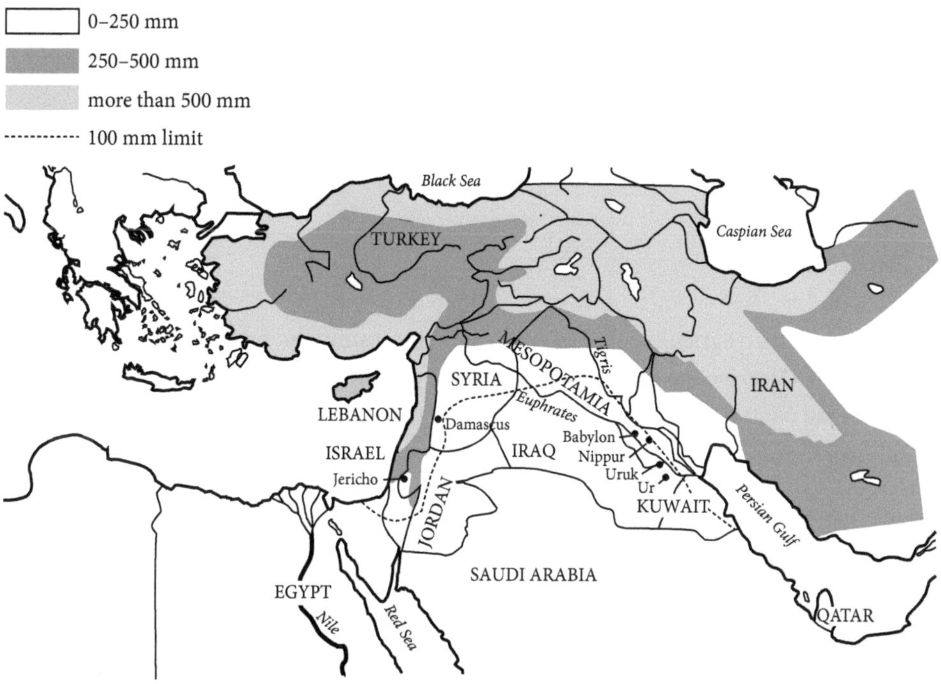

MAP 2.1 **Rainfall in the Near East**

Notes: In the areas with less than 250 mm rainfall no crops can be grown without irrigation. In the areas to the south of the 100-mm limit too little grows to allow stock-keeping.

groundwater level of the low-lying, flat land was very high and the salts migrated to the surface of the land via capillary cracks in the clay. Protracted irrigation without sufficient drainage could ultimately make the soil unfit for cultivation owing to complete salinization. That this indeed happened can be inferred from the crops that were cultivated: in southern Mesopotamia the amount of barley cultivated gradually increased, whereas the amount of wheat decreased. The reason for this is that barley is more resistant to salt. Egypt, on the contrary, is believed to have grown more wheat than barley throughout antiquity.

Another important difference between Egypt and Mesopotamia concerns the surrounding areas. In Egypt the transition from arable land to desert sand was so abrupt that it was possible to stand—literally—with one foot in a green field and the other in the dry desert sand. In Mesopotamia the transition from fertile to less fertile land was more gradual. Secondly, being totally surrounded by uninhabitable deserts, Egypt was far less accessible than Mesopotamia, and consequently far more isolated from the outside world. This difference had major political consequences: whereas the history of Egypt is fairly stable and static, with relatively little interference from outside, that of Mesopotamia is characterized by constant invasions of foreign peoples, many of whom assumed control and founded new empires. Nevertheless, a considerable degree of continuity was preserved in Mesopotamia too, as most of the newcomers adapted themselves to the original occupants' cultural traditions.

Topic Two Suggested Supplemental Reading

North, Douglass C., and Robert Paul Thomas. 1977. “The First Economic Revolution.” *Economic History* Review 30, no. 2 (May): 229–241.

Topic Two Questions

1. Explain how settled agriculture led to civilization (meaning economic specialization and interdependence). Describe the governmental structure of the early civilizations.
2. Compare and contrast Sumerian cuneiform and Egyptian hieroglyphic scripts in terms of their structure and reasons for development.

Topic Three

Economic Development in the Ancient Empires

CHAPTER THREE

Technology

From *The Cambridge Economic History of the Greco-Roman World*

Helmuth Schneider

I. Ancient Technology in Modern Historiography

Ancient technology has been a subject of controversial scholarly debate since the beginning of the twentieth century. So far, a consensus has proved unattainable, whether about the issues and topics of a modern history of ancient technology, about the criteria of evaluation of technological developments in pre-industrial societies, or about the actual spread of technological innovations. In such circumstances, this chapter must begin by taking up a position in relation to the views expressed in earlier research, and at the same time offering some methodological justification for my own view.

Almost all work on the history of technology published before 1984 espoused the opinion that technological development in antiquity never implemented advances that were actually quite possible; that ancient technology had, on the whole, been characterized by stagnation; and that it had only few inventions to show which could be compared in importance to the accomplishments of the ancient civilizations in such areas as literature, art, philosophy, mathematics or medicine. It was further held that those few technological innovations which are documented had scarcely been put to economic use, and had therefore only had scant influence on work, production, and productivity. Various reasons were given for the perceived primitive and backward nature of ancient technology, such as a reverence for nature that was rooted in religion, the preponderance of thought structures shaped by rhetoric and therefore unsuitable for the understanding of technical facts, or the elitist self-perception of ancient scholars who had had no interest in making practical use of their scientific knowledge. Economic factors were also brought into play, such as the lack of markets for the yields of mass-production based on the mechanization of work processes, the lack of capital for the building up of industries, the lack of suitable energy sources for industrial

Translation by Annemarie Künzl-Snodgrass, with the help of Anthony Snodgrass.

production and, not least, the existence of slavery, which had supplied the ancient economy with sufficient cheap labor, so as to make the use of labor-saving machinery superfluous.[1]

This critical view of ancient technology is in many cases based less on a comprehensive evaluation of the sources for the history of technology in antiquity, than on generalized statements that can hardly be adequately substantiated. A characteristic example of this can be found in Finley's observations at the beginning of his much-cited 1965 essay on "Technical innovation and economic progress in the ancient world." His statement "it is a commonplace that the Greeks and Romans together added little to the world's store of technical knowledge and equipment," an older position in scholarship, which should have been critically evaluated, is instead accepted as a *communis opinio* and used as the starting point for the deliberations on ancient technology which follow. In this same context it is significant that Finley, after giving a (by no means comprehensive, yet still impressive) list of technical innovations, comprising amongst others the cog wheel, screw, rotary and water mill, screw press, glass production, concrete, hollow-cast bronzes and torsion catapult, comments on this list by saying that "it adds up to not very much for a great civilisation over fifteen hundred years."[2] The criteria for such an evaluation of ancient technology remain unclear; the question arises whether, in the light of the inventions listed by Finley, it would not be more appropriate to credit ancient society with a considerable potential for technological innovation and to analyze the causes of the technological development achieved, rather than to postulate a technological backwardness in antiquity and then discuss the reasons for the perceived stagnation.

Behind much of the work published in the twentieth century on ancient technology lies an understanding of technology which is, to a high degree, shaped by technological progress in the age of industrialization. Since the beginning of the Industrial Revolution, an acceleration in technological change has taken place, which through the mechanization of work processes and the use of machinery led, from the first, to a fundamental change of production and thus to a hitherto unimagined increase in productivity. The interdependency of technological progress and economic growth, so characteristic for modern industrialized societies, is reflected in the fact that inventions are very swiftly put to economic use. From early on, industry went over to pushing technological developments ahead in their own research laboratories, in order to secure advantages for themselves in the competition of the markets. Through competition between businesses as well as between nation states, through patency laws which guaranteed the economic utilization of inventions, and through the development of joint-stock companies, these processes were still further accelerated, so that innovations followed each other in ever quicker succession. Railways, motor cars, and aeroplanes revolutionized transport in the nineteenth and early twentieth centuries, as did telephone and radio with communication systems and electricity and power stations

1 Lombroso-Ferrero 1920; Lämmli 1968: 44–9, 58–67; Kiechle 1969; Vernant 1974; Gille 1980: 170–95; Greene 1990; Schneider 1992: 22–30; Wilson 2002; compare also the criticism of such positions in Persson 1988.

2 Finley 1965b: 29.

with power supply. Technological change spread beyond industry into agriculture, private households and, with electronic data-processing in the past two decades, into office work as well as the whole area of communication. Far-reaching social change sprang from industrialization: while the number of workers in farming decreased strongly, the number of industrial and office workers increased, production came to be concentrated in industrial cities, which developed into conurbations with millions of inhabitants; in the longer term, the supply of food and consumer goods to the population improved.

Impressed by the technological progress of the nineteenth and twentieth centuries, ancient historians had to grant the superiority of modern technology over ancient; yet at the same time it was held that it had been in principle possible for antiquity to anticipate modern technological developments. It was pointed out in this context that the principle of steam power had been known in antiquity and that the building of steam engines had thus been a possibility.[3] On this premise, it needed to be explained why technological progress comparable with that of the Industrial Revolution had not taken place in the Roman empire, although the empire had at its disposal considerable technical means and great progress had been made in the understanding of nature.

Such argumentation understands industrialization as the model for a technological development which can serve as a yardstick for other epochs and societies; every deviation from this model therefore needed an explanation. What was not taken into account was the fact that the Industrial Revolution was based on specific economic and technological, not to mention social, scientific and political, conditions which only became present in the eighteenth and nineteenth centuries; it is impossible to detach industrialization from the context of European, and particularly British, history of that time.

The conditions for technological development changed fundamentally with the Industrial Revolution; therefore, when describing the technology of pre-modern agricultural societies, it makes little sense to take as a starting point the expectations and horizons of modern industrialized societies. Rather, the attempt should be made to understand technological development and the potential for innovation in agricultural societies from the standpoint of their own conditions. One part of this is the examination of individual inventions or minor improvements precisely in terms of their importance in the context of agriculture and craft.

A new view of ancient technology was formulated in 1984 by White and Wikander. In a longish section of his *Greek and Roman Technology*, White gives an impressive overview of "Innovation and Development" in antiquity, taking into account all areas of technology ranging from agriculture and craftsmanship to the military sector. Independently of White, Wikander addressed the problem of "technological stagnation" in a study of the diffusion of the water mill in antiquity, contradicting the accepted opinion that water power had scarcely been put to economic use in the Roman empire, even though the principle of constructing a water mill had already been known in Augustan times. Lately, Greene and

3 Diels 1920: 29–33; Kiechle 1969: 148–55.

Wilson have pointed in a series of articles to the technological advances of Roman times especially, decisively supporting the view that ancient technology must be freshly evaluated.[4]

More recent studies of the history of technology increasingly take as their theme, besides invention, the transfer of technology, that is the adoption of technological knowledge from other societies or the transfer of one's own technology to other regions. This aspect is of considerable importance for the history of antiquity, in as much as the development of Greek civilization in archaic times was to a high degree based on the appropriation of the technological achievements of Egypt and Mesopotamia; while the historically relevant process of Romanization, especially in the western Mediterranean and in north-western Europe, also included the spread of Roman technology in the provinces.

One of the most important results of modern research in the history of technology is, without doubt, the insight into the interdependency of technological and economic developments. Economic activities are, on the one hand, dependent on the technological equipment of a society; on the other, they favor innovation and thus create the conditions for technological progress. This by no means applies to modern industrial societies only, but also—within limits—to pre-modern agricultural societies. Economic development in antiquity can only be understood when studies of economic history sufficiently take into consideration the technological levels reached in Greece and in the Roman empire. The production and distribution of goods depended on the use of tools, equipment, and means of transport, as well as on the application of technological procedures in the production and transformation of substances; the use of certain tools and equipment shaped the work processes, and the productivity of agriculture and craft had a considerable influence on the prosperity of urban centers.

II. The Technological Systems in Antiquity: Agricultural Technology, Tools, Energy

Agricultural technology, mining, the various branches of craftsmanship and transport represent areas of technology by no means independent of each other, but showing numerous mutual dependencies and thus forming a technological system.[5] For example, the level of metal-working is of decisive importance for building, the working of wood for ship-building. Plato already clearly sees this connection: he points out that craftsmen produce the tools for other crafts—thus a carpenter produces a loom for a weaver—and emphasizes the specialization of the individual craftsman. Thus, in a bigger city, craftsmanship is directed not only to goods for consumption, but also to tools and equipment for production.[6]

For an adequate and comprehensive description of a technological system it is necessary, first to establish the economic significance of the various branches of the economy; then

4 White 1984: 27–48; Wikander 1984: 5–15; Greene 2000; Wilson 2002.

5 Gille 1978: 19.

6 Pl. *Cra.* 387d–389d; *Resp.* 370c–e; *Leg.* 678c–679b.

to work out the characteristics of the means of production typical for the system; finally to record the energy sources at the disposal of the economy. For the technological system of antiquity, three fundamental facts call for notice:

1. Ancient societies were agricultural societies: agriculture was their economic basis. This means that particular weight must be given to agricultural technology in the description of ancient technology.
2. Ancient technology must primarily be characterized as a tool-based technology; the use of tools was indispensable for all important processes of work and production.
3. Human and animal muscle power remained the crucial sources of power until the end of antiquity. The thermal energy needed for the preparation of food, as well as for metal-working or for the production of glass or ceramics, was delivered by wood or charcoal. From Augustan times, water power was used for the grinding of grain; for late antiquity it is also documented for the sawing of marble.

Agriculture had as its primary function the production of food, with the cultivation of grain, wine and olive trees being prominent; fruit and vegetable growing also played an important part. The mainly vegetarian diet was supplemented by products of animal husbandry, in particular cheese and pork. It must not be overlooked here that agriculture also delivered the raw materials for the production of textiles—wool and flax—and that animal breeding supplied both agriculture and transport with work animals—oxen, mules, and donkeys—and the army with horses for the cavalry. The most important aim of cattle husbandry was the rearing of oxen.[7]

In ancient agriculture there existed not only farmsteads where farmers farmed either their own or leased land, but also bigger estates specializing in a market-oriented production with particular products, and gigantic *latifundia*, which were normally managed extensively. While small farmers usually clung to traditional equipment and procedures and hardly had the economic scope for experimentation with new technologies, the owners of big estates in Roman times were really interested in using new or improved equipment and adopting new methods of cultivation or animal husbandry; they had financial resources at their disposal to increase the output of their estates through the acquisition and use of new or improved equipment.

In ancient agriculture, certainly, much of the work hardly changed over long periods of time: for example, ploughing with a pair of oxen, hoeing of the ground to eliminate weeds, harvesting the grain with a simple sickle, winnowing, or harvesting olives with long sticks. Numerous innovations are however attested, for example in the threshing of grain; in many estates in Italy, grain was not trodden out by animals, but rotating sledges were used. At the same time, threshing with threshing sticks was common. Wine- and oil-presses were significantly improved in Roman times. Yet in many cases, innovations in agricultural technology were not established throughout the empire, but only in individual regions.

7 Isager-Skydsgaard 1992; White 1970b; White 1984: 58–72.

Moreover, inventions did not at all always result in the immediate suppression of the older technology. This is especially true of wine- and olive-presses: they were expensive acquisitions and had a relatively long life-span; therefore they were not replaced immediately even when construction had been partially improved. Thus it was possible to have various types of press simultaneously in use.

For ancient craftsmanship, working with a tool was characteristic; both Plato and Aristotle analyzed the function of tools and described it in precise terms. According to Aristotle, it is his soul, which already bears in itself the form of the product, and his knowledge that move the hands of the craftsman; his hands in turn move the tool which has an effect on the material.[8] Thus the structure of craft-production can be understood in its essence: the craftsman directs a tool with his hand and so shapes the material; the work of the craftsman is based on a clear idea of the object which is to be produced, on knowledge of the properties of the material used for working and not least on manual dexterity. Craftsmanship of this kind dominated many branches of manual work in antiquity.

Under ancient technological conditions, a mechanization of production, that is the transfer of individual steps in the course of the work to a machine, could be realized only within certain limits. Besides tools, use was also made of mechanical equipment, which either made certain work easier or else made it possible at all. In an illuminating section, Vitruvius differentiates between tools (*organa*) and mechanical equipment (*machinae*), which in his opinion differ from each other in that *machinae* are moved by several workers and by bigger forces, whereas a tool is used by a single craftsman in a intelligent way.[9] So the operation of mechanical equipment did not need the technical expertise of a craftsman, and was therefore not comparable with the use of a tool. The effectiveness of mechanical equipment was based on the use of mechanical instruments such as the roller, the pulley, the lever, the winch or the screw; examples are on the one hand lifting equipment, which enabled heavy stone blocks to be lifted on building sites; on the other, the big wine- and oil-presses. This by no means rendered superfluous the use of human labor; rather, the physical force needed for certain work was reduced through the use of mechanical equipment. The analysis of simple mechanical instruments such as roller, pulley, lever, winch or screw, and the construction of mechanical equipment needed a kind of competence which far exceeded the knowledge and experience of a craftsman: a new scientific discipline emerged in mechanics, which employed mathematical methods to enable the most efficient use of mechanical instruments.

Under the conditions of ancient technology, human muscle power remained one of the most important energy sources.[10] Agricultural work in particular was highly physical work, done with simple tools such as hoe, sickle, or scythe. Craftsmen use muscle power to handle their tools: this is true for all branches of craft, for the working of metal or ceramics as

8 Arist., *Gen. an.* 730b.

9 Vitr. *De arch.* 10. 1. 3.

10 Halleux 1977; Landels 1978: 9–33; Casson 1984a; White 1984: 49–57.

well as for textile production; in a similar way, the mechanical crushing of ore, the forging of iron by hammering the piece, the shaping of silver or bronze objects by cold-working, the shaping of clay vessels, the weaving or fulling of cloth all demanded the use of human labor. On top of that, human muscle power served as driving-force: thus the potter's wheel was driven by an assistant while the potter shaped the vessel, and the big water-sluicing installations in Roman mines were operated by manpower, as were the Archimedean screws used for irrigation in Egypt. As is shown on Roman reliefs, the big cranes used to lift big loads on building sites were equipped with tread-wheels, set in motion by manpower.

Above all, the part played by human labor in the transport of goods should not be underestimated; in particular, it was people who carried the loads at harbors or in the middle of cities—amphoras filled with wine or oil as well as sacks of grain. The distances were usually fairly short, but such transports made up a substantial portion of the whole. Even in the transport of human beings, people as carriers played a considerable part: the sedan-chair carried by slaves served as a normal means of transport for the members of the upper classes in the cities, but also in rural districts.

After human labor, animal muscle power was the second most important source of energy in antiquity. In the ancient economy, the prime function of animals was that of supporting people in their work, and many of the domesticated animals were work animals.[11] Oxen were used in agriculture above all for ploughing, for the necessary preparation of the soil for sowing; oxen also pulled heavy, mostly two-wheeled carts and thus transported loads such as the monumental stone blocks which had to be carried from the quarries to the building sites. Donkeys carried loads with the help of pack saddles and baskets; they brought agricultural products from the hinterland to the cities on a daily basis, as Libanios describes for Antioch; in particular, the transport of wood for fuel by donkeys is also widely attested.[12] Mules, which were better suited to certain tasks than horses or donkeys, were harnessed to light carts or even ploughs and were also valued as riding or transport animals. In the eastern parts of the Roman empire the camel, which is superbly suited to the climatic conditions of desert regions, became quite important for transport.

Although horses are more powerful than oxen, their use in ancient economies remained problematic: not because the type of ancient harness presented a decisive obstacle, as an older thesis held, but because of the difficult temperament of the horse, and in addition its susceptibility to injury and illness, as well as the need for high-quality food. Only when overland transport in the north-western provinces grew commoner and wider inland regions were increasingly opened up to carriage-roads did the use of the horse as a draught animal catch on.[13]

In many cases animal power was confined to the simple function of driving a mill or raising water. The grinding of grain is widely documented, and represented in images

11 Xen. *Mem.* 4.3.10; Pl. *Resp.* 370d–e; Cic. *Nat. D.* 3.159.

12 Lib. 50; Dem. 42.7; Apul. *Met.* 7.17f.

13 Amouretti 1991; Raepsaet 2002.

too, as the work of donkeys, mules and, above all, horses. Harnessed to a rotary mill, the blindfolded animal had to drive the heavy millstone in the narrowest of circles and with extreme flexion of its body; in addition, the use of oxen for the scooping of water is documented for Roman Egypt.[14]

Thermal energy was as necessary for the preparation of food, the baking of bread, or the cooking of meat as for the smelting of ore, the forging of iron, the casting of bronze, the firing of lime, bricks or ceramics, or for glass production. The fuel most used in the Mediterranean lands was wood and charcoal, the use of coal being widespread only in the Roman province of Britannia. Charcoal has several advantages in comparison with wood; its calorific value is higher than that of wood, so that higher temperatures can be reached, and it burns more or less smoke-free. Since charcoal kilns were often situated in remote forest areas, charcoal had to be transported over longish distances to the consumers. Charcoal from different woods was used for different purposes; young trees were mostly used for the production of charcoal, which could have negative consequences on forestation.[15]

Wind power was used only for shipping: Greek merchantmen had a high mast and a square-rigged sail, which offered a big enough surface to the wind to drive the ship. Merchantmen made use of rowers only in exceptional cases; there was a type of fast ship which could deliver wares to their destination even when the wind failed. Warships, on the other hand, having to remain capable of maneuver even when the winds were unfavorable, were driven by crews of oarsmen during military operations.[16]

The use of water power is without doubt to be considered as a break-through in technological history; it was probably the construction of water-wheels that constituted the first use of machines driven by running water. A transmitting mechanism then made it possible to transfer the rotary movement of the water-wheel to the grindstone. With the mill driven by water power, which according to recent research was in widespread use throughout the Roman empire, the foundation for the technological system of the Middle Ages was created.[17]

III. Areas of Technological Progress

Technical advances that were of economic relevance can be substantiated in various areas of the ancient economy: these at times changed fundamentally the processes of production, the kinds of work and the products themselves, or generated new products. In building, technological innovations such as the use of concrete (*opus caementicium*) and the superior command of the construction of the arch had opened up completely new possibilities for architecture and had, more especially, made possible an accelerated development of the

14 Moritz 1958: 74–102.

15 Reece 1969: 43–6.

16 Casson 1971; Landels 1978: 133–66.

17 Landels 1978: 16–26; Wikander 1981; 1984.

infrastructure of the Roman empire. The sources may not allow us to follow these processes in detail; but a few examples can nevertheless well demonstrate the characteristics, the economic consequences and the limitations of technological change in antiquity.

(a) The Development of the Grain Mill

Since grain, containing in sufficient quantity almost all the nutritional elements needed by human beings, plays a decisive role in ancient nutrition, the grinding of corn, along with ploughing, sowing, and harvesting, was part of the agricultural work necessary for sustaining life. The machine used for this was the mill, which underwent several significant changes in the course of antiquity. For any evaluation of ancient technology, it is indispensable to describe these changes, together with their effects on the work process and work productivity, with precision.[18] The earliest reference in Greek literature to the grinding of corn is in Homer: in Odysseus' palace on Ithaca, twelve women work on the mills;[19] these would be saddle querns, which had a firmly fixed lower stone and a smaller moveable upper stone. The upper surface of the lower stone was inclined at about 25 degrees; the corn was usually ground by women who knelt at the upper end of the lower stone, moving the upper stone forwards and backwards; this procedure had to be interrupted frequently to remove the flour and to put more corn grains between the millstones. Corn-grinding was labour-intensive, and tiring and monotonous work for those who undertook it.

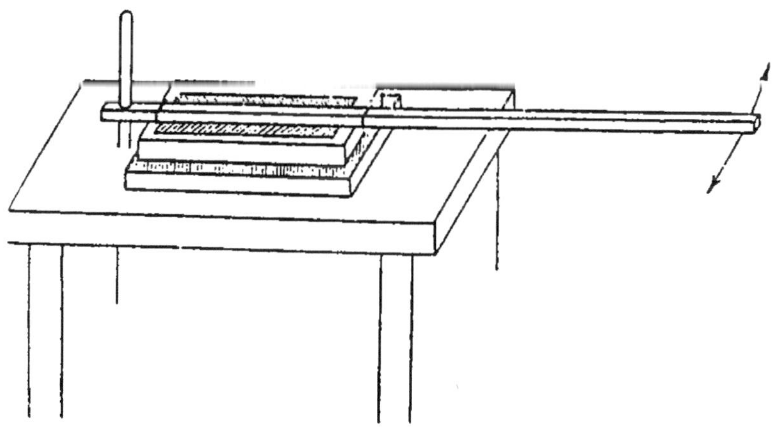

FIGURE 3.1 Olynthian grain mill with upper stone and long handle

Source: Moritz 1958: 45

18 Moritz 1958; Maróti 1975; Wikander 1981; Wikander 2000: 371–400; Wilson 2002: 9–15.

19 Hom. *Od.* 20.106–11.

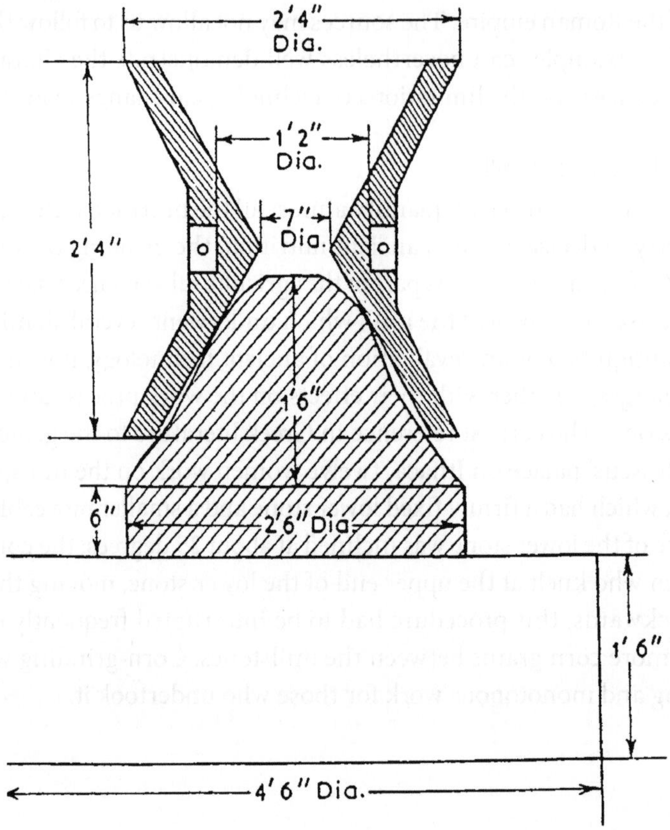

FIGURE 3.2 Pompeian mill with *meta* and *catillus*, the upper stone

Source: Moritz 1958: 75

Millstones found at Olynthus, which was destroyed in 348 BC, show that in classical times the grain mill was considerably improved by two innovations. The upper millstone was now fitted with a large funnel, so that grains fed into it while grinding could run slowly down into the space between the millstones. The lower, horizontal millstone rested on a table, while a long horizontal pole was fixed to the upper millstone, which was attached at one end to a vertical upright, while the other end, protruding beyond the upper stone, served as a handle. With this device, efficient use could be made of leverage in the grinding operation.

The rotary mill probably originated in the western Mediterranean, through the use of two circular millstones; a rotary movement now replaced the backward-and-forward one. This type of mill was probably first used as a hand mill. Soon it proved possible to have an animal carry out the continuous rotary movement. Portrayals of this donkey mill can be found on several Roman reliefs, while numerous actual mills have survived in Pompeii. It consisted of a bell-shaped lower stone and a hollow, hour-glass shaped upper stone. This was not in direct contact with the lower stone, but was suspended on a wooden frame,

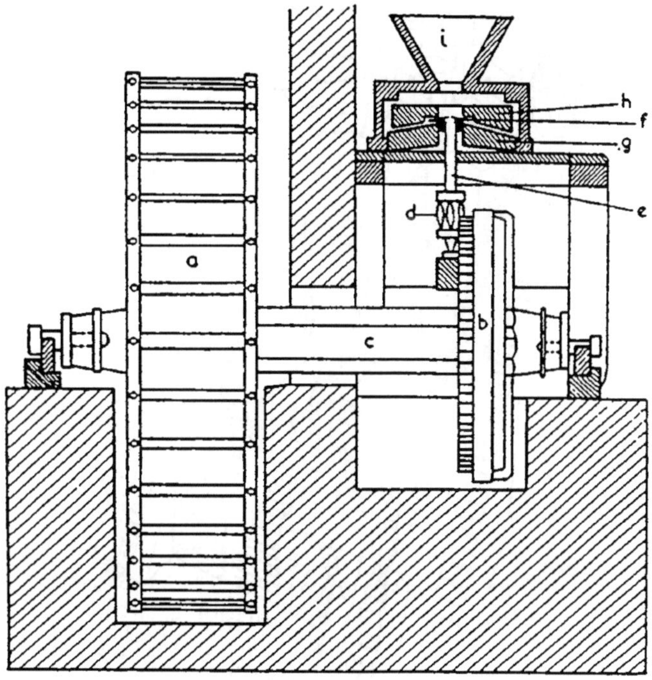

FIGURE 3.3 Water mill as described by Vitruvius (10.5.2)

Source: Moritz 1958: 123

whose center rested on a vertical iron axis. In this way, the mill could be adjusted exactly to different types of flour, while abraded stone was prevented from getting mixed in with the flour. In comparison with the saddle quern and the rotary hand mill, which were above all for domestic use, the Pompeian donkey mill was a complex appliance, which brought a higher level of mechanization to grain milling and was used mainly by commercial bakeries to produce flour for bread production. The donkey mill freed people from a monotonous labor which was now loaded on to animals.

From the first century BC on, water power generated by water mills was used for the grinding of grain; knowledge of the cog wheel was the prerequisite for the mechanism of transmission by which the rotary movement of the water wheel was brought to bear on the millstone.

Besides single water mills in various provinces of the Roman empire, large mill complexes, which were erected on slopes and had several milling stations, are documented in archaeological remains and literary sources; water was supplied by aqueducts. One such facility near Barbegal, in the vicinity of Arles, has now been dated to the period of Trajan.[20]

20 Leveau 1996.

FIGURE 3.4 **Barbegal multiple system with 16 wheels**

Reproduced from Sagui 1948: 225–31

In fourth-century Rome, the mills on the Janiculan hill delivered the flour for the city's population.[21] When the Goths at the siege of Rome interrupted the water supply for these mills, Belisarius in AD 537 had mills installed on ships moored by a bridge over the Tiber. The ship mill, originating in a military crisis, has been shown to have existed in many European cities down to early modern times. Its advantage lay above all in the fact that the water wheel could be adapted without difficulty to the changing water level of the river.[22]

An overview of the development of the mill, from the primitive saddle quern to the water mill and then the ship mill, makes it clear that the step-by-step improvement of this invention had achieved a notable lightening of the work necessary for everyday subsistence. People were relieved from heavy physical labor; human labor as the driving force was replaced first by animal muscle power and then by water power. The transition from backward-and-forward to rotary movement was a precondition for the mechanization of the mill. For the construction of the water mill, a transfer from one area of technology to another was necessary: the water wheel driven by running water, which combined the

21 *Cod. Theod.* 14.15.4.

22 Procop. *Goth.* 1.19.8–29.

functions of a driving wheel and scooping wheel, was now used, by the transmission of power through cog wheels, as the drive for the mill.

(b) Oil and Wine Presses

For the production of olive oil and wine, which together with grain were an important component of the ancient diet, equipment was needed for the pressing of the olives or the grapes. Although it was not at all unusual to tread grapes with the feet, from archaic times use was also made of the lever-press, whose press-beams were pulled down by weights, such as large stones, so that continuous pressure was put on the material to be pressed. The improvements made to this press were generally aimed at increasing the efficiency of the pressing process by technical means and, at the same time, decreasing the danger of injury to the people working with the press; in addition, it was desirable to save as much space as possible when setting up the press-beam, so as to limit the size of the press-rooms.[23]

While the press-beams of the early Roman presses were pulled down by a rope winch and a long lever, attempts were made in the ensuing period to construct a press in which continuous pressure could be applied to the material, without the need to employ uninterrupted human labor. For that purpose, a heavy stone was used as weight, but the rope winch was retained. This was now used to lift the stone, which in turn pulled down the press-beam by its weight. There were, however, serious disadvantages to this construction: the long levers turning the winch could break or jump out of their fastenings; the rope, too did not always run smoothly over the roller. These problems were only overcome when the

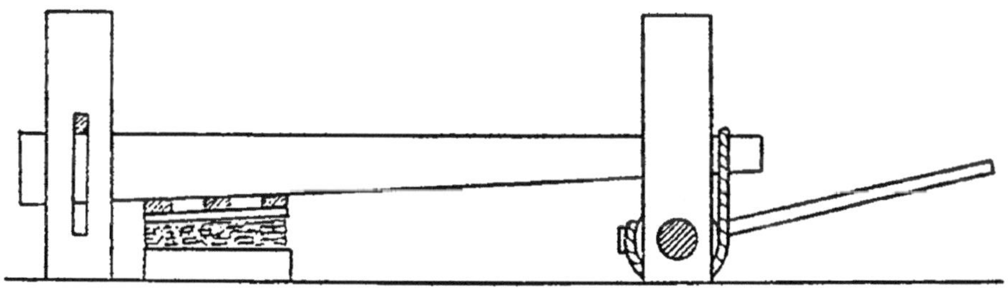

FIGURE 3.5 Roman lever-press as described by Cato the Elder

Reproduced from Drachmann 1967: 31

rope winch had been replaced by a big wooden screw, which was fitted into a thread on the press-beam and had the weight at its lower end.

Through rotation of the screw the weight, which to start with was on the floor, could be lifted up, and the press-beam lowered accordingly. There were various types of screw-press,

23 Drachmann 1932; Rossiter 1981; White 1984: 67–72; Brun 1986; Amouretti 1986: 166–75; Cato, *Agr.*18–22; Vitr. *De arch.* 6.6.3; Plin. *HN.* 18.317; Heron, *Mechanica* 3.13–21.

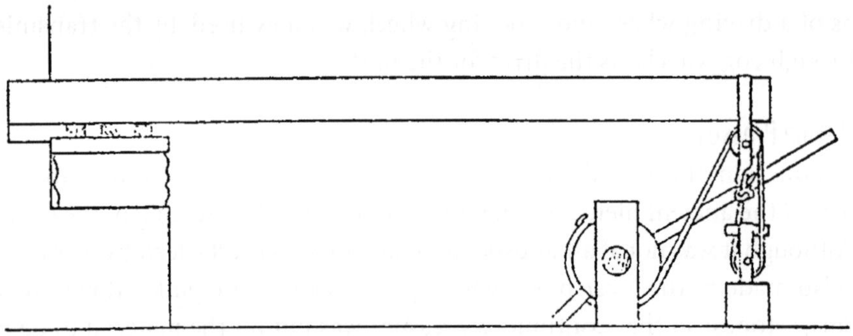

FIGURE 3.6 Lever-and-stone press according to Heron's *Mechanika* (3.13f.)

Source: Drachmann 1967: 32 (top)

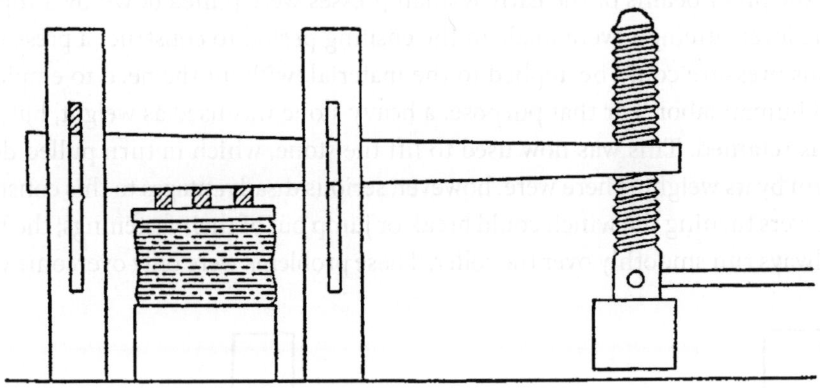

FIGURE 3.7 Lever-and-screw press according to Pliny the Elder (18.317)

Source: Drachmann 1967: 33

amongst them also presses without a stone weight, where the press-beam was pulled down by a screw fixed to the floor.

Towards the middle of the first century AD a new type of press emerged, where direct pressure was put on the material to be pressed by the rotation of a screw fitted vertically into a wooden frame. There were several advantages to this type of press: since there was no need for a long press-beam, this press needed very little space and could be easily transported.

This type of screw press appears relatively quickly in the urban context; it is remarkable that it was already used as a cloth press in Pompeii, that is before AD 79. The conditions of ancient technology clearly made it quite possible for equipment designed for agricultural use to be employed in craft production.[24]

24 Moeller 1976: 25–7.

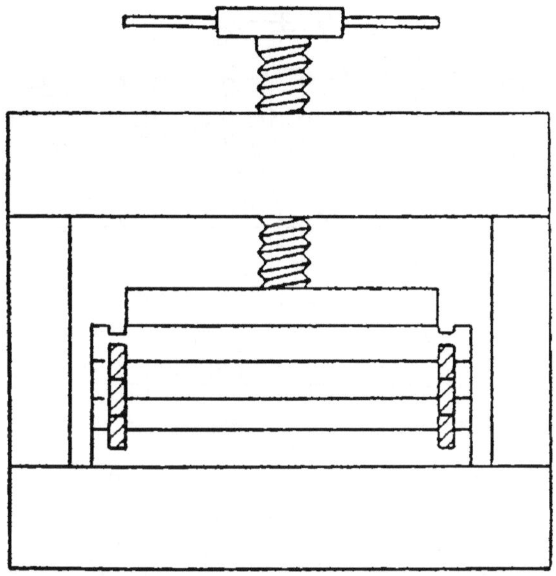

FIGURE 3.8 Screw-press according to Heron (3.20)

Source: Drachmann 1967: 36

Ancient presses proved to be so efficient that it was not possible to make fundamental improvements in them in the Middle Ages and in early modern times. In the Mediterranean lands, presses with press-beams and wooden screws were used until the early twentieth century; the screw press which put direct pressure on the material to be pressed was used in trade for other purposes, such as the book press for the printed book.

The development of the mill and the press is exemplary for technical change in antiquity: equipment that was important for production was improved; new mechanisms, such as the transmission of power through cog wheels or the generation of pressure through the turning of a screw, were introduced. Such technological progress is hardly to be rated as marginal.

(c) Innovations in the Production of Ceramics and Glass

The commercial production of ceramics supplied many families and households in antiquity with vessels and dishes of high quality; production of one's own clay pots for domestic use seems to have continued to be of importance only in remote rural regions. In these conditions, the potters produced large quantities of ceramic vessels for local and inter-regional markets from archaic times onwards. Technical innovations in ceramic production thus involved a trade which was of some economic importance.[25]

25 Peacock 1982; Bémont and Jacob 1986; Noble 1988.

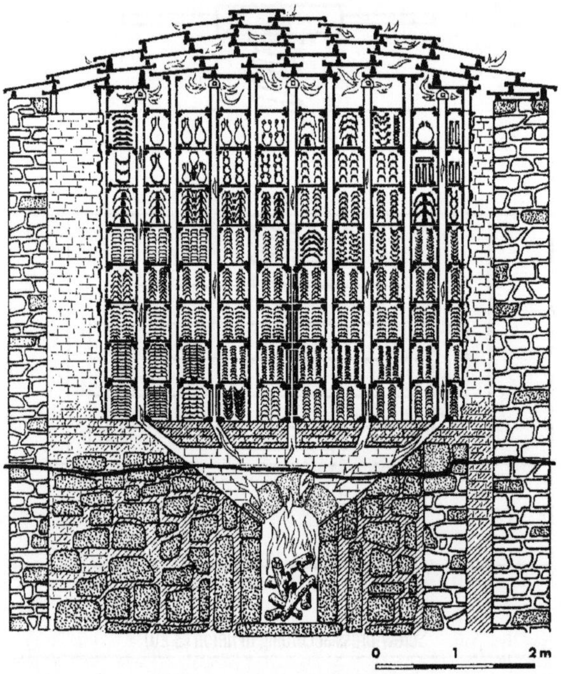

FIGURE 3.9 A large pottery-kiln at La Graufesenque

Reproduced from Vernhet 1981: 38

Already in archaic and classical times, the production of black- and red-figure Attic vases was based on considerable technical and manual skills: the clay had to be prepared diligently before the shaping of the pots, and the firing process required exact regulation of the temperature in the kiln and the oxygen supply during the separate phases of firing. In traditional ceramic production, the potter's work was limited to the shaping of the pot on the potter's wheel, while a vase painter painted the pots before firing. In Roman times, this working process was fundamentally changed for the production of the relief-decorated *terra sigillata* vessels, with the employment of moulds. Smooth *terra sigillata* pots, shaped without a mould, were still in mass production at the time of the Principate but, in addition, relief-decorated vessels from the pottery centers of Southern Gaul were marketed in many parts of the Empire during the first century AD. The thick-walled shaping bowls used as moulds carried on their inner side decoration in relief, executed by pressure with an incising tool (*poicon*). The production of relief-decorated ceramics was thus separated into three stages of work: first, the burins were cut; then the shaping bowl was prepared, with the hollow relief on its inner side; lastly, the mould was fired and used to shape the relief-decorated vessels. The potter put the mould at the center of his wheel, pressed the clay into the inside of the shaping bowl with the wheel turning, and thus drew up the wall of the pot. While the pot was being shaped, the relief decoration was simultaneously created, and the individual vessel did not require separate and time-consuming decoration. Once the clay had dried (and simultaneously shrunk), the pot was taken from the shaping bowl, which then could be used again. In this way it was possible to produce identical pots in great numbers; relief-decorated ceramics became an article of mass production.

In the pottery centers of Gaul, big kilns were erected for the firing of ceramics, which can hardly be compared with the kilns in Greek potteries. At La Graufesenque, such kilns were 4 meters wide and 3 meters high, and had a capacity of approximately 30,000 pots; lists, preserved as graffiti on bowls and plates, show that several potters delivered their products for simultaneous firing.[26]

In certain pottery centers, the existence of big installations for clay preparation can be demonstrated: it seems to have been already then appreciated that productivity in ceramic production could be increased by wider cooperation at the stages of clay preparation and firing.

Glass production provides a further example of the way in which technological innovations could have far-reaching economic consequences. Glass is a material which does not occur in nature, but has to be produced from various natural components (quartz sand, soda, lime); it was used, before the first century AD, primarily for the production of small containers. This glass was colored and opaque; small bottles were shaped by the sand-core method, in which a solid sand core was immersed into the molten glass. Two technological innovations made it possible to open up completely new production possibilities for glass as a material: with the glass-blowing pipe, bigger vessels could be shaped through glass bubbles, and certain additional ingredients made it possible to produce colorless, transparent glass. Thus the glassmakers were able to produce bottles, glasses, little jugs, and bowls which displayed their content for all to see. An anecdote about a glassmaker in Rome at the time of Tiberius and the representations of glass vessels on murals in Pompeii show that this new material exercised widespread fascination. Glass objects were soon distributed widely, and glass production in the western Mediterranean and the north-western provinces was accordingly soon on the increase. The gravestone in Lyon of the glassmaker Julius Alexander, who was of African origin, is testimony to the fact that this craft offered the opportunity for a certain prosperity. New techniques were repeatedly developed in ancient glass production: at the time of the early Principate, two-colored and two-layered glasses were created, with the use of moulds making it possible to decorate bottles in relief or shape vessels in the form of fruits. In late antiquity *diatreta* glass, with the appearance of being enveloped in a net, was created by intricate cutting methods. Finally, even glass plates with applied figural images made of gold were produced. Besides the plain glassware for domestic use, the products of glassmakers included precious luxury items. The development of Roman glass production proves the craftsmen's ability to innovate and to

26 Marichal 1988.

be in total command of new techniques. In addition, it is clear that technical innovations spread and put to economic use fairly rapidly.[27]

(d) New Building Techniques: Arch Construction and *Opus Caementicum*

Ancient architecture underwent a complete change during the Hellenistic age and the early Principate, thanks to two technological changes; this transition was not limited to the aesthetic dimension, but opened up entirely new possibilities for creating large interior spaces, without the use of many supports, and for bridging large spans. Arch construction undoubtedly had an effect on the design of façades, in particular of Roman monumental architecture; but its wider use was in the construction of installations for the infrastructure, for instance in the building of the bridges so important for the network of Roman roads. Similarly, aqueducts were led across wide valleys on top of high arches, as for example in the Pont du Gard in the south of France. In order to bring water to Rome in an open channel at the highest possible level, arched stretches more than 9 km in length were in several cases constructed in the plains outside the city.

From the second century BC a new building material, *opus caementicium*, came into use. This was a kind of liquid concrete which could be poured into wooden boarding and which, when it dried, was of such firmness that it was also suitable for the building of vaults and domes. Examples of this new building technique are the Pantheon, constructed at the time of Hadrian, which has a dome bigger than that of St. Peter in Rome or the Duomo in Florence, and the Frigidarium of the Baths of Diocletian (today S. Maria degli Angeli). In particular, utilitarian buildings used for trade, such as the market halls at Ferentinum or in Trajan's Forum in Rome, had large vaults made of *opus caementicium*. During the early Principate, in particular after the fire in Rome at the time of Nero, fired brick came into wide use as a building material for walls; the walls of larger buildings were often furnished with a core of *opus caementicium*, with the brick walls having the function of a boarding. Since *opus caementicium* retained its firmness even under water, it could also be used for the building of harbors.[28]

The construction of building complexes for inner-city trade, as well as the intensified improvements in the infrastructure of transport and traffic, were without a doubt of considerable importance for the Roman economy. In the big inland spaces of the western and north-western provinces especially, the transport of goods was dependent on a network of good and passable roads; bridges made river crossings possible without passing through fords. Improvements in Mediterranean harbors, such as the construction of the mole at Puteoli or of the harbor basin at the mouth of the Tiber, supported long-distance trade and thus secured the supply of the big cities.

---

27 Strong and Brown 1976: 111–25; Newby and Painter 1991; Schneider 1992: 108–19; Plin. *HN*. 36.189–99; Strabo 16.2.23; Petron. *Sat.* 51; Sen. *Ep.* 90.31; Dessau, *ILS* 7648.

28 White 1984: 73–90; Adam 1984; Hodge 1992; O'Connor 1993; Vitr. *De arch.* 2.6.

(e) Shipping and Land Transport

There were numerous innovations in shipping in antiquity, closely connected with the expansion and intensification of trade and the exchange of goods in the Mediterranean. Already in the archaic period, the long, slim galleys were no longer adequate for the demands of longer trading journeys. From the sixth century, therefore, ships were built with a thick-set body, high sides, high masts and a big square-rig sail. These ships were wind driven and therefore no longer needed rowers; because of their bigger loading capacity, they could be used for the transport of mass-produced goods such as grain, wine, and oil. In the time of the early Principate, grain for the city of Rome was transported from Egypt to central Italy by ships that could carry loads of over 450 tonnes in weight. One problem with such ships was that they often had only one sail; in order to increase the size, some Roman trading ships had two further masts installed at the bow and at the stern, besides the mainmast in the middle of the ship; and a triangular upper sail was fixed above the mainsail on the central mast. At the same time, the rigging and thus the maneuverability of the ships was improved. In figural representations, the lateen sail appears besides the square rig: its main use was probably for coastal shipping in the eastern Mediterranean. Ancient ships were perfectly capable of navigating the high seas: after the discovery of the monsoon winds, Roman ships traveling in convoy took the direct route to India by the Red Sea and across the Indian Ocean. The lighthouse of Brigantium (La Coruña) in north-western Spain proves the existence of Roman seafaring on the Atlantic.[29]

The construction of the boats used for the transport of goods on the rivers of the north-western provinces also underwent a series of technical changes. As is demonstrated by the finds of wrecks at Mainz, the Romans on the Rhine went over from the shell construction common in the Mediterranean, to skeleton construction, which made the building of the hull noticeably easier. Another characteristic of these boats is that the single rudder is firmly fixed to the stern post; this is clearly visible on several reliefs.

In the Mediterranean world until late antiquity, overland transport of heavy loads was mostly carried on in the traditional manner, that is, with pack animals or two-wheeled ox-carts; but at the same time, the fundamental change in overland transport in the north-western provinces, and also in northern Italy, should not be overlooked. Strabo already appreciated the close connection between improvements in traffic infrastructure and technological developments in transport; in comparing Roman and Greek building activities, he notes that Roman roads were constructed in such a way as to allow the transport of entire ship's cargoes by cart. As is documented by numerous reliefs and mosaics, new methods of harnessing were experimented with, especially in Gaul and northern Italy; at the same time, carts were constructed which were better suited to the long-distance transport of heavy loads than the usual ox-carts with their big disc-wheels. While in archaic and classical Greece two oxen—more rarely two mules—were normally harnessed to a yoke fixed to the cart's shaft, during the Principate horses began to be increasingly used

29 Casson 1971; Landels 1978: 133–66; White 1984: 141–56.

for overland transport. The harness was now adapted to the horse's anatomy, so that the animals were not handicapped when pulling. In Roman Gaul, heavy carts with two axels and spoked wheels were used for the transport of goods. They were usually pulled by two horses: a relief from Langres even shows a team of horses harnessed in couples behind each other. It was also possible to harness a single horse to a two-wheeled cart; the horse then walked between two poles, which were connected to the harness around the horse's neck.[30]

From Augustan times, wooden barrels were used in Gaul and northern Italy as containers for wine; their decisive advantage over amphoras was the better ratio between the weight of the container and the weight of the fluid; moreover, since vats did not have to be carried like amphoras but could be rolled, the transport of fluids, for example when loading or unloading ships, was made considerably easier. While smaller barrels were used for river transport, bigger carts were sometimes loaded with a single barrel of considerable capacity.[31]

(f) Water-lifting Equipment

In ancient Egypt as well as in archaic Greece, devices for the lifting of water already existed: the *shaduf*, a swing-beam to which a scooping container and a counterweight were fastened, was used in Egypt for the irrigation of fields and gardens; with the *shaduf*, water could be taken from a river or canal and led to a field higher up. In Greece, such swing-beams were fixed directly to the well, in order to make the lifting of the water-filled clay vessels easier.

Two new devices for the raising of water were the scoop-wheel and the Archimedean screw. The scoop-wheel was either fitted at its circumference with boxes to take up the water, or else had containers attached there, which were then emptied at the highest point of the wheel. If the scoop-wheel was located on a river with strong enough currents, it could be driven by water power. The Archimedean screw, on the other hand, set up in a slanting position, had to be turned by human power; it could lift water only over a small vertical interval, but was an efficient device for the irrigation of agricultural land in Egypt.[32]

But the preeminent economic importance of water-lifting equipment lay in its use in Roman mines, much more than in its agricultural uses. When the Romans in Spain started to mine precious metals below ground-water level, they had to tackle the problems of drainage. For this, water-lifting equipment, long since used for the irrigation of fields, was installed in the mines. The contemporaries of the Romans were much impressed by their ability to pump whole streams of water out of mines with the help of the Archimedean screw: it was a precondition for the mining of gold and silver. Besides Archimedean screws, scoop-wheels were also set up in mines; since their size made it impossible to take them to their final position through the narrow shafts and galleries, they were put together from their components underground.

30 Landels 1978: 170–85; White 1984: 127–40; Raepsaet 2002.

31 Plin. *HN* 14.132; Strabo 5.1.8; 5.1.12; White 1984: 133; Zimmer 1982: 218–19; 229–30.

32 Oleson 1984; Landels 1978: 58–83; Wikander 2000: 217–302; Vitruvius, *De arch*. 10.4–6.

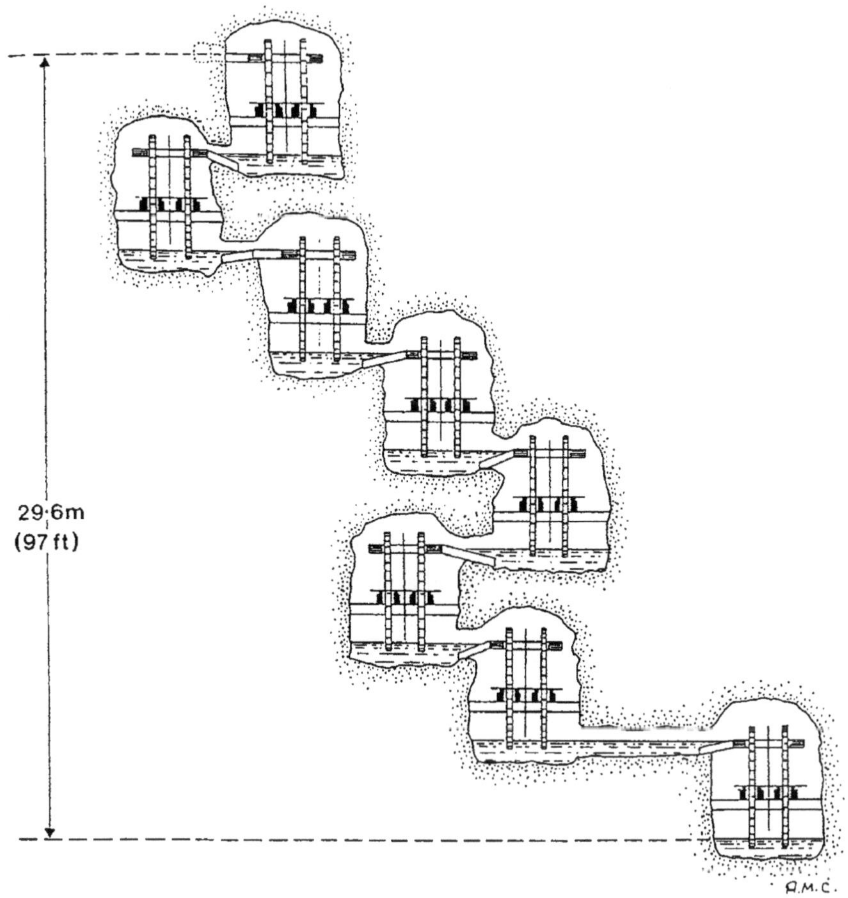

FIGURE 3.10 **Water wheels used for drainage at Rio Tinto**

Source: Wacher 1987: vol. II, 621

Only through the Roman solution of the technical problem of water containment in the silver and gold mines could sufficient quantities of precious metal be mined for the minting of coins under the late Republic and the early Principate.[33]

IV. Technical Knowledge and Economic Development

At many levels in ancient societies, technical knowledge was passed on orally: experiences and knowledge were handed down from the older to the younger generation in the context of the rural family, without the need to record them. Similarly, in the field of craftsmanship,

33 Diod. Sic. 5.37.3f.; Healy 1978: 93–100; Domergue 1990: 443–60.

apprentices gained the necessary competence for the practice of their craft through direct contact with an older craftsman.[34] Apart from this knowledge gained through experience by farmers and craftsmen, a body of technological knowledge grew up in classical Greece, which was used to employ mechanical instruments with maximum efficiency, or to construct equipment designed for certain purposes. Architects in particular faced grave problems with the construction of monumental buildings, and needed a great deal of technological creativity to solve them. Examples are the lifting of heavy ashlar blocks, the transport of stone blocks from the quarry to the building site, or the laying of foundations in soft ground. Already in early classical times architects self-consciously recorded their achievements in their own writings. Later, Vitruvius systematically summarized the specialist knowledge of architecture, with technical aspects taking up a substantial part of his work.[35]

In the field of engineering, the aim of specialist knowledge was to understand exactly the causes behind the effectiveness of mechanical instruments; for example, much attention was paid to the lever and its effects. A specialist literature developed in the fourth century BC for this area of ancient technology, which was by no means confined to theoretical knowledge, but was quite attuned to practical application, for example, the *Mechanica* of Heron of Alexandria. Heron was interested in the improvement of presses, and was able to expound exactly the advantages and disadvantages of the various types of press, taking also the safety of the workers into consideration. It was specifically in the field of engineering that considerable progress, of importance for general technology and consequently for the economy, was made. A precise description of the transmission of power by cog-wheel, or the use of a combination of rollers (block and tackle) for the lifting of heavy loads, was achieved; the screw and the advantages of the screw press are also the subject of longish explanations.[36]

An enlightened attitude towards technological innovation is clearly expressed in the Roman literature on agriculture, by Cato, Varro, and Columella; fairly long treatises are devoted to the devices for pressing olives, the equipment used for threshing, or the methods of fertilization. Pliny likewise mentions, in his *Natural History*, new devices such as the heavy plough pulled by four oxen, the mowing machine used in Gaul, or the screw press.[37] The work of Pliny undoubtedly contributed to the spread of technological knowledge. The recording of technological knowledge in writing did not, however, lead to a permanent process of technological innovation; technological change remained in many cases spasmodic and dependent on specific contexts.

34 Meissner 1999.

35 Vitr. *De arch.* 10.2.11f.; cf. 7, *Praefatio* 12; Plin. *HN* 36.95–8.

36 Arist. [*Mech.*]; Heron, *Mechanica*; Drachmann 1963; Gille 1980.

37 Cato, *Agr.* 18–22; Varro, *Rust.* 1.29.1; 1.52; Columella, *Rust.* 12.52.6f.; Plin. *HN* 18.171–3; 18.296; 18.317.

V. Conclusion

The recent debate on the ancient economy distinguishes clearly between two forms of economic growth in pre-industrial societies: on the one hand, with the level of productivity remaining stable, growth depends on the extension of the land available for agriculture, on the opening up of new mines, or on an increase in the number of workshops. A precondition for this type of growth (extensive or aggregate growth) is a numerical increase in the labor force. Per capita growth, on the other hand, is dependent on an increase in work productivity; its prerequisites are normally technological innovation and an increase in financial expenditure on technical provision at production sites.[38]

In the debates of economic history, two fundamental facts are perhaps beyond dispute: on the one hand, that in antiquity as in other pre-industrial societies, considerable extensive growth took place, visibly represented by urbanization, the growth of urban settlements and the foundation of new cities, the development of wider regions for intensive agricultural use and the extension of mining activities; on the other hand, that economic growth since the beginning of the Industrial Revolution has essentially been attributed to an increase in work productivity, which in turn is highly dependent on increasing division of labor, technological innovation and rising capital investment.

The question that faces ancient historians is whether, and if so to what degree, technological innovation in antiquity contributed to a growth in productivity, and thus generally to intensive economic or per capita growth. First, the way in which working processes in agriculture, craft, and building were changed through technological development must be clarified. In antiquity, there were various possibilities for increasing the productivity of work processes: the introduction of new tools, the improvement of known tools and equipment, or the construction of complex mechanical devices. An example of the introduction of a new tool is the use of handled shears for sheep shearing in Roman Italy.[39] The importance of improvements in the details of technical equipment is often underrated. This is true for the vertical loom, which in Roman times had an upper and a lower beam, while the Greek loom possessed only the upper cloth-beam, the warp-threads being held taut by weights. At first glance, this change seems insignificant, but it made it possible to push the weft-thread downwards on to the already woven fabric and to weave sitting down, while with older looms the women had to work standing, and with raised arms. In this case, technological improvement certainly led to a considerable reduction in physical exertion. As is demonstrated by the development of the grain mill, there was even the possibility of a partial mechanization of work processes, resulting in the use of animal muscle power and finally of water power as the driving force. Mill complexes such as those near Arles and on the Janiculan hill in Rome had a high capacity of output and could meet the demands of several thousand people. A targeted use of the laws of mechanics also characterizes the construction

38 Saller 2002.

39 Varro, *Rust.* 2.11.9.

of oil- and wine-presses or water lifting equipment, and the use of block-and-tackle for lifting heavy loads in the construction of large buildings. The Romans were also capable of adapting traditional technology to new conditions: many technological innovations can be traced in Gaul, for instance the wheeled plough mentioned by Pliny, which was better suited to the heavy soil of the regions north of the Alps than the Mediterranean plough; or the mower specific to Gaul, which allowed the harvest to be brought in in the quickest possible way and with little expenditure of labor.[40] By comparison with the archaic epoch, such technological developments certainly increased the productivity of work processes in Hellenistic and Roman times.

But at the same time the limitations of technological development in antiquity must be emphasized. In the area of craftsmanship, manual tools were never replaced by machines nor, by and large, was manual production ever pushed aside. Such a division of labor as is described by Adam Smith in the famous first chapter of *The Wealth of Nations* was therefore hardly possible in the ancient sites of production. In contrast with the factories of the Industrial Revolution, the introduction of larger workshops barely influenced working processes. Such workshops were therefore essentially no more productive than the small ones in which one craftsman worked with his assistants. Normally, the workshops were not elaborately fitted out and it was quite cheap to set up a workshop; a craftsman usually needed only a few tools for his craft and often practiced it in a shop connected with his living quarters. There were some crafts, however, which were dependent on bigger production sites with more expensive equipment: bakeries had their ovens and mills, smithies their forges for bringing iron to red heat, and fulling plants their big water basins for the working of cloth. Bakers and fullers in particular were sometimes quite well-off: the baker Eurysaces, for example, was able to have erected for himself a pretentious monument at the Porta Maggiore in Rome, and the fullers of Pompeii were able to donate money for a statue for Eumachia.

In such conditions as these, it hardly made sense for the members of the upper classes to invest part of their wealth in large-scale enterprises for commercial production: the chances of obtaining high returns from craft-based production were clearly lower than in agriculture or in money-lending. One of the few exceptions, from the time of the early Principate, was brick production: here, some big land-owners made economic use of the clay from their estates by setting up brickworks, which delivered building materials even to distant cities. The chances of a profitable return arose from the building boom in Rome and in other cities, such as Carthage, ensuring the sale of large amounts of brick.

The dominant feature of urban trade continued to be the small workshop, and even production centers that were of inter-regional importance comprised not large-scale concerns, but a multitude of small businesses.[41] In special cases a number of craftsmen, each working in their own small workshop, were able to use certain production facilities in

40 Pliny, *HN* 18.171–3; 18.296.

41 Manning 1987: 587.

common, for example at La Graufesenque, where many potters were able to fire their pots simultaneously in the big kilns. Ancient craftsmanship achieved its highest possible quality and productivity by the specialization of individual craftsmen or workshops in certain products; production and products were crucially governed by the experience and practice of the individual craftsman. Antiquity was characterized not by the large concern, where the work process would be divided (vertical specialization) into a multitude of individual operations with a marked division of labor, but by a specialization, as far-reaching as was possible, of craftsmen and workshops (horizontal specialization). The degree of specialization was dependent on the size of particular markets: a small rural settlement undoubtedly offered fewer opportunities for craft specialization than a bigger town with an affluent group of consumers.[42] That specialization in individual trades and professions makes economic sense and leads to a better supply of goods for a *polis* was a claim already recognized, and extensively supported through theory, by Plato.[43]

In any analysis of the role which technological innovation played in economic growth, it must be borne in mind that productivity could be increased not only through technological progress, but also through improvement in the organization of labor. This is especially true for the big estates of Hellenistic and Roman times: the control over slaves, the exact listing of individual duties, the establishment of work norms, the motivation of the slaves through rewards, even the fixing of food rations aimed at securing the highest possible income for the owners of the big estates. Labor organization and technological advance complemented each other nicely in estate management: estate owners like Cato paid attention to both.

But technological progress should not only be seen from the point of view of increase in productivity: the new possibilities of arch construction and of *opus caementicium* were employed in architecture in order to create an efficient infrastructure for transport, trade and exchange, both in the cities and in rural regions; water supply for urban populations was secured by the building of aqueducts; in this way, technological change also has an effect on health and welfare. The effects of an efficient infrastructure on the economic growth of pre-industrial societies are difficult to evaluate, but it can safely be assumed that the infrastructure of the Roman empire contributed substantially to the standard of living and the prosperity of Roman society. Urbanization in the Mediterranean lands had been possible only on the condition that agriculture and craft were able to provide the growing urban populations with food and consumer goods, and that the erection of public buildings, which served the benefit of the population, was technically and financially possible.

Technological change in the ancient Mediterranean never changed production in agriculture and craft as fundamentally as did the Industrial Revolution, and never increased productivity to a degree that would have resulted in change to the economic or social structure. On the contrary, technological progress in antiquity always took place within the framework of the agricultural society and never achieved the same dynamic as the innovatory

42 Xen. *Cyr.* 8.2.5.

43 Pl. *Resp.* 369d–371e; 374a; 397e; Harris 2002; compare with Rome also Treggiari 1980.

processes of modern industrial societies. To point out the technological innovations of antiquity and their economic effects is by no means to express agreement with a modernist view of ancient technology and economics; rather, it is meant to contribute to an adequate recording of the importance of technological change for ancient agricultural societies.

Bibliography

Adam, J.-P. (1984) *La construction romaine. Matériaux et techniques.* Paris.

Amouretti, M.-C. (1986) *Le pain et l'huile dans la Grèce antique. De l'araire au moulin.* Centre de Recherche d'Histoire Ancienne vol. 67/ ALUB 328. Paris.

——. (1991) "L'attelage dans l'antiquité. Le prestige d'une erreur scientifique," *Annales ESC* 46: 219–32.

Bémont, C. and Jacob, J.-P., eds. (1986) *La terre sigillée gallo-romaine. Lieux de production du Haute Empire: implantations, produits, relations.* Paris.

Brun, J.-P. (1986) *L'oléiculture antique en Provence. Les huileries du département du Var.* Revue archéologique de Narbonnaise Suppl. 15. Paris.

Casson, L. (1971) *Ships and Seamanship in the Ancient World.* Princeton. ed. (1984a) *Ancient Trade and Society.* Detroit.

Diels, H. (1920) *Antike Technik.* Leipzig.

Domergue, C. (1990) *Les mines de la péninsule ibérique dans l'antiquité romaine.* Paris and Rome.

Drachmann, A. G. (1932) *Ancient Oil Mills and Presses.* Copenhagen.

——. (1963) *The Mechanical Technology of Greek and Roman Antiquity.* Copenhagen.

——. (1967) *Grosse griechische Erfinder.* Zürich.

Finley, M. I. (1965b) "Technical innovation and economic progress in the ancient world," *Economic History Review* 18: 29–45.

Gille, B. ed. (1978) *Histoire des Techniques. Technique et civilisations. Technique et sciences.* Paris.

——. (1980) *Les mécaniciens grecs. La naissance de la technologie.* Paris.

Greene, K. (1990) "Perspectives on Roman technology," *Oxford Journal of Archaeology* 9: 209–19.

——. (2000) "Technological innovation and economic progress in the ancient world: M. I. Finley re-considered," *Economic History Review* 53: 29–59.

Halleux, R. (1977) "Problèmes de l'énergie dans le monde ancien," *LEC* 45: 49–61.

Harris, E. M. (2002) "Workshop, marketplace, and household: the nature of technical specialization in classical Athens and its influence on economy and society," in Cartledge et al., eds. (2002): 67–99.

Healy, J. F. (1978) *Mining and Metallurgy in the Greek and Roman World.* London.

Hodge, A. T. (1992) *Roman Aqueducts and Water Supply.* London.

Isager, S. and Skydsgaard, J. E. (1992) *Ancient Greek Agriculture.* London.

Kiechle, F. (1969) *Sklavenarbeit und technischer Fortschritt im römischen Reich.* Wiesbaden.

Lämmli, F. (1968) *Homo Faber: Triumph, Schuld, Verhängnis?* Basel.

Landels, J. G. (1978) *Engineering in the Ancient World.* London.

Leveau, P. (1996) "The Barbegal water mill in its environment: archaeology and the economic history of antiquity," *JRA* 9: 137–53.
Lombroso-Ferrero, G. (1920) "Pourquoi le machinisme ne fut pas adopté dans l'antiquité?" *Revue du Mois* 21: 448–69.
Manning, W. H. (1987) "Industrial growth," in Wacher, ed. (1987): 586–610.
Marichal, R. (1988) *Les graffites de la Graufesenque. XLVII*e supplément à "Gallia". Paris.
Maróti, E. (1975) "Über die Verbreitung der Wassermühlen in Europa," *Acta Antiqua* 23: 255–80.
Meissner, B. (1999) *Die technologische Fachliteratur der Antike. Struktur, Überlieferung und Wirkung technischen Wissens in der Antike (ca. 400 v. Chr.—ca. 500 n. Chr.).* Berlin.
Moeller, W. (1976) *The Wool Trade of Ancient Pompeii.* Leiden.
Moritz, L. A. (1958) *Grain Mills and Flour in Classical Antiquity.* Oxford.
Newby, M. and Painter, K., eds. (1991) *Roman Glass: Two Centuries of Art and Invention.* London.
Noble, J. V. (1988) *The Techniques of Painted Attic Pottery.* London.
O'Connor, C. (1993) *Roman Bridges.* Cambridge.
Oleson, J. P. (1984) *Greek and Roman Mechanical Water-Lifting Devices: The History of a Technology.* Toronto.
Peacock, D. P. S. (1982) *Pottery in the Roman World: An Ethnoarchaeological Approach.* London and New York.
Persson, K. G. (1988) *Pre-Industrial Economic Growth: Social Organization and Technological Progress in Europe.* Oxford.
Raepsaet, G. (2002) *Attelages et techniques de transport dans le monde gréco-romain.* Brussels.
Reece, D. W. (1969) "The technological weakness of the ancient world," *G&R* 16: 32–47.
Rossiter, J. J. (1981) "Wine and oil processing at Roman farms in Italy," *Phoenix* 35: 345–61.
Sagui, C. L. (1948) "La meunerie de Barbégal (France) et les roues hydrauliques chez les anciens et au moyen âge," *Isis* 38: 225–31.
Saller, R. (2002 = 2005) "Framing the debate over growth in the ancient economy," in Scheidel and von Reden, eds. (2002): 251–69, and in Manning and Morris, eds. (2005): 223–38.
Schneider, H. (1992) *Einführung in die antike Technikgeschichte.* Darmstadt.
Strong, D. and Brown, D. eds. (1976) *Roman Crafts.* London.
Treggiari, S. (1980) "Urban labour in Rome: mercennarii and tabernarii," in P. Garnsey, ed., *Non-Slave Labour in the Greco-Roman World*: 48–64. Cambridge.
Wacher, J., ed. (1987) *The Roman World.* London.
White, K. D. (1970b) *Roman Farming.* London.
———. (1984) *Greek and Roman Technology.* London.
Wikander, Ö. (1981) "The use of water-power in classical antiquity," *Opuscula Romana* 13: 91–104.
———. (1984) *Exploitation of Water-Power or Technological Stagnation? A Reappraisal of the Productive Forces in the Roman Empire.* Lund.
———. ed. (2000) *Handbook of Ancient Water Technology.* Leiden.
Wilson, A. (2002) "Machines, power, and the ancient economy," *JRS* 92: 1–32.
Zimmer, G. (1982) *Römische Berufsdarstellungen.* Berlin.

CHAPTER FOUR

Late Roman Social Structures and the Late Roman Economy

Averil Cameron

Understanding the late Roman economy presents a particular challenge. Because of the deep-seated disposition to think in terms of 'decline', attention has traditionally been focused on the supposed negative indicators. Certain topics, such as slavery, taxation and the so-called 'colonate' (see pp. 85ff.), have occupied a special place in the secondary literature. All have undergone re-evaluation in recent years, and many other older assumptions have been questioned as well. In addition, the increased interest in this period shown by archaeologists in the past two decades or so, and the vast amount of new evidence that is becoming available mean that the old questions can be looked at in new ways. This has meant that the late Roman economy in general is now one of the most lively areas of current research. It is not too much to say that the large volume of new material is dramatically changing the look of the subject.

The Older Model

As I have suggested, the whole subject of the late Roman economy (which involves also the consideration of groups such as landowners, tenants and slaves) is closely tied to conventional historiographical models of decline and collapse, and economic collapse, or at the very least severe strain, has been adduced by many historians anxious to explain Rome's fall. The resulting scenario is however more a convenient myth than a realistic analysis.

In the first place much of the evidence is impressionistic. Complaints about tax collectors or soldiers billeted in towns are indeed extremely common, but similar examples can be found in almost any society, and need to be read with caution. Whether things had really changed significantly for the worse is equally hard to establish; it is possible to find plenty of evidence from the Principate which suggests that the condition of the peasant then was hardly better.[1] Individual instances of peasants taking evasive action at the tax collector's approach (see p. 98) do not necessarily add up to a general picture of flight and collapse. A more fundamental problem is posed by the legal evidence, especially the often repeated laws in the Theodosian Code, by which successive emperors legislated to keep decurions in place in their towns and *coloni* on the estates in which they are registered (see p. 86). The picture of oppression and authoritarianism which these laws seem to suggest has been endorsed by many scholars, who have represented the later Roman empire as virtually collapsing under its own weight, and described it in terms such as 'totalitarian' and 'repressive'.[2] But when laws are constantly repeated they must be presumed to be ineffective; moreover, laws need enforcement. Where the necessary apparatus for the latter is lacking, it may be comforting for those in authority to repeat the law itself, but it does not necessarily follow that it was actually carried out in practice.

The literary sources may also distort the picture, and taking them at face value can lead to equally overstated conclusions. Many modern discussions take literally the apparent statement by the Christian Lactantius (*De mortibus persecutorum* 7), a biased and hostile source, that Diocletian quadrupled the size of the army, and then used this as the basis for a highly negative view of the economy in general. Similarly, despite Diocletian's measures to ensure better collection of revenue, it is far from certain that the level of taxation itself increased, as many scholars have assumed.[3] The few general statements that we have on such matters as taxation tend to come from writers as biased and as unsubtle as the pagan Zosimus or the fifth-century Christian moralist Salvian, and must be treated with considerable caution. Finally, in considering these methodological issues, it is also necessary to consider the relative weight of internal factors versus external ones like the impact of barbarian invasion and the question of east versus west. After all, if the structure of the state in the late fourth and fifth centuries was as top-heavy and as liable to collapse from its own internal contradictions as many scholars assert, why is it that the eastern empire seems to have gone from strength to strength?

1 See for instance Peter Garnsey and Richard Saller, *The Roman Empire. Economy, Society and Culture*, London, 1987; and Peter Garnsey, *Famine and Food Supply in the Graeco-Roman World*, Cambridge, 1988, ch. 15.

2 Among them A. H. M. Jones; see especially his articles on the colonate and on taxation in P. Brunt (ed.), *The Roman Economy*, Oxford, 1974; M. I. Rostovtzeff, *SEHRE*, ch. 12. cf., e.g., C. G. Starr, *The Roman Empire, 27 bc to ad 476*, Oxford, 1982, 164–5: 'politically the structure of the Later Roman Empire is one of the grimmest of all ancient times'; 'to modern man, the corrupt, brutal regimentation of the Later Empire appears as a horrible example of the victory of the state over the individual'. Peter Brown's review discussion of Jones, *LRE*, in his *Religion and Society in the Age of St. Augustine*, London, 1972, 46–73, is still worth reading.

3 For example, A. H. M. Jones, 'Over-taxation and the decline of the Roman Empire', in Brunt (ed.), *The Roman Economy*, 82–9.

An Alternative Approach

It is the contribution of archaeology in particular which has led historians to question the older view, and it is worth noting that A. H. M. Jones published his great work, *The Later Roman Empire,* in 1964, well before the current interest in late Roman and early medieval archaeology. Such a book would look very different today. But it is also a matter of new ways of looking at the subject. While the older assumptions of decline are still very much with us,[4] many historians have been influenced by different approaches, especially comparative ones. Perhaps most interestingly, the lively debate about the ancient economy in general which has been going on since the publication of M. I. Finley's *The Ancient Economy* in 1973,[5] has taken in the later empire as well as the Principate, thus to some extent bypassing the supposed great divide that came with the third century and the reforms of Diocletian.[6] The older model depends on the view of a massive tightening up of government control and consequent increase of government expenditure, generally attributed to Diocletian. If, however, those reforms were actually merely revisionist in character, this in turn should cause us to question the general model, and in particular to pay more attention to the underlying economic structures which held good throughout the long history of the empire.[7]

East and West

There are of course certain obvious issues which do affect the later period specifically, including that of the increasing divide between east and west. Here it is important to remember that the basic administrative, economic and military structures of the Roman state established in the early fourth century were still in place in the eastern empire at least up to the reign of Justinian, and often beyond. We must therefore look for special factors, such as those described in Chapter 2, to explain why the west should have been different.

The late Roman tax system was designed to cope with a situation in which continual debasement of the coinage had led to near collapse and revenues had to be collected and payments made to the troops in kind; the regular census and the five-year indiction aimed at ensuring reliable collection of tax revenue for the state, and the scheme also involved elaborate matching of need and supply. The main item of expenditure as before was on the army, who were now paid in kind as well as money (Chapter 2). Certain obvious consequences followed: army units (themselves far more varied in type and organization than

4 Alföldy, *Social History,* ch. 7.

5 *The Ancient Economy,* Berkeley and Los Angeles, Calif., 1973, 2nd rev. edn, London, 1985.

6 For a useful introduction to the issues and for further reading see Kevin Greene, *The Archaeology of the Roman Economy,* London, 1986, 45–66.

7 For a good general introduction to the Roman economy in the early empire, emphasizing its structural features, see Garnsey and Saller, *The Roman Empire.*

previously) now tended for instance to be stationed near to the sources of supply, and thus in or near towns, instead of on the frontiers. While by the end of the fourth century more payments were made in cash, the central role of the state in collecting and distributing the *annona* (the army supplies) remained an important feature of the economy, both in terms of organization and stimulus to production; the cessation of this state function in the fifth century was a major factor leading to economic fragmentation, as was the end of the grain requisitions for the city of Rome (Chapter 7).

In contrast, basically the same system was in force in the east as in the west, but apparently with more success. A number of factors contributed to this. The east, for instance, had been much earlier and more successfully urbanized than the west and, despite the ceaseless complaints of municipal councils and their spokesmen, most of these cities continued in existence or were even flourishing during the fifth and sixth centuries. We hear a great deal about their problems, not least because our written sources tend to come from just this kind of milieu; thus Ammianus Marcellinus, Libanius, Julian and later Procopius all took up the cause of the cities versus the central government (see Chapter 7). But many of their complaints had an ideological basis; in practice, the fifth and early sixth centuries seem to have been a time of prosperity for many eastern regions, especially parts of Syria and Palestine (Chapters 1 and 8). Another obvious difference between east and west in economic terms relates to the constant and in the end more serious barbarian incursions suffered by the west in the fifth century; not only was the economic base itself weaker than in the east (see p. 95), but the demands on it were greater. As we have seen, the western government had great difficulty in maintaining military forces adequate for their task. But a deeper and more structural difference lay in the growth of an immensely rich and powerful class of senatorial landowners in the west during the fourth century, whereas wealth in the east was by comparison more evenly spread. The combination of a weak government and wealthy and powerful landowners was crucial in determining the shape of the western economy.

Thus east and west were both similar and dissimilar in this period. Local factors are increasingly important from AD 395 onwards, yet many shared features remain and some similar trends can be observed, even though the rate of change may differ. The standard accounts of decline and collapse obscure these real differences. In contrast, the present lively state of archaeological investigation invites us to compare one site or area with another, and encourages the broader view; it also invites the question of how the traditional textual evidence and the increasing amount of material evidence relate to each other. By the end of our period, while it is still possible in some ways to speak of a Mediterranean world,[8] the west has largely fragmented, while the eastern government and its provincial and defensive structures are clearly in a far weaker position than before. It is possible to argue, as we shall see, that Justinian's wars of reconquest (Chapter 5) actually contributed to this weakness, as did the catastrophic plague which first hit the empire in AD 541. In addition there were

8 cf. Peter Brown, 'Eastern and western Christendom in late antiquity: a parting of the ways', in id., *Society and the Holy in the Late Antiquity,* Berkeley and Los Angeles, Calif., 1982, 166–95.

also structural factors which we can see reflected in the gradual metamorphosis of many cities in the eastern empire either into medieval towns or (more often) into villages, a process which had begun before the end of the sixth century (see Chapter 7). In many areas, the signs of prosperity evident earlier were already beginning to tail off when the Persian invasions of the early seventh century dealt another severe blow to the east, and made it unable to resist the first Arab conquests of the 630s (see Chapter 8). Taking a long view, it is possible to argue that the east and west underwent similar processes, but at different times, the speed of change being regulated by the operation of local factors.[9]

The Organization of Labour

It has been argued, notably by M. I. Finley, that large-scale slavery declined in the Roman empire for a variety of reasons, of which the most important was a drying-up of the main supply of slaves when the more or less continuous wars of conquest ceased in the early empire. Yet the sources for the late Roman empire make it clear that slaves continued to exist;[10] sometimes indeed they existed in very large numbers, for example on the vast estates of senatorial landowners. When such landowners became Christian, they sometimes sold their property in order to use the wealth for Christian purposes, in which case the slaves were sold too; we know that this was the case with certain estates which belonged to Melania the Younger in the early fifth century (see p. 78). Legal sources also demonstrate the continued existence of slaves on the land and elsewhere, and the church itself soon became a major owner of slaves. We can assume that part of the labour force on the land and in many forms of production will still have been servile. However, it is less clear what this meant in practice or how slaves related to *coloni*, technically free tenants who were, in many areas, theoretically tied to their particular estates by imperial legislation, and over whom the landlords had rights which can look very like the rights of owner over slave. It was for instance possible to be described as *servus et colonus* (both a slave and a *colonus*), and it is clear that slaves could themselves be tenants.

This apparent confusion illustrates very well one of the basic problems we have in understanding the late empire. Are we to take the mass of imperial legislation at face value? How reliable a picture does it present of the way in which society really worked? As we can see from the *Codex Theodosianus* under Theodosius II, and from the *Codex Justinianus* a century later, late Roman emperors passed repeated laws which on the face of it sought to restrict the freedom of movement of *coloni* and tie them to the land; if these laws were really

9 This is essentially the view of K. Randsborg, *The First Millennium ad in Europe and the Mediterranean. An Archaeological Essay*, Cambridge, 1991.

10 cf. Finley, *The Ancient Economy;* the main thesis of de Ste Croix, *Class Struggle*, is premised on the view that the numbers of slaves had declined in the late empire. For some of the problems, see R. MacMullen, 'Late Roman slavery', *Historia* 36 (1987), 359–82; C. R. Whittaker, 'Circe's pigs: from slavery to serfdom in the later Roman world', *Slavery and Abolition* 8 (1987), 87–122.

successful, we would have to conclude that the late empire was a time of real repression, in which the population was reduced to virtual serfdom.[11] In law, this was certainly the case. The difference between slave and free may often have been slight or non-existent in practical terms: by the time of Justinian, for instance, tenants who are *adscripticii* (bound to the soil) were treated in the legal texts more or less as if they were slaves (*CJ* XI.48.21.1; 50.2.3; 52.1.1). Yet the impression we get of these classes from saints' lives and other more popular sources is far from being one of total repression and alienation, and social mobility was surprisingly common at slightly higher levels. There was thus evidently a large gap between theory and practice.

It is very important to realize that late Roman law often followed, rather than led, social practice. The frequently repeated and often contradictory pronouncements of emperors do not signify authoritarian intrusions on the lives of individuals so much as vain attempts to regulate a situation which was in practice beyond their control. Once this is fully recognized it is easier to understand why there is so much confusion and inconsistency between the laws themselves, and to discard the idea of Diocletian as the initiator of some kind of rigid and repressive regime. Rather, the legislation on *coloni* grew out of the difficulties experienced in collecting the poll-tax (*capitatio*), for tax due from *coloni* could only be collected if their whereabouts were known. Thus the state legislated essentially to help landlords to control and trace the labour force on which the tax was due. Not surprisingly, given the ways of late Roman government, this legislation developed only gradually and piecemeal during the fourth century, and uncertainty as to the relation of slave and *colonus* in individual areas, and inconsistency between geographical regions, were among the results of the untidy process that was adopted.

Legislation on the apparent reduction in the status of *coloni* was thus introduced at differing rates in different geographical areas, in Illyricum and Palestine not until the end of the fourth century. Furthermore, as the evidence of the Egyptian papyri suggests, there were many possible variations at the level of actual arrangements between landlord and tenant; loans, effectively mortgages, from large landowners to small were common, and defaulting borrowers were subjected to coercive measures from the lenders which were of more immediate concern than any imperial legislation.[12] The 'colonate' itself is thus an institution more theoretical than real.[13] In general, it seems doubtful whether conditions for the lower classes had in practice significantly deteriorated since the early

11 See A. H. M. Jones, 'The caste system in the Roman empire', in Brunt (ed.), *The Roman Economy*, 396–418; id., 'The Roman colonate', in ibid., 293–307; de Ste Croix, *Class Struggle*.

12 J. Gascou, 'Les grands domaines, la cité et l'état en Egypte byzantine', *Travaux et Mémoires* 9 (1985), 1–90, questions the older view of self-sufficient large estates in late Roman Egypt; see also Alan Bowman, *Egypt after the Pharaohs, 322 bc–ad 642*, Berkeley and Los Angeles, Calif., 1986.

13 This is naturally a very simplified account; for the theoretical issues see especially J.-M. Carrié, 'Le "colonat" du Bas-Empire: un mythe historiographique?', *Opus* 1 (1982), 351–70; id., 'Un roman des origines: les généalogies du "colonat du Bas-Empire"', *Opus* 2 (1983), 205–51; with A. Marcone, *Il colonato tardoantico nella storiografia moderna*, Como, 1988. See in general, Alföldy, *Social History*, 202ff. (but overstated).

empire. The condition of the poor, whether urban or rural, remained hard at all times. There had indeed been over the imperial period a progressive intensification of penalties applied to those convicted under the law, with an ever-widening division between the treatment of the rich and powerful and the cruel treatment (torture, chains, mutilation) meted out to the poor.[14] But the same process coincided during our period with a new consciousness of 'the poor' as a class, no doubt inspired by Christian teaching, which found some expression, as far as the urban poor were concerned, in various forms of Christian charity. Moreover, a number of saints' lives attest the role of the local bishop in alleviating economic distress in the country areas, and especially in providing food in times of famine (Chapter 6).

The economic changes which took place in the late empire were not of a revolutionary nature. This was still a basically agrarian society, and much of the land was owned by large landowners and worked by tenants, whether slave or free; for slavery as such certainly continued into our period. Again, though comparisons with medieval feudalism are tempting, especially for Marxist historians, they can be very misleading: there was no simple chronological transition from late Roman *coloni* to medieval serfs, and the institutions of late antiquity and of the medieval kingdoms need to be examined separately from each other. It would also be a mistake to suppose that peasants in earlier centuries had had much possibility or inclination de facto to move away from their area, or that they had not been dependent before; terms like 'serf' are liable to carry value judgements with them, and for this and the other reasons given should only be applied to the late empire with extreme caution.[15] As for the lower classes in the towns, it is equally difficult to get a fair picture of their lot when so much evidence is anecdotal and when so many of the literary sources are liable to exaggerate for their own purposes. Naturally it is very easy, as in most periods, to find evidence in the sources of both urban and rural poverty, especially in relation to tax debts.[16] But again one should be cautious about generalizing too much on the basis of this evidence. In the same way we hear many complaints in this period from the town councillors, the *curiales* or decurions, about their difficulties in continuing to finance urban life. But while we can certainly detect a slow process of increased imperial intervention in the affairs of cities, especially their financial affairs, and, at any rate towards the later part of the period, a degree of weakening of the traditional ways of urban government (Chapter 7), it is not until the later sixth century that the city structures of the eastern empire suffer real change. When they do, it is often the local bishop who steps into the breach, and even then, with the exception of the not inconsiderable part now played by Christian charity,

14 See R. MacMullen, 'Judicial savagery in the Roman empire', *Chiron* 16 (1986), 147–66.

15 For a Marxist view which overstates its case in relation to the late empire, see P. Anderson, *Passages from Antiquity to Feudalism*, London, 1974; see C. Wickham, 'The other transition: from the ancient world to feudalism', *Past and Present* 103 (1984), 3–36.

16 As is done by modern historians who wish to stress the gloomy aspects of the late empire in order to explain its 'decline'; cf., e.g., Alföldy, *Social History*, 203–10. The same approach goes hand in hand with an emphasis on social unrest (cf. ibid., 210–20).

one may suspect that the condition of the people remained much the same. On the whole the economic role of towns remained similar to what it had been during the early empire.

But if there was no economic revolution, certain new factors did become operative—on the one hand, barbarian settlement on a large scale; on the other, the growth of the church as a major economic institution in its own right, with the profound implications which we have already seen, ranging from the role of bishops as urban and rural patrons and the diversion of resources into church building, to the growth of monasteries and their potential impact on the local economy. It was factors such as these, together with the severe damage caused in some areas and to some towns by invasion and war, which severely disturbed the balance of landholding and wealth and which inevitably brought profound change with them.

The Classes of Late Antique Society

The senatorial class of the west had been a major beneficiary of the disturbances which took place in the third century, and was, moreover, at least in part itself a product of the patronage of Constantine and his successors. One of the main features of the early fifth-century west is the enormous wealth, by which we mean the enormous landholdings, of the western senatorial class. Perhaps because of unsettled conditions in many areas, it had become possible to acquire vast estates—the size of towns, we are told. A landowner would also expect to have at least one town house in which he lived in extreme luxury, as we learn from Ammianus' famous (and scathing) description of the fish ponds and table delicacies of the Roman nobility of the late fourth century (14.6, 28.4). Owning estates on this scale was a business in itself, even if the landlord was an absentee. According to Ammianus, 'a journey of fair length to visit their estates or to be present at a hunt where all the work is done by others seems to some of them the equivalent of a march by Alexander the Great or Caesar' (28.6). None the less, upkeep of these estates required armies of retainers and an elaborate system of production and supply of goods. Owners were naturally interested in profits, and had perforce to devote a good deal of time simply to keeping things going. Much of it was occupied not as it might be nowadays by arranging how to sell surplus produce, or how best to invest in their estates, but in dealings for mutual benefit with others in a similar position, transactions which reinforced the gift element and the importance attached to display which were typical features of the late Roman economy. Sulpicius Severus and Paulinus provide evidence in their writings of typical gifts from one landowner to another of such commodities as oil and fowl, a practice continued by Sidonius, and indeed by bishops and kings in the Merovingian period; Pope Gregory the Great was no different in this respect from a secular landowner of earlier times.[17] While therefore a landlord might well become

17 See C. R. Whittaker, 'Late Roman trade and traders', in P. Garnsey, K. Hopkins and C. R. Whittaker (eds), *Trade in the Ancient Economy*, London, 1983, 170–3.

involved in production and engage in long-distance transport, both might take place within an exchange system involving either simply his own estates, or those of himself and his friends; this is less an economic activity than a patronal relationship. Even the widespread appearance overseas of African pottery during our period may be partly a product of this mutual exchange rather than the result of new market or production systems.[18] Emperors and the church, not surprisingly, behaved in essentially the same way. If then it is true that the amount of land in the hands of great proprietors (the *potentes*) increased, it may also be the case that overall markets—never greatly developed—were correspondingly diminished as a result of this increase in reciprocal exchanges between the estates of the rich.

During the same period the enlargement and transformation of the senatorial class, greatly increased in numbers from the time of Constantine on, as well as by the creation of a senate at Constantinople as well as Rome, rendered the old equestrian class otiose; the latter eventually disappeared as its former offices were progressively renamed and redefined as senatorial. Nor was it enough to be called simply *vir clarissimus* (the standard senatorial rank in the early empire). Valentinian I in AD 372 laid down a hierarchy of *clarissimi*, and above them *spectabiles* and (at the top) *illustres*; these grades were attached to the holding of particular offices, and other privileges of rank, such as the seats allotted at the Coliseum in Rome, also followed. The senate of Constantinople, on the other hand, differed from that of Rome since it was an artificial creation; while the Roman senate comprised families of vast wealth and pretensions to aristocratic lineage (even if in many cases they did not go further back than the third century), that of Constantinople was filled with new men. However, this feature in the long run helped its future continuance; being based on Constantinople itself, and lacking the enormous estates of its counterparts in Rome, the eastern senate was also likely to be able to avoid the tensions which developed between the Roman senate and the imperial government.[19] But eastern senators too enjoyed substantial privileges, and their role as members of the traditional landowning class, allegedly preyed upon by the rapacious emperor, is emphasized by Procopius, who himself identified with their interests, in his *Secret History*.[20] Like their western counterparts, eastern senators were not only undertaxed but also no doubt in a good position to evade the special tax (*collatio glebalis* or *follis*) which had belatedly been imposed on them by Constantine. In the example of the senatorial class we can in fact see the combination of tradition and innovation which is typical of the late empire; for while, on the one hand, the late Roman senate was essentially a service aristocracy which differed considerably from the senate of the early

---

18 Whittaker, 'Late Roman trade and traders', 176–7. On the other hand, the large estates of late Roman Egypt, such as that of the Apiones at Oxhyrhynchus, were not self-sufficient; they hired local craftsmen and bought necessities such as mats and ropes from local monasteries.

19 On the senate, see Jones, *LRE*, II, ch. 15; M. T. W. Arnheim, *The Senatorial Aristocracy in the Later Roman Empire*, Oxford, 1972 (far too schematized); stratification: T. D. Barnes, 'Who were the nobility of the Roman empire?', *Phoenix* 28 (1974), 444–9. The senate was still important in sixth-century Constantinople: see H.-G. Beck, *Senat und Volk von Konstantinopel*, Sitz. bayer. Akad. der Wiss., Munich, 1966.

20 See Cameron, *Procopius*, chs 4 and 13.

empire, it did not occur to anyone not to maintain existing social patterns, so that many of the outward signs of senatorial status and privilege were retained or even enhanced. In such circumstances, the Christianization, and in particular the conversion to asceticism, of members of leading senatorial families, which began to occur in Rome in the late fourth century, could seem to present a threat to status, wealth and tradition, and therefore met with considerable opposition.[21]

The later Roman empire is characterized by a high degree of competition for status and access to wealth and privilege, which we can see operative also in the centralized bureaucracy. Since posts in the imperial service could be highly lucrative, and released the holder from burdensome existing obligations, the bureaucracy drew off talent from the ranks of the *curiales* in the cities even as imperial legislation, conscious of economic and administrative needs, sought to keep them in their places. One of the most persistent of modern myths about the late empire is that of a top-heavy and rigid bureaucracy which wielded the hand of repression, yet whose size made it unsustainable from the existing resources of the empire. In fact the empire was engaged in a constant balancing act between what was perceived to be necessary and what was in fact possible. Paradoxically, there was in practice a high degree of social mobility, and the court and the officeholders had a natural tendency to proliferate in view of the attractiveness of the posts. The nomenclature and emoluments of the imperial service paralleled those of the army; office-holders held titles of military equivalence and received military stipends. This had little to do with modern concepts of efficiency, though the government had at least an interest in filling the administration with people it deemed suitable; at the same time however it also needed to maintain the numbers of *curiales* in each city (the obvious candidates for openings in the imperial service), since on them fell financial responsibility and tax obligations at local level.[22] Jones rightly emphasizes the very large number of posts (*dignitates*) that had to be filled on a regular basis, and the law-codes make it very clear that *curiales* were constantly endeavouring to escape their lot and better themselves, in the administration, the church or the army. This class as a whole was the subject of what Jones calls 'a vast and tangled mass of legislation', whereby the state attempted ineffectually to prevent the seepage and maintain the councils on whom the cities depended.[23] Earlier attempts to return *curiales* to their cities if they had managed to secure a post in the administration failed, and in principle after AD 423 individuals could no longer escape their obligations in this way. Similarly, the fifth-century emperors were still attempting to stop the loophole opened by Constantine when he freed clergy from curial obligations, as was Justinian, when in AD 531 he allowed ordination of *curiales* only if they had spent fifteen years in a monastery first, and were willing to surrender a substantial part of their estate (*CJ* I.3.52). The double bind in which the government found itself was

21 Peter Brown, 'Aspects of the Christianization of the Roman aristocracy', *JRS* 51 (1961), 1–11, is still basic.

22 The government's dilemma is well brought out by F. Millar, 'Empire and city, Augustus to Julian: obligations, excuses and status', *JRS* 73 (1983), 76–96.

23 *LRE*, I, 748; see 740–57.

further complicated by the willingness of individuals effectively to buy their way into the administration, and that of the government to sell offices within it—the attraction for the purchaser being the emoluments that went with the position, and often the possibilities for favour and extortion that it carried in addition. To a modern observer this is not likely to seem an acceptable way of going about things, but we should remember that for all its impressive state apparatus, the late Roman empire was still a very traditional society. The 'government' lacked both more sophisticated means for coping with these problems, and an understanding in modern terms of where the problems lay.

The practice of selling offices in the imperial administration provides a particularly delicate example; on the one hand, the late Roman and Byzantine governments were concerned to stop the abuse of the practice, while at another level each used it as a financial tool and mechanism for selection. In AD 439 an oath was exacted from all those appointed to provincial governorships that they had not paid to secure office:

> we ordain that men appointed to provincial governorships should not be promoted by bribe or payment but by their own proven worth and your [i.e., the prefect's] recommendation; let them testify on oath that in gaining their responsibilities they have neither made any payment nor will they make any subsequently.
>
> (*CJ* IX.27.6 pr.)

Yet later emperors actually sold offices: Zeno for instance, raised the price for the governorship of Egypt from 50 lb of gold to nearly 500 (Malchus, fr. 16, Blockley). Justinian again tried to stop the practice, repeating the earlier demand for an oath from those appointed; again, however, Procopius claims that Justinian himself was selling offices again within the year (Just., *Nov.* 8; Procopius, *Secret History*, 21.9f.).[24] The example illustrates both the weakness of the government and the lack of effective remedies at its disposal. The corollary, and the underpinning of the sale of offices was, of course, extortion by the officials themselves in order to recoup the moneys paid, the prospect of which had been a powerful attraction to purchase in the first place. Corruption, both in the sense of buying favours in a more or less blatant way and of rapacious behaviour by office-holders, was evidently all-pervasive, just as it is in any similar society where more overt procedures are lacking. It does not however follow, as is sometimes argued, that corruption in itself was a major element in the decline and fall of the Roman empire, and we should be careful not to import modernizing (and moralizing) assumptions into the study of a traditional system.

One of the hallmarks of the late Roman administrative system was patronage. Recent work has increasingly emphasized the importance of patronage in understanding ancient society as a whole, especially in the context of the Roman empire,[25] and this should make

24 Jones, *LRE*, I, 391–6; and more generally MacMullen, *Corruption*, 148–67.

25 See A. Wallace-Hadrill (ed.), *Patronage in Ancient Society*, London, 1989, in particular Peter Garnsey and Greg Woolf, 'Patronage of the rural poor', at 162–6; R. P. Saller, *Personal Patronage under the Early Empire*, Cambridge, 1982.

understanding the late empire somewhat less daunting. Patronage, in the sense of a more or less systematized protection of the poor, has existed and does exist in many—perhaps even all—societies, but is present typically where the protection offered by the state is weak, as here, where the social bonds are loose or where there is change and competition for place in the new scheme of things. In late antiquity, 'traditional patrons found themselves supplanted as patrons, but also impeded as landlords—and as tax collectors—by men with local authority, secular or religious. Their protests were echoed with legislation representing the fiscal interests of the central government.'[26] For when new actors—bishops, state officials—entered a stage on which patronage already operated on every level, and when the interests of the poor, the landlords and the state diverged, any existing equilibrium was broken. In such conditions the poor and the helpless looked where they could for protection. The state for its part made repeated attempts to declare this form of protection (*patrocinium*) illegal, representing as it did an evasion of the responsibilities of those who were its subjects, and an illicit appropriation of authority by those who took it on, not to mention the extra tips which they doubtless imposed. A law of AD 415 allowed the churches of Constantinople and Alexandria to retain villages which had come under their protection, provided that all taxes were paid and other obligations fulfilled (*CTh* 11.24.6), but later emperors such as Marcian and Leo continued to try to end the practice, and Leo attempted to forbid all patronage contracts from 437 in Thrace and from 441 in the east (*CJ* XI.54.1, AD 468). Again, the practice itself and the government's inability to deal with it demonstrate not so much endemic corruption as the weakness of the bureaucratic system in comparison with the vast and fragmented areas which it was attempting to control.

Financing the State

Behind many of the problems which the state experienced, and which gave rise to these social difficulties, lay the need for tax revenue and the difficulties of collection. Many scholars have believed that late Roman taxes were higher than before—so high in fact as to contribute substantially to increased extortion and consequent decline. Before considering this question a brief excursus is necessary on taxation and the ancient economy in general.

Fortunately there is no shortage of guides; indeed, the nature of the ancient economy was one of the liveliest topics of research in the 1970s and 1980s, and the increased interest in late Roman archaeology is guaranteeing that the later period is not neglected.[27] It is probably fair to say that since the early 1970s the model of the ancient economy associated

26 Garnsey and Woolf, 'Patronage of the rural poor', 167; see also Alföldy, *Social History*, 215–16 (though too highly-coloured).

27 Much of volume III of Giardina (ed.) (*Le merci, gli insediamenti*), is devoted to these questions; cf. the review by C. Wickham, 'Marx, Sherlock Holmes and late Roman commerce', *JRS* 78 (1988), 183–93. See also the important collection, C. Morrisson and J. Lefort (eds), *Hommes et richesses dans l'empire byzantin I, IVe–VIIe siècle*, Paris, 1989.

with Moses Finley's *The Ancient Economy* (Berkeley and Los Angeles, Calif., 1973) has been modified but not essentially given up. According to this model, the ancient world was basically an agrarian society in which towns were not centres of industrial production and in which markets and profit were comparatively undeveloped, as were notions of 'economic rationality' in general. More recently, scholars including Finley himself have laid more emphasis than this model would allow on the extent of monetarization, and on the level of trade, while Keith Hopkins in particular has argued for a slow degree of economic growth, at least up to the end of the second century AD. Some recent archaeological work in our period now suggests both a surprising degree of prosperity in the east and more long-term exchange than had previously been supposed. One is therefore led to ask how far if at all the arguments put forward in the general debate apply to the later empire. This section will therefore focus on issues relating to taxation, money and state revenues and expenditure, while the next will take up the questions of production, rural prosperity or decline and long-distance exchange.

Certain premises about the ancient economy have been generally accepted, and there is no reason to doubt that they apply equally to the later empire. These are (in the case of the Roman empire) that the wealth of the empire came largely from its land, which also provided the bulk of the state's revenues; that the army, or at least the defences generally, constituted by far the biggest part of the state budget;[28] and that other state expenditure was extremely limited by comparison with that of modern states. The extent of monetarization has been seen as low on this model, and the state's purpose in issuing coin as political or military rather than economic or commercial, though this has indeed been strongly challenged of late.[29] Hopkins has usefully listed the factors which in his view may have been conducive to a certain degree of economic growth. Taking these as a base we may ask how many of them were present in the late empire, and whether there is likely to have been growth or recession, assuming these concepts to be applicable at all.[30] They include: an increased amount of land being brought under cultivation; a greater population size, with more division of labour and consequent growth in non-agricultural production; and higher productivity per capita (including the increase attributable to the fact that in peacetime some of those who would otherwise have been engaged in warfare are available as part of the labour force). Finally, two propositions important for the late empire are the suggestions, first, that increased government exaction acted as a stimulus rather than a damper on productivity and, second, that government expenditure of the money raised by taxation itself in turn benefited the economy.

28 Also recognized by contemporaries: see M. Hendy, *Studies in the Byzantine Monetary Economy c. AD 300–1450,* Cambridge, 1985, 158.

29 See C. Howgego, 'The supply and use of money in the Roman world, 200 BC–AD 300', *JRS* 82 (1992), 64–94.

30 See Garnsey, Hopkins and Whittaker (eds), *Trade in the Ancient Economy,* xiv–xxi; the argument is set out more fully in Hopkins's article, 'Taxes and trade in the Roman Empire', *JRS* 70 (1980), 101–25.

If we apply these suggestions—which have been derived largely from the period *c.* 200 BC to AD 200—to the period covered here, certain points are immediately apparent. In the west, the available land from which the state was able to collect taxes actually diminished through the processes of war and settlement. Further, the population itself may already have dropped during the period of crisis in the third century, and at any rate the Roman population in the western provinces was partially displaced during the later fifth century by new barbarian settlers with whom it was forced to share its land on terms which were heavy whichever interpretation of the evidence we may adopt (Chapter 2). The question of peace versus war also raises the question of the difference between west and east; thus the east could prosper at least during much of the fifth century and into the sixth, while the wars with the Sasanians were enjoying something of a lull, but as we have seen, the west saw continuous warfare and fragmentation of territory, with all the obvious consequences of damage to land and urban centres as well as the cost in manpower.

On several of Hopkins's criteria, then, it looks as though the western empire must have suffered a degree of economic decline even before the main period of barbarian settlement. Some other indicators point in the same direction. Both the smaller units and the stationing of the late Roman army within the empire rather than in large numbers on the frontiers will have reduced its former role in the circulation and redistribution of coin through army pay and expenditure, even without the large element of its needs now supplied in kind. If correct, the postulated trend towards exchange within the network of large estates rather than via the open market should have operated in the same direction. And finally, the disruption of so much of the land-base of the empire, combined perhaps with other natural factors, may in itself have led to a reduction in available raw materials.[31]

Added to these factors is the sheer cost of maintaining the late Roman army (Chapter 2). If it were true that Diocletian had really doubled, let alone quadrupled, the size of the army, as well as increasing the bureaucracy, the economic problems of the later empire would indeed have been insuperable. Jones put the problem neatly in his famous statement that the late empire had too many 'idle mouths', that is, non-producers, who therefore had to be paid for out of the diminishing resources of the empire.[32] But few historians today would be as confident as Jones was in 1964. As we have seen already (Chapter 2), Diocletian is more likely to have regularized the status quo than actually doubled the army in size, and it must be regarded as doubtful whether even that figure could be maintained after the late fourth century. At 400,000 plus, the late Roman army was still an extremely large

---

31 For mining see J. Edmondson, 'Mining in the later Roman empire and beyond: continuity and disruption', *JRS* 79 (1989), 84–102.

32 Jones, *LRE*, II, 1045, 'the basic economic weakness of the empire was that too few producers supported too many idle mouths'. Jones believed however that the late Roman army had doubled in size since the Principate (ibid., 1046).

force, notably bigger than the Augustan army of the early Principate, and such an army must certainly have represented a great drain on resources.

Yet historians may have got the issue the wrong way round when they emphasize the contribution of this military expenditure to eventual collapse. What is remarkable is rather that the system continued as long as it did. One might equally argue that while the cost was indeed heavy, the empire's most intractable military problems lay in the sheer size of its borders and the difficulty of maintaining defence on such a scale. Had the west not had to endure decades of barbarian attack, the story there might have been very different. As for the east, Justinian did indeed encounter severe financial problems in conducting his wars, which he passed on in turn to his successors, but here too it was a combination of external factors which was operative in causing his most severe problems (Chapter 5). The state had already found partial answers to the difficulties of cost in that by the sixth century much of the defence of the south-eastern part of the frontier area from Transjordan to Arabia had been left to Arab allies, and, even in the regular armies, barbarians were regularly used.[33] Finally, the equation worked both ways: the presence of the army in a particular area, with all that it required for its maintenance—not just the pay and supplies of the troops, but also a good road system and transport and local support systems—could in itself be a powerful economic stimulus. This was no doubt one of the factors behind the undoubted prosperity and density of settlement in the fifth century in the south-eastern frontier areas even in barren and difficult places such as the Hauran and the Negev, where there were many small military settlements in addition to the major fortresses.[34]

From all this it is clear that generalizations about the late antique economy as a whole are likely to be misleading, and that we must always allow for regional variations and the intervention of external factors. The difficulty of computing the cost of the army, as of its size, is also partly a matter of methodology, in that while we have in the sources a number of figures for tax revenue and budgetary expenses, it is far from clear whether they are reliable or not, or how far they may have changed over the two centuries we are considering.[35] There was at least in the late empire a regular tax period (indiction) for which levels were fixed, and the system had been changed to take into account both labour force and quality of land. Constantine had imposed special taxes on senatorial wealth and on commerce, and had thus at last brought these sectors into the tax net. Basically, however, the taxes still fell mainly on the land and on agricultural production; the government had little recourse in response to loss of land and shortage of manpower apart from often repeated

33 See S. Thomas Parker, *Romans and Saracens. A History of the Arabian Frontier*, Winona Lake, 1986, 83–4, 112, 149; and Chapter 8 below; for barbarians, see Chapter 2; and cf. J. L. Teall, 'Barbarians in the armies of Justinian', *Speculum* 40 (1965), 294–322.

34 See Parker, *Romans and Saracens*, 143; and Chapter 8.

35 Hendy, *Studies in the Byzantine Monetary Economy*, contains a wealth of information not easily available elsewhere on the late Roman financial system, though the arrangement of the book makes it difficult to use and obscures understanding of diachronic change.

legislation such as that seeking to restrict movement of *coloni* and thus help landlords to keep their tenants:

> whereas in other provinces which are subject to the rule of our serenity a law instituted by our ancestors holds tenants down by a kind of eternal right, so that they are not allowed to leave the places by whose crops they are nurtured or desert the fields which they have once undertaken to cultivate, but the landlords of Palestine do not enjoy this advantage: we ordain that in Palestine also no tenant whatever be free to wander at his own choice, but as in other provinces he be tied to the owner of the farm.
>
> (*CJ* XI.51.1)

The tax collector indeed looms large in contemporary literature as a hated and dreaded figure, and the danger to those who could not pay was very real. Paphnutius, a hermit near Heracleopolis in the Thebaid, met a former brigand who told him how he had once come upon a woman who had suffered in this way, and asked her why she was crying:

> she replied, 'Do not ask me, master; do not question me in my misery but take me anywhere you wish as your handmaid. For my husband has often been flogged during the last two years because of arrears of taxes amounting to three hundred gold coins. He has been put in prison and my beloved three children have been sold as slaves. As for me, I have become a fugitive and move from place to place. I now wander in the desert but I am frequently found and flogged. I have been in the desert now for three days without eating anything.' 'I felt sorry for her,' said the brigand, 'and took her to my cave. I gave her the three hundred gold coins and brought her to the city, where I secured her release together with that of her husband and children.'
>
> (Russell, *Lives of the Desert Fathers,* 95)

The repeated laws show, however, how little the government could actually do to enforce collection of revenue. The taxes were highly regressive: small peasant proprietors paid the same as great landlords for the same amount of land. And despite Constantine's reforms, the traditional emphasis on the land still meant that they failed to tap major sources of wealth, whether from trade or, importantly, from senatorial incomes. In the latter case, especially, it was in part the nature of the tax laws themselves which enabled senators to amass colossal fortunes while the government went short. Emperors themselves shared the traditional view that exemption from taxation was a privilege to which rank and favour allowed one rightfully to aspire, and thus their grants of exemption were an expression of this traditional attitude as well as a way of gaining popularity. Cancelling arrears was another common device, either in the face of real inability to enforce the law, or in response to these traditional attitudes, and there was little conception of budgeting for the future. On the other hand, as Jones points out, the eastern government at any rate seems to have been able to collect very substantial sums on a continuous basis;[36] this was despite the outflow of large sums of gold to buy peace with Persia, or for 'subsidy' payments to barbarian groups.[37] As for commerce, the so-called *chrysargyron* (gold and silver tax, so-called because it had to be paid in gold and silver, usually, in practice, gold) was consistently unpopular; it was actually abolished in AD 499 by the Emperor Anastasius (*CJ* 11.1.1), as the *collatio glebalis* (*follis*), levied on senators, had been by the Emperor Marcian (*CJ* 12.2.2). Then, as now, taxation was an ideologically charged issue, and emperors who raised taxes, even if like Justinian they did so for military purposes, are uniformly criticized in contemporary sources.

The late Roman taxation system was thus a complicated and unwieldy affair, full of inequities and far from perfectly administered. Its most important part, the *annona*, the supplies for the army, was also the most difficult to organize. From the later third century much of the *annona* had been collected in kind, by means of a cumbersome system which one is surprised to find working at all; even so, while the method of calculation varied from province to province, it was possible from time to time to reduce the demand on a particular province, as with Achaea, Macedonia, Sicily, Numidia and Mauretania Sitifensis in the fifth century. However, the regular censuses necessary to keep the registers of land and population accurate tended not to be held, and great discrepancies could arise. Once collected, finally, the goods had to be transmitted to the necessary unit—a further process requiring complicated organization. Other forms of taxation were also of great importance throughout the imperial period, especially the grain requisition for the food supply of Rome, a system Constantine also extended to his new foundation of Constantinople (Chapter 1). Since the Republic, the Roman government had considered it a priority to ensure the food supply for the capital, and had maintained free bread doles for the purpose.[38] The corn came in the main, though not only, from North Africa and Egypt, where in each case its provision had a major impact on the local economies;[39] equally, its eventual cessation as conditions changed in the west must have exercised a material effect. At Rome, the loss of North Africa to the Vandals caused severe disruption, but the distributions went on and were eventually taken over by the church. In the east, Egypt continued to supply Constantinople, but the link was abruptly broken by the Persian invasion of Egypt in the early seventh century. Before this, however, the tickets on which the actual distributions were made had come to be passed on by sale or inheritance; the government tried at times to

36 Jones, *LRE*, I, 468–9 (and in general on finance, 411–69; see also J. Durliat, *Les finances publiques de Dioclétien aux carolingiens (284–889)*, Sigmeringen, 1990).

37 See R. C. Blockley, 'Subsidies and diplomacy: Rome and Persia in late antiquity', *Phoenix* 39 (1985), 62–74.

38 Jones, *LRE*, I, 691–705; at Rome there were also free distributions of pork and of oil, the former causing some awkward problems of supply.

39 See Peter Garnsey, 'Grain for Rome', in Garnsey, Hopkins and Whittaker (eds), *Trade in the Ancient Economy*, 118–30; with his *Famine and Food Supply*, ch. 15 (up to AD 250); J. Durliat, *De la ville antique à la ville byzantine*, Rome, 1990; B. Sirks, *Food for Rome. The Legal Structure of the Transportation and Processing of Supplies for the Imperial Distributions in Rome and Constantinople*, Amsterdam, 1991.

regulate these practices too, but as time went on, as with other late Roman taxes, the match between those theoretically qualified and those actually receiving the dole had already become less and less close.

By the beginning of our period payment in kind was beginning to be commuted into gold, especially in the west, at varying rates of commutation which at times had to be regulated by the government, and in the sixth century payment in gold (pounds or *solidi*) was the norm. Though Constantine was able to introduce the gold *solidus,* which remained standard henceforth, later emperors were unsuccessful in their attempts to reintroduce silver coinage on a stable basis. Inflation itself also continued, as can be seen from prices given in papyri, probably because the government minted far too much of the small base-metal coinage, but the *solidus* remained stable throughout the period and for long afterwards. By the fifth century, however, there was effectively nothing between the gold *solidus* and the tiny copper denominations, whose rate, valued against the *solidus,* was constantly changing. The later fifth-century emperors, in particular Anastasius (AD 491–518), were more successful in introducing some stability; here it is interesting to find that Anastasius' reform continued trends already to be seen in the Vandalic and Ostrogothic coinages of the west.[40] It is extremely difficult to assess the economic consequences of this state of affairs. On a priori grounds alone, the collection and distribution of taxes in kind, which continued in part well into the fifth century, and the constant fluctuation of value against the *solidus* of the base-metal/copper coinage (*pecunia*) cannot but have had a depressive effect on the existence of a market economy. But the roots of third- and fourth-century inflation lay with the monetary policy of the state rather than with the economy itself, and we have seen that revenue levels in our period were apparently maintained, at least in the east. One must conclude that shaky though its control may have been, so long as the late Roman government continued to operate well itself, as it did in the east during our period, the economy as a whole also continued to function. Local and unforeseen factors such as famine, pestilence or the like constantly threatened a traditional agrarian economy with no obvious technological advances, but were also part of the expected range of possibilities and could therefore be contained, whereas external factors such as invasion, settlement and demographic change were another matter altogether.

Trade and Traders

Given its date, the 'Pirenne thesis' (see p. 4) was necessarily based mainly on literary evidence; now, with the growth of interest in this period by archaeologists, far more material is available, and this, together with the more sympathetic approach to the role of trade in assessing the ancient economy to which we have referred above (p. 94), puts a new light

40 See Jones, *LRE*, I, 438–48; Hendy, *Studies in the Byzantine Monetary Economy,* 475–92, and in general on these very difficult questions.

on the old controversy. We shall return to the theme later (Chapter 7); for now, we can conclude this chapter with some brief comments on the controversy concerning the role of long-distance trade in our period.

Much of the question turns on pottery evidence, in particular the diffusion of African Red Slipware and African amphorae outside North Africa, which continued even during the Vandal period. On this base an extensive hypothesis about trading patterns has been built, especially in relation to the fifth to seventh centuries.[41] A clear curve is evident from the finds: first, between the second and fourth centuries, African pottery gradually comes to dominate sites in the west in a striking way, while the former exports from Gaul and Baetica diminish;[42] next, with the growth of Constantinople and the diversion of Egyptian grain to the eastern capital, an eastern axis, Carthage/Constantinople, comes into being; export along these two lines, north and east, continues into the fifth century, with no break at the Vandal conquest of North Africa in 439;[43] however, decline can be seen by the early sixth century, along with certain changes in production, the former to be connected not only with circumstances in North Africa itself but also with the reduction in markets as a result of the establishment of the barbarian kingdoms—nevertheless, the eastern axis continues in existence throughout the period, as the importance of Constantinople reaches its peak; finally, further and clearer decline is evident in the seventh century, where however evidence is also much more sparse.

Many questions suggest themselves as a result of these conclusions, of which the following are only the most obvious. For example, whether these findings actually represent trading links at all (the evidence of pottery will not tell us the *why* of transmarine exchange, only the *how*). What if anything can these results tell us about the impact of the barbarian kingdoms on the Mediterranean economy? Finally, how far does this evidence tally with that of urban change to suggest that a significant weakening of the Mediterranean system of classical antiquity can best be located in the later sixth to early seventh centuries, that is, after the Justinianic attempt at reconquest and before the Arab invasions?

---

41 The issue is well discussed by Wickham, 'Marx, Sherlock Holmes and late Roman commerce', 190–3, who provides a good introduction to the fundamental Italian work by A. Carandini and others (especially C. Panella, 'Le merci: produzioni, itinerari e destini', in Giardina (ed.), III, 431–59; see also Carandini, in ibid., 3–19, for a more theoretical exposition; and C. Panella, 'Gli scambi nel Mediterraneo Occidentale dal IV al VII secolo dal punto di vista di alcune "merci"', in Morrisson and Lefort (eds), *Hommes et richesses dans l' empire byzantin I,* 129–41, who provides a very clear picture of the evidence). The typology of late Roman pottery, established only since the publication of John Hayes, *Late Roman Pottery,* London, 1972, depends on a number of important recent excavations, among which that by the British team at Carthage, like that of the Italians, is central: see M. G. Fulford and D. S. Peacock, in H. Hurst and S. Roskams (eds), *Excavations at Carthage: the British Mission,* I, part ii, Sheffield, 1984.

42 For the prosperity of North Africa in the pre-Vandal period and for the increasing scale of senatorial holdings there see C. Lepelley, *Les cités de l'Afrique romaine an Bas-Empire,* I–II, Paris, 1979, 1987; id., 'Peuplement et richesses de l'Afrique romaine tardive', in Morrisson and Lefort (eds), *Hommes et richesses dans l'empire byzantin I,* 17–30; Whittaker, 'Trade and the aristocracy in the Roman empire'.

43 For the North African economy during the Vandal conquest see M. Fulford, 'Carthage—overseas trade and political economy, AD 400–700', *Reading Medieval Studies* 6 (1980), 68–70.

It is important to note that all these issues are still the subject of ongoing debate and considerable disagreement, not least because they raise ideological issues about trade and the nature of the ancient economy. Carandini, Panella and their colleagues see the evidence as reflecting trading patterns in a market economy. This emphasis may need to be qualified. Among the questions still to be settled is that of the economic impact of the Vandal conquest, including that of the effect on North Africa (and the other conquered areas) of the cessation of Roman taxation. Wickham rightly underlines the importance for North Africa of the grain requisitions for Rome, which would have had the effect of requiring a highly developed navigation and export system from which other products could also benefit, and whose cessation was therefore likely to have serious and widespread effects. According to this argument, while the enforced grain exactions for Rome and Constantinople called forth a considerable level of production that was itself non-commercial, their ending, in the case of Rome, with the collapse of Roman government in the west, should have had serious repercussions on such market economy as did exist. And since North African wares were so completely dominant previously, a major change of this kind which affected North Africa directly will have had widespread effects in other regions.

Conclusion

There is no simple way to characterize the late Roman economy, or the actual effect on society of the government's attempts to control it. Certain trends are evident, not simply the profound impact of barbarian invasion and settlement during this period, but also more general developments such as the tendency towards the amassing of vast amounts of land by individuals, the return to taxation in coin (gold) instead of in kind, the growing gulf between east and west and the difficulty experienced by the government in ensuring the collection of revenues and staffing its own administration. Not surprisingly, the existence of the barbarian kingdoms in the west and the effects of the wars of reconquest had major economic repercussions; these will be discussed in Chapter 5. In the east, by contrast, there is evidence of population increase and of intensified agriculture and cultivation in areas such as the limestone massif of northern Syria and even in such unpromising areas as the Hauran and the Negev; this evidence will be discussed further in Chapter 8. On the other hand, by the late sixth century, following the effects of war and perhaps also plague, the Roman military presence in the east was clearly becoming harder and harder to maintain.

Clearly it is misleading if not impossible to generalize over so wide an area and so eventful a chronological span. Unfortunately, however, modern historiography abounds in confident value-judgements about the decline or the end of antiquity, many of which rest on unacknowledged assumptions about the late Roman system itself. That system was certainly cumbersome and had many defects. Lacking modern communications, it could neither operate efficiently nor respond easily to change. The government resorted all too easily to empty and hectoring legislation; the officials did what they could; the people learnt how to cheat the system. There is nothing surprising in that, and the power of inertia was also great. What *is* surprising, in such a context, is rather that this highly traditional society did manage to survive so comparatively well.

Topic Three Suggested Supplemental Readings:

Finley, M. I. 1965. "Technical Innovation and Economic Progress in the Ancient World." *Economic History Review* 18, no.1 (August): 29–45.

Starr, Chester G. 1958. "An Overdose of Slavery." *Journal of Economic History* 18, no. 1 (March): 17–32.

Topic Three Questions

1. Briefly summarize the development of mills in the ancient world. Briefly summarize the development of presses in the ancient world.
2. How does Schneider characterize the differences in technological progress in the ancient Mediterranean versus the Industrial Revolution?
3. Provide two specific reasons why the Late Roman Empire fell into fiscal crisis. Provide three examples of policies enacted to alleviate these fiscal woes.

Topic Four

The Medieval Economy

CHAPTER FIVE

The Causes of Slavery or Serfdom

A Hypothesis

Evsey D. Domar

I

The purpose of this paper is to present, or more correctly, to revive, a hypothesis regarding the causes of agricultural serfdom or slavery (used here interchangeably). The hypothesis was suggested by Kliuchevsky's description of the Russian experience in the sixteenth and seventeenth centuries, but it aims at a wider applicability.[1]

According to Kliuchevsky, from about the second half of the fifteenth century Russia was engaged in long hard wars against her western and southern neighbors. The wars required large forces that the state found impossible to support from tax revenue alone. Hence the government began to assign lands (*pomest'ia*) to the servitors, who were expected to use peasant labor (directly and/or via payments in kind and/or money) for their maintenance and weapons. In exchange, the servitor gave the peasants a loan and permitted them, free men as yet, to work all or part of his land on their own. The system worked rather badly, however, because of shortage of labor. Severe competition among landowners developed, the servitors being bested by lay and clerical magnates. Things became particularly difficult for the servitors after the middle of the sixteenth century when the central areas of the state became depopulated because of peasant migration into the newly conquered areas in the east and southeast. Under the pressure of the serving class and for certain other reasons, the government gradually restricted the freedom of peasants, already hopelessly in debt to their landlords, to move. They became enserfed by the middle of the seventeenth century, though the process itself continued for many decades to come.

This is a very rough summary of Kliuchevsky's story which hardly does him justice but which will serve my purposes until Part II. Like many a historian, he assembled and

1 V. Kliuchevsky, *Kurs russkoĭ storii* (Moscow: Gosudarstvennoe sotsial'no-ekonomicheskoe izdatel'stvo, 1937). The original work was published in 1906. All my references apply to the 1937 edition. An English translation by C. J. Hogarth, *A History of Russia,* was published in New York by Russell and Russell in 1960. For specific references, see Part II.

Evsey D. Domar, "The Causes of Slavery or Serfdom: A Hypothesis," *The Journal of Economic History*, vol. 30, no. 1, pp. 18–32.

described the relevant facts (and in beautiful Russian at that) and stopped just short of an analytical explanation.

The economist would recast Kliuchevsky's account as follows: The servitors tried to live off rents (in one form or another) to be collected from their estates. But the estates could not yield a significant amount of rent for the simple reason that land in Russia was not sufficiently scarce relative to labor, and ironically, was made even less scarce by Russian conquests. The scarce factor of production was not land but labor. Hence it was the ownership of peasants and not of land that could yield an income to the servitors or to any non-working landowning class.

A simple economic model may sharpen the argument (if any sharpening is needed) and help to develop it further. Assume that labor and land are the only factors of production (no capital or management), and that land of uniform quality and location is ubiquitous. No diminishing returns in the application of labor to land appear; both the average and the marginal productivities of labor are constant and equal, and if competition among employers raises wages to that level (as would be expected), no rent from land can arise, as Ricardo demonstrated some time past. In the absence of specific governmental action to the contrary (see below), the country will consist of family-size farms because hired labor, in any form, will be either unavailable or unprofitable: the wage of a hired man or the income of a tenant will have to be at least equal to what he can make on his own farm; if he receives that much, no surplus (rent) will be left for his employer. A non-working class of servitors or others could be supported by the government out of taxes levied (directly or indirectly) on the peasants, but it could not support itself from land rents.

As a step toward reality, let us relax the assumption of the ubiquity of uniform land, and let capital (clearing costs, food, seeds, livestock, structures and implements) and management be included among the factors of production. Owners of capital, of superior skill and of better-than-average land will now be able to pay a hired man his due (or to use a tenant) and still obtain a surplus. But so long as agricultural skills can be easily acquired, the amount of capital for starting a farm is small, and the per capita income is relatively high (because of the ample supply of land), a good worker should be able to save or borrow and start on his own in time. Most of the farms will still be more or less family-size, with an estate using hired labor (or tenants) here and there in areas of unusually good (in fertility and/or in location) land, or specializing in activities requiring higher-than-average capital intensity, or skillful management. But until land becomes rather scarce, and/or the amount of capital required to start a farm relatively large, it is unlikely that a large class of landowners, such as required by the Muscovite government, could be supported by economic forces alone. The American North in the Colonial period and in the nineteenth century would be a good example of an agricultural structure of this type.

So far the institutional structure has been shaped by economic forces alone without direct interference by the government.[2] Suppose now that the government decides to create, or at least to facilitate the creation of, a non-working class of agricultural owners. As a first step, it gives the members of this class the sole right of ownership of land. The peasants will now have to work for the landowners, but so long as the workers are free to move, competition among the employers will drive the wage up to the value of the marginal product of labor, and since the latter is still fairly close to the value of the average product (because of the abundance of land) little surplus will remain. The Russian situation prior to the peasants' enserfment corresponds to this case.

The next and final step to be taken by the government still pursuing its objective is the abolition of the peasants' right to move. With labor tied to land or to the owner, competition among employers ceases. Now the employer can derive a rent, not from his land, but from his peasants by appropriating all or most of their income above some subsistence level.[3] That Russian serfs could stay alive, and even to multiply, while working for themselves half-time and less suggests that the productivity of their labor (with poor technique, little capital, but abundant land) must have been quite high.

To recapitulate, the strong version of this hypothesis (without capital, management, etc.) asserts that of the three elements of an agricultural structure relevant here—free land, free peasants, and non-working landowners—any two elements but *never all three can exist simultaneously.* The combination to be found in reality will depend on the behavior of political factors—governmental measures—treated here as an exogenous variable.

The presence of this exogenous political variable seriously weakens the effectiveness of my model: it makes the presence of free land by itself neither a necessary nor a sufficient condition for the existence of serfdom. It is not a necessary condition because so long as marginal productivity of labor is high, serfdom may continue to exist even if free land is no longer present; it may even be imposed at this stage, as it was in the Russian Ukraine in the eighteenth century. Free land is not a sufficient condition because, as I stated above, without proper governmental action free land will give rise to free farmers rather than to serfs.

For the same reasons the model cannot predict the net effect of a change in the land/labor ratio on the position of the peasants. Suppose that with constant land, technology, and per capita stock of capital, population increases. The economic position of the peasants will worsen (even serfs can be exploited more), but the landowners will be less inclined to interfere with the peasants' freedom. Let population decline instead. The peasants will be better off provided they do not become less free. Thus a change in the land/labor ratio can set in motion economic and political forces acting in opposite directions.

The strength and usefulness of the model could be increased by making the political variable endogenous. But this I cannot do without help from historians and political scientists.

---

2 I mean by the "government" any organization capable of maintaining some measure of law and order and particularly of using non-economic compulsion. It can be a king, an assembly of landowners, a magnate, etc.

3 He may be restrained by custom and by the fear that his serfs can run away—a common occurence in Russia.

These difficulties notwithstanding, I would still expect to find a positive statistical correlation between free land and serfdom (or slavery). Such a correlation was indeed found by H. J. Nieboer of whom you'll hear more in Part III.

What about the end of serfdom (or slavery)? Traditionally it was assumed that it would or did disappear because of the inherent superiority of free labor. This superiority, arising from the higher motivation of the free man, was supposed to increase with greater use of capital and with technological progress. Let us disregard the possibly greater reliability of the slave and the longer hours he may be forced to work (particularly in traditional societies where leisure is highly valued), and let us assume that the economy has reached the position where the net average productivity of the free worker (P_f) is considerably larger than that of a slave (P_8). The abolition of slavery is clearly in the national interest (unless the immediate military considerations, such as of the Muscovite government, overwhelm the economic ones), but not necessarily in the interest of an individual slave owner motivated by his profit and not by patriotic sentiment. He will calculate the difference between the wage of a free worker (W_f) and the cost of subsistence of a slave (W_8) and will refuse to free his slaves unless $P_f - P_8 > W_f - W_8$, all this on the assumption that either kind of labor *can* be used in a given field.[4]

As the economy continues to develop, the difference $P_f - P_8$ can be expected to widen. Unfortunately, the same forces—technological progress and capital accumulation—responsible for this effect are apt to increase W_f as well, while W_8 need not change. We cannot tell on a priori grounds whether $P_f - P_8$ will increase more or less than $W_f - W_8$. Therefore we cannot be sure that technological progress and greater use of capital *necessarily* reduce the profitability of slave as compared with free labor. Much will depend on the nature of technological progress. Thus Eli Whitney's gin greatly increased the profitability of slavery,

---

4 Actually, it is not easy to compare the relative profitability of free and slave labor. Since the free worker is paid more or less concurrently with his work, while a slave must be either reared or purchased, and may have children, etc., the streams of receipts and expenditures from the two kinds of labor must be properly discounted. It is assumed in the text that all indirect costs of using slaves, such as medical expense, extra supervision, etc., are included in W_8.

In a well-organized slave market, the price of a slave will approximate the present value of his discounted net lifetime marginal product. A buyer who pays this price will discover that he will earn not much more than the going rate of interest; he will complain about the high cost of slaves and express doubt regarding the profitability of slavery in general, because at the margin he will be fairly indifferent between employing free or slave labor. But so long as the supply of food and of similar items for the maintenance of slaves is elastic (which it is likely to be), the slave-breeder should do very well. He benefits from the chronic perpetual disequilibrium in the slave market created by the abundance of land and by the limited human capacity to procreate (assuming no importation of slaves). But if the slave-breeder computes his rate of return on the current value of his slaves and land, he may not record much more than the market rate of interest either. In other words, the market mechanism transforms the profit from slaves into capital gains.

On this see Lewis Cecil Gray, *History of Agriculture in the Southern United States to 1860*, published in 1933 and reproduced in part in Harold D. Woodman, *Slavery and the Southern Economy: Sources and Readings* (New York: Harcourt, Brace & World, Inc., 1966), pp. 106–09, and Alfred H. Conrad and John R. Meyer, *The Economics of Slavery and Other Studies in Econometric History* (Chicago: Aldine Publishing Company, 1964), pp. 43–92.

while a transition from raising crops to breeding sheep in medieval England might have acted in the opposite direction by creating a surplus of workers. (See Part II.) American planters must have used better agricultural techniques and more capital than their Latin-American and particularly Russian colleagues, but the Americans defended slavery with much greater zeal.

In a traditional society without technological progress and capital accumulation, the end of slavery is, paradoxically, more certain. As population continues to increase and the society eventually becomes Malthusian, the marginal product of labor descends to the subsistence level. Now the free man costs little more to employ than the slave, while, hopefully, being less bothersome and more productive. The ownership of human beings becomes pointless because of the great multiplication of slaves, and they become free provided they stay poor.[5] It is land that becomes valuable, and rents collected from estates worked by free laborers or tenants without any noneconomic compulsion are sufficient to support an army of servitors or idlers. If the Muscovite government could have only waited a few hundred years!

II

Where I come from, an economic model without empirical testing is equated with a detective story without an end. My attempts to test the present model, however, merely taught me that the job is not for the amateur. I shall report to you the results of my skin deep investigation in the hope that my mistakes will stimulate the specialists. I concentrate on the Russian case, with short excursions into the histories of Poland-Lithuania, Western Europe and the United States.

1. *Russia.* The phenomenon to be explained here is not only the development of serfdom but its particular timing: before 1550 Russian peasants were free men; a hundred years later they were serfs. The relevant variables are:

   (1) the number of servitors required by the military needs of the Moscow state, and
   (2) the population density.

   According to Kliuchevsky, prior to the middle of the fifteenth century, Moscow, still a Tatar vassal surrounded by other Russian lands, fought very few foreign wars; its population became dense because Moscow was the safest spot in the area with

5 It is possible that even in a Malthusian society slavery (or serfdom) may linger on. Slaves may be kept for reasons of social prestige (a relic from the times when slavery was profitable), or simply because a slave is more reliable than a hired man. On the other hand, the use of a tenant (with a limited lease) or of a hired man allows the landowner to choose the best among several applicants with much greater ease than among slaves or serfs protected by custom.

few outlets for emigration.[6] We may conclude that there was no need as yet for a large class of servitors, and that the landowners could derive rents from their estates (patrimonies, to be exact) without enserfing the peasants. It is true that Russia, from the Kievan times onward, always had a substantial number of slaves. At the time, these were mostly household servants and retainers rather than peasants.[7]

From the middle of the fifteenth century the situation changes drastically. Having become independent from the Tatars (officially in 1480, actually earlier), and having gathered a number of Russian lands, Moscow was confronted with powerful enemies: with Poland-Lithuania and Sweden in the west and northwest, and with the Crimean Tatars in the south. The struggle with the latter went on continuously, while 50 out of the 103 years from 1492 to 1595 were spent in wars against Poland-Lithuania and Sweden, as were the following 30 out of 70 years from 1613 to 1682, not to mention the Time of Troubles, 1598-1613, filled with both civil and foreign wars.[8]

The military proficiency of the Muscovite armies being poor, refuge was sought in large numbers. More than 300,000 men were reported to have been under arms during Ivan the Terrible's Livonian War. There must have been a great increase in the number of servitors. With trade and industry making no significant progress, the government had to assign land to them. This process began on a large scale in the second half of the fifteenth century and was accelerated throughout the sixteenth century.[9]

In the meantime, the central areas of the country became depopulated. The conquest of the whole expanse of the Volga river (begun in 1552) opened up large areas of better soil and attracted large masses of peasants fleeing from high taxes, Ivan the Terrible's oppression (the famous *oprichnina)* and Crimean invasions. And then came the Time of Troubles which devastated the country once more. Already in the sixteenth century there was fierce competition for peasant hands among the landowners. It must have intensified after 1613.[10]

Thus both ingredients for the development of serfdom—a high land/labor ratio and the government's determination to create a large class of servitors—were present. In addition, there were several other forces working in the same direction. The first was the decline in the power of the great magnates, both at the hands of Ivan

---

6 Kliuchevsky, Vol. I, p. 379; Vol. III, pp. 9–10, 121. Blum, however, talks about depopulation already in the fourteenth and fifteenth centuries. See Jerome Blum, *Lord and Peasant in Russia from the Ninth to the Nineteenth Century* (Princeton: Princeton University Press, 1961), pp. 60–61. It is possible that Kliuchevsky describes the relative position of Moscow among other Russian lands, while Blum refers to the whole country.

7 Kliuchevsky, Vol. I, pp. 282–83; Vol. II, pp. 182–83.

8 *Ibid.*, Vol. II, pp. 121, 125, 221–22; Vol. III, p. 135.

9 *Ibid.*, Vol. II, pp. 221, 229–42, 248; Vol. III, pp. 63–64, 230–31, 257, 283. Blum, pp. 93, 157.

10 Kliuchevsky, Vol. II, pp. 254–57, 339–44; Vol. III, pp. 182, 244. Blum, pp. 147, 152–54, 157, 160, 252. B. D. Grekov, *Krest'iane na Rusi s drevnelshikh vremen do XVII veka* (Moscow-Leningrad: Izdatel'stvo Akademii Nauk SSSR, 1946), pp. 794–96, 849.

the Terrible and during the Time of Troubles. By offering the peasants privileges and protection, these magnates had been quite successful in bidding the peasants away from the servitors; for this reason the magnates favored the free movement of peasants, while the servitors, quite naturally, opposed it. Now the peasants lost the support of their "friends."[11] The second reason lay in the fiscal interest of the state: peasant migrations, particularly from the center to the periphery of the state, disorganized tax collections.[12] And finally, the peasant communities objected to the emigration of their members because the community carried a collective responsibility for the tax liabilities of its members (until in later years this responsibility was taken over by the masters); the departure of several members would leave the rest overburdened until the next census.[13]

Space does not allow me to give additional details of the process which gradually enserfed the peasants, or to discuss the disagreement between Kliuchevsky, who emphasized the hopeless indebtedness of the peasants to their landlords as the main obstacle to their movement, and Grekov and Blum who put greater stress on legislative enactments (particularly on the so-called "Forbidden Years," *zapovednye gody).*[14] Let me mention instead two further reflections of the scarcity of labor in Russia: the first manifested itself in the replacement of the basic land tax by a household tax in the seventeenth century, and by a poll tax under Peter the Great.[15] The second is an interesting cultural trait which remained long after its cause had probably disappeared: as late as in the first half of the nineteenth century, the social position of a Russian landowner as described in contemporary literature, depended less on the size of his land holdings (which are seldom mentioned) than on the number of *souls* (registered male peasants) that he owned.[16]

---

11 Kliuchevsky, Vol. II, pp. 259, 307. Blum, pp. 253–54. Grekov, pp. 870–71, 903, 909. Grekov, , *Glavneĭshie etapy v istorii krepostnogo prava v Rossii* (Moscow-Leningrad: Gosudarstvennoe sotsial'no-ekonomicheskoe izdatel'stvo, 1940), p. 46.

It is interesting to note that when the leaders of the gentry militia were negotiating a treaty with the Polish king Sigismund regarding the accession of his son to the Moscow throne in 1610 and in 1611, they demanded the inclusion of a provision forbidding the movement of peasants. Kliuchevsky, Vol. II, p. 349.

12 Kliuchevsky, Vol. III, p. 188.

13 *Ibid.*, Vol. II, pp. 317–18, 336–37, 340. Blum, pp. 96, 234.

14 Kliuchevsky, Vol. II, pp. 321–23, 331–50; Vol. III, pp. 181–88. Blum, pp. 254–55. Grekov, *Krest'iane,* pp. 826, 850. Grekov, *Glavneĭshie,* pp. 64–65.

If the peasants' debts tied them to their lords as strongly and as hopelessly as Kliuchevsky asserts, it is puzzling that the government had first to limit and then to forbid their movement by law.

15 Kliuchevsky, Vol. III, pp. 243–46; Vol. IV, pp. 142–48. Grekov, *Glavneĭshie,* pp. 71–72.

16 Here are a few examples: In Pushkin's *Dubrovsky,* the old Dubrovsky is identified as the owner of seventy souls, and Prince Vereisky, of three thousand; in *The Captain's Daughter,* the commandant's wife is impressed by Grinev's father's ownership of three hundred souls; in Gogol's *The Dead Souls,* Pliushkin owns more than a thousand souls; in Goncharov's *Oblomov,* the principal hero owns three hundred and fifty; in his *A Common Story,* a certain Anton Ivanich has twelve, mortgaged over and over again. ...

2. *Poland-Lithuania.* On the theory that the length of a report should be proportional to the intensity of research done, this section will be very short. The relevant facts are as follows:

   (1) In the fourteenth century vast open and very sparsely populated territories in the Ukraine were conquered by the Lithuanians.[17]
   (2) In the fifteenth and sixteenth centuries, Ukraine was repopulated by immigrants from the more central areas of the state. The migration depopulated the central areas to such an extent as to constitute, according to Grekov, a threat to the Polish state.[18]
   (3) By the end of the sixteenth century, the peasants were enserfed.[19]

What is not clear to me is the time sequence of events (2) and (3). In Vol. III (p. 110), Kliuchevsky dates the repopulation of the Ukraine in the sixteenth century; in Vol. I (p. 293), in the fifteenth century. But in both places he attributes the migration of peasants to the intensification of serfdom in Poland-Lithuania. Polish serfdom, according to him, had been established already in the fourteenth century, and Lithuanian, in the fifteenth century.[20] On the other hand, Grekov asserts that according to the Polish constitution of 1493, each peasant could still leave the land, having settled accounts with his landlord. But he also reports that in 1444 the Galician gentry demanded that the government prevent other landlords from interfering with the peasant movements.[21] Evidently, such interference was taking place even then.

In Poland-Lithuania great gaps between legal enactments and the actual state of affairs were quite possible. There were probably considerable regional variations, both in law and in practice as well. I would be happier if it could be established that migration to the Ukraine preceded the development of serfdom, but I am certainly not in a position to settle the matter. It is quite possible that migration and serfdom were reinforcing each other.

Since I have not studied the development of serfdom in other East European countries, I can make only two brief comments on Blum's well-known and very interesting article on "The Rise of Serfdom in Eastern Europe." His stress on the increasing power of the nobility and on the general depopulation of the area "from the Elbe all the way across to the Volga ..." is heartily welcome.[22] But his use of

---

17 Kliuchevsky, Vol. I, p. 293.

18 *Ibid.*, Vol. I, pp. 293–94. Grekov, *Krest'iane*, p. 387.

19 Jerome Blum, "The Rise of Serfdom in Eastern Europe," *American Historical Review*, LXII (1957), pp. 807–36. See particularly pp. 821–22.

20 Kliuchevsky, Vol. III, pp. 101–02.

21 Grekov, *Krest'iane*, pp. 381–83. There seems to be considerable disagreement among the authorities he cites. He mentions a number of legislative enactments passed at the end of the fifteenth century and in 1510, 1519, 1520, 1532 limiting the freedom of peasants to move (p. 387).

22 Blum, "The Rise of Serfdom," p. 819.

alternating periods of prosperity and depression as important causes of the rise and decline of serfdom cannot be evaluated until he presents an analytical explanation of the causation involved.

3. *Western Europe.* We shall deal here very briefly with four events:

 (1) The emergence of serfdom in the late Roman Empire
 (2) The decline of serfdom by 1300
 (3) Its non-recurrence after the Black Death
 (4) The relationship between sheep breeding and serfdom.

The depopulation of the late Roman Empire is, of course, well known. Referring to Byzantium, Georg Ostrogorsky states: "And so ever-increasing masses of the rural population were tied to the soil. This is a particular instance of the widespread compulsory fastening of the population to their occupation which scarcity of labour forced the later Roman Empire to pursue systematically."[23]

This is the clearest statement on the relation between scarcity of labor and the development of serfdom that I have come across in my reading of European economic history.

Similarly, the great increase in population in Western Europe by the end of the thirteenth century when serfdom was declining is also well known. Thus Ganshof and Verhulst talk about "... a considerable and growing reserve of surplus labor ..." in France, and Postan discusses signs of overpopulation in England: a growing number of wholly landless men, sub-holdings of many tenants, shortage of pasture, etc.[24] The same information for Western Europe in general is supplied by Smith, who adds that: "The problem therefore for western landowners, at any rate before the demographic collapse of the mid-fourteenth century, was not to keep tenants, but how to get the most out of them.[25] Since these facts fit my hypothesis so nicely, let me stop here while I am still winning.

But when we come to the depopulation caused by the Black Death after 1348 (though, according to Postan, English population stopped growing even earlier),[26] my hypothesis is of little value in explaining the subsequent course of events. (See

23 Georg Ostrogorsky, "Agrarian Conditions in the Byzantine Empire in the Middle Ages," *The Cambridge Economic History of Europe,* Second Edition (Cambridge: Cambridge University Press, 1966), I, 206. See also pages 11, 27–28, 33, 66 and 257 of the same volume. Also, W. R. Brownlow, *Lectures on Slavery and Serfdom in Europe* (London and New York: Burns and Oates, Ltd., 1892), pp. 49–50.

24 François Louis Ganshof and Adriaan Verhulst, "Medieval Agrarian Society in its Prime: France, The Low Countries, and Western Germany," *Cambridge Economic History,* I, 294; M.M. Postan in his essay on "England," same volume, pp. 552–56, 563–64, 624; Blum, "The Rise of Serfdom," pp. 810–11.

25 R. E. F. Smith, *The Enserfment of the Russian Peasantry* (Cambridge: Cambridge University Press, 1968), p. 4.

26 Postan, essay on "England," *Cambridge Economic History,* I, 566–70.

Part I.) Why did serfdom fail to come back after such a sharp increase in the land/labor ratio?

I address myself only to England. Except for one rather queer economic explanation to be discussed presently, I have none to offer and have to fall back on political factors. Serfdom could not be restored unless the landowners were reasonably united in their pressure on the government, and unless the latter was willing and able to do their bidding. But it is most unlikely that every estate lost the same fraction of its peasants. Hence, those landowners who had suffered most would welcome the freedom of peasant movement, at least for a while, while those who had suffered least would oppose it. If so, the landowners could not be united. Postan also suggests the probability that the main pressure behind Richard II's legislation came not from feudal landowners, but from smaller men;[27] English magnates, like their Russian colleagues (see above), could evidently take care of their own interests. Though I cannot judge the "spirit" of medieval legislation, it seems to me that the measures undertaken by Richard's government were somewhat halfhearted.[28] In any case, they were ineffective. So economic forces could reassert themselves and help the peasants.

The queer economic explanation which I have just mentioned would delight an economist if only it squared with facts. It is the expansion of sheep breeding, an activity which is land-using and labor saving.[29] Unfortunately such data as I could find do not support the contention that there was an expansion of sheep breeding in the hundred years following the Black Death. The legal exports of English wool, in raw and in cloth, fell from 12 million pounds in 1350 to 8.7 million in 1400—a drop of 27 percent. Another fall of 12 percent (of the 8.7 million) took place by 1450.[30] My authorities do not state the proportions of wool consumed at home and smuggled out of the country.[31] Perhaps these were affected by the Hundred Years' War. But as things stand, I certainly cannot claim that an expansion of English sheep breeding took place after 1350 and that it helped to save the peasants from the return of serfdom.[32]

27 *Ibid.*, p. 609.

28 Brownlow, *Lectures on Slavery*, pp. 157–83. Smith, *Enserfment*, pp. 4–5.

29 The idea that sheep-breeding may have had something to do with serfdom was suggested by Nieboer in his book (pp. 371–75) discussed in Part III.

30 K. G. Ponting, *The Wool Trade Past and Present* (Manchester and London: Columbine Press, 1961), p. 30. The figures are based on a chart facing p. xviii of *Medieval Merchant Ventures* by E. Carus Wilson.

31 According to Postan, p. 568, domestic consumption of cloth is not known. Peter J. Bowden arbitrarily assumed it to be 50 percent. See his *The Wool Trade in Tudor and Stuart England* (London: Macmillan & Co., Ltd., 1962), p. 37.

32 Data on the size of the sheep population, or more correctly on increments in it, would not be sufficient for our problem. We would have to know how many cropraising peasants were replaced, say, by 1,000 extra sheep.

Judging by Thomas More's famous passage about sheep devouring men, by Bishop Latimer's "Sermon of the Plough" (1549), and by other more direct evidence, there must have been considerable expansion of sheep breeding at the expense of crops and of people in the sixteenth century.[33] By that time, however, English peasants hardly needed the help from the sheep in staying free.

But is it possible that the early expansion of sheep breeding which must have taken place sometime prior to 1350 *had* helped the English serfs to gain their original freedom after all?

4. *The United States.* The American South fits my hypothesis with such embarrassing simplicity as to question the need for it. The presence of vast expanses of empty fertile land in a warm climate, land capable of producing valuable products if only labor could be found seems to me quite sufficient to explain the importation of slaves. What is not clear to me is the failure of the North to use them in large numbers. Besides social and political objections, there must have been economic reasons why Negro slaves had a comparative advantage in the South as contrasted with the North. Perhaps it had something to do with the superior adaptability of the Negro to a hot climate, and/or with his usefulness in the South almost throughout the year rather than for the few months in the North.[34] I have a hard time believing that slaves could not be used in the mixed farming of the North; much food was produced on southern farms as well, most of the slave owners had very few slaves, and many slaves were skilled in crafts.[35] A study of the possible profitability of slavery in the North, along Conrad and Meyer's lines, which could show whether the North could have afforded paying the market price for slaves, would be most welcome.

   I have not come across any good evidence that slavery was dying out in the United States on the eve of the Civil War, and I side here with Conrad and Meyer, though, in truth, I am not sure that such a thorough investigation was required to prove the profitability of slavery in the South.[36]

33 See E. Lipson, *The History of the Woollen and Worsted Industries* (London?: Frank Cass & Co., Ltd., 1965), p. 19; E. Nasse, *On the Agricultural Community of the Middle Ages, and Inclosures of the Sixteenth Century in England* (London: Macmillan & Co., 1871), pp. 77–78; Brownlow, *Lectures on Slavery*, p. 184; Bowden, *Wool Trade*, p. xvi.

34 Woodman, *Slavery and the Southern Economy*, p. 7.

35 Conrad and Meyer, *Economics of Slavery*, p. 80; James Benson Sellers, *Slavery in Alabama* (University, Alabama: University of Alabama Press, 1950), pp. 71, 120, 162–63; Rosser Howard Taylor, *Slaveholding in North Carolina: An Economic View* (Chapel Hill: University of North Carolina Press, 1926), p. 72; Harrison Anthony Trexler, *Slavery in Missouri* (Baltimore: The Johns Hopkins Press, 1914), pp. 13, 19; Woodman, *Slavery and the Southern Economy*, pp. 14–15.

36 As the authors practically admit on p. 78. On the profitability debate see Stanley L. Engerman, "The Effects of Slavery Upon the Southern Economy: A Review of the Recent Debate," *Explorations in Entrepreneurial History*, Second Series, IV (1967), pp. 71–97.

III

In conclusion, let me say a few words about the origin of my hypothesis and about its place in economic history. Although I had discussed it in my classes for a good dozen years, I did not write it up until 1966 because I had been told on good authority that the idea was old and well known. My source was indeed correct because a brief search in the library revealed quite a few predecessors. The most important of them was the Dutch scholar Herman J. Nieboer whose magnum opus of 465 pages under the title of *Slavery as an Industrial System: Ethnological Researches* was published in 1900. [37] The hypothesis which I have immodestly called "mine" was stated by him time and again, and tested against a mass of anthropological and historical data. As you might expect, he was satisfied with his results.

But the hypothesis was not really original with Nieboer. He in turn referred to A. Loria's *Les Bases Economiques de la Constitution Sociale* of 1893, and to E. G. Wakefield's *A View of the Art of Colonization* published in 1834. Some glimpses can be found even in Adam Smith's *The Wealth of Nations.*[38]

I have two disagreements with Nieboer. First, his definition of free land has too much legal and not enough economic content to my taste, though he seems to have been unclear rather than wrong. Second, he exaggerated the importance of the hypothesis by claiming, though not in so many words, that free land or other free resources are both necessary and sufficient for the existence of slavery or serfdom: "… Only among people with open resources can slavery and serfdom exist, whereas free labourers dependent on wages are only found among people with close resources."[39] He protected himself with a note on the same page by excluding simple societies of hunters, fishers, and hunting agriculturists, hardly a fit company for the farmers of the American North. He disregarded the possibility that serfdom, once established, could exist for a long time after its initial cause—free land—had disappeared, or that serfdom may be even introduced in the absence of free land. He ignored the role of government. These, however, are minor defects in an important major contribution.

On the other hand, my source may have been a bit wrong. If historians have always known about the relation between the land/labor ratio and serfdom (or slavery), they must have tried hard not to scatter too many good, clear statements in places where I could find them, though the students of the American South have been much kinder to me than

37 It was published in The Hague by Martinus Nijhoff. A republication is scheduled in 1970 by Burt Franklin, Publisher, New York.

38 Adam Smith, *The Wealth of Nations* (London: Cannan's edition, 1922), II, 66–68. There is another book by Wakefield on the same subject: *England and America: A Comparison of the Social and Political State of Both Nations* (London: Richard Bentley, 1833), Vol. II. Other sources: J. E. Caimes, *The Slave Power* (London: Parker, Son, and Bourn, 1862); J. S. Mill, *Principles of Political Economy,* 1848 (New York: D. Appleton and Co., 1920), I, 316.

39 Nieboer, *Slavery as an Industrial System,* pp. 312, 389.

others?[40] Nieboer could also lodge some complaints. His name can be found neither in the bibliography nor in the index of the 1966 edition of the first volume of *The Cambridge Economic History of Europe.* And it is absent from Blum's classic study of Russian serfdom. I did find Nieboer's name in Genovese's *The Political Economy of Slavery* in connection with some insignificant point, but with a further notation that "Phillips read and referred to this book." Phillips had read it, and confirmed that "hired labor was not to be had so long as land was free."[41]

Perhaps in history this hypothesis occupies a place similar to that enjoyed by economic growth in economic theory not long ago. That place was once described as "always seen around but seldom invited in." If so, why not invite it? After all, the land/labor ratio is readily quantifiable.

Evsey D. Domar, *Massachusetts Institute of Technology*

40 A clear statement by Ostrogorsky was quoted in Part II. For the American views, see Woodman's collection.

41 Eugene D. Genovese, *The Political Economy of Slavery* (New York: Vintage Books, 1967), p. 84. Ulrich B. Phillips, "The Economic Cost of Slaveholding in the Cotton Belt," *Pol. Set. Q.*, XX (June 1905), partially reproduced in Woodman, *Slavery and the Southern Economy,* p. 36.

Topic Four Suggested Supplemental Reading:

North, Douglass C., and Robert Paul Thomas. "The Rise and Fall of the Manorial System." *The Journal of Economic History* 31, no. 4 (December 1971): 777–803.

Topic Four Questions

1. Explain Domar's theory of slavery and serfdom as it relates to population and land endowments.
2. Compare and contrast the manorial system in Western Europe with Russian serfdom.

Topic Five

Europe and China on the Eve of the Industrial Revolution

CHAPTER SIX

The Economy in the Fifteenth Century

Preconditions for European Expansion

Paola Massa

An Integrated Economic System: Europe in the Fifteenth Century

The Geographical Background

Geographers describe Europe, or the Old Continent as it is sometimes called, as a large indented peninsula extending for thousands of kilometres seawards. This circumstance has had a decisive effect on Europe's climate and greatly influenced the lives of its people, motivating them to navigate, explore and colonize new lands. Over the course of centuries the internal territorial divisions of Europe have undergone considerable variations as a result of numerous wars and subsequent political changes. However, despite their impact and influence, and despite enduring political divisions, economically we can consider fifteenth-century Europe as a single unit, as a community united by similar, or at least complementary, interests.

The French historian Fernand Braudel identified a process of integration in the economic fabric of Europe, occurring between the Middle Ages and the modern period, and he took the Old Continent as the basis for a model of economic development that he defined as a 'world system' or 'world economy'.[1] In his model, the population was subdivided into different social groups. These had differing demands for goods and manufactured products, and were largely self-sufficient for their requirements; thus they did not recognize any great economic advantage, or chance of enough profit, in exchanges with other groups beyond their boundaries. A further interesting aspect of Braudel's development model of modern Europe is how the territory and economy of the Old Continent ultimately came to include not only the whole Mediterranean area, but also the North African countries that had economic links with it. The waters of the 'internal' sea of the Mediterranean were an important point of intersection for the movement of goods, precious metals and people.

1 F. Braudel, *Civiltà materiate, economia e capitalismo*, voi. III, *I tempi del mondo*, Turin, 1982, pp. 5–50.

This idea of Europe is one that embraces an economic world with physical boundaries, limited by mountain chains, the North Pole and the African desert. It is a view of Europe that perhaps we can still look to today as we reflect on its political and cultural characteristics and historical traditions.

Urban Poles of Development and Markets

An important aspect of the 'world economy' model in its application to fifteenth century Europe[2] is the way it underlines the dynamic changes that lead to successive and increasingly advanced stages of development. Braudel argued that a number of urban centres emerged, which he defined as 'poles', and which provided 'leadership' at different times. It was under their motivating force that certain sectors of the economy were expanded and formed bodies that, in different periods of history, acted as nuclei attracting greater numbers of productive resources, because of the more advantageous operating conditions.

At least until the mid-fifteenth century, apart from the textile industry (particularly the manufacturing of woollen cloth), it was in commerce where good profits could be made. Commerce, which could be called 'commercial capitalism', had existed since the early thirteenth century. Marco Cattini has described it as 'the merchant acting as middleman between producer and consumer and closing the great gap in time and space that lay between the place where certain goods were acquired and where they were sold'.[3] Merchants were men with considerable financial means and credit, and were considered reliable. They had a close technical knowledge of their wares in addition to being well versed in commerce, law and accounting.

During the fifteenth century two key areas of trade became increasingly important for the whole European economic system. The first coincided with the Italian cities of the Mediterranean including Genoa, Venice, Pisa, Amalfi, Ancona, Naples, Messina and also Sienna and Lucca, which specialized in trade with the East and supplied Europe with indispensable products such as spices.[4] They also engaged in trading primary goods such as cereals and raw materials. The second was in the Baltic Sea area, where as far back as the mid-thirteenth century a group of ports, including Bruges and Antwerp, Hamburg, Danzig, Stettin, and Novgorod on the Russian coast, had joined to form part of the Germanic Hanseatic League. Hansa ships sailed from the Baltic Sea to the North Sea through the Sound, and all the northern European countries, including England, depended on them for their supplies.

Political factors complicated the pre-existing social and economic balances however. Overland trade was made difficult during the Hundred Years War (1337–1453), but it

2 Braudel considered that a slightly modified model could also be applied to the next two centuries.

3 'nell'interporsi del mercante tra produttore e consumatore, grazie alla enorme distanza spaziale e temporale che, per certi merci, separava i luoghi di approvvigionamento da quelli di vendita'. M. Cattini, *La genesi della società moderna contemporanea*, Parma, 1992, pp. 170–1.

4 Spices form the great exception to F. Braudel's 'self-sufficiency' model.

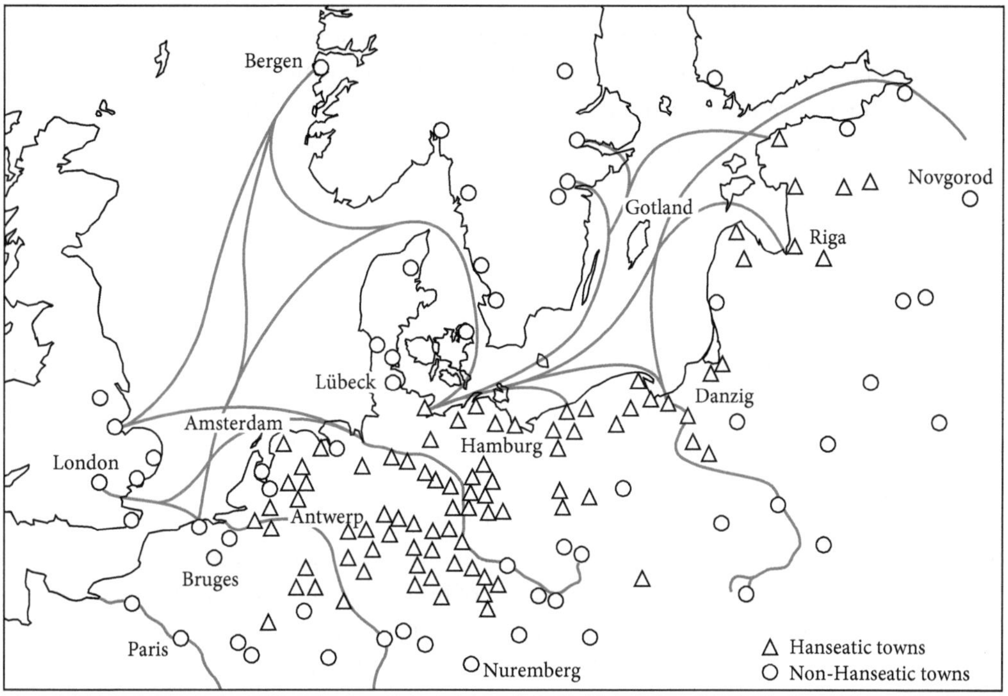

MAP 6.1 **Areas of Hanseatic trade around 1400.**

Source: F. Braudel, *Civiltà materiale, economia e capitalismo*, III, *I tempi del mondo*, Turin, 1982 [1979], p. 89.

enabled Bruges to succeed in establishing itself as a midway port. When, at the end of the fifteenth century, Bruges fell out of favour with the Habsburg dynasty, its place was taken by the cosmopolitan mercantile centre of Antwerp, which was also the venue for one of the first international commodity exchange markets.

Goods, Routes and Means of Transport

Throughout the fifteenth century, and for much of the sixteenth, the most important economic sector in Europe continued to be the production and trading of textiles. Tens of thousands of lengths of wool and silk cloth were traded and redistributed from Flanders, the Venetian hinterland, Tuscany and the important Italian 'silk cities' such as Lucca, Venice, Florence and Genoa. There was also a significant seaborne trade, involving bulk commodities such as grain, salt and timber. Important raw materials like iron, lead, tin, copper, leather, wax and furs, as well as grains such as rye, oats and barley, were transported to the North Sea ports by the Hanseatic League, while cargoes of Asian and Mediterranean produce such as oil, wine, spices, rice, dried figs, raw wool, dyes, alum[5] and textiles arrived

5 Phocaea had been the source of this substance until the fall of Constantinople in 1453 when it was replaced by Tolfa, near Rome. Alum was used as a mordant in dyeing textile fibres, and in the tanning of leather.

from the opposite direction. Goods with a high unit value and low bulk were exchanged at international trade fairs such as the one in Champagne, which had been taking place since the thirteenth century, or in Geneva and Lyons since the fourteenth century. Every three months these fairs provided important meeting places for merchants, who came from the main countries, both north and south, to exchange goods and conduct their business transactions.[6]

Transporting goods along the various trade routes was not always easy. Mule caravans loaded with goods and people had to cross the Alps over passes that were often deep in snow. In the interior of Europe there were plenty of regular services and shipments along the rivers and canals, but there were still numerous obstacles, such as water mills or fulling works in mid-stream, that made costly transfers necessary. There were also dues and tolls to pay, or services that were under the monopoly of the corporations. The route of choice was therefore the sea; the transport it provided was slow and hazardous, owing to mishaps caused by human error or acts of nature, but it was undoubtedly less costly. Sailings did not usually take place in winter, but this was offset by the greater distances that could be covered and the high profits from the transport of both expensive goods and the relatively cheap bulk commodities. Before the explorations and geographical discoveries at the end of the fifteenth century, ships still sailed within sight of the coast wherever possible, but there was a gradual increase in the tonnage of the vessels. These were now being equipped with a greater number of masts and with stern rudders, and were making better and more rational use of sail power. Alongside the rowing galleys,[7] ships known as carracks, or *navis,* were appearing, and caravels later in the fifteenth century. For coastal navigation smaller boats were used. They were similar one to another but often had very different names. Throughout the century improvements to instruments, and developments in cartography, gradually reduced the margins of error and lowered the risks that were an integral part of navigation.

The Gradual Development of an Efficient Money Market

In medieval tradition, going back to the time of Charlemagne, the treasury held the right to mint coins. It was a right that the most important cities also claimed for themselves, and when after lengthy and often difficult negotiations they succeeded in winning that right, they guarded it closely. Monarchs resisted this, since coins were seen as a symbol of sovereignty, but also, and perhaps more important, because the mint was a primary source

6 The next section of this chapter explains how, in an economic system based only on metal currency, the possibility of transacting business without it reduced the need to have it in circulation; this was a great advantage, since obtaining the precious metal usually involved long and hazardous journeys. The trade fairs were precisely where the bill of exchange originated; this was an instrument of credit used throughout Europe and acted as a draft in a foreign currency deferring payment in time and space, whether to settle a business deal or grant a loan. It enabled trading houses to expand their range of business and to operate more efficiently.

7 Allowing for defence requirements, in the fifteenth century the average crew-load ratio was one sailor for every four to five tons.

of financial revenue. The revenue was acquired either legally through the right of 'seigniorage'[8] or illegally through gains the treasury could make by issuing coins of increasingly poor quality but whose legal value remained unchanged.

During the early Middle Ages the only coin actually in circulation was the silver *denaro,* whose weight and fineness varied considerably from one mint to another and from one year to the next. However, the general tendency was for these to decrease, one reason being the scarce supply of the metal on the markets. With rare exceptions, gold, as a means of payment, was used in the form of objects or bars whose value was measured by weight, or in the form of Byzantine or Arab coins. The wide availability of these coins delayed monetization in the western areas of Europe even after 1000, which was a period of strong recovery in trade that coincided with the first Crusades, a considerable increase in population and a steady decline in barter.

In the period until the eleventh century, exchanges were typically made using forms of payment that the French historian Frédéric Mauro has defined as 'borderline'. For example a family made use of any surplus goods, produced beyond its own needs, for the purpose, though this arrangement was more common in country areas and generally in closed economies. Barter was widely practised on regional or international markets, and for this purpose salt was one of the most enduring commodities. Another widespread form of payment' was the free provision of care and medical treatment for much of the population, by the Church and the monastic orders. Before the spread of printing, parishes and convents provided education and culture. They also organized water supplies in the urban centres.

After the mid-thirteenth century, coin gradually made its way into every field of economic life; even feudal taxes that had been payable in kind were now starting to be paid in money. Some historians maintain that the first gold coin of any importance was the *genovino,* which was coined in Genoa and dated back to the second half of the twelfth century. The *fiorino,* issued in Florence, and the Venetian gold ducat, later called the *zecchino,* belonged to a slightly later period. France followed the example set by the Italian cities and in 1266 issued the *parigino,* while some years later England did the same with the *noble.* However, the development of a money market was delayed because there was insufficient precious metal in circulation suitable for coining. Thus, until the mid-fifteenth century, there was a considerable discrepancy between supply and demand. Only modest quantities of precious metals were being extracted and, in any case, these were only partly used for coinage. Gold, as well as silver, was required for making jewellery and plate, church and convent treasures, which were considered as risk-free investments.

In the second half of the century the bimetallic system developed in Europe, and the search for new deposits of gold and silver produced positive results; meanwhile the increasing price of metal provided a further impetus. The application of new mining techniques that were being developed led to better exploitation of the known deposits. The availability of silver increased with the improved exploitation of German, Austrian and Hungarian

8 The right of a feudal lord. (*Translator's note.*)

mines, and at the end of the century there were increases in the quantities of gold. Two simultaneous circumstances caused an increase in the availability of gold. First there was the exploitation of the gold reserves in Guinea and Senegal, following the Portuguese explorations along the African coasts. These sources boosted the circulation of European money, supplementing the gold supplies that had long been coming from the Sudan, across the Sahara to North Africa, where they were exchanged for Italian and Spanish products. Second there was the result of the early voyages of Columbus that brought the 'gold of the isles' from Santo Domingo, Porto Rico, Cuba and the Antilles into Spain.

However, even this was still very little compared with the growing needs of the economic system of Europe, the development of which was closely linked with variations in the available quantities of precious metals and the instability of their value. Here it should be pointed out that the monetary organization of all states was based on a distinction between real, or coined, money and money of account, between which the state fixed a ratio. Money of account acted as a unit of measure for the currency in circulation,[9] and, at least until the sixteenth century, was rock-solid.

All in all there were many different coins circulating in Europe, yet, at the same time, attempts were being made to bring stability to the international money market. Apart from money of account, there was also a tendency towards trying to keep the exchange ratios constant. Two examples illustrate the efforts that were made to bring order and innovation to a technically archaic system. First there was the formation of the Rhenish Monetary Confederation in the fifteenth century; eleven sovereigns and seventy-four German cities signed an agreement whereby, for a certain period, the Rhenish florin was to act as the only legal currency. Second there was the *scudo di marco,* which had a more sophisticated and significant purpose; this type of money of account had first circulated in the thirteenth century fairs of Champagne, and during the course of almost three centuries had gradually merged in such as way as to meet the needs of merchants from different countries.

It is more difficult to assess how rapidly money circulated in the fifteenth century. Gold was circulating less rapidly than silver (through the effects of Gresham's law[10]); this circumstance was further conditioned by individual territorial circumstances, the role of credit, and the slow recovery of capital invested in commerce and manufacturing. The consequences were to be much greater in the following century, when the first great period of European inflation occurred, and when there was exceptional development in commercial and financial business on an international level. From this point of view the fifteenth century, particularly the second half, was a time when the European economic system was adapting to pressures of all kinds.

9 This was a *lira*, which was made up of twenty *soldi*, each of which consisted of twelve *denari*.

10 The hypothesis formulated by the English financier Thomas Gresham in the sixteenth century that bad money drives good money out of circulation. (Translator's note.)

The Merchant Bankers: The First Instruments and Institutions of Credit

While economic activity was still carried on within a feudal framework the lack of money was not seen as an important problem, but the gradual development of trade—which postulates the need for a suitable substitute for money—led to attempts to get round this deficiency. The granting of credit long remained an unregulated and often illegal practice, and as a result, though average rates of interest in western Europe varied between 5 per cent and 10 per cent, merchants and artisans did not acquire the capital they needed for an investment, since its cost would certainly have been greater than any profit from it. Initially the clientele of banker-moneylenders consisted mainly of people requiring money for the purchase of consumer goods. But the fifteenth century was still dominated by the medieval conviction that any payment for the loan of money was immoral, which was the official view of the Church. Even the bill of exchange was viewed with suspicion and considered as a loan in disguise (which indeed it did become), despite its use for a commercial transaction. The only case where it was permissible was if it was negotiated on another market and in a different currency from the drawer's, in which case the interest was camouflaged within the exchange rate.

The leading figures in the sector of credit were the merchant bankers. They were non-specialist financial dealers who opened current accounts and received deposits without, initially, paying any interest, at least not overtly. An account would be opened to facilitate a client's payments, withdrawals and giro operations 'in writing', which meant that the transaction was entered into the merchant banker's account books at his *banco,* or 'bench'. The banker could use the sums he received to carry out his own business, which might be mercantile or entrepreneurial or in the field of insurance, and at the same time gain greater professional and social credibility for himself. When changes in the doctrinal attitudes of the Church allowed greater freedom, it meant that the depositor could now be paid a 'fair' interest rate. Business deals, which were initially negotiated only on the local *piazza,* or market place, gradually moved to other markets, or *fuori piazza.* Venice, Genoa and Barcelona, but especially towns in south Germany and Tuscany,[11] were flourishing centres for this type of activity, which now saw the progressive development of a wide range of instruments of credit, including advance payments on goods and associated banking techniques such as endorsements and cheques.

Apart from the large and dynamic families of merchant bankers, who operated mainly out of Italy with branches and correspondents throughout Europe, there were also a number of public institutions of credit, particularly in Spain and Italy. One of the oldest of these was the Banco di San Giorgio (Bank of St George), which was founded in Genoa in 1408. Other forms of credit also existed, and these would be further refined over the next centuries. They included loans to sovereigns or cities, securities, annuities and investments for partnership in companies. The midfifteenth century was especially marked by the spread of pawnbroking under the management of the Monti di Pietà, whose main purpose was to

11 Florence had over thirty banking houses in 1470.

provide charitable aid. These organizations were founded by the Franciscan monks, and the first Monte, in Perugia, dates from 1462. The Monti were an alternative to usury for people who, though poor, were not destitute; the money was required in the short term, and the borrower was confident of soon finding the resources to pay back the debt and redeem the items he had pawned. By the end of the century this typically Italian institution had spread to most of the peninsula. Its strong point lay in the low interest rates, which did not usually exceed 10 per cent and in some cases were much lower. In the case of particularly small amounts they were even zero. The capital the Monti used for their activities initially came from their own sources of revenue, and was not subject to any charges. A century later some of them started gathering deposits, but for a long time no interest was charged.

The Supply of and Demand for Goods: Agricultural and Manufactured Goods

Population Patterns

In quantitative terms the major factor conditioning the demand for goods is population. However, no definite or complete data for population patterns and structure between the Middle Ages and the modern period are available, since the first censuses and reasonably accurate figures date only from the early nineteenth century. However, some estimates, especially those concerning urban areas, can provide a certain degree of reliability, and even on a wider territorial scale it is possible to make some statistical observations and hypotheses.

The medieval period was marked by a long-term steady growth in the European population, despite a high mortality rate that could be defined as 'catastrophic' and which was caused by wars, famines and epidemics.[12] There was also the 'normal' mortality rate, which in itself was very high, especially as regards the death of infants and children under the age of ten. Such a mortality rate was a direct consequence of the poverty and hardships that the population endured. Its effect on the demographic structure of the Old Continent was almost paradoxical; it was always a 'young' population, with the average life expectancy calculated by Carlo M. Cipolla as never being more than forty to forty-five years.[13] Cipolla had addressed the immense problem of calculating the overall population of Europe, including European Russia and the Balkans, and concluded that in 1000 it was about 30 million to 35 million inhabitants. He calculated that in the midfourteenth century it had grown to 80 million, amounting to almost a third of the total world population of around 300 million. Between 1247 and 1351 the population of Europe was reduced by a third, as a result of the enormously high number of deaths during the great epidemic known as the Black Death,

12 According to Cipolla, the other two ills became more common or were worsened because of war; famine resulted from the destruction and pillaging of crops and cattle by the passing armies, while epidemics were often the result of the poor state of health and sanitary conditions of the armies, and spread more rapidly among a malnourished population.

13 C.M. Cipolla, Storia economica delle'tà preindustriale, Bologna, 1990, pp. 13–17 and 171–84.

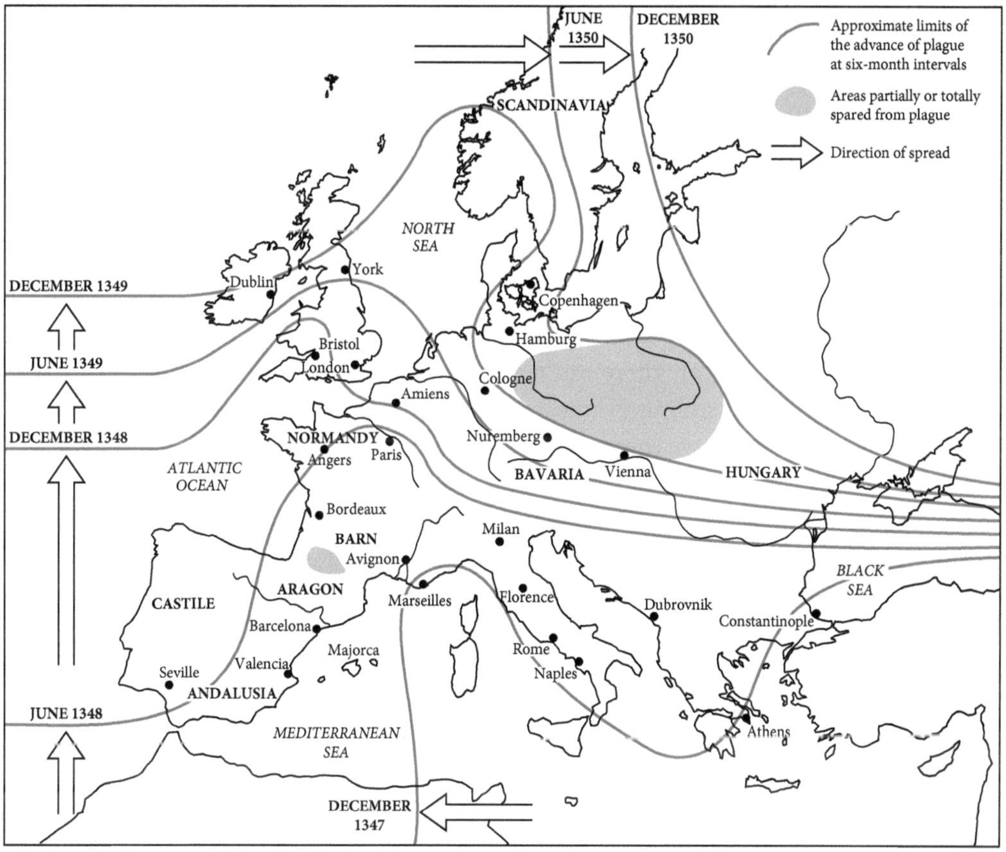

MAP 6.2 The spread of the Black Death in Europe from 1347.

Source: E. Carpenter, 'Autour de la Peste Noire: famines et épidémies dans l'histoire du XVI siècle', *Annales E.S.C.*, 17, 1962.

which had started in the East and spread very rapidly.[14] Besides the high number of deaths, there were two further consequences. The first was that, from then on, the plague became endemic in Europe, with scattered focal points and serious outbreaks at regular intervals. The second was that, for over a century, the European population remained at considerably reduced levels compared with the pre-1347 levels. It was not until the end of the fifteenth century that the overall population again reached the 80 million mark, although during the first half of the century there were marked regional imbalances. Growth was slow in France owing to the Hundred Years War (1337–1453), and in Italy the upward trend was also very slow. On the other hand the Iberian peninsula, Germany and England showed much stronger rates of growth. A more generalized upward trend started after 1450 with

14 For example, in England the mortality rate was over 20 per cent of the population. In some Italian cities over three-quarters of the inhabitants died. During epidemics and famines, there was an increase in the number of deaths but there was also a decrease in the number of births, so the two results were compounded.

the recovery of the economic system, which had been heavily affected by the plague. The reduction in population, and hence in demand, increased the availability of resources somewhat, and led to improved living conditions for people for several decades, though it did not activate the economy as a whole.

The European population was also showing a tendency towards concentrating in towns. This was mainly to seek better protection, but also to search for more lucrative employment. It has been calculated that in the pre-industrial period the population living in urban centres averaged 10 per cent, with peaks of 15–20 per cent in some areas.[15] The movement towards the towns usually followed one of two trends; either from rural areas or from smaller to larger towns. In Italy there was a movement of people from Padua and Verona to Venice, while Milan was an important magnet for other Lombard centres. In the early fifteenth century, in Italy alone, there were about ten cities of around 50,000 inhabitants[16] while the rest of Europe had no more than nine.[17] Such movements of people inevitably had consequences for the urban areas, and the greater concentrations of population in the towns obliged the public authorities to provide a more wide-ranging and efficient system for the supply and distribution of primary consumer goods.

Consumption and Investment

Expenditure in fifteenth century Europe was primarily on consumption, and largely to meet private demand; the amount of capital invested in manufacturing activities was considerable, but this was more a result of the slow market process than because it was tied up in plant and machinery, and in any case it concerned only a small minority of the population. Public expenditure on goods and services was not very different from private expenditure, except in times of war; investment in the productive sectors was negligible, with the mining industry as practically the only exception. Means of communication were the only infrastructure in which states showed any real interest; there was state involvement in the building of ports, canals, road networks and shipyards as well as civic authority buildings. The Church and the Roman Curia similarly invested in building activities. F. Mauro has debated the question of whether the financing of maritime enterprises in remote countries could also be considered as public investment:[18] the conclusion is probably that it could. This applies not so much to the Spanish conquests, but certainly to the policy of the Portuguese sovereigns who, throughout much of the fifteenth century, financed shipbuilding as well as trading expeditions.

Private individuals, especially from the aristocracy, channelled their profits from land, and other investments, into expenditure on goods such as fine furniture, tapestries, paintings and jewellery, which are not easily separated into luxuries and investments. In any

15 P. Malanima, *Economia preindustriale. Mille anni: dal IX al XVIII secolo*, Milan, 1995, pp. 19-20.

16 Genoa, Milan, Venice and Florence had almost 100,000 inhabitants each.

17 Paris (almost 100,000), London, Cologne and Barcelona were among the most important.

18 F. Mauro, *L'Europa del XVI secolo. Aspetti economici*, Milan, 1974, pp. 138–48.

case, the greatest share of individual income was absorbed by primary needs such as food, housing and heating. Even the spiritual relationship a person had with the Church needed to be paid for, not to mention the compulsory payment of tithes. In 'normal' years, around 80 per cent of a person's income went on primary goods, and the demand for these goods was constant even during the frequent agricultural crises. If people ate little and badly an important reason lay in the very low average of individual incomes. Clothing was a further item that involved considerable expense but this increased in relation to income, unlike food.

The staple 'diet' of the poor classes consisted of cereals (which apart from wheat also included rye, barley, oats and spelt), chestnuts and almost a litre per head per day of drinks such as wine and beer (which provided energy). Income levels varied according to wage patterns and price levels and set natural limits to people's wants and needs. Social and economic differences were reflected in calorie intake and diversification of foodstuffs. Apart from differences between rich and poor, there were those between town and country, as well as the different geographical areas of Europe. In the central and eastern parts of Europe the consumption of meat and animal fats needs to be reassessed, and the same applies to vegetable oils in the Mediterranean area. The intake of fish protein in areas by the sea should not be underestimated, and salted or dried fish was also widely consumed, despite its high cost. The demand for salt and spices remained steady though it was limited to small quantities *per capita.*

The Primary Sector: Forms of Cultivation and Innovations

The primary sector includes industries such as agriculture, forestry and fishing, which involve natural raw materials.[19] Agriculture, in particular, has been the main occupation of populations for centuries, and in the pre-industrial period it engaged over 65 per cent of people. According to some economists,[20] an important indicator of the structural change of an economic system is when the great changes resulting from the industrial revolution lead to equal numbers of workers in both the agricultural and the industrial sectors. Indeed, when a person's income increases, there is a corresponding decrease in the proportion he invests in food resources.

At the end of the Middle Ages land was still the major resource of the European economy in terms of value, what it produced and the labour force it employed. It is difficult to provide a clear, overall picture of agricultural yields, organization and produce, because of the many differences determined by the climate and geography of the continent. In the Mediterranean areas of Europe, cereals were cultivated alongside a number of crops such as vines, olives, mulberries and citrus fruits, in addition to sugar cane and cotton in the most southerly areas. Oats, barley and rye, as well as plants such as flax and hemp used

19 There are some anomalies. Mining really belongs to the primary sector, but is normally considered a secondary activity; transport, which is often included in the secondary sector, is a service (considered a tertiary activity).

20 In particular W.W. Rostow, *The World Economy. History and Prospect*, Austin x, 1978, p. 778, and S. Kuznets, *Economic Growth of Nations. Total Output and Production Structure*, Cambridge, 1971, p. 14

in manufacturing textiles, were grown in the northern and Atlantic areas. Cereal crops, which were also an important source of supplies for the rest of the Old Continent, were cultivated in central and eastern Europe.

The population increases in Europe, which became more generalized from the middle of the fifteenth century, had a number of wider consequences in the long term. One was the gradual break-up of the closed medieval *curtis*[21] of western Europe and its opening up to the market. Another was deforestation, which in the second half of the fifteenth century made new areas available for agriculture, at a time when all usable land was already under cultivation. There were also land reclamation projects, as well as the introduction of new agrarian contracts, such as the *mezzadria* sharecropping system in Tuscany at the end of the century and ricefields in the plains of the Po valley, where pre-capitalist forms of management and large-scale land leases were introduced. These were all indications that the fifteenth century, rather than being a period of crisis, was one of readjustment after violent upheavals, and that the economic system was going through a transitional stage. During the first decades the negative consequences of the wars, famines and epidemics of the previous century were being felt, with serious effects on the economy because of the decrease in population and reduced trade, not to mention the difficulties in organizing production. However, after 1450 the process was reversed and the population once again started to increase, though already there had been signs that wages were increasing and that a new equilibrium between the quantity of cultivable land and the supply of labour was being found.

In agriculture, the most important innovation was the replacement of the classic binary rotation system, in which fields were left fallow every other year, with a three-yearly rotation system. This brought several advantages: soil productivity was improved, since the amount of cultivated land increased by a third; work was more equally distributed throughout the year, since crops were now sown in autumn and spring; in addition, there was less risk of famine. There were also two significant innovations closely linked with the new form of crop rotation. First a new type of heavy wheeled plough was introduced, which was no longer made of wood but of iron, and second draught horses were used, with important changes being made to harnessing and equipment. Contemporary writers calculated that each horse could carry out the work of three or four oxen. However, their maintenance was three times as costly, and they were also required for transport and military operations. The cost effectiveness of adopting horse power thus depended on circumstances and had to be carefully assessed.

The Secondary Sector

The goods and manufactures required by the population, apart from those produced for its own consumption, gave rise to activities that involved the processing of raw materials, and since they were located in different areas important flows of traffic developed for their redistribution. The fifteenth century was a 'pre-industrial' period, in the sense that it came

21 The heart of a large medieval estate was the interior courtyard, or *curtis*, which by its very nature was 'closed' with respect to the economy of the period. (*Translator's note.*)

before the period of industrialization that started with the English industrial revolution in the mid-eighteenth century. However, if the expression is limited to meaning the use of technology appropriate to that particular period, then the fifteenth century can be considered 'industrial'. The raw materials subjected to industrial processes included agricultural products such as cereals, wood for building ships and making tools, plants such as flax for manufacturing textiles, or the mulberry which was important in the production of silk. One extremely important raw material was wool, while leather, used for many different manufactures, was also worked in countries along the Mediterranean coast of Africa. In the second half of the century, paper was produced from rags as well as from fibres containing cellulose. Important centres of paper production in Italy were located in Tuscany and Fabriano, but also in other parts of Europe such as the Vosges and the Dauphine.

The sector that employed by far the greatest number of workers was textile manufacturing, particularly wool products, which had been the case for centuries. England and Spain were the most important areas providing the raw wool, while the manufacturing centres were mainly urban centres such as the cities of Flanders and those of central and northern Italy. Their high quality products were much in demand on the international market and were bought and sold at the fairs and ports. Associated with this was a heavy demand for dyes and the previously mentioned alum, as well as the manufacture of clothing and other goods in common use. The mining and metallurgical industries, as well as early attempts at working iron, especially in the central and western areas of Europe, provided tools, ploughs, building materials and arms. A wide range of metals, especially precious metals, became available and their particular locations often meant they had to be transported long distances by sea.[22]

The sea itself provided an abundance of resources such as coral, fish and salt, which were the basis for a variety of manufacturing processes and employed people living in its vicinity. Salt in particular was an important commodity, used not only for everyday purposes but also for salting meat and tanning leather. In the mountain areas it was in great demand from the cattle farmers, who used it for feeding to their animals. In northern Europe, where the seas had a lower salt content, people needed it in order to preserve fish. Indeed, salt was perhaps one of the best examples of long established exchanges between European peoples. The Mediterranean areas produced it from the sea and exported it in considerable quantities to northern Europe, while at the same time the countries of central Europe supplied the rock salt they obtained from mines. In their turn, the fishermen in northern Europe sent back the fish they had caught and preserved with the imported salt.

22 For instance copper was found only in Sweden and Germany, tin in Cornwall and Ireland, lead in Austria and Hungary.

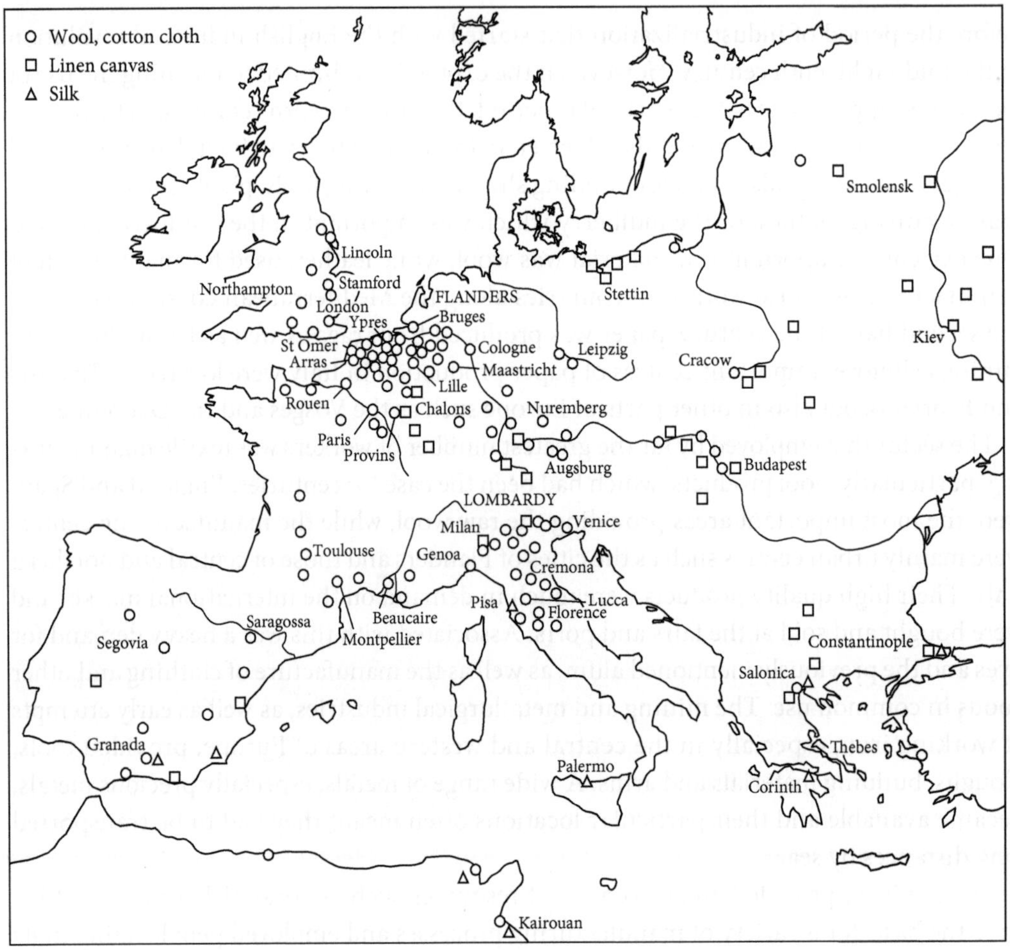

MAP 6.3 **Leading centres of the textile industry in twelfth century Europe.**

Source: R.S. Lopez, *La rivoluzione commerciale del Medioevo,* Turin, 1974, p. 170.

Imports from the Asian Continent

In F. Braudel's model of the European economic system, with its self-sufficiency as regards goods,[23] there was one important exception, which was spices. Europeans had depended on imports from the Asian continent for centuries, and since precious metals were the only form of payment accepted on the Eastern markets before the arrival of the Portuguese, the Old World's economic system suffered from a significant and constant trade imbalance.

The trade included spices such as pepper, nutmeg, ginger, cinnamon and cloves but other commodities like perfumes, medicinal herbs and roots, in addition to the dyes, arms, silks, carpets, cotton, precious stones and ivory all gave rise to one of the most flourishing and ancient international trades. There were two phases to the trading operations. First the

23 F. Braudel, *Civiltà materiale*. III, pp. 5–50.

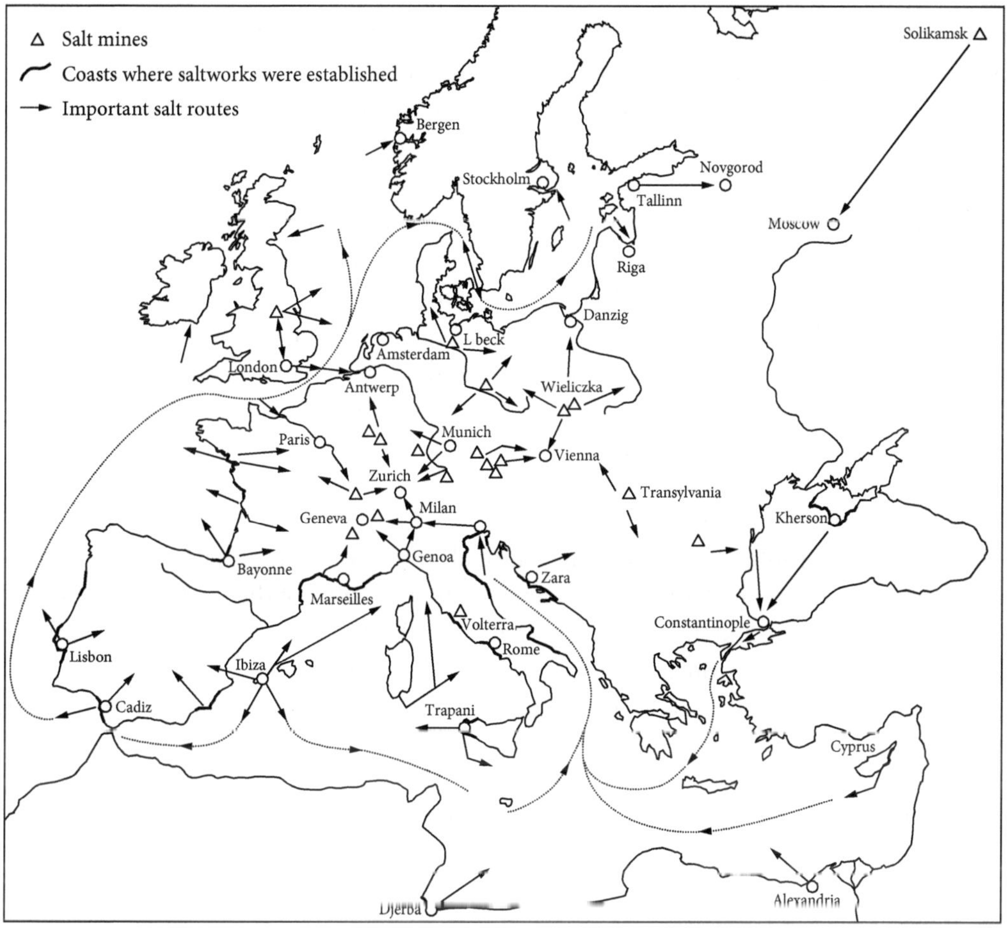

MAP 6.4 **The main saltworks and mines in Europe and salt traffic routes, fourteenth to sixteenth centuries.**

Source: J.F. Bergier, *Una storia del sale*, Venice, 1984, p. 70.

Eastern merchants, from countries such as Malaysia or India, consigned their products to Arab agents on the shores of the Indian Ocean, at places like Calicut in Malabar. The goods were then transported to the shores of the Mediterranean via sea and/or land, or up the rivers from the Caspian and the Black Sea, even as far as northern Europe. European merchants were involved in the second phase, acting as intermediaries between East and West. In the fifteenth century, the most important merchants in the Mediterranean area were from Venice and Genoa, and, to a lesser extent, from Provence or Catalonia. Throughout the period spanning the twelfth and sixteenth centuries, Venice was the greatest spice market in Europe and attracted large numbers of merchants from the European interior. Other maritime centres also made huge fortunes from this trade in costly luxury goods, which for European society had by now become a 'need', creating a steady demand for them. In order to acquire them, people were prepared even to sacrifice part of their income, though the way they were used determined the level of the demand.

Historians do not all agree as to their uses. Some argue that it was part of a vogue, a longing for an unnecessary extravagance or a way of displaying wealth, in view of their high cost. Others maintain that therapeutic and aphrodisiac properties were attributed to spices, and that they were also used to preserve food, or to camouflage the poor state of the food itself when it was being cooked. Doctors recommended the use of spices, and spice sellers would sell them to the sick at high prices. In food preparation and seasoning they played a comparable role to that of salt. The quantity of pepper that was traded was the same as that of all the other spices put together, and it is calculated that at the end of the fifteenth century Asian production was more than 100,000 cwt, almost all of which found its way into Europe. Other products included betel, rhubarb, opium, amber and musk, sandalwood, incense and camphor, and from the medical point of view were considered to have therapeutic functions.

The enormous profitability of this international traffic continued to attract capital and interest, even in the second half of the fifteenth century in spite of the long depression following the Black Death, and the situation in the Middle East that was becoming increasingly complex, after the fall of Constantinople and the subsequent Turkish conquest of Egypt. But, as Roberto Lopez has stated,[24] the Golden Age of the Mediterranean merchants had ended, and capital and interest no longer came from them but from the sovereigns of the Atlantic states. However, Italian entrepreneurs, for whom the pepper trade had driven the economy for almost two centuries, continued to play a significant role.[25]

Work Organization and Techniques

The Organization of Labour

Rural Domestic Industry

By using raw materials that were easily accessible and did not need to be acquired from the market, farming families had long met their own needs in the way of manufactured goods—especially textiles and utensils made out of wood and iron. These subsistence manufactures were produced when the family nucleus was not occupied in farming activities, and they went a considerable way to meeting the agrarian population's demand for primary goods. This was therefore *rural family* (or *domestic) industry* for auto-consumption.

24 R.S. Lopez, 'Market expansion: the case of Genoa, *Journal of Economic History*, 24, 1954, pp. 445–54.

25 C.M. Cipolla, *Allegro ma non troppo*, Bologna, 1988.

Artisans and Corporations

On the other hand, in the urban areas of Europe since the Middle Ages, the main economic activities had been organized into professional or trading associations. These were based on two common principles: equality and solidarity between members, and remaining separate from everybody else. Stipulations regarding the way specific forms of production were co-ordinated went even further: raw materials were to be purchased collectively; inside competition was prohibited and quality standards and common prices for the manufactured goods were expressly laid down. There were set procedures for membership and for learning individual trades. Members of the group, who were united by formal bonds under a specific set of regulations, or statute, enjoyed social benefits and took part in various forms of religious worship, with each trade having its own patron saint and very often its own devotional chapel inside a church. In Italy these groups were known as *corporazini* or *Arti,* and in other parts of Europe as trade guilds. Their workshops or laboratories, which were often concentrated in a particular area of a city, were owned by master artisans assisted by apprentices and various underlings who were taught the trade but whose entry into the guild was carefully controlled by the ruling elite. The guilds enjoyed a monopoly over specific products and were able to safeguard their positions to a greater or lesser extent depending on the market trends for their goods. Before a guild member was able to become autonomous he had to undergo a tough examination at the end of a lengthy period in the workshop; however, relatives of the master artisan, who was already enrolled or 'matriculated', were exempted.

This system, on which artisan production was based, lasted several centuries and was still the pillar of urban labour organization in the fifteenth century. It was viewed benignly by the town government authorities, who saw in it a means of exercising control and guaranteeing social harmony, as well as securing tax payments. The corporations guaranteed product quality and regarded any innovation with suspicion, so much so that technological development in the sector was delayed and labour negatively affected. They went so far as to demand a ban on the entry of potentially competitive foreign products and thus achieved true customs protectionism. At the same time they were committed to safeguarding their own technical expertise and severely punished members who left the town and the guild and divulged trade secrets to the outside world.

The master artisan's workshop was thus the technical unit of production, but as Carlo M. Cipolla has pointed out, concentration of labour and capital was minimal and waged labour practically non-existent.[26] Tools were personal property, and the working hours were extremely long, extending from dawn to dusk, as many town statutes testify. As a rule the artisan produced goods for the market, which was not just the local one, or on commission, and was unlikely to produce any for stock; nevertheless he still took on a risk, though it was minimal (see Table 6.1). The sectors ranged widely: food, textiles, clothing, building, the working of wood, metal (from iron to precious stones) and leather. It was only when

26 C.M. Cipolla, *Storia economica*, pp. 130–1.

the guilds, instead of being self-governing bodies safeguarding group interests, started to become the means of gaining privileges that their interests clashed with those of society as a whole, and they began to be resented in the towns.

Domestic Industry

In many regions of Europe, artisans were sometimes involved in complex production processes where semi-worked products were passed on to other workers with different specific skills. This was especially so with textile manufacturing, but also in other sectors such as metal and leather working. The artisan lost the direct link that he had had with the supply markets and the outlets for his products, and the production process became dominated by the merchant-entrepreneur, who owned not only the raw materials and working tools but also the finished product. Under him were the artisans, who only worked on what they were provided with, and had no economic autonomy, and over whom he had technical control.[27] The artisans were paid by the piece, within a system that greatly reduced the risks; they ended up becoming workers in their own homes as part of a network of independent workshops, all co-ordinated and managed by a single individual. It was a relatively flexible system of production. However, since the manufacturing cycle was often quite long (as much as six months in the silk sector), the merchant-entrepreneur needed to have a good knowledge of the markets, which often were international because of the range of his business, so that he could judge the degree of investment he required in raw materials and wages. Wages were paid in advance instalments; on the one hand this meant that the merchant-entrepreneur constantly required available supplies of money, and on the other that the artisan ended up by being a waged worker. This situation was further accentuated in cases where the artisan was categorically prevented from working on his own, and the relationship with the employer became an exclusive one. Conflicts often arose over the amount of pay and became even more acute when an important change in employment conditions was introduced whereby the employed worker could not refuse to be paid in kind. This was the 'truck system', which was still common at the time of the English industrial revolution.

The organization of the cottage industries did not change significantly when they became partly or completely ruralized. In some areas (such as Flanders) this change was already taking place in the fifteenth century, but it became more widespread in the rest of Europe in the following centuries. Textile production carried out in the countryside was a way of supplementing family incomes, but it also meant that supplies of primary goods could be obtained more cheaply and the excessive rigidity of the urban centres and guilds could be eluded. Furthermore, even though it meant relaxing controls on production quality, it did lead to important social changes, since female labour was now introduced into the production process, playing a role that was well defined and by no means marginal.

27 It is noteworthy that even in the fifteenth century he was still not specialized: he was a merchant-entrepreneur as regards textiles, but was also banker, insurer, dealer in spices, metals and grains.

TABLE 6.1 **The Structure of Industry in Medieval and Modern times**

	Artisan Industry	Home Industry	Capitalistic or Manufacturing Industry
A Location	City or town	Countryside	Near source of energy or raw materials
B Workplace	Workshop or laboratory of master artisan	Worker's dwelling	Factory (plant, mill, works, etc.)
C Worker	Master artisan, *garzone* (apprentice) and casual worker	Peasant	Worker
D Work cycle	Continuous	Alternating with agricultural work	Continuous and co-ordinated
E Head of enterprise	Master artisan	Merchant entrepreneur	Capitalist entrepreneur
F Owner of:			
raw materials	Master artisan	Merchant entrepreneur	Capitalist entrepreneur
work tools	Master artisan	Peasant (not always)	Capitalist entrepreneur
finished product	Master artisan	Merchant entrepreneur	Capitalist entrepreneur
G Most widespread industrial sector	Textiles and clothing, manual processing of wood and metals, leather, building, food	Textiles and clothing	Iron foundries, copper works, flourmills, sawmills, fulling mills, papermills, tanning works, glassworks, etc.

Source: G. Felloni, *Profilo di storia economica dell' Europa dal medioevo all' età contemporanea*, 2nd edn, Giappichelli, Turin, 1997, p. 157.

Technical Innovations

In recent centuries the most dynamic factor of economic change and development has been technological innovation. During the fifteenth century there was a flourishing of technical improvements in several significant productive sectors. They affected the various fields of economic activity in different degrees and with different consequences, but were seen mainly in the mining and metallurgical industries, and in a number of manufacturing processes. However, as with agriculture, there was no clear-cut dividing line between the Middle Ages and the modern period.

One of the most important inventions ever, and certainly of the fifteenth century, was the printing press with its movable types, and the techniques of the printing process remained almost unchanged until the eighteenth century. Though there were no immediate consequences as regards the number of workers involved, it unquestionably increased the productivity of the book trade and enormously increased the availability of information, particularly the circulation of technical and economic information. A further consequence was a heavy increase in the demand for paper, the production of which had been an active concern since the fourteenth century and now experienced a boom. The superiority of paper over previous writing materials, such as parchment, lay in its lower cost. The number of readers, both inside and outside the universities, as well as those of the copyists' workshops, had already been increasing in the fourteenth century, and now experienced an upsurge. Only fifty years after the invention of movable type, Europe had 236 cities with printing shops, and around 20 million books, produced with the new technique, were in circulation.

The improvements in the art of navigation and shipbuilding also played a fundamental role in the success of the geographical explorations and discoveries. The introduction of gunpowder and its application to firearms, which were also carried on ships, was likewise important for European overseas conquests. This, together with the use of firearms and artillery in wars, accounts for the greater strategic importance of the metallurgical industries. The application of gunpowder in the mining industry ultimately led to other improvements such as pumps to extract air, and wagons with wooden wheels to transport material, all of which contributed to making it more cost-effective to mine at greater depths. Similarly, the first blast furnaces, which benefited from associated innovations such as hydraulic bellows, mechanical hammers and grinding mills for crushing the ore, first made their appearance in the fifteenth century, especially in Sweden and the southern part of the Low Countries and Luxembourg, but also in some areas of Italy such as Tuscany and Brescia. Methods of textile production and building remained more traditional during this period, but discounting agriculture they were still the sectors with the greatest number of workers overall.

C.M. Cipolla has pointed out that in Europe areas of great innovation (such as fifteenth century Italy) existed alongside others that were less innovative. This resulted in the movement of 'human capital', closely connected with which was the knowledge and spread of new techniques to a greater or lesser degree. It is perhaps too soon to talk of the mobility of labour, but it should be remembered that as early as the fifteenth century, and right up to the industrial revolution, countries were well aware that the emigration of specialist and technical workers could have negative consequences for the economy. The power to control the movement of people nevertheless seems to have been extremely limited at that time.

The Development of Sources of Energy

The scarcity of available energy meant that the known sources had to be rationally exploited, but it also led to experiments in more advanced technologies with the aim of increasing their efficiency. The search for new resources was equally important, but in practice was conditioned by the availability of the land on which they were found.

In the Middle Ages animal power played an important role alongside human energy, as we have seen in relation to agriculture. In transport it was used directly, or for drawing boats along the internal watercourses and canals, and horse power was particularly important in mining. Non-animal power, such as energy from wind and water, involved a different approach. Though cost-free it was discontinuous, and required investment to be exploited by means of mills and waterwheels, that could be used in many manufacturing processes.

Besides being used for heating, wood and charcoal provided over 50 per cent of the energy required for economic activities despite the small size of many workshops, as Paolo

Malanima has shown.[28] The example of ironworking is particularly interesting and it has been calculated that at the end of the fifteenth century 2 cwt of mineral ore and 25 m^3 of wood were still required to obtain half a hundredweight of iron. In this period only a few countries had begun to use coal, which had been mined in England and central Europe since as early as the thirteenth century. Its use was limited to a few areas such as Liège where the first blast furnaces were located, and was of no real importance to the economy for at least another two centuries.

Geographical and Economic Expansion

New Horizons

A particularly significant aspect of the second half of the fifteenth century was the widening of geographical horizons, and that the era of the great explorations and territorial discoveries coincided almost exactly with a period of demographic growth. An important consequence was the search for sea routes between Europe and Asia, and the colonization of new lands in the west. Over the next century Europe would benefit from a greatly increased availability of resources of food and precious metals, though at the same time the Mediterranean would lose the central position it had gained in trade, and in particular its monopoly of the spice trade.

Two countries on the Atlantic Ocean, Portugal and Spain, were to play the leading role in this expansion, though ultimately they did not succeed in taking full advantage of the gains they had made, or of the new wealth they had conquered, as we shall see when we examine the sixteenth century. The areas of central, eastern and northern Europe would not be involved to any significant extent in the prosperity of the sixteenth century, partly because the most important trade routes were changing, but also because of the dynastic and religious wars that diverted energy away from economic activities. Only later, in the seventeenth century, would the Low Countries, England and northern France ultimately become the area of Europe deriving the greatest benefit from the economic changes associated with the great discoveries.

Portugal

Portugal was a small and relatively poor country that in due course came to dominate a vast maritime empire in Asia, Africa and America, achieving a considerable feat in the context of European expansion during this period. By 1515 the Portuguese already held sway over the Indian Ocean.

Portugal's territorial borders had become firmly established by the fifteenth century, but the country was still sparsely populated, with a limited number of small towns and a largely

28 P. Malanima, *Economia preindustriale*, pp. 84–91.

subsistence economy, with the main exception of fishing and saltworks in the coastal areas. Despite its sparse population, it was not totally self-sufficient in food products, especially in cereals, and it had to import corn as well as manufactured products. Besides salt and fish it also exported a few Mediterranean products such as oil, wine, fruit, cork and hides.

The explanation for the great Portuguese expansion overseas lay in the knowledge built up from designing ships and developing navigation techniques. These skills were part of the shrewd policy pursued by two members of the reigning family; first the king's younger son, Prince Henry, known as 'the Navigator' (1393–1460), and second King John II, who ascended the throne in 1481. Henry set about encouraging the explorations of the African coast, with the ultimate aim of reaching the Indian Ocean. By 1415 the Portuguese had already ventured ashore in Morocco and occupied Ceuta, a small fortress and important Christian outpost in Arab territory, which acted especially as a strategic base for a country that was aiming at commercial expansion. Henry set up a study centre, as it were, in his castle on the Sagres promontory in the extreme south of Portugal, where he gathered together astronomers, geographers, cartographers and navigators of every nationality. This continued a strong tradition dating back to the previous century, when the Portuguese crown collaborated with Genoan navigators and Italian merchants in several ventures of exploration. Almost every year from 1418 until his death, he organized expeditions during which seamen mapped the coasts and currents with painstaking precision, and updated the already known portolans.[29] They also rediscovered and colonized the Atlantic islands of Madeira and the Azores, as well as the Canaries (later ceded to Spain), established trading relations with the indigenous chiefs along the African coast, and had no qualms about searching for gold and slaves. Henry did not live long enough to realize his greatest ambition, and at his death the Portuguese navigators had sailed only a short way south of Cape Verde. But the scientific and explorative work that had been carried out under his patronage laid the foundations for subsequent discoveries.

After his death the impetus to exploration was lost through lack of royal support, but apart from this there was competition from the lucrative trade in ivory, gold and slaves that Portuguese merchants were carrying on with the indigenous kingdom of Ghana. When King John II came to the throne in 1481 exploration was revived once again, and in the space of a few years his navigators had almost reached the extreme southern tip of Africa. Eventually, in 1488, Bartholomew Diaz sailed round the Cape of Good Hope, which he had named the Cape of Storms. The next year, after crossing the Mediterranean, Pedro de Covilhao reached the Red Sea by land and went on to explore the west coast of India. The next voyage he made paved the way for Vasco da Gama, who reached Calicut by sailing round Africa between 1497 and 1499. Many ships and men were lost during this expedition because of disease, mutiny, storms and other difficulties, but the ships that did come back were laden with spices that more than compensated for the heavy cost of the voyage. Once they had seen the size of the profits, the Portuguese, in as little as ten years, and

29 Precise nautical charts of the coasts. (*Translator's note.*)

using military force as necessary, managed to oust the Arabs from the Indian Ocean and organize fortified trading posts as far afield as the fabulous Spice or Moluccan Islands. In 1513 one of their ships anchored at Canton in southern China, and by the mid-sixteenth century they had also established trade and diplomatic relations with Japan.

During the first decades of the sixteenth century the Portuguese continued to strengthen and expand their settlements in Asia. They did not, however, push towards the interior of these regions, but confined themselves to controlling the sea routes. These routes were already completely transforming the geography of exchange between Europe and Asia, and the limits of the economic interests of the Old Continent were reaching farther and farther eastward.

The Spanish Economy and the New World

The other country that played a leading role in European expansion was Spain, but in this case it was westward. Economic conditions in Spain created their own particular problems and there were also serious difficulties relating to internal unity.[30] The varied nature of the territory gave rise to difficulties and conflicts. There were fertile coastal regions to the east and south, mountainous areas to the north and in other parts of the country, and a high plateau area known as the *meseta* that embraced the central part of the peninsula. In the field of agriculture the Arab and Moorish peoples, who had populated Andalusia before the Christian reconquest, had left a considerable heritage. They had been excellent market gardeners and had brought the art of irrigation to a high level, but the religious fervour of the Spanish sovereigns led to this legacy being wasted. At the same time as many Muslims were already leaving the country, and in the same year as the reconquest of the kingdom of Granada and the discovery of America by Columbus, they also ordered the Jews, who were skilled artisans and traders, to be expelled from the kingdom.

The productivity of Spanish agriculture was among the lowest in western Europe. One of its main problems derived from the conflict between the peasants and the large landowners. The land had remained intact as a result of particular property laws such as the *fideicommissum*,[31] and was largely given over to sheep rearing. Wool had a very profitable outlet on the international market, because of the strong demand from the textile centres, especially in the Mediterranean area. The unique practice of transhumance was widespread among shepherds, who moved their flocks between the summer mountain pastures and the winter quarters on the lower plains. It was unique because of the enormous distances that had to be covered, and the way it was organized, not to mention the royal protection it enjoyed. The sheep farmers formed a corporation known as the Company of the Mesta and were a powerful lobby at court. Putting a tax on the migrating flocks at strategically

30 The last Arab territorial outpost, the Caliphate of Granada, fell only in 1492. Though Isabella of Castile and Ferdinand of Aragon had been joined in marriage in 1476 the two kingdoms continued to be ruled separately, sometimes following different policies, until their grandson Charles came to the throne.

31 A type of arrangement in a will whereby the heir was obliged to pass on the entire inherited property, or a part of it. (*Translator's noted.*)

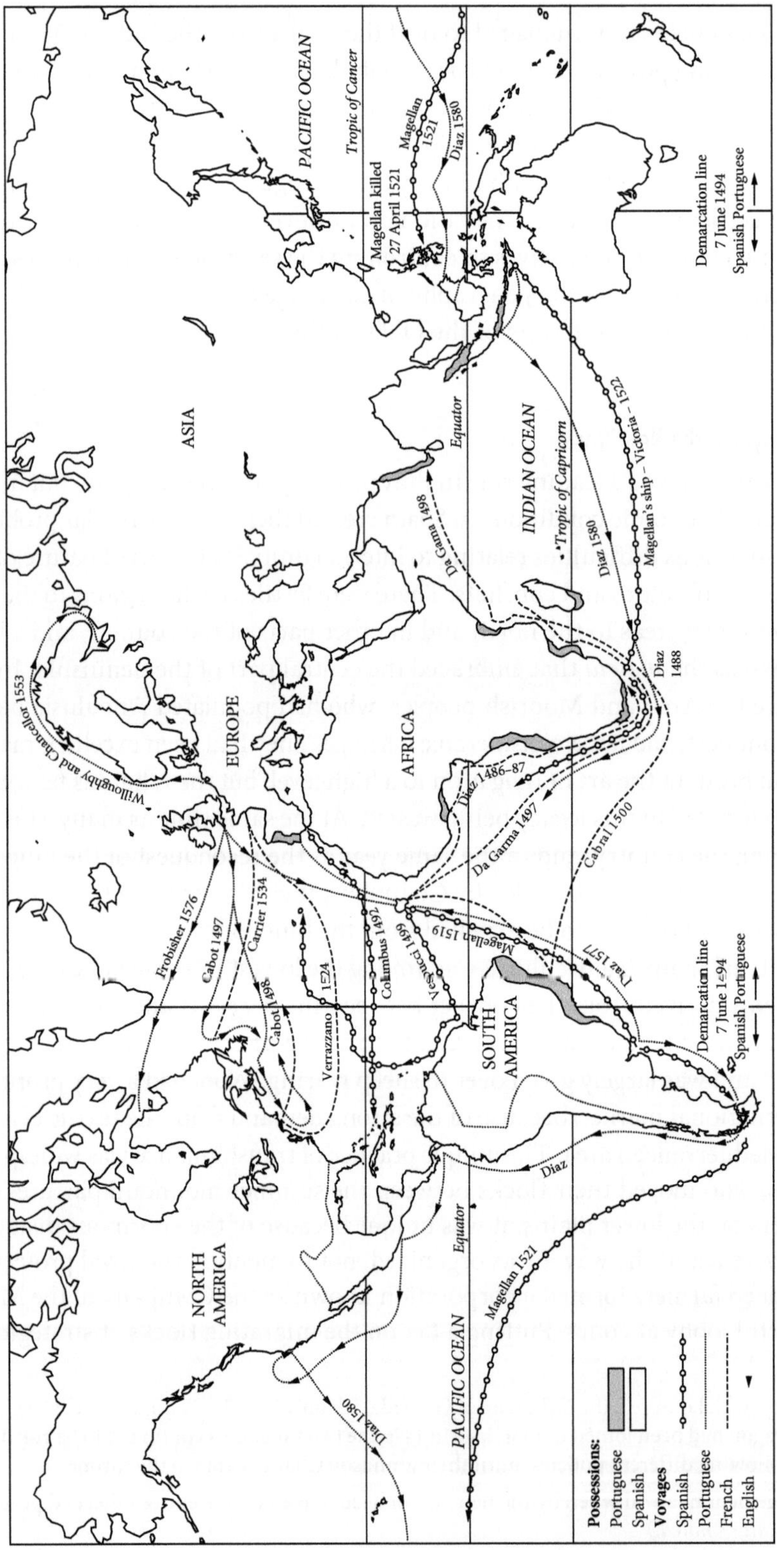

MAP 6.5 **Voyages of discovery in the fifteenth and sixteenth centuries.**

Source: R. Cameron, *Storia economica del mondo*, Bologna, 1998, p. 164.

located toll stations was an easy matter. Wool was a valuable goods item that brought money, unlike many agricultural crops, and it could be easily taxed when it was exported. In exchange for paying higher taxes, the Mesta was granted special privileges, including the right to unlimited grazing on common land, to the detriment of agriculture.

Spanish expansion was perhaps more fortuitous, and less concerned with seeking new economic horizons for trade, than that of Portugal. Cameron has succinctly described how in 1483 or 1484, when the ships sent by John II of Portugal were still opening up routes along the African coast, a Genoese named Columbus, who had served in the Portuguese navy and married a Portuguese woman, petitioned the king to finance an expedition over the Atlantic to reach the east by sailing westwards.[32] The proposal was not altogether an unusual one, since there was already a widely held belief that the earth might be spherical. John II had already authorized privately financed expeditions westwards, but resources were being concentrated on the more realistic project of sailing round Africa. Columbus's proposal was consequently rejected. However, Columbus would not admit defeat and turned instead to the Spanish sovereigns Ferdinand and Isabella. However, they were involved in war against the Arabs, and did not think the enterprise was feasible. The English and French sovereigns thought likewise; finally, in 1492, to celebrate the victory over the Moors at Granada, Isabella of Castile agreed to finance his expedition. On 12 October that year, after sailing for over two months, he reached the islands that were to be called the West Indies, since it was thought he had actually reached Asia. Columbus called the indigenous people Indians, though their evident poverty caused him dismay. He sailed back to Spain, and the following year returned with a much larger and better equipped expedition of seventeen ships and 1,500 men, taking cattle and other animals to start the real work of colonization.

New Conflicts on the Seas and the Treaty of Tordellisas

At the close of the fifteenth century there were thus two states up against each other on the seas. Both were perhaps convinced they had reached the same rich Eastern markets, but by opposite routes.

As soon as Columbus arrived back from the first expedition, Ferdinand and Isabella turned to Pope Alexander VI so that a 'demarcation line' could be drawn confirming Spanish rights over the lands that had just been discovered. This ideal line was to be drawn between the two poles, at a longitude of 100 leagues (about 330 miles) west of the Azores and Cape Verde. It was to divide the non-Christian world into two halves for the purpose of further explorations, with the western part being reserved for the Spaniards, and the eastern part for the Portuguese. A year later, in 1494, when the Treaty of Tordillas was being drawn up, the King of Portugal persuaded the Spaniards to mark out a new line that was to lie about 210 miles farther west of the 1493 line. This seems to point to the fact that the Portuguese already knew of the existence of the New World, since the area of South America bulging eastwards, which would form the bridgehead, and later become Brazil, was in the Portuguese hemisphere in the second treaty. In 1500, during the first great Portuguese trading

32 R. Cameron, *Storia economica del mondo*, Bologna, 1993, pp. 158–65.

expedition after the return of Vasco da Gama, Pedro de Cabral headed straight for this area and claimed for Portugal the territory on which he landed, before continuing for India.

In the meantime explorers from other countries were following in the footsteps of Columbus. John Cabot, an Italian at the court of Henry VII of England, undertook a voyage in 1497 with financial backing from a number of Bristol traders, and reached the island of Newfoundland and Nova Scotia. The following year he explored the northern coastline of North America with his brother; but the results were considered so economically insignificant that the king compensated them with a mere £10. At the beginning of the next century, French merchants financed another Italian, Verrazzano, to search for a western route to the Indies. Ten years later the Frenchman Jacques Cartier carried out the first of three voyages that would lead him to discover and explore the St Laurence river. All this marked the beginning of a process of liberation from the restrictions of medieval knowledge towards a new and different geographic and economic outlook.

As Cameron has also observed,[33] the most dramatic and significant aspect of European expansion—the premises of which were laid down in the fifteenth century—was the transfer of European culture, and the way it modified non-Western cultures, even leading to their extinction. The economic changes, whether quantitative in terms of the amount of goods circulating, or qualitative in terms of new products and markets, need to be seen against the cultural, social and political repercussions that these events were to have over the following centuries.

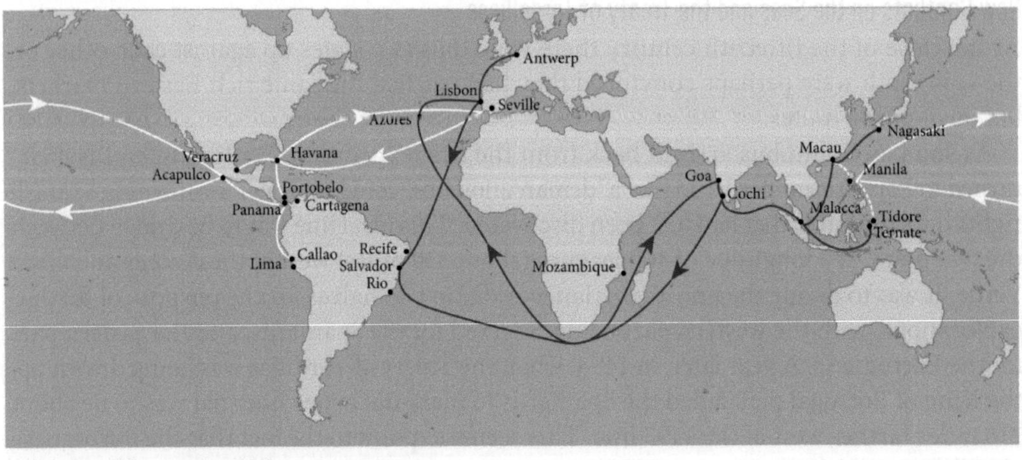

MAP 6.6 **16th century Spanish/Portuguese trade routes.**

Source: https://commons.wikimedia.org/wiki/File:16th_century_Portuguese_Spanish_trade_routes.png.

33 *Ibid.*, p. 167.

CHAPTER SEVEN

Why Did the West Win (Temporarily)?

Andre Gunder Frank

> *To confront world history is to confront the ultimate questions of human destiny. … One must look at history, particularly world history, as the reflection of a desired future. … To avoid the challenge of a global perspective is to abdicate in the face of the historian's central task—to decipher the meaning of history. To reject world history in a time of crisis is to renege on the historian's ultimate responsibility of confronting society with its past in a meaningful and useful way. … World history has become a pursuit of world unity.*
>
> Paul Costello (1994: 213, 8–9, 215)

This chapter poses the question *why* the West won (temporarily). It offers two answers and inquires into the possible relations between them. One answer is that the Asians were weakened, and the other answer is that the Europeans were strengthened. That may sound platitudinous, but it is not if we consider what weakened Asians, what strengthened Europeans, and what may in turn have related these two processes. Moreover, this very question/answer combination is not platitudinous: virtually all other contending "explanations" rest on the supposition or assertion that Asia was and supposedly remained "traditional." They also allege that Europe first pulled itself up by its own bootstraps to "modernize" itself and then graciously offered this "modernization" to Asians and others. According to the West and thanks to its "demonstration effect," this offer of "civilization" and "progress" was accepted voluntarily by some. Others had to have it imposed by the force of colonialism and imperialism. Allegedly, other Asians, not to mention Africans, Latin Americans, and even some Europeans (and quite a few North Americans) languish in their traditional juices.

The evidence and argument in the previous chapters show that Asians were no more "traditional" than Europeans and in fact largely far less so. Moreover as we will argue below, the Europeans did not do anything—let alone "modernize"—by themselves. That contention turns the tables on the historiography and social science of the last century or so, and indeed also on the humanities of the type "the East is East, and the West is West, and never the twain shall meet." They *did* meet, albeit not at all on the alleged Eurocentric terms, and the question is why?

This book has sought to build up, chapter by chapter, the global scaffolding that will permit the construction of at least preliminary answers derived from the structure and dynamic of the world economy as a whole. Chapter 2 outlined the productive and trade framework and regional interconnections of the global economy. Chapter 3 signaled how money went around the world circulatory system and provided the lifeblood that made the world go round. Chapter 4 examined the resulting world population and economic quantities, technological qualities, and institutional mechanisms, and noted how several regions in Asia maintained and even increased their global preponderance. Chapter 5 proposed a global marcohistory analysis, with which we can perceive how events and processes are often cyclically related around the world.

This chapter inquires whether and how the world economic advantage of Asia between 1400 and 1800 may have been turned to its own disadvantage and to the advantage instead of the West in the nineteenth and twentieth centuries. Some world economic connections and a possible mechanism that may have generated or at least permitted this interchange were explored in chapter 5: the long, expansive cycle (or "A" phase) that began in 1400 appears to have lasted into the eighteenth century but then turned into a "B" phase decline, at least for Asia. World economic cycles and especially crises generate both danger and opportunity—as the Chinese understand the word "crisis." However, these differ from one economic sector and region to another in accordance with their place and role in the world economy as a whole. So now we can use these lessons and the scaffolding from the previous chapters to inquire into the whys and wherefores of "the Decline of the East and the Rise of the West." The present chapter is organized into four main sections: (1) Is there a several-centuries-long world economic "roller coaster" cycle, whose expansive "A" phase turned into a contractive "B" phase for Asia? (2) When and how did the "Decline" of Asia manifest itself? (3) How did Europe and the West "Rise"? (4) How are this decline and rise related by the world economic structure through global and regional population, economic, and ecological dynamics?

Is There a Long-Cycle Roller Coaster?

We found in chapter 5 that, in the absence of a general "seventeenth-century crisis," the long global economic expansion lasted from 1400 in Asia into at least the mid-eighteenth century. This finding now permits us to pursue the Gills and Frank half-millennium-long cycles into early modern times. One of the initial incentives to write this book, we may recall, was to inquire about what the recognition of the existence of an old world system with its long "A/B" cycles beginning long before 1500 (Frank and Gills 1993) implies for Immanuel Wallerstein's "modern world-system" after 1500. These cycles had expansive

"A" phases followed by contractive "B" phases, each of which lasted from two to three centuries. We traced, identified, and dated these cycles common to most of Afro-Eurasia since 1700 B.C. (Gills and Frank 1992; also in Frank and Gills 1993) and then back to 3000 B.C. (Frank 1993a). The question becomes whether these long cycles continued into early modern times and if so to what effect.

Without seeking to review the entire history of these long cycles again here, it may be noted that a new major period of expansion spanned the years A.D. 1000/1050 to 1250/1300. That was the period especially of the major technological, productive, commercial and general economic development under the Song dynasty in China. William McNeill (1983) regards China to have been the most important "center" of the world at that time. George Modelski and William Thompson (1996) place in China the first four of their approximately fifty-year long Kondratieff cycles, beginning with A.D. 930. Also Wallerstein (1992: 586–8) notes that "the patterns of expansion and contraction are clearly laid out and widely accepted among those writing about the late Middle Ages and early modern times in Europe. ... Thus 1050–1250+ was a time of expansion in Europe (the Crusades, the colonizations) ... The 'crisis' or great contractions of 1250–1450+ include the Black Plague." Janet Abu-Lughod (1989) characterized the first century from this last phase, 1250 to 1350, as at first expansionary, but then contractionary after 1300. She did so on the basis of her analysis of a "thirteenth-century world system" in all of Afro-Eurasia. Gills and Frank (1992; also in Frank and Gills 1993) sought to review both periods as first an expansionary "A" phase until about 1250 and then a contractive "B" phase crisis until about 1450, and in the Afro-Eurasian world economy and system as a whole.

Gills and Frank (1992) dated the renewed period of "A" phase expansion as beginning about 1450, perhaps too closely following Wallerstein (1974) in his analysis of the European world-economy. We did not give adequate weight even to Ravi Palat and Wallerstein (1990), who identify the beginnings of a major expansion in India in 1400. The present review of the world economy also suggests that this expansion began in 1400, not only in India but also in Southeast Asia and probably in China.

At its marginal western end, Venetian and Genovese activities in the Black Sea and eastern Mediterranean, as well as the Genovese expansion westward through the Mediterranean and into the Atlantic, were minor parts of this world economic expansion. So were the Spanish "reconquista" on the Iberian Peninsula and all Iberian initiatives into the Atlantic. These went first to the Azores and to the Madeira and Canary islands and then around and along the shores of West Africa. This Iberian expansion laid the basis in turn for the search and discovery of a way to the prosperous and golden East Asia. The Iberians went both westward around the globe via the Atlantic and then onward via Cape Horn and Panama and/or Mexico across the Pacific, and eastward around Africa via the Cape of Good Hope. The latter would have been not only the shorter route but also the one that offered earlier and greater economic benefits from the riches of the regions bordering the Indian Ocean and the South China Sea. Only the discovery of the Americas with its golden and silver monetary riches then made the westward journey profitable. It offered the Europeans their first real opportunity to ante up in the Asian-dominated global casino. Moreover, it was initially and primarily the Asian economy that was again open for business and flourishing since 1400.

The question then becomes until when did this expansive "A" phase in the aforementioned long cycle last? When this cycle was first traced back to 1700 B.C., we really stopped at 1450 and "provisionally accepted the main outlines" of other students of cycles since then (Gills and Frank 1992; also in Frank and Gills 1993: 180).

In the revision of his test of this cycle and its phase datings on the basis of urban growth data, Andrew Bosworth (1995: 224) now writes that "it seems hasty of Gills and Frank to sound the death knell for longer term cycles ... and embrace instead shorter Kondratieff waves (if that is in fact their position). The two phenomena ... are not necessarily incompatible." Well, that may have been our pragmatic position de facto; but de jure we also considered that in principle the two kinds of cycles may nest within each other. That is indeed the thesis in the discussion of the "Monetary Analysis and the Crises of 1640" in chapter 5 above, even if I have not yet pursued how several Kondratieffs may nest in one long-cycle phase (but see our discussion of Modelski and Thompson in chapter 5).

But the more examined question is how long this (possible) "A" phase lasted. The answer is—to at least 1750. Bosworth also pursued a similar question with his urban growth data and concludes that they also "reinforce" the view of a longer "A" phase: for all twenty-five largest cities in the world, the fit to the long cycle is not good because of a sixteenth-century dip. However, "the relative urban hierarchy for East Asia (measuring the growth of its largest cities within the set of the 25 largest cities) is high until about 1650, after which it proceeds along with the ratio of the European/Atlantic city system. This 'tottering' lasts for more than a century" (Bosworth 1995: 221–2). In his Figure 8.4 the lines for relative urban hierarchy among East Asian and European/Atlantic cities do not cross until about 1825, when Asian economic and political power waned. London displaces Beijing as the world's largest city in 1850. As noted in chapter 4, Rhoades Murphey (1977) also puts the crossover between the decline of the East and the rise of the West at about 1815.

Therefore it again appears that this (so far last) world economic long cyclical phase of expansion lasted—at least in Asia—over three centuries, from the fifteenth through the seventeenth centuries and into at least the first part if not to the end of the eighteenth century. The evidence on the seventeenth century reviewed above also lends support to the notion of a continuation of the "long sixteenth-century" expansion from 1400/1450 throughout the seventeenth and into at least the early eighteenth century. Moreover, the major expansion of production and growth of population remained in Asia, as already noted in chapter 4, while Europe only caught up very belatedly. Both expansions were fueled by the inflow of American money brought by the Europeans. In terms of world historical reality and development, it was really (only) American money that permitted the Europeans to increase their participation in this mostly Asian-based productive expansion of the world economy. Moreover, we must conclude that the strongest and most dynamic parts of the world economy still remained in China and India.

I argue therefore that these and other major Asian economies had, and continued to have, a pattern of long cyclical economic growth reaching the upper turning point of its expansive "A" phase, then passing on to a contractive "B" phase. Moreover, these Asian economies were of course all connected to each other. Therefore, it cannot be "coincidental" and should not be surprising that they were experiencing such expansive and contractive phases nearly simultaneously, if that is what was happening. However, these Asian economies were not only related to each other, they were all part and parcel of a single global economy, which presumably had its own long cycle of development. The argument here is that the upward "A" phase since about 1400 of such a long cycle reached its upper turning point and gave way to a succeeding long "B" phase, especially for the more central economies in Asia between 1750 and 1800. Moreover, as I argued in Frank (1978a) and again in chapter 5, the shorter Kondratieff long cycle was in a "B" phase from 1762 to 1790.

That long "A" phase of expansion that came to an end in Asia in the late eighteenth century and its subsequent (cyclical?) decline offered the still marginal West its first real opportunity to improve its relative and absolute position within the world economy and system. Only then could the West go on to achieve a (temporary?) period of dominance. The contemporary analogy is that the present world economic crisis permits the rise of what are now called the "Newly Industrializing Economies" (NIEs) in East Asia, again at the "margin" of the world economy. We may note that like these East Asian NIEs now, Europe then engaged first in import substitution (at that time in what was the "leading" industry of textiles previously imported from Asia), and increasingly also in export promotion—first to their relatively protected markets in West Africa and the Americas and then to the world market as a whole.

There are also earlier historical analogies in which some but not all marginal and peripheral "marcher states" innovatively challenged "core" economies, societies, and polities (or, empires), as Christopher Chase-Dunn and Thomas Hall (1997) argue. The previously (semi-) peripheral economies took advantage of the opportunities (and tried to avoid the dangers) generated by crises at the center/s of the world economy/system (Gills and Frank 1992; also in Frank and Gills 1993). It cannot be emphasized too much or too often that this positional change (as in musical chairs) each time owed more to the relatively sudden system-wide crisis at its center than to any long "preparation" or previously predictable "rise" of the previously (semi-)peripheral region or its newly "leading" sectors.

Thus, we are led to inquire whether the late eighteenth century may have begun a "B" phase world political economic decline in Asia to the benefit of the previously relatively marginal and now rapidly ascending Europeans. The previously identified world system cycle (Gills and Frank 1992; also in Frank and Gills 1993) implies that the simultaneous "fall" of so many important powerful states—the Ottomans, Mughals, Safavids, Qing, and Hapsburgs—would be the accompaniment of a world system crisis and "B" phase. We will speculate a bit at the end of this chapter about the historical continuation of this long cycle, whose "B" phase appears to have begun in Asia at the end of the eighteenth century. The consideration of related theoretical problems is postponed to chapter 7.

We must still pose the important historical question of just when, not to mention why, political economic declines really began in Asia and whether they were part of a long-cycle "B" phase or not. These related questions also have far-reaching theoretical and ideological implications: were these declines in the East also initiated and caused, or only accelerated—if even that—by "the Rise of the West"?

The Decline of the East Preceded the Rise of the West

This heading is borrowed from Janet Abu-Lughod's masterful *Before European Hegemony* (1989). Alas, she did not pursue the matter beyond A.D. 1350. We have seen that the "East" took several centuries more to "decline," and that the "West" did not really "rise" until very belatedly. We are able to say very little about why the Asian economies and the Ottoman, Safavid, Mughal, and Qing empires declined. Indeed, the discussion of the eighteenth century in Asia has been ambiguous and confusing:

> For a considerable time now, in the historiography of Indonesia, India and the Arabic countries, the eighteenth century has been seen as a period of decline. The English saw the decline as justification for empire; the Dutch saw in the period an eclipse of the noble Company; the Arabs only regarded it as background to their modern period. In recent years this notion of decline has been criticized by historians working in each of these major regions. ... [Some warn] about the danger of taking political fragmentation as evidence of decay. ... [Yet] for most features of the economy the meagre evidence processed so far suggests continuity rather than sharp change. (Das Gupta and Pearson 1987: 132–3)

Nonetheless, we must follow Fletcher's admonition and look for possible systemic processes and causes in Asia's eventual "decline." Moreover, that has been my procedure for earlier periods, which has produced some significant tentative findings reported in Frank and Gills (1993) and Frank (1993a). So we should also inquire if and how the decline of the East and the rise of the West may have been systemically related.

M. Athar Ali has recently addressed the same issue. How he poses the question is worth quoting in full, although his own tentative answer seems less than satisfactory. He notes that the fall of the Mughal empire has been attributed to all manner of "internal" factors—from too much bad influence of women to institutional inadequacies that made peasant exploitation inefficient but therefore all the more severe, which generated growing nationalism. He observes that a synthesis of all relevant factors is yet to be attempted; but, before even trying, we first need to place them in "the proper context." Ali observes that

> In following the scholarly discussion over the break-up of the Mughal Empire, I have been struck by the fact that the discussion should have been conducted in such insular terms. The first part of the eighteenth century did not only see the

> collapse of the Mughal Empire: The Safavid Empire also collapsed; the Uzbek Khanate broke into fragments; the Ottoman Empire began its career of slow, but inexorable decline. (Ali 1975: 386)

Ali goes on to suggest that it would be straining one's sense of the plausible to assert that it was coincidental for the same fate to overcome all these large regions at the same time. Therefore, also following Fletcher (1985), we should inquire whether it is possible to discover some common factor that caused these simultaneous events. Ali continues:

> There is one remarkable point too, which may serve as a guideline in our search. The break-up of the empires directly precedes the impact from the armed attack of the Western colonial powers, notably Britain and Russia. But it precedes the impact with such a short interval that the question must arise whether the rise of the West was not in some ways, not yet properly understood, subverting the polity and society of the East even before Europe actually confronted the eastern states with its superior military power. It is a regrettable gap in our study of economic history of the Middle East [sic!] and India, that no general analysis has been attempted of the changes in the pattern of trade and markets of these countries, as a result of the new commerce between Europe and Asia. (Ali 1975: 386)

Ali's own attempts at a tentative answer are not satisfactory however, because of how he begins: "the major event between 1500 and 1700 was certainly the rise of Europe as the centre of world commerce" (Ali 1975: 387). The evidence amassed in this book contradicts this point of departure and obliges us to look for a different explanation. Ali goes on to suggest that European economic influence must have disrupted and weakened the Asian economies, not only relatively but also absolutely (Ali 1975: 388). This supposition is also contradicted by the evidence for the sixteenth century, especially for the seventeenth century, as well as for part of the eighteenth century, during which the Asian economies were, on the contrary, strengthened.

Then Ali argues that the supposed diversion of Asian income to Europeans and its denial to the ruling classes in Asia obliged the latter to increase agrarian exploitation to keep themselves afloat, and that "of course, spell[s] the end of the great empires" (Ali, 1975: 388). However, increased exploitation, especially of those working on the land, is usually not so much the result of declining income by those who rule them, as the result of greater and rising market opportunities to generate income for the latter from those who work the land for them. That has been the common experience in plantation and other agrarian export economies (Frank 1967). That polarizes the economy and society, making the rich richer and the poor poorer. Below, we will observe ample evidence for this in the seventeenth and eighteenth centuries in India and China as well.

In that way, economic expansion combined with polarization of income and status also resulted in atrophy in the very process that generated it. Therefore, the political stability of the Asian empires may have been undermined not so much by European competition in their economies, as Ali suggests. The growing economic and political strains in Asia may instead have been generated more by the Europeans' supply of silver and by the resultant increased purchasing power, income, and demand on domestic and export markets in the world economy and especially in Asia. That presumably increasingly skewed the distribution of income, which could have led to constraints on effective demand and growing political tensions, as we will see below.

Only in the second half of the eighteenth century, especially in the last third, did trends toward decline accelerate in the Ottoman, Indian, and Chinese empires. The decline was earliest and most accelerated perhaps in Persia and then in India, with the gradual loss of competitive advantages in textiles and the reversal of bullion flows (that is, outward rather than inward) after mid-eighteenth century.

So unless it was in Safavid Persia or in Timurid and/or Bukharan Central Asia, the earliest decline seems to have occurred in India; and it is also the one for which the most studies are readily available to us. So let us start with India, and go on to examine other parts of Asia after that.

The Decline In India

Historiography on India has long debated whether and to what extent especially British colonialism was responsible for famine and deindustrialization first in Bengal and then elsewhere in India. Ironically, Western-aligned and Indian nationalist observers agree that the British victory at the Battle of Plassey in Bengal in 1757 marked the most important disjuncture. Western-aligned observers tended to argue that Britain brought civilization and development to India. Some Indian nationalist writers in the nineteenth century (reviewed by Chandra 1966) and many Soviet, Indian, and other "anti-imperialist" ones (including Frank 1978a) in the twentieth century have seen the decline of India as the result of the defeat in that battle, which led to British colonization. That began the "Rape of Bengal" by the British East India Company, the destruction of the textile industry, the zamindari (large holdings) and *ryotwari* (small holdings) structure of landownership, the "drain" of capital from India, and so on.

Without wishing to pursue this dispute here, there is nonetheless legitimate doubt about just when and where economic decline began in India and elsewhere. Those who argue that it only began after 1757, or, like Amiya Bagchi, only after 1800, or indeed really only from about 1830 as Burton Stein (1989) suggests, must confront at least some evidence that significant economic decline had already started before any of these dates. Contrary to received allegations about "stagnation" in India and elsewhere in Asia prior to the arrival of the Europeans, we observed in chapters 2, 3, and 4 and in the section on a "seventeenth-century crisis" in chapter 5 that substantial economic growth continued in India well into the eighteenth century. That is also the summary judgment of the historical evidence about eighteenth-century India by Stein (1989). In his view, however, British policy did not cause significant economic damage in India until about 1830.

Yet others have observed beginnings of economic decline in India about a century earlier. "There is a definite decline in *both* silk and cotton production in Bengal from the early 1730s" (Rila Mukherjee, private communication 1995). Mukherjee (1994) offers evidence from Kasimbazar, a major Bengali silk-producing center, where the number of merchants supplying silk to the British East India Company declined from an average of 55 merchants with investments of 17,000 rupees in the period 1733–1737 to 36 merchants with 7,000 rupees in 1748–1750. After a crisis in 1754, these merchants vanished from the factory records overnight. Procurement/supply problems had been on the increase, and the hinterland was breaking down as elsewhere in coastal India. However, Bengal was also suffering from declining demand for its silk as Chinese competition grew in Bombay and Madras. Mukherjee (1990/91) also studied Jugdia, the most important Bengali cotton-producing area. There too, matters were "coming to a crisis in the production sphere" at the same time. There were problems of procurement such as late deliveries, shortfalls in supply, deteriorating quality, sudden price hikes, and general unreliability, so that "by the mid-eighteenth century we can already foresee some of the signs of deindustrialization" under the impetus of both stronger foreign capital and weaker local mercantile organization (Mukherjee 1990/91: 128). It seems strange then that Richard Eaton's (1993) study of the Bengal frontier finds little or no economic decline, and at most a shift of economic activity from west to east toward and within Bengal before the mid-eighteenth century.

P. J. Marshall (1987: 290) also observes that "the stability of Bengal itself, which had lasted for several decades, began to crack in the 1740s. A stark picture is painted in a recent assessment. …" Then he quotes from K. N. Chaudhuri (1978), who refers to a "push [of] the economy of Bengal towards the brink of general collapse." Chaudhuri (1978: 308) himself goes on to refer to "the disruption of textile production. …" Moreover, Chaudhuri (1978: 309, 294) observes that "the 1730s were a bad time for southern India" and that "the great Anglo-French wars of the mid-eighteenth century further dislocated trade that was already in serious difficulties; Madras suffered particularly severely." Sinnappah Arasaratnam (1986: 211), questioning whether the Coromandel trade underwent stagnation or decline, writes that especially after 1735, "there is no doubt that the region saw a downturn in economic activity and therefore in commerce."

Tapan Raychaudhuri and Irfan Habib, in volume 1 of *The Cambridge Economic History of India,* add that

> considerably more important than the decline of shipping in Bengal was the downfall of the great commercial marine of Gujarat in the early eighteenth century. Here again it is worth noting that the decline of Gujarat's maritime trade, although hastened by the growing political insecurity, had begun before the breakdown of law and order really began to bite. … The decline of the Mughal port of Surat and the disappearance of the fleet which was based at that port—the actual figures falling from 112 vessels in 1701 to 20 in 1750—were arguably the

> most important developments in the trade of the Indian Ocean during the period. (Raychaudhuri and Habib 1982: 433)

Yet, Surat in the west and Masulipatam and other Coromandel coast centers and their hinterlands to the east had declined in the early decades of the eighteenth century, as a consequence of the simultaneous weakening of the Mughals, Safavids, and Ottomans (Das Gupta and Pearson 1987:140). Europeans were able to take commercial competitive advantage of this Asian decline and of their Asian competitors' distress elsewhere as well. Marshall observes that these

> would have been difficult times for Asian ships whether the Englishman was offering his services in competition with them or not. ... Only when their Indian counterparts were drastically weakened ... did the English influence on western Indian trade begin to grow. ... All Asian ships appear to have been losing ground in southeast Asia and China to British ships from Madras and Calcutta in the early eighteenth century. (Marshall 1987: 293, 292)

However, the Indian economic difficulties seem to have spread and/or deepened in the third and fourth decades of the century, and also seriously to have affected the heretofore competitively strongest regions, like Bengal. Moreover, the average annual imports (based on invoice values and sales values) from Asia by both the Dutch and British East India companies declined in the decades of the 1730s and 1740s (but recovered in the 1750s), "confirming the assumption that this was a period of marked competition in the European-Asian trade" (Steensgaard 1990d: 112–3). Chinese merchants were massacred in Dutch Batavia in 1740. It was also a time of "a general European recession in the colonial trade" (Steensgaard 1990d: 110) and a time of war—of Jenkins' Ear beginning in 1739 and of the Austrian Succession in 1740, which Walter Dorn (1963: 164) characterized as "in essence a commercial one, a struggle of rival merchants" fought about overseas commerce (Frank 1978a: 110). But this observation is not limited to Dorn: "The last war which was undertaken altogether on account of the colonies [was] the Spanish war of 1739," observed Adam Smith ([1776]1937: 899).

Returning to India, it does seem important to inquire further whether political problems and then European colonialism may well have come on the heels of and only accelerated an already earlier and still ongoing economic decline in various parts of India—and elsewhere. At the same time, it is also important to inquire whether, how, and to what extent such decline was related to or even in part generated by a European rise, even *before* European political/military colonial intervention in the declining region.

Arasaratnam (1995) considers this matter with regard to the Coromandel coast. Dutch colonial intervention in Southeast Asia and British efforts to profit more from the China trade simultaneously disadvantaged the Coromandel coast and its Indian merchants. Growing Dutch VOC political and commercial control in Indonesia and especially in Java and its choking effects on Malacca also cut into the long-standing Coromandel ties with

Southeast Asia. These had been both bilateral and multilateral as part of the wider trading network outlined above, and both were severely damaged. The British East India Company's growing direct links with China also served to cut Coromandel out of previously important trading business. Arasaratnam summarizes some commercial changes in the early and mid-eighteenth century and "the single most decisive feature" for Coromandel, the decline in its trade with Southeast Asia:

> As far as Coromandel was concerned, European trade, in its new forms and directions, cut deep into the trade that had been traditionally carried on in that region. … It was this [Southeast Asian] artery that was punctured violently by the Dutch in the course of the seventeenth century. Indian trading links were cut off one by one with the Moluccas, Macassar and the Celebes, Bantam and the north Javanese ports, [and the] west coast of Sumatra. In a series of military and naval actions, these ports and markets were shut off from competitive trading. It meant denial of a lucrative export market in textiles for the Coromandel shippers. It meant the wresting from their hands of the import trade in spices to Coromandel. And it meant the denial of mineral—gold and tin—which had formed a profitable import to India. It must be emphasized that these were achieved by brute force and not by superior commercial expertise. … The boom in the China trade in the second half of the eighteenth century and the consequent changes to the inter-regional trade of Asia constituted the final blow to the Coromandel trade. … Coromandel like Bengal, was drained of bullion to purchase Chinese exports, leading to a general shortage of capital. The Coromandel merchants had little or no role to perform in this newly emerging trade pattern. … The extension of direct English control over important parts of the country dispensed with their role as middlemen. … As the amount of power wielded by the Europeans grew, so also did [the Indian political power brokers'] dependence on it and their commitment to it. They were decidedly on the side of the European in their confrontation with the merchants and helped to undermine the interests of the merchants. Likewise they took the side of their European masters against the hinterland power and contributed to undermining the latter in the interest of the former. (Arasaratnam 1995: xiv–28, 29, 41, 40)

In summary, there is substantial evidence that economic decline in India and in particular in the Bengali textile industry had already began before the Battle of Plassey in 1757. The accompanying political disarray of the Mughals and others rendered Asians vulnerable to predatory European merchant, naval, and ultimately political power. The Europeans captured the carrying trade from the indigenous shipping and merchants in the mid-eighteenth century in Indian waters on a new scale. India was the first Asian political economic power to begin the "fall" to European hegemony.

The Decline Elsewhere in Asia

The same issue arises with regard to other regions of Asia, in particular in West, Southeast, and East Asia. In the Ottoman Empire, economic expansion seems to have peaked in the late seventeenth century. The Ottoman economy became gradually weaker during the first half of the eighteenth century and decline accelerated in the last third of the century. Ottoman economic power was gradually undermined in the late eighteenth century by the ascendance of new industrial centers and the increasing commercial dominance of the Europeans. Political power began to be eclipsed by the Europeans at the turn of the eighteenth to the nineteenth centuries, following Napoleon's expedition to Egypt.

In the eighteenth century, Ottoman foreign trade as a whole stagnated and therefore declined as a share of growing world trade. In particular, trade with Europe declined, and among Europeans the French increasingly replaced the British as Ottoman trading partners. Moreover in the late eighteenth century, Ottoman exports and even domestic markets began to suffer from foreign competition and apparently from the French connection, especially with the Americas. Cheaper cotton from North American began to displace that from Anatolia, and cheaper Caribbean coffee to displace Arabian coffee exported through Cairo. Caribbean sugar invaded the domestic market. All these competing products were produced by slave labor in the Americas.

The Ottoman economic "decline" seems to have accelerated after 1760. Among the indications are the following: Migration from rural to urban areas increased. More and more agricultural land, both absolutely and relative to the total, owned by the relatively landed rich was exempted from taxes. Concomitantly, tax-farming increased on the remaining agricultural population, already poor. That increased their poverty further, contributed to driving them off the land, and made the distribution of property and income increasingly unequal. The production and export of agricultural and other raw materials increased only slowly. However their share of total exports increased rapidly, as cotton textiles and manufacturing exports decreased. Especially after 1760, the weaving and export of cotton cloth declined; and some of the foreign trade was replaced by Ottoman interregional trade. Ottoman state control weakened as the strength of its central institutions waned, and regional decentralization grew. Market-derived state revenue declined at Istanbul and several other cities. Contemporary documents quoted in Charles Issawi (1966: 30–37) also testify to increasing French and decreasing Ottoman competitiveness at one Ottoman port city after another.

The 1760s were also years of inflection and subsequent decline, according to various studies of Ottoman textile and other industries (see Islamoglu-Inan 1987), especially by Mehmet Gene. In Aleppo, the beginnings of decline were already evident in 1750 (Masters 1988: 30 ff). Halil Inalcik and Donald Quataert (1994: 703) summarize: "These trends are based on incomplete evidence, but they fit with a general impression of faltering commercial conditions in the last decades of the eighteenth century and the first decade of the subsequent century." Huri Islamoglu-Inan (private communication 1996) questions even this "decline" of the Ottoman economy in view of its partly successful competition with British textiles both at home and abroad in the midnineteenth century.

What these observers do not inquire about but we may consider is whether, how, and to what extent this Ottoman "faltering of commercial conditions" at the end of the eighteenth century was also part of the European-Atlantic economy's Kondratieff "B" phase since 1762, which presumably helped to reduce Ottoman markets in the West and may be to increase the competition from colonial slave production in the West. Apparently, the Ottomans were not able, or at least were less able, to benefit from the renewed "A" phase recovery at the turn of the century, while the Europeans did. The cotton textile exports Islamoglu-Inan refers to may have derived some benefit from this recovery. However later in the nineteenth century, the Europeans destroyed much of the Ottoman textile industry and prevented its establishment in Egypt by Mohammed Ali, despite his desperate efforts to do so (Issawi 1966).

In Qing China, the decline came later. In the eighteenth century, China undoubtedly experienced economic and population growth. Its recuperation from the crisis in the middle of the seventeenth century, discussed in chapter 5, may have been "delayed" by the Ming/Qing succession and reorganization of the country until say 1683, when Taiwan was reincorporated and all restrictions on trade were lifted. Then, a veritable economic boom started in China. However, silver imports declined drastically in the 1720s and even more so at mid century, before increasing again after 1760 and being especially high in the 1780s (Lin 1990). In 1793 Emperor Ch'ien-lung (Qianlong) wrote King George III through the English ambassador to China the oft-quoted letter that "as your ambassador can see for himself, we posses all things. I set no value on objects strange or ingenious, and we have no use for your country's manufactures. ... There was [is] therefore no need to import the manufactures of outside barbarians in exchange for our own produce" (Frank 1978a: 160).

Wolfram Eberhard (1977) dates the beginning of Qing Chinese internal decline to the Shantung rebellion in 1774 and the resurgence of the White Lotus Society in 1775 (the same time, we may observe, as the American Revolution and other events during the 1762–1790 Kondratieff "B" phase analyzed above). Europeans replaced Chinese traders in the China Sea only at the end of the eighteenth century; and even then the balance of trade remained heavily in China's favor (Marks 1996: 64). As is well known, it was only the British recourse to opium grown for them in India that finally reversed this situation in the nineteenth century.

Thus in China, rapid economic dislocation occurred only in the early nineteenth century, via the opium trade and its bullion drain of silver out of China, which destabilized the entire economic system. This weakening process culminated in the Opium wars and the "fall" of China. Victor Lippit's "The Development of Underdevelopment in China" (in Huang 1980) deals almost exclusively with the nineteenth century. Lippit does rather well in denying the historical or theoretical basis of most received attempts to explain China's underdevelopment. These attempts at explanations have been made in terms of "the family system" (Marion J. Levy), "pre-industrial stage theory" (A. Eckstein, John King Fairbank,

L. S. Yang), and "the vicious circle of poverty" (Ragnar Nurske), none of which can account for any of China's success before 1800, nor for much of the lack of the same after 1800 (also see Lippit 1987).

However, Lippit attributes too much causative influence to the weight of Chinese bureaucracy and class structure. Indeed, as I already argued in my own contribution to C. C. Huang's book (Frank 1980), Lippit's contribution is mistitled for several reasons, only one of which is that he sees stagnation in China while its economy was still expanding before 1800. Indeed, he later rectifies this judgment himself in Lippitt (1987: 40, 42) when he recognizes "renewed economic expansion" and "thriving economic activity" between the sixteenth and eighteenth centuries. Nonetheless in both books, he attributes nineteenth-century "underdevelopment" to class-generated internal weaknesses and virtually dismisses all influences of China's position in the world economy.

Evidence of some economic decline and sociopolitical crisis can also be found in mainland Southeast Asia during the last third of the eighteenth century (Tarling 1992: 572–95). However new research by Anthony Reid (1997) and his colleagues complicate this picture. Their revisionist thesis is that "there was a distinct commercial expansion in the region from about 1760" accompanied by a decline in most indices of Dutch VOC activity. The arrival of ships at Malacca grew from 188 in 1761 to 539 in 1785, of which 54 and 242, respectively, were captained by Malays, 55 and 170 by Chinese, and 17 and 37 by British. Almost half of these and almost all of the increase represent ships arriving from Siak, only 20 from China and about 40 from India (Reid 1997: tables 1, 2). Yet Reid also finds that Southeast Asian sugar exports reached a (temporary) peak in 1760 and that Dutch VOC imports of textiles to archipelago Southeast Asia declined from 272,000 pieces to 102,000 (Reid 1997: table 5). And Reid's comment is that "assembling the relevant data suggests that for imported textiles, as for exports, the new upturn occurred precisely in the period when documentation is most difficult at the end of the eighteenth century" (Reid 1997). These findings, and/or the lack of them, then also raise the question: was there really such an upturn precisely after 1760? Not only is the documentation scarce, but the declining Dutch VOC trade from India may reflect not only the economic decline of both (perhaps to the benefit of the British East India Company since arrivals from Indian ports remained stable between 1765 and 1785). Also arrivals from the still relatively flourishing Chinese ports tripled from 7 to 21 ships but remained quantitatively quite modest compared to the intra-Southeast Asian ones (Reid 1997: table 2). Moreover, any purported "distinct commercial expansion" in Southeast Asia would have had to go against the cyclical trend elsewhere in the world. Indeed, according to Reid's table 4, the value of average annual Southeast Asian exports of pepper, coffee, and sugar were (in thousand Spanish dollars) 864 in the 1750s; 1,236 in the 1760s, 1,043 in the 1770s, 1,076 in the 1780s, and 1,310 in the 1790s. That makes for a 50 percent increase over the fifty years from 1750 to 1800, including a 5 percent increase after 1760 (even with the absolute decline in the 1770s and 1780s)! That hardly sounds like a "distinct commercial expansion," which on further reflection seems more like a storm in a Southeast Asian teacup. So Southeast Asia as well may have remained in step with other regions.

We need more empirical confirmation of major regional and/or even pan-Asian economic decline, accompanied or followed by an inflection in the population growth rate by the mid-eighteenth century. That would place the late eighteenth- and then nineteenth-century rise of Europe to relative dominance into a rather different light and historical perspective. In that case, neither the Eurocentric European exceptionalist nor the Indo-, Sino- and other Asian nationalist interpretations of this period would be adequate. Perhaps there really *was* a long economic cycle in whose downward "B" phase one after another region and empire in Asia declined. Then, the previously rather marginal Europeans and later the North Americans were able to take advantage of this Asian cyclical "B" phase decline, like the East Asian NIEs today: it is *then* that the Europeans staked out their own claim to leadership and hegemony in the world economy—temporarily! However, not only did "the Rise of the West" follow "the Decline of the East." The two were also otherwise structurally and cyclically dependent on each other as inextricably interrelated parts of a single global economy. That is what I seek to demonstrate in the following sections.

How Did the West Rise?

So how did the West rise to win this competition—temporarily? The introduction to this book reviewed a number of received theories and answers, all of which allege one or another or a whole combination of European and by extension Western exceptionalisms. The introduction also contended that all of these theories, Marxist, Weberian, and/or whatever, are fundamentally flawed by their Eurocentrism. J. M. Blaut's (1993a) *The Colonizer's Model of the World: Geographical Diffusionism and Eurocentric History* analyzes a dozen of these answers and their flaws chapter and verse. Our first chapter cites Goody, Said, Bernal, Amin, Hodgson, Tibebu, and Lewis and Wigen, who also demystify this Eurocentrism. However, they mostly concentrate on ideological critiques of the manifest and hidden ideologies under review. Also cited is my own critique (Frank 1994, 1995) of the "modern capitalist world-economy/system" alternative proposed by Braudel and Wallerstein. But my earlier work too is limited mostly to a critique, although Frank and Gills (1993) offers an alternative world system interpretation of world history before 1500.

The historical/empirical sections of the present book demonstrate that the real world during the period from 1400 to 1800, not to mention earlier, was very different from what received theory has alleged. Eurocentric history and "classical" social theory, but also still Wallerstein's "modern world-system" suppose and/or allege European predominance, which simply did not exist. Until about 1800 the world economy was by no stretch of the imagination European-centered nor in any significant way defined or marked by any European-born (and European-borne) "capitalism," let alone development. Still less was there any real "capitalist development" initiated, generated, diffused, or otherwise propagated or perpetrated by Europeans or the West. That occurred only by the stretch of the Eurocentric *imagination,* and even that only belatedly after the nineteenth century, as Bernal has already emphasized. A related question then is whether there had already been any "capitalist [development of] underdevelopment." For Latin America and the Caribbean, that argument (Frank 1966, 1967) can probably still stand, and perhaps for the slave trade regions of Africa as well. The argument was that in India, this process only began after the Battle of Plassey in 1757 (Frank 1975, 1978a). However, this historical review does raise some question as to what extent the Indian and other Asian decline was "imposed" by Europe, not to mention by "capitalism."

For, the data in the preceding sections have shown unequivocally that the world economy was preponderantly Asian-based. Europeans had been clamoring to attach themselves to it for centuries before Columbus and Vasco da Gama, which is what propelled them to seek some, any, and especially a golden way to do so in the first place. And yet for centuries after these European (not world!) pioneers, other Europeans still only clambered very belatedly, slowly, and marginally to attach themselves to the Asian economic train. Only in the nineteenth century did they succeed in finding a place in the locomotive.

Climbing up on Asian Shoulders

So how did the West rise? The answer, literally in a word, is that the Europeans *bought* themselves a seat, and then even a whole railway car, on the Asian train. How were any—literally—poor Europeans able to afford the price of even a third-class ticket to board the Asian economic train? Well, the Europeans somehow found and/or stole, extorted, or earned the money to do so. Again, how so?

The basic answer is two-fold, or three-fold. The most important answer is that Europeans obtained the money from the gold and silver mines they found in the Americas. The secondary answer is that they "made" more money, in the very good business first of digging up that silver—or more accurately, obliging the indigenous peoples of the Americas to dig it up for the Europeans. The Europeans also engaged in a variety of other profitable businesses they ran in—and to—the Americas. These were first and foremost the slave plantations in Brazil, the Caribbean, and the North American South; and, of course, the slave trade itself to supply and run these plantations. The Europeans employed and exploited perhaps a million workers at any one time in this profitable business, by Blaut's estimate (1993a: 195). Europeans were able to make still more money selling their own European-made products to these and other people in the Americas, products for which Europe otherwise would have found no other market, since they were not competitively salable in Asia.

The Keynesian multiplier did however operate also in Europe, first through the infusion of the American-derived money itself, and then also through the repatriation and investment in Europe of profits from the Americas, Africa, and from the "triangular"—including especially the slave-trade among them. Of course, Europe also derived profits from the aforementioned European production and export of its goods to the Americas and Africa. All these European sources of and machines for finding and making money have been alluded to in the earlier empirical sections of this book. They need not be elaborated on here, because they have already been researched and demonstrated countless times over, without however seeing some of their implications nor drawing the necessary conclusions, outlined below.

In order to avoid a tedious recounting or Marx's language of "capital dripping with blood and sweat," it should be sufficient to allude to everybody's favorite observer, Adam Smith:

> Since the first discovery of America, the market for the produce of its silver mines has been growing gradually more and more extensive. First, the market of Europe has become more extensive. Since the discovery of America, the greater part of Europe has improved. England, Holland, France and Germany; even Sweden, Denmark and Russia have all advanced considerably both in agriculture and manufactures. … Secondly, America is itself a new market for the produce of its own silver mines; and as it advances in agriculture, industry and population … its demand must increase much more rapidly. The English colonies are altogether a new market. … The discovery of America, however made a most essential [contribution]. By opening up a new and inexhaustible market to all commodities of Europe, it gave occasion to a new division of labour and improvements of art, which, in the narrow circle of ancient commerce could never have taken place for want of a market to take off the greater part of their produce. The productive powers of labour were improved, and its produce increased in all the different countries of Europe, and together with it the real revenue and wealth of the inhabitants. … (Smith [1776]1937: 202, 416)

As Smith knew, it was America (in a word) that accounted for the increase in the real revenue and wealth of the inhabitants of Europe. Moreover, Smith repeatedly argues that even Poland, Hungary, and other parts of Europe that did not trade with the Americas directly, nonetheless also derived indirect benefit for their own industries from the same. Moreover of course, as Ken Pomeranz (1997) emphasizes and analyzes, the European exploitation of native, bonded labor and slave labor imported from Africa in combination with the resources of the Americas not only afforded Europe additional resources for its own consumption and investment but also lightened the pressure on scarce resources in Europe itself.

Smith also recognized Asia as being economically far more advanced and richer than Europe. "The improvements in agriculture and manufactures seem likewise to have been of very great antiquity in the provinces of Bengal in the East Indies, and in some of the eastern provinces of China. … Even those three countries [China, Egypt, and Indostan], the wealthiest, according to all accounts, that ever were in the world, are chiefly renowned for their superiority in agriculture and manufactures. … [Now, in 1776] China is a much richer country than any part of Europe" (Smith [1776]1937: 20, 348, 169).

Moreover, Smith also understood *how* the poor Europeans were able to use their new money and increased wealth to buy themselves tickets on the Asian train. Continuing with the third point in his discussion excerpted above, Smith writes:

> Thirdly, the East Indies [Asia] is another market for the produce of the silver mines of America, and a market which, from the time of the discovery of those mines, has been continually taking off a greater and greater quantity of silver. … Upon all these accounts, the precious metals are a commodity which it always has been, and still continues to be, extremely advantageous to carry from Europe to India. There is scarce any commodity which brings a better price there [and it is even more advantageous to carry silver to China]. … The silver of the new continent seems in this manner to be one of the principal commodities by which the commerce between the two extremities of the old one is carried on, and it is by means of it, in great measure, that those distant parts of the world are connected with one another. … The trade to the East Indies, by opening a market to the commodities of Europe, *or, what comes to the same thing, the gold and silver* which is purchased with those commodities, must necessarily tend to increase the annual production of European commodities. … Europe, instead of being the manufacturers and carriers for but a small part of the world … have now [1776] become the manufacturers for the numerous and thriving cultivators of America, and the carriers, and in some respect the manufacturers too, for almost all the different nations of Asia, Africa, and America. (Smith [1776]1937: 206, 207, 417, 591; my emphasis)

The Asian market for the Europeans was the same thing as silver, as Smith remarked, for two related reasons: One is that silver was their only means of payment. The other is that therefore the Europeans' main business was the production and trade of silver as a commodity itself. That was the main source of the profits Europeans derived from their trade both within Asia and between Asia and Europe.

Braudel declares himself "astonished," "as a historian of the Mediterranean," to find that the late eighteenth-century Red Sea trade was still the same "vital channel" in the outflow of Spanish-American silver to India and beyond as in the sixteenth century. "This influx of precious metal was vital to the movements of the most active sector of the Indian, and no doubt Chinese economy" (Braudel 1992: 491). India "had in fact been for centuries subject to a money economy, partly through her links with the Mediterranean world" (Braudel 1992: 498). "Cambay (another name for Gujarat) could only survive, it was said, by stretching out its arm to Aden and the other to Malacca" (Braudel 1992: 528). Gold and silver "were also the indispensable mechanisms which made the whole great machine function, from its peasant base to the summit of society and the business world" (Braudel 1992: 500). Braudel himself concludes that "in the end, the Europeans had to have recourse to the precious metals, particularly American silver, which was the 'open sesame' of these trades" (Braudel 1992: 217). "From the start, Spanish America had inevitably been a decisive element in world history" (Braudel 1992: 414). "Is not America … perhaps the true explanation of Europe's greatness?" (Braudel 1992: 387).

Precisely that is also the explanation of Blaut (1977, 1992, 1993a), who in all these regards seems to be the modern alter ego of Adam Smith. Both understand and explain the first two answers to the question of how the poor Europeans managed access to the thriving Asian market: (1) they used their American money, and (2) they used the profits of both their production/imports from and their exports to America and Africa, and their investment of the proceeds of all of these in Europe itself.

However, the third answer alluded to above is that Europeans also used both the American silver money and their profits to *buy into* the wealth of Asia itself. As Smith noted, and all the evidence reviewed above shows, Europe used its commodities, or what comes to the same thing, the *only* commodities it could sell in Asia, that is its American gold and silver, to buy Asian products. Moreover, as also documented above, Europe used its silver purchasing power to muscle in on the intra-Asian trade, which the Europeans called "country trade." As noted above, it was the silver—and gold—trade itself that was really the mainstay of the European companies. Consider for instance this summary of Dutch VOC strategy:

> The European precious metals, the Japanese silver obtained mainly against Chinese silk and other goods, and the gold obtained in Taiwan mainly against Japanese silver and Indonesian pepper were invested primarily in Indian textiles. These textiles were exchanged largely for Indonesian pepper and other spices but also sent to Europe and various Asian factories. The bulk of the pepper and other spices was exported to Europe but a certain amount [was] used for investment in various Asian factories such as those in India, Persia, Taiwan and Japan. Raw silk from Persia and China also found its way to Europe. ... The pattern of Dutch participation in intra-Asian trade was determined in part by the requirements of the trade with Japan which was by far the most important Asian source of precious metals for the Company during the seventeenth century. ... In certain years precious metals procured in Japan were of greater value than those received at Batavia from Holland. (Prakesh 1994: 1–192,193)

More graphical still is a frequently quoted description of Dutch trade in 1619 from VOC director Jan Pieterszon Coen himself:

> Piece goods from Gujarat we can barter for pepper and gold on the coast of Sumatra; rials and cottons from the coast [of Coromandel] for pepper in Bantam; sandalwood, pepper and rials we can barter for Chinese goods and Chinese gold; we can extract silver from Japan with Chinese goods; piece goods from the Coromandel coast in exchange for spices, other goods and gold from China; piece goods from Surat for spices; other goods and rials from Arabia for spices and various other trifles—one thing leads to another. And all of it can be done without any money from the Netherlands and with ships alone. We have the most important spices already. What is missing then? Nothing else but ships and a little water to prime the pump. ... (By this I mean sufficient means [money] so that the rich

> Asian trade may be established.) Hence, gentlemen and good administrators, there is nothing to prevent the Company from acquiring the richest trade in the world, (quoted in Steensgaard 1987: 139 and by Kindleberger 1989, who cites Steensgaard 1973 [same as 1972] but writes "sufficient money" and omits the last—and for present purposes the most significant—sentence!)

That is, Europeans sought to muscle in on *"the richest trade in the world,"* but it took the Dutch rather more than just "a little water *[meaning* money]" to pump this Asian well of treasures and capital, and of course *that* money came from the Americas. Thus, Europeans derived *more profits* from their participation in the intra-Asian "country trade" than they did from their Asian imports into Europe, even though many of the latter in turn generated further profits for them as re-exports to Africa and the Americas. So the Europeans were able to profit from the much more productive and wealthy Asian economies by participating in the intra-Asian trade; and *that* in turn they were able to do ultimately only thanks to their American silver.

Without that silver—and, secondarily, without the division of labor and profits it generated in Europe itself—the Europeans would not have had a leg, or even a single toe, to stand on with which to compete in the Asian market. Only their American money, and not any "exceptional" European "qualities," which, as Smith realized even in 1776, had not been even remotely up to Asian standards, permitted the Europeans to buy their ticket on the Asian economic train and/or to take a third-class seat on it. That is looking at this European "business" in Asia from the demand side. The concomitant supply side, emphasized by Pomeranz (1997), is of course that their American money permitted the Europeans to buy real goods, produced with real labor and resources in Asia. These goods not only increased consumption and investment beyond what it otherwise could and would have been in Europe; they also diminished the pressure on resources in Europe itself.

To refer to another analogy, their American-supplied stakes permitted the Europeans an entry into the Asian economic casino. Why were they ultimately able to prosper there? Only because of their unending, albeit fluctuating, flow of American silver and gold. That is what provided the Europeans with their one competitive advantage among their Asian competitors, for these did not have money growing on American trees. However, even with that resource and advantage, the Europeans were no more than a minor bit player at the Asian, indeed world, economic table. Yet the Europeans gambled their American stakes for all they were worth in Asia and held out there for *three* centuries. Even though the Europeans also reinvested some of their Asian earnings to buy into still more and better seats at the Asian economic table, they were able to continue doing so only because their supply of cash was being continually replenished from the Americas. Witness that even in the eighteenth century, the Europeans had nothing else to offer any Asians, for European manufactures were still not competitive. However, Smith exaggerated worldwide sales of European manufactures, unless we read his qualification of "to some extent" as meaning almost nothing.

Certainly, the Europeans had no exceptional, let alone superior, ethnic, rational, organizational, or spirit-of-capitalist advantages to offer, diffuse, or do anything else in Asia. What the Europeans may have had, as we will consider further below and in our conclusions, is some of what Alexander Gerschenkron's (1962) calls the advantages of "backwardness" afforded by their position, as Chase-Dunn and Hall (1997) also observe, at the (semi-) periphery of the world economy!

So how is it that this otherwise apparently hopeless European gamble in Asia panned out—and finally hit the jackpot? Only because while the Europeans were gathering strength from the Americas and Africa, as well as from Asia itself, Asian economies and polities were also becoming weakened during part of the eighteenth century—so much so that the paths finally crossed, as in Rhoades Murphe's (1977) diagram, at about 1815. However, in the half century before that, another—fourth—element entered into the European/Asian equation. Adam Smith is also known for arguing that colonies did not pay, even though he wrote a chapter "On Colonies" and argued primarily against colonial monopolies. Moreover, Smith wrote just before the major technological inventions and innovations of the industrial revolution in Britain and Europe. This is not the place to enter into the arguments about whether there really was such a "revolution" and whether European rates of capital accumulation really did "take off," as W. W. Rostow (1962) and others have contended.

Supply and Demand for Technological Change

R. M. Hartwell, who was one of the foremost students of the industrial revolution, observed that

> J. H. Clapham wrote in 1910 that "Even if … the history of 'the' industrial revolution is a 'thrice squeezed orange', there remains an astonishing amount of juice in it." Indeed, half a century later interest in the industrial revolution is increasing. … On the causes of the industrial revolution, for example, there is silence, simplicity or confusion. What was the prime mover, or what complex of movers was responsible? Agricultural revolution? Population growth? Improved technology? Increased trade? Capital accumulation? All of these have their supporters. Or must explanations be sought in noneconomic forces? Changes in religion, social structure, science, philosophy and law? … There seems to be little agreement. … The most difficult problem is to determine the extent to which this stimulus was *exogenous* (i.e., independent of the economy)—for example, an increase in demand through international trade … and to what extent it was *endogenous* (i.e., generated within the economy) … ? (Hartwell 1971: 131, 110, 115)

However, the real problem is what economy? My contention is that the key to the confusion is to be found in Hartwell's last sentence: Clapham's orange that was already thrice squeezed almost a century ago and innumerable times since then has always been regarded as only a British, European, or at most a "Western" fruit. Yet Graeme Snooks (1994: 1–2) writes "we have only begun to scratch the surface of a field that needs to be ploughed long and deep … [and] we need to view the Industrial Revolution from an entirely different vantage point to those traditionally used." Snooks and his contributors propose several different ones, but all of them continue to search for root and cause in Europe alone, in the "dynamic quality of England (and of Western Europe generally) throughout the pre-modern period" and over the entire past millennium at that (Snooks 1994: 11, 43 ff.). So despite their "entirely different" vantage point, in all this time and even still today, no one has really even attempted a globally holistic world economic/systemic explanation of the whole orange tree that could satisfy the maxim cited from Leopold von Ranke in my opening epigraph: "There is no history but universal history—as it really was"!

The question is how and why beginning around 1800 Europe and then the United States, after long lagging behind, "suddenly" caught up and then overtook Asia economically and politically in the one world economy and system. It is important to see that this pursuit and victory was part of a competitive race in the single global economy, whose structure and operation itself generated this development. That is, a number of well-known technological and other developments and investments in new productive processes took place in (Western) Europe and then in the United States. But it simply will not do to attempt to account for these departures by looking for their roots only or even primarily in a thousand years of history only in Europe, as Snooks (1994, 1996) still proposes in his "new perspectives on the industrial revolution" or as Robert Adams (1996) does in his "inquiry into Western technology," which also examines only Europe, except when he goes back to the Iron and Bronze ages in the eastern Mediterranean and West Asia.

Yet, these technological developments of the industrial revolution should not be regarded as only European achievements. Instead, they must be understood more properly as world developments whose spatial locus moved to and through the West at that time after having long moved about the East. The relevant question is not so much what the "distinctive" European features or factors are of the industrial revolution as how and why this industrial shift took place from East to West.

We have already observed above that the answers to the reasons for this shift must be sought in both the decline of the East and in the rise of the West. The heretofore received "answers" to the "why/how?" question suffer doubly or triply. They suffer first from the misattribution of the reasons for the supposed exceptionalisms of superiority to Europe, which Blaut and others have already shown to be without any foundation in historical fact. Moreover, they suffer from looking for the reasons for the rise of Europe within Europe itself in the first place, and therefore neglecting analysis of the related decline of the (several) Easts. However, these two cases of misplaced concreteness also imply a third failure: they fail to look for the reasons of "the Rise of the West" and "the Decline of the East" in the structure and operation of the whole world economy itself. We have already observed how and why Europe was such a laggard in the economic race until well into the eighteenth century and how it improved its position by buying a ticket on the Asian train and then displacing some of its passengers, primarily through the European access to and use of American money.

The question remains, however, why and how Western Europeans and Americans then bested the Asians at their own game through recourse to the technological advances of the industrial revolution. How and why were these made then and there? A fully satisfactory answer may be still beyond us—but certainly no more than it is beyond all the erroneous ideological Eurocentric answers that others from Marx to Weber and their latter-day followers have proffered. A world economic analysis can certainly and easily do better than that even with the still limited elements, hypotheses, and evidence offered in an only very preliminary way below.

Technological progress through the invention and application of labor-saving machinery has frequently been attributed to the profitability of the same in a high-wage economy, particularly in North America. High wages create an incentive to reduce costs of production by replacing this high-wage labor with labor-saving machinery. And wages in North America were relatively high from early on, as so many observers including Marx pointed out, because the population/land-resource ratio was low and the expanding frontier offered an escape from low-wage drudgery. Therefore, it has been argued that in the nineteenth and twentieth centuries, the incentive to invent, innovate, and use labor-saving machinery increasingly shifted across the Atlantic from Europe to America—in the world market competition to reduce costs of production and maintain or gain market share.

We can and should apply the same kind of analysis and argument to the invention, innovation, and application of labor-saving machinery during the industrial revolution in Europe. Of the increase in the British growth rate in the eighteenth century, 80 percent—and 30 percent of the total growth between 1740 and 1780—have been attributed to increased productivity alone (Inkster 1991: 67). Europeans also, even more so than Americans, were in a race and struggle in the world economy, in which they had to compete for their markets primarily with Asians. However, Europeans were also relatively high-wage/high-cost producers. That is precisely why, as we observed above, Europeans were unable to sell virtually anything to Asians, who were much more productive and competitive with much lower wage costs. How and why so? Well, because also the population/land-resource ratio was relatively higher in many parts of Asia, certainly in China and India, than it was in the more sparsely settled Europe.

Moreover, Europe also had a frontier—in the Americas and later also in Australia, as Benjamin Higgins (1991) has pointed out. Certainly during much of the nineteenth century, European emigration across the Atlantic to the Americas served to lower the population/land-resource ratio well beyond what it otherwise would have been. Thus, the lower European population and its safety-valve emigration to the Americas both served to generate incentives for labor-saving machinery in Europe far more than the Asian population/resource base did.

Adam Smith was writing just as the inventions of the industrial revolution were getting up steam; he observed at the end of his chapter on "The Wages of Labour" that

> the liberal reward of labour ... increases the industry of the common people. The wages of labour are the encouragement of industry, which, like every other human quality, improves in proportion of the encouragement it receives. ... where wages are high, accordingly we shall always find the workmen more active, diligent and expeditious, than where they are low. ... the high price of provision, by diminishing the funds destined for the maintenance of servants, disposes masters rather to diminish than to increase the number of those they have. ... [When there is an] increase in wages of labour ... the owner of [capital] stock which employs a great number of labourers, necessarily endeavours, for his own advantage ... to supply them with the best machinery which either he or they can think of. What takes place among the labourers in a particular workhouse, takes place, for the same reason, among those of a great society. The greater their number, the more they naturally divide themselves into different classes and subdivision of employment. More heads are occupied in inventing the most proper machinery for executing the work of each, and it is, therefore, more likely to be invented. There are many commodities, therefore, which, in consequence of these improvements, come to be produced by so much less labour than before, that the increase of its price is more than compensated by the diminution of its quantity. (Smith [1776]1937: 81, 83, 86)

In a later section on the "effects of the Progress of Improvement upon the real Price of Manufactures," Smith observes that so far in his and the preceding century the cost of production had already declined and in the future could decline most remarkably in manufactures made of coarser metals. On the other hand, he reports that in the clothing manufacture there had been "no such sensible reduction of price" (or cost of production). However, Smith does remark on three capital improvements and many smaller ones in coarse and fine woolen manufactures; but Smith does not yet in 1776 mention any such technological progress or "industrial revolution" in the cotton textile industry!

As A. E. Musson (1972) observes in the introduction to his *Science, Technology, and Economic Growth in the Eighteenth Century,*

> there seems little doubt, however, that—whatever the motives of inventors—innovators or entrepreneurs were certainly much influenced by economic factors, such as relative prices, market possibilities, and profit prospects. Of this there is plentiful evidence in specialized historical studies of particular firms, too well known and numerous to list here. (Musson 1972: 53)

However, these relative prices and profit prospects, of course, were relative to *world* market possibilities, especially in competitive industries like textiles, which began the industrial revolution in Britain.

Indeed, Smith himself had already compared Europe, India, and China in this respect in 1776. Discussing their relative costs of transportation, he observed that in comparison to the expense of land-carriage in Europe the availability of inland navigation in China and India was already labor-saving and reduces the real and the nominal price of many manufactures. Analogously, there was a certain rationale that chlorine bleaching of textiles, which had previously been done by exposing them to much sun, was invented and introduced where there was little sun to be had—in Britain. Similarly, its use of coal as the fuel for the industrial revolution was certainly induced and rendered economical by the growing shortage of wood for charcoal (that shortage also existed in China, but there capital was in shorter supply and coal more expensive).

Hartwell (1971: 268) observed that "there is general agreement that there was no capital shortage [in Britain] in the eighteenth century, although the implication of this admission is not always appreciated." The main implication that is not always appreciated—indeed apparently not ever and also not by Hartwell himself—is that Britain and all of these other "economies" were connected through a single worldwide division of labor and circulation of goods and money. Therefore, the competitive forces of relative demand-and-supply shortages and availabilities of labor and capital operated not just in Britain, but also worldwide. That is, the combined demand-and-supply, both-sides-of-the-coin analysis must also be extended to the single global economy as a whole. Indeed, Smith himself began to do so in his above noted comparison of labor and other costs of transportation in Europe and Asia. It is difficult to understand let alone to accept therefore that although Snooks (1996) also stresses relative factor prices, contributors like E. A. Wrigley (in Snooks 1994) limit their analysis of competition to Britain and Western Europe. Indeed, Wrigley reexamines the writings of the classical economists from Adam Smith to David Ricardo regarding the relative prices of labor, capital, land, and other natural resources; yet unlike them (for example, Ricardo's law of international comparative advantage), Wrigley's focus is on Britain alone. Snooks goes further but writes that "the Industrial Revolution emerged from a thousand years of fierce competition between a large number of small, equally matched Western European kingdoms" (Snooks 1994: 15).

Yet most certainly in the textile market, which was the primary locus of the industrial revolution, Britain and Western Europe had to compete primarily with India and China, as well as West Asia. Thus, relative supply-and-demand differences generated differential regional and sectoral comparative costs and comparative advantages in relation to each other around the whole world. These structural differences could then be the basis of differential rational microeconomic labor, land, capital, and labor-saving technological responses by the various enterprises, sectors, and regions of the single global economy. The argument here is that this (and not so much "internal" European circumstances) is where we must look for the real explanation of the incentive and option for investment in and application of technological advance in some parts of the world economy. The argument is not that "internal" European circumstances were not relevant to the economic decision-making process there. It is that circumstances "internal" to Europe (or to Manchester, or to James Watt's steam-engine shop) were created by its participation in the world economy. That is, the structure and dynamic of the world economy/system itself generate the differential comparative costs, advantages, and rational responses to the same all around the world and everywhere in the world.

It is gratifying to find a the similar, albeit more limited argument, by Giovanni Arrighi:

> Our thesis has been that the main historical link between the three moments of the industrial expansion [in the fourteenth, sixteenth/early seventeenth, and late eighteenth centuries] in England was integral to an ongoing financial expansion, restructuring, and reorganization of the capitalist world-economy, in which England was incorporated from the very start. Periods of financial expansion were invariably moments of intensifying competitive pressures on the governmental and business institutions of the European trade and accumulation system. Under these pressures, agro-industrial production declined in some locales and rose in others, primarily in response to the positional disadvantages and advantages of the locales in the changing structure of the world-economy. (Arrighi 1994: 209)

Indeed, except that the world economic structure and process in question was not only that of Europe but the entire world as a whole. Also noteworthy is the period, industry, and the extent of the restructuring involved: Arrighi, following Nef (1934), Wallerstein, and others, stresses centuries-long industrial "expansion" and not "revolution." In each cyclical occasion, the sectoral locus centered in textiles, which was probably the productive industry (as distinct from the financial service sector) in which competition was most rife. However, the first adjustment improved England's competitive position only relative to Flanders and the second one relative only to northern and southern Europe. Only the third adjustment managed significantly to alter Britain's competitive position worldwide. Even that required over half a century, as net textile imports to the previous competitive leader, India, did not exceed its exports until 1816.

We cannot accompany this world development here, but we may illustrate it by citing a couple of testimonies from the beginning of the eighteenth and nineteenth centuries. Reference was already made in chapter 5 to the 1703 Anglo-Portuguese Treaty of Methuen that consolidated British access to the Portuguese market, which had been opened by three prior treaties since 1642. The British statesman J. Methuen waxed loud and clear about it in December 1702: "This agreement will have this consequence in Portugal that all their own manufactures, which at this time make a vast quantity of ill cloth and dear, will be immediately laid down and totally discontinued; and the cloth or stuffs of no other nation will be able to come into competition with those of England" on the Portuguese market. His Portuguese critic Luis da Cunha agreed at least on the facts that "what the British want is to improve their manufactures, and to ruin those started in Portugal" (cited in Sideri 1970: 57, 59). And so it turned out, as related in Frank (1978a,b), which also signals the irony that a century later Ricardo would defend British industry by exemplifying his "law of comparative costs/advantage" with the exchange of British textiles for Portuguese wine!

Regarding competition in the world textile market, we may return to Braudel:

> The incentive worked the other way round—providing a stimulus to the threatened industry in Europe [by Indian exports]. England's first step was to close her own frontiers for the greater part of the eighteenth century to Indian textiles, which she reexported to Europe and America. Then she tried to capture for herself this profitable market—something that could only be achieved by making drastic reductions in manpower. It surely is no coincidence that the machine revolution began in the cotton industry. ... England, held back by high domestic prices and labour costs which made her the most expensive country in Europe, could no longer cope with the competition from the French and Dutch on the markets closest to home. She was being beaten to it in the Mediterranean, in the Levant, in Italy and in Spain. ... [but] remained ahead in Portugal, which was one of her most ancient and solid conquests ... and in Russia. (Braudel 1992: 522, 575)

In 1776, Adam Smith observed that "the perfection of manufacturing industry, it must be remembered, depends altogether upon the division of labour ... [which] is necessarily regulated, it has already been shown, by the extent of the market"; Smith then added in the same paragraph that "without an extensive foreign market, they could not well flourish" (Smith [1776]1937: 644). Perhaps Smith had read Matthew Boulton's 1769 letter to his partner James Watt: "It is not worth my while to manufacture [your engine] for three countries alone; but I find it very well worth my while to make it for all the world" (cited in Mokyr 1990: 245). Why then in their analysis of the factors that account for the industrial revolution do Mokyr, Snooks, and others view factor price and product competition primarily in British and at most in West European terms? By 1800, four out of seven pieces of cotton cloth produced in Britain were exported (Stearns 1993: 24); and these in turn accounted for one fourth of all British exports and one half by 1850 (Braudel 1992: 572). By 1839, the Belgian Natalis Briavoinne was able to look back and observe:

> Europe was for centuries dependent on India for its most valuable products and for those of most extensive consumption: muslims, printed calicoes, nankeens, cashmeres ... for which she could only pay in specie. ... There was hence impoverishment for Europe. India had the advantage of less expensive and more skilled workforce. By the change brought about in the mode of fabrication ... Indian workers cannot compete ... [and] the balance of trade is henceforth in our favor, (cited in Wallerstein 1989: 24)

The next competitive struggle (or the struggle long ongoing but now altered) was in transportation, in which the Asian economies had also excelled. European steam-powered railroads and ships finally made far-reaching incursions on world trade only in the nineteenth century, after having failed to reduce transportation costs significantly during the three preceding centuries, as we observed in chapter 4.

The zillions of microeconomic decisions in the world market also have macroeconomic effects and causes as well. These macroeconomic relations have given rise to analyses by

Marxist and other "supply-side" economists as well as by Keynesian and other "demand-side" economists. Both in turn have been combined, albeit so far rather inadequately, in attempts by L. Pasinetti (1981) and others to understand technological progress and also by Joseph Schumpeter (1939) and others to trace its long cyclical ups and downs. We cannot really assess and pursue these analyses here, other than to note how essential a real "revolution" still is in economics, which would finally achieve a double, quadruple, or indeed sextuple marriage of micro- and marcoanalysis, and also of supply-side and demand-side analysis, as well as of cyclical and "development" analysis, and finally would create an "extended family" of such economic analysis on a world economic/demographic/ecological scale. For a critical assessment and a very general indication of where and how to pursue such an economic analysis, see Frank (1991c, 1996).

What we can and must do, however, is at least to pose the question of how and where the technological advances of the industrial revolution may have been part and parcel—and therefore must also be accounted for and explained by—microeconomic options in macroeconomic contexts, and vice versa, within a pattern of Kondratieff long cycles and perhaps even longer world economic cycles.

Therefore perhaps, world economic conditions were ripe for some enterprises, sectors, and regions to improve their micro- and macropositions through measures of the "Newly Industrializing Economy" (NIE) type. Moreover, these measures could only be applied when world economic conditions became ripe for them; and these were more critical than any prior, long "preparation" by those who invoked them.

We have observed how this European noncompetitiveness in the world economy and in Asian markets in particular was counterbalanced, and even then only partly so, by the recourse Europeans had to American sources of money. Moreover, this flow and supply of money had to be constantly replenished. But even a temporary supply failure or decline in the American supply of money, as in part of the seventeenth century, a fortiori left Euro peans essentially out of business in Asia. This American money-supply problem therefore generated either temporary and/or growing incentives for Europeans to compete in the world market by lowering their costs of production. The alternative would have been to be able to maintain or even increase their access to and reliance on American silver, as well as to the Asian credit that was guaranteed by this silver money. Can it be shown that after the mideighteenth century the availability to Europe of American money began a relative decline that threatened European market (share) penetration? That would have generated incentives for Europeans to protect and enhance their competitiveness on the world market by lowering their labor costs of production instead.

I have long since argued that the period after 1762 was a Kondratieff "B" phase in which profits declined at home and abroad for Europeans, especially from Caribbean sugar plantations and the slave trade, although the Mexican supply of silver rose again (but the Brazilian supply of gold petered out) (Frank 1978a). I have also argued that it was this Kondratieff "B" phase that generated the inventions of the industrial revolution (as well as the American and French political revolutions) in the last third of the eighteenth century.

The simultaneous progressive (long cyclical?) weakening—for whatever reason—of the Asian economies and empires and the European Kondratieff "B" phase offered the typical opportunities and incentives for some previously rather marginal economies and sectors to vie for a better competitive position in the world economy. Some regions and sectors in Europe grabbed this opportunity to become in effect NIEs (like some East Asians today). They reduced their costs of production through labor-saving and energy-generating mechanization, which offered new possibilities to increase world market share—first by import substitution in European markets and then by export promotion to world markets. The higher European wages and factor costs of production supplied the opportunity and incentives to do so.

At least two other—and mutually related—circumstances offered a helping hand: One was the aforementioned economic and political difficulties of their indigenous and other competitors in some Asian markets.

However, the political economic weakening of their Asian competitors by their respective and common (cyclical?) decline also facilitated the greater European incursions in Asia. There, competitive indigenous market access, not to mention export, was also suppressed by political/military oppression. They underlay both the "Rape of Bengal," in what had been the richest region of India, as well as its extension through conquest and colonization by the British to other parts of India, and the semicolonization of China through the "open door" to European capital in the nineteenth century. These and other European colonial enterprises simultaneously opened colonial markets for industrial production and supplied capital to support British investment in its own industry. At the turn of the century, productivity in China still remained high, indeed still in the nineteenth century perhaps higher than in Japan (Inkster 1991: 233). So since China was economically still too productive and politically still too strong to be easily penetrated, the British had recourse to Indian-grown opium to force "open the door" in an attempt to take over—which despite all nineteenth-century efforts never succeeded very far.

Though we do not yet have a fully adequate "explanation" of these economic and political difficulties, the suggestion here is that it should be sought in the context of the microeconomic demand-and-supply conditions analyzed by Adam Smith for Europe and by Mark Elvin (1973) for China. But we must extend it to the world economic scale. The other circumstance, supplies and sources of capital, is discussed in the following section.

Supplies and Sources of Capital

The other circumstance aiding greater European incursion is their, and especially the British, supplies and sources of capital. Regarding the supply of capital, Hartwell (1971: 268) reviews the works of several experts and is very explicit: "There is general agreement that there was no capital shortage [in Britain] in the eighteenth century, although the implication of this admission is not always appreciated." One implication Hartwell discusses (citing Hill 1967) is that capital from agriculture and commerce was the result of "spectacularly large sums flow[ing] into England from abroad—from the slave trade, and, especially, from the seventeen-sixties, from organized looting of India" (Hartwell 1971: 269). This is what Marx called "primitive" accumulation of capital through colonial exploitation.

The question of whether colonies pay has given rise to a long debate. Adam Smith wrote that

> the profits of a sugar-plantation in any of our West Indian colonies are generally much greater than those of any other cultivation that is known either in Europe or in America. And the profits of a tobacco plantation though inferior to those of sugar, are superior to those of corn [meaning the wheat grown in Britain]. (Smith [1776]1937: 366)

Nonetheless, like Paul Bairoch among many others, Patrick O'Brien (1982, 1990) has on several occasions dismissed any significant contribution of overseas trade and colonial exploitation to capital accumulation and industrialization in Europe. There could not have been any such, since by his calculations this trade, not to mention profits therefrom, amounted to no more than 2 percent of European GNP in the late eighteenth century. Yet he also goes on to argue that "neither quantification nor more historical scholarship will settle debates about the significance of oceanic trade for the Industrial Revolution. ... For the history of European (and even British) industrialization the 'perspective of the world' [the reference is to Braudel's title] for Europe emerges as less significant than the 'perspective of Europe' for the world" (O'Brien 1990: 177). Alas, O'Brien and so many others could not get it more wrong. For as Braudel well put it, Europe was able to consume beyond its means and invest beyond its savings. However, it did and was able to do both primarily as a function of the structure and development of the entire world economy as a whole.

Though Bairoch, O'Brien, and others deny these foreign contributions, José Arruda again reviews the debate on colonial sources of capital and markets, and concludes that

> in short, commercial investments made in the colonies, integrated into the circuit of mercantile capital and tied to the bonds of mercantile policies, substantially and strategically contributed to the economic growth of Western Europe. They opened new areas for investments—areas essential for the growth and mobility and circulation of capital. ... THE COLONIES DID PAY. (Arruda 1991: 420, capitals in original)

Indeed, the colonies did pay. They supplied not only almost free money, but also servile labor and the cheap sugar, tobacco, timber, cotton, and other goods produced in the Americas for European consumption. Moreover, it was their American money that afforded Europeans access to the silk, cotton textiles, and spices they were able to buy from Asia and the additional money they were able to make from their participation in intra-Asian's "country trade."

Therefore, it is relevant to our present concerns to record the profits Europe derived directly from its colonies (including also from India after the Battle of Plassey) before the 1815 crossover date in European and Asian "effectiveness." Ernest Mandel (1968: 119–120) estimated the European colonial booty between 1500 and 1800 at 1,000 million gold pounds sterling, of which 100 to 150 million reached Britain from India alone between 1750 and 1800. This inflow of capital facilitated if not financed Britain's investments in the new industrial revolution, especially in steam engines and textile technology. For instance, as Eric Williams (1966: 102–3) recalled "it was the capital accumulated in the West Indies that financed Watt and the steam engine. Boulton and Watt received advances. ... " Yet by 1800 the capital invested in steam-operated industry in all of Europe was still less than what its colonial profits had been. The most scrupulous student of the British economy for that period, Phyllis Deane (1965), detailed "six main ways in which foreign trade can have helped to precipitate the first industrial revolution" (quoted in detail in Frank 1978a: 227).

Perhaps, as Robert Denemark suggests, another "test" of whether and how much this influx of colonial capital did pay is whether that drove down the rate of interest and thereby rendered the investments cheaper and more possible in Britain and other parts of Europe. The monetary historian John Munro (private communication 1996) responded to my query that in Britain the rate of interest declined from 12 percent in the early 1690s and 8 percent after the establishment of the Bank of England in 1694 to 3 percent in 1752. By then, the rate of interest in Britain had become competitive with that on the Amsterdam money market, which had been funneling capital into Britain, where the Bank of England increasingly "managed" it.

This trend, which was only interrupted by temporary wartime increases in interest rates, is confirmed by P. G. M. Dickinson (1967: 470 and passim), who records interest rates on British public debt at 7 to 14 percent in the 1690s, 6 to 7 percent from 1707 to 1714 and 5 percent after that until the 1730s, when they declined to 3 to 4 percent and then to 3 percent by 1750. Moreover, Dickinson finds interest rates on private debt closely following that of public debt, in particular as massive Dutch funds flowed into the British market. Though much of that was managed by the Bank of England to support the public debt, some of that capital also flowed into private investment, and the public debt itself freed private capital to be invested elsewhere in the economy in turn.

British contemporaries were well aware of and welcomed this decline in interest rates and debated a myriad of domestic "English institutional" considerations to promote and extend them into the farthest reaches of the British Isles (Dickinson 1967). Adam Smith ([1776]1937:38–39) remarked that the maximum legal rate of interest was reduced in steps from 10 to 5 percent by one king and queen after another, but "they seem to have followed and not gone before the market rate of interest," which in turn he saw to be related to the demand for, and inversely related to the supply of, capital.

In addition to the Bank of England, the two other of the "three sisters," the British East India Company and the South Sea Company, also made significant contributions to the flow into and the management of the stock of capital in Britain.

All of these and other sources of capital including the Amsterdam funnel were of course derived directly from the colonies. However, these also had influences that were indirect but no less significant, for this decline in the interest price of money in London and Amsterdam was derived from their participation in the worldwide structure and operation of the global economy as a whole.

Therefore, until any and all of these domestic institutional considerations can be shown to be more important than the underlying increase in the flow and stock of capital and its world wide sources, Denemark's hypothesis seems amply confirmed. Nonetheless, having capital was only a necessary but not a sufficient reason to invest it. The mere availability of a supply of potentially investable capital, as emphasized by Hartwell, with its source in colonial exploitation in particular and in international trade in general, would not be enough to induce or account for its actual investment in the cost-reducing, labor-saving, and power-generating equipment of the industrial revolution. That required marco- and microeconomic incentives.

In a global economy, however, even such local and or sectoral micro-economic incentives anywhere were related to and indeed derived from competitive participation in the macroeconomic world economic structure and dynamic as a whole. This is my third and main argument: in that single global economy and system, "the Decline of the East" and "the Rise of the West" must have been related. The question is how?

A Global Economic Demographic Explanation

Let us review this entire process of Asian decline and European rise once again in global demographic and economic terms. Doing so suggests that paradoxically it may have been the very expansion of economic production and population in Asia in the previous centuries that militated against its continuation after 1800: previous chapters have looked at the long global economic expansion, particularly in Asia, which was fueled—but not started—by the European-supplied American money. We also noted that this expansion was even greater in Asia than in Europe. The new American money seems to have generated inflation in Europe and relatively more expansion of production, settlement, and population in Asia, as noted in chapters 3 and 4. However, the population/land-resource ratio had already been higher in Asia to begin with; and this expansion significantly increased pressure on resources in much of Asia. If the same happened less so in Europe (or as is argued below the latter had more escape valves), the global expansion may well have increased the relative and absolute population/resource gap between East and West.

A Demographic Economic Model

The relations between population and economic growth in general and with technological development in particular have been the subject of long debate at least since Adam Smith, David Ricardo, and Thomas Malthus. Disagreement and/or uncertainty continues today among the most expert demographers and development economists. Dominick Salvatore (1988: xiii) notes for instance that conflicting conclusions still emerge from recent reports by the United Nations, the World Bank, and the Working Group on Population Growth and

Economic Development of the U.S. National Research Council (1986). The latter's oft-cited report reviewed a vast literature on the subject, posed nine different summary questions, and arrived at only very tentative conclusions.

Thus, it may be vain indeed for someone as uninstructed as I to enter into the fray. For, with regard even to the explanation of the acceleration of population growth from the mid-eighteenth century onward in Europe alone, the weight of expert opinion has shifted from attributing it to a decline in mortality to an increase in fertility instead. Nonetheless the recent judgment by the eminent historian William Langer (1985: 5) is that it "can never be explained with any high degree of assurance or finality." Far more hazardous therefore is any speculation about the possible relations of population, economic, and technological growth on the scale of the world as a whole and about its regional differentiation. Indeed, as Ronald Lee (1986: 96–97) writes of his own expert modeling and analytic attempts, "can we explain the relative technological performance of Africa, China and Europe in a framework of this sort? … Of course there are great difficulties, perhaps even absurdities, addressing issues at such a high level of abstraction and in such generality. None the less, I believe the questions are sufficiently interesting to warrant exploration." I agree; not only are the issues interesting, but addressing them is vital for any comprehension of what really happened in the world. However, as this entire book has argued, that requires addressing the issues at an even greater—global—level of generality. Since the experts fear to tread there if only for fear of having their efforts dismissed as absurd, it falls to a foolish nonexpert to risk even more absurdity.

Lee (1986) himself reviews the "debate" between Thomas Malthus and Esther Boserup (1981), and proposes a "dynamic synthesis." Malthus, it will be recalled, argued that through the law of diminishing returns, increasing pressure on resources itself will limit the growth of population. Prior to the latter-day revival of Malthusianism, Malthus seems to have been challenged by the rapid and massive population growth in the world, made possible by repealing the law of diminishing returns through technological development, which increases the supply of resources and/or their returns. Boserup (1981), in her study of long-term trends in population and technological change, went a step further—or rather, returned to Smith, for whom population growth generated increasing returns. Boserup proposed that the growth of population and its concomitant pressure on resources can itself generate technological advance, which abolishes these decreasing returns. Lee, following F. L. Pryor and S. B. Maurer (1983), whom he credits as pioneers, seeks a "synthesis" of the Malthus thesis and the Boserup antithesis. Along the way, he constructs at least six different models of how changes or the lack of changes in population and technology might hypothetically interact.

The micro- and macroeconomic "explanation" of rapid technological change in Europe before Asia around 1800 that I propose turns out to be a variation on one of Lee's hypothetical models. My explanation is not Malthusian, which does not contemplate this technological change; and it is also not Boserupian, which attributes such technological development to rapid population growth itself. Therefore and unlike Lee's, my proposition is not a synthesis of their thesis/antithesis. Instead it is a denial of both. Indeed, my proposition is another antithesis to Boserup's, but not to Malthus. My even more "abstract and general" proposition than Lee's is that higher population growth in Asia impeded technological advance generated by and based on demand for and supply of labor-saving and power-generating machinery and that lower population growth in Europe generated the incentives for the same—in competition with Asia! One or two of Lee's "hypothetical models" contemplates such a possibility, but Lee does not seem to pursue this possibility. My reasoning is far less sophisticated than Lee's models, graphs, and equations, but my procedure may be much more realistic because I introduce three additional variables to complicate Lee's models—but eventually to simplify a real-world explanation. These three additions are (1) I put Asia, Africa, and Europe into the same globally competitive world economic bag, which is the major thesis and procedure of this book; (2) I differentiate the distributions of income, supply of labor and its price, and demand for products within economic regions, and therefore also relatively among these same regional economic parts within the competitive world economy as a whole (as per the first addition); and (3) I allow for the supply of potentially investable capital and for sources of such capital from—and indeed also its absence in or drain to—regions other than the economic region in which that capital is invested to produce labor-saving and/or energy-generating equipment and facilities.

I can briefly anticipate the resulting "dynamic," to whose plausibility Lee devotes scant attention if only because he does not give these three variables the attention they deserve in reality: around 1800, technological advance takes place in Europe, but not in Asia, which had higher population growth but also more polarization in its distribution of income and scarcity of capital. Yet it also does not take place in Africa, where the population/resource ratio was even lower than in Europe; Africa had no access to sources of investable capital from the outside, as Europe did.

A High-Level Equilibrium Trap?

So let us again review this long "A" phase expansion since 1400 and suggest why and how the economies and societies of Asia and Europe may have become more differentiated. The world economic expansion since 1400 was accompanied by large increases in production, as observed in chapters 2, 3, and 4. This also permitted significant population growth in the major economies of Asia, notably since the mid-seventeenth century, as observed in chapters 2 and 4. Thus, it was the world economic expansion that produced these effects in the major core economies and societies of Asia, and it did so there more than in the more marginal Europe. For it was the more productive Asian economies that had responded "better" to the influx of new American money.

The less productive and more marginal economies of Europe, the Americas, and Africa were not able to respond as fast or as much through higher production (as we saw in chapter 4), and Europe at least experienced higher inflation instead (as noted in chapter 3). Moreover, population growth also remained low in Europe until 1750, as we saw in chapter 4.

Between 1600 and 1750 the rate was only one-fourth of what it would become in the century thereafter (Livi-Bacci 1992: 68). Therefore, wages remained higher in Europe than in Asia.

In the major economies of Asia on the other hand, world and regional economic growth increased the population and productive pressure on the resource base, polarized the distribution of income, and thereby constrained effective domestic demand for mass consumer goods. The same structure and process pushed down the wage costs of production without increasing price incentives to invest capital in labor-saving or energy-generating techniques of production, as we will note below. Adam Smith ([1776]1937: 72) observed that, compared with Europe, the higher supply of labor and especially the greater poverty of laborers "of the lower ranks of people in China" depresses the wages at which they are willing to work. Moreover, Marks (1997a) suggests that in China faster growth in the production of rice and slower increases in its price than in population militated against incentives to invest in further improvements in productivity, especially through labor-saving devices. Indeed as already suggested in chapter 4, agricultural improvements in China and perhaps elsewhere in Asia (and probably also increased fertility and reduced mortality) outpaced those of Europe. "But the irony, of course, is that the subsequent growth in China's population may well have precluded the emergence of self-sustaining economic growth based on industrial development" (Marks 1997a).

Elvin quotes Smith to this effect as part of his own well-known argument (1973) about the "high-level equilibrium trap." He seeks to explain the absence of an industrial revolution in China when all the other conditions and "prerequisites" seemed to be abundant, as we observed in our review of production, trade, institutions, and technology. The essence of Elvin's thesis is that China had "gone about as fer as ya' can go" (to quote the observation about Kansas City in the musical *Oklahoma)* with the agricultural, transport, and manufacturing techniques developed in the preceding centuries on the basis of abundant human labor combined with scarce land and other resources. For instance, grazing lands were particularly scarce, because all agricultural land is scarce with a high and growing population; however, that made labor cheap. Therefore, low costs of transport by water and high costs of fodder for animals made heavy reliance on human-powered transport the rational alternative choice. For example, a 1742 reference to a water pump argued that it could save four-fifths of the labor needed to irrigate agricultural land. However, construction of the machine required copper, which was too expensive—indeed, literally was money sacrificed, since circulating cash coin was made out of copper. Therefore, investment in the making of such pumps was not economical or rational.

Elvin argues that it was not any institutional or other failure to "develop" but rather precisely the opposite, rapid growth of production, resources use, and of population based on the same, which rendered all resources scarce—other than labor:

> Clearly the shortages of many resources grew more severe. In many areas there was a lack of wood for building houses and ships, and indeed machinery. There was a shortage of fuels ... of clothing fibres ... of draught animals. ... Metals were

> in short supply, particularly copper ... but also iron and silver. Above all, there was a shortage of good farmland: the quality of the new land brought under the plough in this period fell sharply. A major cause of these shortages was of course the continuing growth of population under conditions of relative technological standstill ... [which] had all reached a point of sharply diminishing returns by the later eighteenth century. (Elvin 1973: 314)

Yet Elvin argues that it was these very same developments that

> made profitable invention more and more difficult. With falling surplus in agriculture, and so falling per capita income and per capita demand, with cheapening labor but increasingly expensive resources and capital[,] ... rational strategy for peasant and merchant alike tended in the direction not so much of labor-saving machinery as of economizing on resources and fixed capital. ... When temporary shortages arose, mercantile versatility, based on cheap transport, was a faster and surer remedy than the contrivance of machines. This situation may be described as a "high-level equilibrium trap." (Elvin 1973: 314)

Lee (1986: 124) following Boserup also suggests that China had too high a population density "to support further collective investments ... [for a] technological breakthrough ... China might have become caught up in a high-population, medium-technology attractive equilibrium," like Elvin's "high-level equilibrium trap" discussed above. In that trap, cheap labor due to high population, expensive resources, and scarce capital render investment in labor-saving technology neither rational nor economical. The same would have been the case in India, about which Stein (1989: 11) observes that increased elite consumption and state demands for military expenditures "placed heavier demands upon labourers, diminishing their consumption and the prospects for their very survival, especially during the later eighteenth century," as we observed above in our examination of the decline in India and elsewhere in Asia.

Tradeoffs determined by analogous demand-and-supply underlay the choices and development of fuel supplies and other sources of power. The range of their supplies may have been more locally or regionally restricted by transportation costs for their bulky raw materials, although timber had traveled long distances for millennia. However, the demand for these inputs to generate power for production was vitally affected by cost considerations, which were also derived from the worldwide competitive and/or protected market prices for products like textiles for which these fuels were inputs.

Lippit's (1987) dismissal of Elvin's argument on the grounds that Chinese surplus was high is unacceptable, because it is misplaced. Investable surplus and capital are only necessary but not sufficient conditions for their investment. I have already argued that the issue is not only whether there was an investable surplus or not, but the extent to which it was rational or not to invest it in labor-saving and power-generating technology. The Chinese did after all make huge investments in interregional canals and other infrastructure within China. Elvin argues rightly, I believe, that the Chinese were economically rational, and that that is why they then shunned some investment within a Chinese and regional/local economy-wide demand-and-supply perspective and calculations. That also strengthens my argument that, with regard especially to export industries, this economic rationality must be extended worldwide, in China and elsewhere.

That is, the same argument can and should be applied both elsewhere and worldwide. Much Asian production and export, certainly Chinese silk, was highly labor-intensive to produce under high-labor supply/low-labor cost conditions. In India also, the previous centuries of economic growth and expansion had generated analogous supply and demand relations. There also, not "stagnation" but rather its opposites—economic expansion, population growth, and even institutional change, in a word the (normal?) process of accumulation of capital—must have led to a point of diminishing returns.

The *Cambridge Economic History of India* observes that "the remarkable cheapness of labour ... rendered labour-saving devices superfluous" in India (Raychaudhuri and Habib 1982: 295). Habib also argues elsewhere (in Roy and Bagchi 1986: 6–7) that the abundance of skilled labor and "skill-compensation" in India rendered the adoption of labor-saving devices uneconomical there (although Amiya Bagchi is cited on p. 143 of their appendix as disagreeing with this point).

So, Elvin's approach and analysis may be applied not only in China but also in Southeast Asia, India, Persia, the Ottoman Empire or wherever—and among each of these from a world economic perspective. That includes Europe. There the labor-surplus/capital-shortage argument by Elvin about China (or its application also elsewhere in Asia) is on the opposite side of the coin from the analogous labor-shortage and therefore relative capital-surplus argument that Adam Smith made for Britain and Europe and others more recently for North America.

In Europe, higher wages and higher demand, as well as the availability of capital including that flowing in from abroad, now made investment in labor-saving technology both rational and possible. The analogous argument holds for power-generating equipment. Relatively high prices for charcoal and labor in Britain provided the incentive for the accelerated switch-over to coal and mechanically powered production processes before these also became more economical in areas with even greater surpluses of labor and/or shortages of nonmechanical power, fuel, and capital to develop them. The additional argument here is that, of course, world economic market competition between Europe and China, India, and other parts of Asia rendered such labor-saving and energy-producing technology economically rational for Europeans, but not for Asians.

All this is even more the case if the distribution of income is very unequal. Then, the top of the income pyramid does not generate enough demand for production that might benefit from lower labor costs, while the low incomes at the bottom of the pyramid keep or drive down wages. So a more unequal distribution of income also militates against technological innovation in labor-saving devices and investment in power-generating processes. So what can we say about the distribution of income?

Jack Goldstone (1991a) argues that, regardless of how the use of labor is organized, population growth in agrarian societies concentrates income and wealth and lowers wages and effective demand. Yet, we have argued above that more money and higher population also reinforced each other. All of these common causes could then have undermined economic viability and political stability. Is there evidence for such a process in seventeenth- and eighteenth-century Asia? Yes!

There is indeed reason to believe that it was the very long rise in production and population itself which contributed to subsequent decline at least in the growth rates of both. Evidence from Asia suggests that its rise in production and population put pressure on the resource base and polarized both economy and society: the distribution of income became increasingly unequal.

The changing distance between rich and poor modified the "upper" end of the social pyramid. Upward mobility and conspicuous consumption, especially by merchants and speculators, was enhanced, as documented for Ming China economy and society in Timothy Brook's (1998) history, *The Confusions of Pleasure.* Lippit (1987: 90) estimates the size of the economic surplus that the gentry and others extracted to have been at least 30 percent of national income in the nineteenth century. Earlier economic boom conditions may well have elicited both absolutely and relatively higher surplus. Analogous processes have also been described in India as a result of economic expansion before its nineteenth-century decline. Indeed his attempts to compare the available evidence from India and China (and Europe) in this regard, lead Pomeranz (private communication 1996) to believe that the distribution of wealth and income was even more skewed in India than elsewhere. That increased demand from the top of the social pyramid for luxury and imported goods diverted purchasing power from the mass market for locally and regionally produced consumer goods.

At the bottom of the social pyramid some people were pushed "down and out" and marginalized altogether. A larger group of displaced peasants became low-wage workers who formed an ever bigger pool of cheap labor. Among this large and perhaps growing segment of people at the bottom of society, low income at the same time reduced their effective demand on the market for goods and increased the supply of their cheap labor to produce goods, also for export.

Regarding India, Habib (1963a: 351) explains how "the Mughal Empire had been its own grave-digger." Its governing class got much of its great wealth through the expropriation of the surplus produced by the peasantry. Habib (1963a: 320) quotes two contemporaries who observed that seldom if ever had the contrast been greater between "the rich in their great superfluity and the utter subjection and poverty of the common people" and "the country is ruined by the necessity of defraying the enormous charges required to maintain the splendour of a numerous court, and to pay a large army for keeping the people in subjection." That must have reduced income and effective domestic mass demand and made for a low supply price of wage labor. Indeed, Habib (1963a: 324–9) testifies both to increasing exploitation over time of the peasants and to their resulting flight from the land, which increased the urban and other supply of labor, presumably at lower wages. This condition also contributed importantly to the downfall of the Mughals and their replacement by the Marahatas, who not only continued but even increased the exploitation of the peasantry. Ali (1975) also cites Habib as arguing precisely that there was intensified exploitation in agriculture and that this led to both the peasant and zamindar rebellion. (Increased earning opportunities would also increase exploitation of workers in British industry during the industrial revolution, as Friedrich Engels and Eric Hobsbawm later noted).

So how did the distribution of income in Asia compare with that in Europe and especially in Britain? Regarding China, Adam Smith ([1776]1937: 72) observed that the poverty of the poorest there was far greater than any in Europe, so that the lowest European incomes were still higher than the lowest Chinese and perhaps other Asian ones. Moreover, Smith ([1776]1937: 206) also observed that both the real wage of labor and the real quantities of the necessities for life that the laborers could purchase with their wages were lower in China and India than in most of Europe.

Nonetheless, Pomeranz (1997, private communications 1996) insists that while the distribution of income was indeed more unequal in India, in China it was more equal than in Europe. However, he also suggests that in China laborers were still able to draw on family support from the countryside for some of their subsistence, which was no longer available to urban workers in Europe, not in Britain. Pomeranz suggests that therefore workers would still have been able to manage on—and employers to pay—wages that were lower in China than in Britain or Western Europe, even if the Chinese distribution of income was not more unequal than that in Europe. So in this regard, rural family support in China could be regarded as the "functional equivalent" of a more unequal distribution of income, as in India.

More significantly however, Pomeranz's suggestion can be translated into still another one: whatever the distribution of income in China, wage goods were still relatively and maybe absolutely cheaper there than in Europe and especially in relatively high-wage Britain. That is, relative to the costs of alternative mechanical inputs and other sources of power, the availability of cheap wage goods would still have made it more economical and rational to employ more labor and less capital in China than in Britain even at similar distributions of income. However, no matter through what institutional mechanisms these cheap subsistence wage goods were or were not distributed, they could only have been made available by an agriculture that was more productive and thereby able to produce these wage goods cheaper in China than in Britain and Europe. These observations in turn confirm, or at least are consistent with, two others: Agriculture was more efficient in China, as Marks (1997a) alleges (see chapter 4). And it was relative productive efficiency in Chinese agriculture that militated against labor-saving innovation and capital-using investment elsewhere in the economy, as Elvin (1973) and I allege.

Another answer may perhaps be sought in concomitant differences in price levels. The quantity theory of money (according to which prices rise proportionately to the quantity of money) may not be foolproof. Nonetheless, the evidence is that in general, the closer the source of and therefore the availability of silver/money, the higher the level of prices; and the more distant the money source and the lower its availability, the lower the level of prices. As we have seen, Europe was certainly closer to the American mines and received a greater and earlier supply of silver than did in turn West, South, and East Asia. Can it be shown that the combination of higher wages and higher prices in Europe, not to mention North America, still left most Europeans no more or even less well off than most Asians, while still affording a greater supply of low-wage labor at the bottom of the Asian social pyramid? In that case high wage levels in Europe and low ones in Asia would also have been compatible with the less certain but probable nearly level standards of living, and the possibly even lower ones in Europe, as Bairoch, Maddison, and others suggest. That would have been particularly the case if the distribution of that income was more unequal in Asia and/or if China or even India also had the cheap wage-good "functional equivalent" suggested above. These circumstances would also have made European goods less competitive than Asian ones in world and particularly Asian and even European markets.

Is there evidence to support, deny, or modify this proposition? Yes, there is. We have evidence both on relative population/land-resource ratios at the end of the period 1400–800 and inferential evidence on earlier changes in the same period, based on previous rates of population growth. Moreover, we also have evidence on comparative population growth rates among major regions in the world and Eurasia, presented in chapter 4.

The Evidence: 1500–1750

So can we test this relative wage level microhypothesis and the related long-cycle macrohypothesis as part of a better world economic theory to account for the industrial revolution taking place in Europe and America and not in Asia—or Africa?

The evidence is certainly abundant, and some of it was cited above, that wages were much lower in Asia than in Europe and that for this reason European production was not competitive. Regarding relative population/land-resource ratios, Bairoch (1969: 154–5) examined ratios of population to hectares of cultivated land and projected them back to about 1800 in Asia. He found Asian ratios to have been three to four times higher, with 3.6 and 3.8 people per hectare in China and India, respectively, and only 1.1 in France and 1.5 in England in 1700 (however the ratio for Japan, albeit for 1880, was 5.0 per hectare).

Of course, data for population and its growth are sparse and uncertain, and on economic growth, not to mention their pressure on resources, even more so. However, tables 4.1 and 4.2 summarized world and regional population data from a large variety of sources, which did reveal a significant pattern. We noted that world population growth recovered after 1400 and experienced an upward inflection after 1600 and especially from the middle of the seventeenth century onward, probably for the economic and nutritional reasons outlined in chapters 2 and 4. Yet as we observed in chapter 4, from 1600 to 1750 Europe continued to account for an unchanging 18 to 19 percent of the world's population. Over the same period, the share of the world's population that lived in Asia increased from 60 to 66 percent. That is because, in the already more densely populated Asia, population grew at about 0.6 percent a year, while in Europe it grew at only 0.4 percent. According to the later figure of Livi-Bacci (1992: 68), the rate of population growth in Europe was only 0.3 percent, that is one-half or two-thirds that of Asia. As a result, according to tables 4.1 and 4.2, while from 1600 to 1750 population grew by 57 percent in Europe, it grew by 87 percent in all of Asia and by 90 percent in China and India. Moreover, the absolute increase was four times greater in Asia on its already scarcer resources, by 100 million from 1600 to 1700 and by 216 million to 1750, compared to increases of only 26 million and 51 million respectively in Europe.

Thus, the population/land-resource ratio increased more in Asia than in Europe. This difference by itself suggests that the availability of cheap labor also increased much more in Asia than in Europe. That would be all the more the case if the inequality in the distribution of income also became greater in Asia than in Europe. That was suggested above both because of the more rapid population increase itself and also because of a greater increase in production and income in Asia. In Africa, population remained stable or declined, with what effect on the distribution of income we do not know. However, we do know that unlike Europe, Africa had no significant inflow of investable capital from elsewhere and also not the same degree of competition with Asia in world markets as Europe had. Therefore, we need not expect any changed incentive to innovative labor-saving technology in Africa. Lee does not mention that reason but suggests that Africa may have been caught in a "low-level equilibrium trap" for other reasons as well.

The 1750 Inflection

How and why did population change especially in the second half of the eighteenth century? Historians and demographers have noted an unexplained inflection in population growth rates beginning about 1750. Table 4.1 shows half-century world population increases of about 20 percent from 1650 to 1700 and again to 1750, but a higher 23 percent from 1750 to 1800. In Asia however, the corresponding rates were 26 percent before 1750 and only 20 percent from 1750 to 1800, and in India they dropped from 30 percent in the half century before 1750 to 20 percent in the half century after that. For this period, rather different growth rates emerge from Clark (1977), as summarized in table 4.2. World population totals increased by 24 percent in the first half century, but only by 14 percent in the second one, and then recovered to 21 percent from 1750 to 1800. In China, population growth rates were about 50 percent in the first and last half centuries but inexplicably only about 40 percent in the intervening one from 1700 to 1750. However, Clark does show a significant decline in Indian population growth rate from 33 percent in the half century before 1700 to zero in the half century after 1750 and an absolute decline of 0.5 percent from 1750 to 1800 (after the Battle of Plassey in 1757).

Other data suggest even greater relative declines of population growth in Asia and an increase in Europe. According to the estimates by Carr-Saunders (1936) that are still used by the United Nations, the world population growth rate declined from about 0.3 percent a year in the century before 1750 to 0.2 or even 0.1 percent in the half century to 1800.

Most of that was due to the even more rapid decline in Asia from 0.6 percent a year to 0.13 or 0.14 percent a year between 1750 and 1800. Within Asia, the growth rate, according to more recent estimates, was 1 percent in China but only 0.1 percent in India, during its economic decline, conquest, and colonization by Britain (Nam and Gustavus 1976: 11). So the eighteenth-century reversal from high to lower population growth rates in Asia emerges clearly from all of these population estimates, despite the differences among them.

In Europe on the other hand according to table 4.1, population growth accelerated from 15 percent between 1650 and 1700 to 22 percent between 1700 and 1750, to 34 percent in the half century between 1750 and 1800 and 41 percent from 1800 to 1850. In table 4.2 the growth rates for Europe are similar, rising from 17 percent in the first of these half centuries and 23 percent in the second one to 33 percent in the third one from 1750 to 1800. That is, in Europe the growth rate of population suddenly took off from the previous annual 0.3 or 0.4 percent to 1.6 percent a year for 1750–1800. The latest Livi-Bacci (1992: 68) figures for Europe are 0.15 percent from 1600 to 1750 and 0.63 percent from 1750 to 1800 (which would make them even lower relative to Asian ones in the earlier period). Notwithstanding the differences in these estimates, no one disputes that population growth rates took off in Europe, while they did not in Asia and indeed may have reversed in India. Moreover, these same trends continued and indeed accelerated in the first half of the nineteenth century.

The once proffered suggestion—that fertility rather than mortality generated this increase in population growth due to increased demand for child labor from the industrial revolution itself—is easily disconfirmed. For the population increase was not limited to newly industrializing Britain or even to northwestern Europe but was greatest in Eastern Europe and Russia. The latter's expansion into Siberia supported and funneled off its population growth, but their industrialization was generally slower than in Western Europe. As Langer (1985) suggests, we may never know exactly why population took off in Europe; but we know that it did and that in Asia it did not.

Does this evidence about the reversal of Asian and European population trends after 1750 tend to disconfirm my suggested explanation for the reversal of Asian and European fortunes and the location of the industrial revolution first in the Europe? No. Can we have it both ways? Yes.

The absolute and relative changes in population growth rates in Asia and Europe after 1750 do not necessarily detract from this explanation and perhaps even offer additional support for it. To begin with, the lower rates of population growth in Asia are a manifestation and confirmation of the decline of Asia, which is central to my explanation. Similarly, the increase in population and its growth rate in Europe are also a manifestation of the economic "Rise of Europe" and the West. Additionally however, it may be argued that under these new circumstances there indeed was a Boserup effect! Boserup (1981) herself suggests that the population/land-resource ratio in Europe did not favor technological innovation in agriculture or industry before the mid-eighteenth century. She emphasizes that European population growth offered this stimulus only after that time and that Europe had no immediately prior increase in agricultural productivity. However especially after 1800, the even faster European population increase could well also have supported innovation in labor-saving technology and less laborious and cheaper generation of power and use and handling of materials, as Boserup claims. For that to become possible however, there had to be a marked expansion of the market for European products not only at home but also abroad.

However, Europe also had to have a source of sufficient capital to make these technological investments possible and affordable, as well as the expanding market to make the investments profitable. Beginning especially after the Battle of Plassey in 1757 and from 1800 onward, these conditions were met by and in the world economy. The very decline of Asia, not to mention European colonialism, simultaneously offered Europeans the necessary increase in markets and market share as well as an additional inflow of investable capital. Moreover, emigration to the Americas made it possible to drain off much of the new surplus population from Europe. This population at the European frontier in combination with the additional new resources available in the New World then further expanded the world market for European production and exports. None of this would have been possible without the structure and conjuncture in the world economy around 1800, on which I have insisted in this book.

Another important aspect of this structure and conjuncture is examined by Pomeranz (1997). He argues that the previous long period of economic and population growth—our long "A" phase which he also finds predominant in China—exerted differential ecological demands and opportunities on the resource base among various regions in the world. By the end of the eighteenth century, according to his analysis, these ecological pressures in turn stimulated and favored the conversion to new sources of power in Britain and Western Europe, especially from coal instead of wood and through steam instead of mechanical and animal traction. This ecological/economic incentive and the demographic/economic structure and conjuncture were of course related and require further analysis in relation to each other.

Challenging and Reformulating the Explanation

This demographic and world macro- [sic] and microeconomic explanation of technological change around 1800 can be challenged on some empirical grounds and with some analytical reservations. However, this will also permit reformulating and strengthening the argument. The evidence and reasoning that follows builds on a tripartite e-mail discussion held between August and October 1996 among Ken Pomeranz, Jack Goldstone, and myself. It attempts to construct a stronger synthesis of our arguments that is empirically and analytically more acceptable to all of us and better defensible to the reader. The main issue is how to account for the technological change around 1800 and whether and where to invest to reduce comparative costs of production and to extend markets in terms of world market-wide competition.

1. The main challenge to the simple demand and supply hypothesis was that the technological innovations of the industrial revolution were less labor "saving" than labor "extending" and increased the productivity of both labor and capital.
2. Direct wage rates or costs may have been as high (or even higher) in some parts of China (for example, in the Yangzi Valley and the South), though probably not anywhere in India, as in some parts of Europe, especially England.
3. The distribution of income may have been similar—and not more skewed, as I contended—in China and Europe, although it probably was more unequal in India.
4. The problem of absolute, relative, and worldwide comparative wage costs—in entrepreneurial calculation as in our analysis of the same—is related also to local and regional problems of labor allocation.
5. There were some economic differences in labor allocation especially between agriculture and industry, which were related to some institutional differences. However, it is less clear to what extent these differences were underlying causes of the observed allocation of labor or whether they were only different institutional mechanisms through which the labor allocation were organized. Particularly important differences were (a) labor was bonded in India; (b) women in China were tied to the village and their labor was restricted to agriculture and domestic industry such as spinning; (c) some industrial workers in China could still draw directly on subsistence goods produced by women tied to the village and agriculture; this was less true in England, where subsistence goods often had to be acquired through the market; and (d) enclosures of more land to produce more and cheaper wool for textiles—the "sheep ate men" saying—expulsed male and female labor from the land into urban employment (and unemployment) in England and perhaps elsewhere in Europe.
6. The industrial revolution was initiated with cotton textiles, but these required both a growing "external" supply of cotton (for Europe it came from its colonies) and a "world" market for all in which everybody had to compete (except China, which still had a growing and protected domestic and regional market).
7. The industrial revolution also required and took place in the supply and production of more and cheaper energy, especially through coal and its use in making and using machinery to generate steam power, first stationary and then also mobile. The critical role of coal and its replacement of wood as a source of fuel in Britain is demonstrated by Wrigley (1994).
8. These sources of power technically and economically first required (and permitted) concentration of labor and capital in mining, transport, and production. Then they also permitted faster and cheaper long-distance transport via steam-powered railway and shipping.
9. Investment in such "revolutionary" industrial power, equipment, organization, and the labor necessary to make them work was undertaken only where it was economically rational and possible to do so, depending on (a) labor allocation and cost alternatives; (b) location and comparative costs of other productive inputs (for

example, timber/coal/animal/human sources of power and transport, as well as raw materials like cotton and iron), which were related to the geographical location of these resources and to ecological changes in their availability; (c) capital availability and alternative profitable uses; and (d) market penetration and potential.

The Resulting Transformations in India, China, Europe, and the World

At the beginning of the nineteenth century these nine factors generated the following transformations in the world economy.

In India. India's competitive dominance on the world textile market was threatened despite cheap and also bonded skilled labor. Domestic supplies of cotton, food, and other wage goods continued to be ample and cheap; and productive, trade, and financial organization and transport remained relatively efficient despite suffering from increasing economic and political difficulties. However, supplies of alternative power and materials, particularly from coal and iron/steel, were relatively scarce and expensive. Therefore, Indians had little economically rational incentive to invest in innovations at this time. They were further impeded from doing so first by economic decline beginning in the second quarter of the eighteenth century or earlier; then by the (resulting?) decline in population growth and British colonialism from the third quarter of the century on; and finally from a combination of both decline and colonialism as well as the "drain" of capital from India to Britain. India switched from being a net exporter to being a net importer of cotton textiles in 1816. However, India did continue to struggle on the textile market and began again to increase textile production—by then also in factories—and exports in the last third of the nineteenth century.

In China. China still retained its world market dominance in ceramics, partially in silk, increasingly in tea, and remained substantially self-sufficient in textiles. China's balance of trade and payments surplus continued into the early nineteenth century. Therefore, China had availability and concentration of capital from both domestic and foreign sources. However, China's natural deposits of coal were distant from its possible utilization for the generation and industrial use of power, so that progressive deforestation still did not make it economical to switch fuel from wood to coal. Moreover, transport via inland canals and coastal shipping, as well as by road, remained efficient and cheap (but not from outlying coal deposits).

This economic efficiency and competitiveness on both domestic and world markets also rested on absolutely and comparatively cheap labor costs. Even if per capita income was higher than elsewhere, as Bairoch notes, and its distribution was no more unequal than elsewhere (as Pomeranz and Goldstone claim), the wage-good cost of production was low, both absolutely and relatively. Labor was abundant for agriculture and industry, and agricultural products were cheaply available for industrial workers and therefore to their employers, who could pay their workers low subsistence wages. Goldstone (1996) emphasizes the importance of one factor: women were tied to the villages and therefore remained available for (cheap) agricultural production. Pomeranz (1997) emphasizes a related factor: urban industrial workers were still able to draw for part of their subsistence on "their" villages (as in Yugoslavia during industrialization after World War II), which was produced cheaply in part by the women to whom Goldstone refers. In other words from the perspective of the entrepreneurial industrial employer and the market, wage goods were absolutely and relatively cheap because agriculture produced them efficiently and cheaply with female labor. The "institutional" distribution of cheap food to urban and other workers in industry, transport, trade, and other services was functionally equivalent to what it would also have been if the functional distribution of income had been more unequal than it was. The availability of labor was high, its supply price low, its demand for consumer goods attenuated; and there was little incentive to invest in labor-saving or alternative-energy-using production or transport. Elvin (1973) sought to summarize such circumstances in his "equilibrium trap." Even so, China still remained competitive on the world market and maintained its export surplus. As Emperor Ch'ien-lung explained to King George III of England, China had "no use for your country's manufactures."

In Western Europe. Western Europe and particularly Britain were hard put to compete especially with India and China. Europe was still dependent on India for the cotton textiles and on China for the ceramics and silks that Europe re-exported with profit to its colonies in Africa and the Americas. Moreover, Europe remained dependent on its colonies for most of the money it needed to pay for these imports, both for re-export and for its own consumption, production, and export. In the late eighteenth and early nineteenth centuries, there was a decline in the marginal if not also in the absolute inflow of precious metals and of other profits through the slave trade and plantations from the European colonies in Africa and the Americas. To recoup and even to maintain—never mind to increase—its world and domestic market share, Europeans collectively, and its entrepreneurs individually, had to attempt to increase their penetration of at least some markets, and to do so either by eliminating competition politically and militarily or undercutting it by lowering its own costs of production (or sometimes both).

Opportunity to do so knocked when the "Decline" began in India and West Asia, if not yet in China. Wage and other costs of production and transport were still uncompetitively high in Britain and elsewhere in Europe. However especially after 1750, rising incomes and declining mortality rates sharply increased the rate and amount of population growth. Moreover, the displacement of surplus labor from agriculture increased its potential supply to industry. At the same time, Britain's imposition of colonialism on India reversed its perennial capital outflow to that country. Moreover, a combination of commercial and colonial measures permitted the import of much more raw cotton to Britain and Western Europe. Deforestation and ever scarcer supplies of wood and charcoal rendered these more expensive. From the second third of the eighteenth century, first relative and then absolute declines in the cost of coal made the replacement of charcoal (and peat) by hard coal increasingly economical and then common in Britain. The Kondratieff "B" phase in the last third of the eighteenth century generated technological inventions and improvements in textile manufacturing and steam engines (first to pump water out of coal pits and then also to supply motive power to the textile industry). At the beginning of the nineteenth century, an "A" phase (the first one so identified by Kondratieff) and the Napoleonic wars generated increased investment in and the expansion of these new technologies, including transport equipment, and also led to the incorporation of ever more available but still relatively high-cost labor into the "factory system." Production increased rapidly; real wages and income declined; and "the workshop of the world" conquered foreign markets through "free trade." Yet even then, British colonialism had to prohibit free trade to India and resorted to the export of opium from there to force an "open door" into China.

The Rest of the World. Most other parts of the world still fall through the cracks of our world economic analysis. But in brief, we can observe that most of Africa may have had population/land-resource ratios at least as favorable to labor-saving investment as Europe. However, Africa did not have an analogous resource base (except the still undeveloped one in Southern Africa), and far from having a capital inflow, Africa suffered from capital outflow. The same was true of the Caribbean. Latin America had resources and labor, but also suffered from colonial and neocolonial capital outflow as well as specialization in raw materials exports, while its domestic markets were captured by European exports. West, Central, and Southeast Asia became increasingly captive markets for (if not also colonies of) Europe and its industry, to which they supplied the raw materials that they had previously themselves processed for domestic consumption and export. In the nineteenth century, only the European "settler colonies" in North America, Australasia, Argentina, and Southern Africa were able to find other places in the international division of labor, and China and Japan were able to continue offering significant resistance. But that is another—later—story, which leads to the reemergence of East Asia in the world economy today.

In short, changing world demographic/economic/ecological circumstances suddenly—and for most people, including Adam Smith, unexpectedly—made a number of related investments economically rational and profitable: in machinery and processes that saved labor input per unit of output, thus increasing the productivity and use of labor and its total output; productive power generation; and in productive employment and productivity of capital. This transformation of the productive process was initially concentrated in selected industrial, agricultural, and service sectors in those parts of the world economy whose comparative competitive position made—and then continually remade—the import-substituting and export-promoting measures of such Newly Industrializing Economies both economically rational and politically possible. Thus, this transformation was and continues to be only a temporally localized and still shifting manifestation of a world economic process, even if it is not spread uniformly around the world—as historically nothing ever has been and is unlikely to be in the foreseeable future. The suggestion is that it was not overall poverty and still less tradition or failure that handicapped Asia in the world economic competition relative to Europe around 1800. Rather, in Marxist and Schumpeterian terms, it was their very success that generated failure. For the competitive handicap of the Asian economies was generated by its previous absolute and relative success in responding to the economic incentives of the long "A" phase expansion that the inflow of American money financed, which lasted through much of the eighteenth century. That turns all received theory on its head.

Past Conclusions and Future Implications

To conclude, we may summarize our findings and argument again and inquire into their implications for the future before proceeding in the next chapter to look into what all this means for social and economic theory as well as for world history—past, present, and future. The argument—and the evidence—is that world development between 1400 and 1800 reflects not Asia's weakness but its strength, and not Europe's nonexistent strength but rather its relative weakness in the global economy. For it was all these regions' joint participation and place in the single but unequally structured and unevenly changing global economy that resulted also in changes in their relative positions in the world. The common global economic expansion since 1400 benefited the Asian centers earlier and more than marginal Europe, Africa, and the Americas. However, this very economic benefit turned into a growing absolute and relative disadvantage for one Asian region after another in the late eighteenth century. Production and trade began to atrophy as growing population and income, and also their economic and social polarization, exerted pressure on resources, constrained effective demand at the bottom, and increased the availability of cheap labor in Asia more than elsewhere in the world.

Europe and then also North America (and if we wish to separate it out, also Japan at the other end of Eurasia) were able to take advantage of this pan-Asian crisis in the nineteenth and twentieth centuries. They managed to become Newly Industrializing Economies, first through import substitution and increasingly also by export promotion to and within the global world market. Yet this success, which was based on their previous marginality and relative "backwardness" in the global economy, may also prove to be relatively short-lived. These new, but perhaps also temporary, world economic centers are now experiencing absolute and relative social and economic atrophy analogous to that of the previously central Asian economies, while some of the latter seem to be recovering their economic and social impulse.

Thus, in analogy to other periods of cyclical decline and transition, the late eighteenth century was still one of competing and "shared" political economic power between the declining Asians and the rising Europeans. Only then was a new "hegemonic" order built, with European power at its center, in which a new period of industrial and economic expansion occurred, now with rapid capital accumulation in Europe itself. This nineteenth-century world hegemonic system was eventually followed by increasing intra-European rivalry and rivalry with the United States and Japan. These culminated in a general crisis and war between 1914 and 1945, leading to the construction of a new hegemonic order and renewed world economic growth under American leadership. However, the "American century" lasted only twenty years. The contemporary economic expansion in East Asia, beginning with Japan, then in the East Asian NIEs, and now apparently also in coastal China, may spell the beginnings of Asia's return to a leading role in the world economy in the future such as it held in the not so distant past.

We may speculate a bit about the continuation of this long cycle, whose "B" phase appears to have begun in Asia around 1800. From a long-term Asian and perhaps more global perspective, the ending of this long nineteenth- and twentieth-century "B" phase may have been signaled since the middle of the twentieth century by renewed political decolonization in the "Third" World, including liberation in China and Vietnam. These political events, of course, were also reflections of longterm political economic changes taking place within the West and the world it dominated, including the shift of hegemony from Western Europe to the United States.

At least two major simultaneous and related economic trends have made themselves felt from the early 1970s onward. One is the marked and still unexplained new slowdown of productivity growth throughout the West since the first major postwar recession beginning in 1973. It has also been accompanied by a decline in the average real wage and also unprecedented rampant polarization in the economy of the United States. This and the succeeding 1979–1982 recession have been wrongly attributed to the "oil shocks" of 1973 and 1979 (Frank 1980). It is notable, however, that oil exporters did pose another political economic challenge to the West and that all this economic turmoil, including "relocating" and "downsizing" its productive operations, as well as the political economic debacle in socialist Eastern Europe, have taken place within the West's long Kondratieff "B" phase since 1967.

Another simultaneous and related trend is the marked economic revival in and world impact of East Asia. It began in Japan and then in its former colonies Korea and Taiwan, but also included Hong Kong and Singapore among the first set of "four tigers." Since then, revived economic growth has been spreading also to other "tigers" or "little dragons" elsewhere in Southeast Asia and to the "big dragon" on the China coast. This is the same South (and East) China Sea region, with its diaspora of "overseas Chinese," which had been so prominent in the world economy in the previous long "A" phase from the fifteenth through the eighteenth centuries. Does that presage a renewed "A" phase there, perhaps also spreading to South and West Asia, in the twenty-first century?

Therefore, it is conceivable that the West and the East will again trade places in the global economy and in world society in the not too distant and already dimly foreseeable future. This inquiry and speculation into long cyclical downs and ups during the last seven centuries also poses a serious theoretical problem about how phases succeed each other in our long cycles. Its consideration, however, is perhaps best postponed to the discussion of cycles in our concluding, "theoretical" chapter.

These contemporary developments and future prospects demand new and better social theory to comprehend them and to offer at least some modest guide to social policy and action. It is my hope that this book's rather different historical perspective on the past can also shed more light on this present and future, which that past still helps generate and constrain. Therefore, the final chapter is devoted to drawing out the implications of this historical account of what errors our historiography and social theory should avoid and to inquiring into how it could do better.

References

Abu-Lughod, Janet. 1989. *Before European Hegemony. The World System A.D. 1230–1330.* New York: Oxford University Press.

Adams, Robert McC. 1996. *Paths of Fire: An Anthropologist's Inquiry into Western Technology.* Princeton: Princeton University Press.

Ali, M. Athar. 1975. "The Passing of Empire: The Mughal Case." *Modern Asian Studies* 9, 3: 385–96.

Arasaratnam, Sinnappah. 1986. *Merchants, Companies and the Commerce of the Coromandel Coast 1650–1740.* Delhi: Oxford University Press.

———. 1995. *Maritime Trade, Society and the European Influence in Southern Asia, 1600–1800.* Aldershot, U.K.: Variorum.

Arrighi, Giovanni. 1994. *The Long Twentieth Century. Money, Power, and the Origins of Our Time.* London and New York: Verso.

Arruda, José Jobson de Andrade. 1991. "Colonies as Mercantile Investments: The Luso-Brazilian Empire, 1500–1808." In *The Political Economy of Merchant Empires,* edited by James D. Tracy, 360–420. Cambridge: Cambridge University Press.

Bairoch, Paul. 1969. *Revolución Industrial y Subdesarrollo.* La Habana: Instituto del Libro.

Blaut, J. M. 1977. "Where Was Capitalism Born?" In *Radical Geography,* edited by R. Peet, 95–110. Chicago: Maasoufa Press.

———. 1992. "Fourteen Ninety-Two." *Political Geography Quarterly* II, no. 4 (July). Reprinted in J. M. Blaut et al., *1492. The Debate on Colonialism, Eurocentrism and History.* Trenton, N.J.: Africa World Press.

———. 1993a. *The Colonizer's Model of the World: Geographical Diffusionism and Eurocentric History.* New York and London: Guilford Press.

Boserup, Esther. 1981. *Population and Technological Change. A Study of Long-Term Trends.* Chicago: University of Chicago Press.

Bosworth, Andrew. 1995. "World Cities and World Economic Cycles." In *Civilizations and World Systems. Studying World-Historical Change,* edited by Stephen S. Sanderson, 206–28. Walnut Creek, Calif.: Altamira.

Braudel, Fernand. 1992. *The Perspective of the World.* Vol. 3 of *Civilization and Capitalism 15th–18th Century.* Berkeley and Los Angeles: University of California Press.

Brook, Timothy, ed. 1998. *The Confusions of Pleasure. A History of Ming China (1368–1644).* Berkeley and Los Angeles: University of California Press.

Carr-Saunders A. M. 1936. *World Population. Past Growth and Present Trends.* Oxford: Clarendon Press.

Chandra, Bipan. 1966. *The Rise and Growth of Economic Nationalism in India.* New Delhi: Peoples Publishing House.

Chase-Dunn, Christopher, and Thomas Hall. 1997. *Rise and Demise: Comparing World-Systems.* Boulder: Westview.

Chaudhuri, K.-N. 1978. *The Trading World of Asia and the East India Company 1660–1760.* Cambridge: Cambridge University Press.

Clark, Colin. 1977. *Population Growth and Land Use.* London: Macmillan.

Costello, Paul. 1994. *World Historians and their Goals. Twentieth-Century Answers to Modernism.* De Kalb: Northern Illinois University Press.

Das Gupta, Ashin, and M. N. Pearson, eds. 1987. *India and the Indian Ocean 1500–1800.* Calcutta: Oxford University Press.

Deane, Phyllis. 1965. *The First Industrial Revolution.* Cambridge: Cambridge University Press.

Dickson, P. G. M. 1967. *The Financial Revolution in England. A Study in the Development of Public Credit 1688–1756.* London: Macmillan.

Dorn, Walter D. 1963. *Competition for Empire, 1740–1763.* New York: Harper & Row.

Eaton, Richard N. 1993. *The Rise of Islam and the Bengal Frontier 1204–1760.* Berkeley and Los Angeles: University of California Press.

Eberhard, Wolfram. 1977. *A History of China.* Rev. ed. London: Routledge & Keagan Paul.

Elvin, Mark. 1973. *The Pattern of the Chinese Past.* Stanford: Stanford University Press.

Fletcher, Joseph. 1985. "Integrative History: Parallels and Interconnections in the Early Modern Period, 1500–1800." *Journal of Turkish Studies* 9: (1985) 37–58. Reprinted 1995 in *Studies on Chinese and Islamic Inner Asia,* edited by Beatrice Forbes Manz. Aldershot, U.K.: Variorum.

Frank, Andre Gunder. 1966. "The Development of Underdevelopment." *Monthly Review* 18, no. 4 (September). Reprinted in Frank 1969: 3–20.

———. 1967. *Capitalism and Underdevelopment in Latin America.* New York: Monthly Review Press.

———. 1975. *On Capitalist Underdevelopment.* Bombay: Oxford University Press.

———. 1978a. *World Accumulation, 1492–1789,* New York and London: Monthly Review Press and Macmillan Press.

———. 1978b. *Dependent Accumulation and Underdevelopment.* New York and London: Monthly Review Press and Macmillan Press.

———. 1980. "Development of Underdevelopment or Underdevelopment of Development in China." In *The Development of Underdevelopment in China,* edited by C. C. Huang, 90–99. White Plains, N.Y.: M. E. Sharpe.

———. 1991c. "The Underdevelopment of Development." *Scandinavian Journal of Development Alternatives* (Special Issue) 10, no. 3 (September): 5–72.

———. 1993a. "Bronze Age World System Cycles." *Current Anthropology* 34, no. 4 (August-October): 383–430.

———. 1994. "The World Economic System in Asia before European Hegemony." *The Historian* 56, no. 4 (winter): 259–76.

———. 1995. "The Modern World System Revisited: Re-reading Braudel and Wallerstein." In *Civilizations and World Systems. Studying World-Historical Change,* edited by Stephen S. Sanderson, 206–28. Walnut Creek, Calif.: Altamira.

———. 1996. "The Underdevelopment of Development." In *The Underdevelopment of Development. Essays in Honor of Andre Gunder Frank,* edited by Sing Chew and Robert Denemark, 17–56. Thousand Oaks, Calif.: Sage.

Frank, A. G., and B. K. Gills, eds. 1993. *The World System: Five Hundred Years or Five Thousand?* London and New York: Routledge.

Gerschenkron, Alexander. 1962. *Economic Backwardness in Historical Perspective. A Book of Essays.* Cambridge: Harvard University Press, Belknap Press.

Gills, Barry K., and A. G. Frank. 1992. "World System Cycles, Crises, and Hegemonial Shifts 1700 BC to 1700 AD." *Review* 15, no. 4 (Fall): 621–87.

Goldstone, Jack A. 1991a. *Revolutions and Rebellions in the Early Modern World.* Berkeley and Los Angeles: University of California Press.

———. 1996. "Gender, Work, and Culture: Why the Industrial Revolution Came Early to England But Late to China." *Sociological Perspectives* 39, 1: 1–21.

Habib, Irfan. 1963a. *The Agrarian System of Mughal India.* Bombay: Asia Publishing House.

Hartwell, R. M. 1971. *The Industrial Revolution and Economic Growth.* London: Methuen.

Higgins, Benjamin. 1991. *The Frontier as an Element in National and Regional Development.* Research Report No. 10. Moncton, Canada: Université de Moncton Institute Canadien de Récherche sur le Développement Regional.

Hill, Christopher. 1967. *Reformation to Industrial Revolution. British Economy and Society 1530/1780.* London: Weidenfeld & Nicholson.

Huang, C. C., ed. 1980. *The Development of Underdevelopment in China.* White Plains, N.Y.: M. E. Sharpe.

Inalcik, Halil, with Donald Quataert, eds. 1994. *An Economic and Social History of the Ottoman Empire 1300–1914.* Cambridge: Cambridge University Press.

Inkster, Ian. 1991. *Science and Technology in History. An Approach to Industrial Development.* London: Macmillan Press.

Islamoglu-Inan, Huri, ed. 1987. *The Ottoman Empire and the World-Economy.* Cambridge: Cambridge University Press.

Issawi, Charles, ed. 1966. *The Economic History of the Middle East 1800–1914. A Book of Readings.* Chicago: University of Chicago Press.

Kindleberger, Charles. 1989. *Spenders and Hoarders.* Singapore: ASEAN Economic Research Unit, Institute of Southeast Asian Studies.

Langer, William K. 1985. "Population Growth and Increasing Means of Subsistence." In *Readings on Population,* edited by David M. Herr, 2–15. Englewood Cliffs, N.J.: Prentice Hall.

Lee, Ronald Demos. 1986. "Malthus and Boserup: A Dynamic Synthesis." In *The State of Population Theory. Forward from Malthus,* edited by David Coleman and Roger Schofield. Oxford and New York: Basil Blackwell.

Lin Man-houng. 1990. "From Sweet Potato to Silver." In *The European Discovery of the World and Its Economic Effects on Pre-Industrial Society, 1500–1800,* edited by Hans Pohl, 304–20. Papers of the Tenth International Economic History Congress. Stuttgart: Franz Steiner Verlag.

Lippit, Victor. 1987. *The Economic Development of China.* Armonk, N.Y.: M. E. Sharpe.

Livi-Bacci, Massimo. 1992. *A Concise History of World Population.* Cambridge, Mass., and Oxford: Blackwell.

Marks, Robert B. 1996. "Commercialization Without Capitalism. Processes of Environmental Change in South China, 1550–1850." *Environmental History* 1, no. 1 (January): 56–82.

———. 1997a. *Tigers, Rice, Silk and Silt. Environment and Economy in Late Imperial South China.* New York: Cambridge University Press. Cited from manuscript.

Marshall, P. J. 1987. "Private British Trade in the Indian Ocean before 1800." In *India and the Indian Ocean 1500–1800,* edited by Ashin Das Gupta and M. N. Pearson. Calcutta: Oxford University Press.

Masters, Bruce. 1988. *The Origins of Western Economic Dominance in the Middle East. Mercantilism and the Islamic Economy in Aleppo, 1600–1750.* New York: New "York University Press.

McNeill, William. 1983. *The Pursuit of Power: Technology, Armed Force and Society since AD 1000.* Oxford: Blackwell.

Modelski, George, and William Thompson. 1996. *Leading Sectors and World Powers: The Co-Evolution of Global Economics and Politics.* Columbia: University of South Carolina Press.

Mokyr, Joel. 1990. *The Lever of Riches. Technologies Creativity and Economic Progress.* New York: Oxford University Press.

Mukherjee, Rila. 1990/91. "The French East India Company's Trade in East Bengal from 1750 to 1753: A Look at the Chandernagore Letters to Jugdia." *Indian Historical Review* 17, nos. 1–2: 122–35.

———. 1994. "The Story of Kasimbazar: Silk Merchants and Commerce in Eighteenth-Century India." *Review* 17, no. 4: 499–554.

Murphey, Rhoades. 1977. *The Outsiders. Western Experience in India and China.* Ann Arbor: University of Michigan Press.

Musson, A. E. 1972. *Science, Technology and Economic Growth in the Eighteenth Century.* London: Methuen.

Nam, Charles B., and Susan O. Gustavus. 1976. *Population. The Dynamics of Demographic Change.* Boston: Houghton Mifflin.

Nef, John U. 1934. "The Progress of Technology and the Growth of Large-Scale Industry in Great Britain, 1540–1640." *The Economic History Review* 5, no. 1: 3–24.

O'Brien, Patrick. 1982. "European Economic Development: The Contribution by the Periphery." *Economic History Review* (2nd series) 35: 1–18.

———. 1990. "European Industrialization: From the Voyages of Discovery to the Industrial Revolution." In *The European Discovery of the World and Its Economic Effects on Pre-Industrial Society, 1500–1800,* edited by Hans Pohl. Papers of the Tenth International Economic History Congress. Stuttgart: Franz Steiner Verlag.

Palat, Ravi Arvind, and Immanuel Wallerstein. 1990. "Of What World System Was Pre-1500 'India' a Part?" Paper presented at the International Colloquium on Merchants, Companies and Trade, Maison des Sciences de l'Homme, Paris, 30 May-2 June, 1990. Revision to be published in *Merchants, Companies and Trade,* edited by S. Chaudhuri and M. Morineau. Forthcoming.

Pasinetti, L. 1981. *Structural Change and Economic Growth.* Cambridge: Cam bridge University Press.

Pomeranz, Kenneth. 1997. "A New World of Growth: Markets, Ecology, Coercion, and Industrialization in Global Perspective" Unpublished manuscript.

Prakash, Om. 1994. *Precious Metals and Commerce.* Aldershot, U.K.: Variorum.

Pryor, F. L., and S. B. Maurer. 1983. "On Induced Change in Precapitalist Societies." *Journal of Development Economics* 10: 325–53.

Raychaudhuri, Tapan, and Irfan Habib, eds. 1982. *The Cambridge Economic History of India.* Vol. 1: *c. 1220–c. 1750.* Cambridge: Cambridge University Press.

Reid, Anthony. 1997. "A New Phase of Commercial Expansion in Southeast Asia, 1760–1850." In *The Last Stand of Autonomous States in Southeast Asia and Korea,* edited by Anthony Reid. London: Macmillan. Cited from Manuscript.

Rostow, W. W. 1962. *The Stages of Economic Growth. A Non-Communist Manifesto* Cambridge: Cambridge University Press.

Roy, Aniruddha, and S. K. Bagchi. 1986. *Technology in Ancient and Medieval India.* Delhi: Sundeep Prakashan.

Schumpeter, Joseph Alois. 1939. *Business Cycles.* New York: McGraw Hill.

Sideri, Sandro. 1970. *Trade and Power. Informal Colonialism in Anglo-Portuguese Relations.* Rotterdam: Rotterdam University Press.

Smith, Adam [1776] 1937. *The Wealth of Nations.* New York: Random House.

Snooks, Graeme Donald. 1996. *The Dynamic Society. Exploring the Sources of Global Change.* London and New York: Routledge.

Snooks, Graeme Donald, ed. 1994. *Was the Industrial Revolution Necessary?* London and New York: Routledge.

Stearns, Peter N. 1993. *The Industrial Revolution in World History.* Boulder: Westview Press.

Steensgaard, Niels. 1972. *Carracks, Caravans and Companies: The Structural Crisis in the European-Asian Trade in the Early 17th Century.* Copenhagen: Studentlitteratur.

———. 1987. "The Indian Ocean Network and the Emerging World-Economy (c. 1550 to 1750)." In *The Indian Ocean: Explorations in History, Commerce, and Politics,* edited by S. Chandra, 125–50. New Delhi: Sage.

———. 1990d. "The Growth and Composition of the Long-Distance Trade of England and the Dutch Republic before 1750." In *The Rise of the Merchant Empires. Long-Distance Trade in the Early Modern World, 1350–1750,* edited by James D. Tracy, 102–52. Cambridge: Cambridge University Press.

Stein, Burton. 1989. "Eighteenth Century India: Another View." *Studies in History* (new series) 5, no. 1: 1–26.

Tarling, Nicolas, ed. 1992. *The Cambridge History of Southeast Asia.* Vol. 1, *From Early Times to c. 1800.* Cambridge; Cambridge University Press.

Wallerstein, Immanuel. 1974. *The Modern World-System.* Vol. 1, *Capitalist Agriculture and the Origins of the European World-Economy in the Sixteenth Century.* New York: Academic Books.

———. 1989. *The Modern World-System.* Vol. 3, *The Second Era of Great Expansion of the Capitalist World-Economy 1730–1840s.* New York: Academic Press.

———. 1992. "The West, Capitalism, and the Modern World-System." *Review* 15, no. 4 (Fall): 561–619.

Wrigley, E. A. 1994. "The Classical Economists, the Stationary State, and the Industrial Revolution." In *Was the Industrial Revolution Necessary?* edited by Graeme Donald Snooks, 27–42. London and New York: Routledge.

Topic Five Suggested Supplemental Readings

North, Douglass, and Robert P. Thomas. 1970. "An Economic Theory of the Growth of the Western World." *Economic History Review* 23, no. 1 (April): 1–17.

Nunn, Nathan. 2008. "The Long-Term Effects of Africa's Slave Trades." *Quarterly Journal of Economics* 123, no. 1 (February): 139–176.

Pomernz, Kenneth. 2001. *The Great Divergence: China, Europe, and the Making of the World Economy.* New Jersey: Princeton University Press.

Topic Five Questions

1. Explain the impact of the Hanseatic League and the Champaign Fairs on European trade.
2. Describe the changes in European population 1200–1500.
3. Contrast Portuguese and Spanish overseas exploration.
4. Provide three reasons given by Frank for the decline of India.
5. How was the Chinese economy different that that of India in the eighteenth century?
6. Contrast China with Western Europe in terms of their textile industries, sources of energy, and transportation systems.

Topic Six

The First Industrial Revolution

CHAPTER EIGHT

Britain's Revolution

New Processes and Economic Transformation

Peter N. Stearns

Before the eighteenth century the most advanced economies in the world featured a combination of craft manufacturing (its most skilled components based in cities) and a large labor force committed to agriculture. Most production, both manufacturing and agricultural, was based on manual household labor, with larger village groups combining for certain operations like harvesting and road building. The use of slave crews for the commercial production of key agricultural goods like sugar and tobacco had spread, particularly in the Americas, though there were no major changes in technology. Several societies had developed sophisticated craft skills for the production of luxury cloth, metal goods, and other items. China, Japan, India, the Middle East (including North Africa), and western Europe stood at the forefront in terms of artisanal technology and the vital capacity to produce iron and iron products. Africa had a well established ironworking tradition, and metallurgy and armaments manufacturing were advancing in Russia by 1700.

West European technology had gained ground from the fifteenth century onward. Western production of guns, based on earlier skills in ironworking developed initially for the production of great church bells, provided a crucial military edge, particularly in naval conflicts. Western metallurgy generally led the world by the sixteenth century. During the seventeenth century, growing dominance in world trade spurred the growth of textile production in many parts of western Europe, and here, too, technological refinements occurred that made the West effectively an international leader. Western biases concerning the rest of the world began to take on a technological cast, with scorn for the many peoples slow to imitate Western developments. A Western missionary in the seventeenth century described how, in his opinion, the Chinese could not be persuaded "to make use of new instruments and leave their old ones without an especial order from the Emperor to that effect. They are more fond of the most defective piece of antiquity than of the most perfect of the modern, differing much in that from us who are in love with nothing but what is new."

With all these developments, however, Western technology remained firmly anchored in the basic traditions of agricultural societies, particularly in terms of reliance on human and animal power. Agriculture itself had scarcely changed in method since the fourteenth century. Manufacturing, despite some important new techniques, continued to entail combining skill with hand tools and was usually carried out in very small shops. Western production methods were not decisively superior to those in places like China and India. The most important Western response to new manufacturing opportunities involved a great expansion of rural (domestic) production, particularly in textiles but also in small metal goods. Domestic manufacturing workers used simple equipment, which they usually bought themselves, and relied on labor from the household. Many combined their efforts with farming, and in general their skill levels were modest. The system worked well because it required little capital; rural householders invested a bit in a spinning wheel or a hand loom, and an urban-based capitalist purchased the necessary raw materials and, usually, arranged for sale of the product. Output expanded because of the sheer growth of worker numbers, not because of technical advancement; indeed, the low wages paid generated little incentive for technical change.

Western Europe in 1700 was an advanced agricultural society, with an unusually large commercial sector and a great deal of manually operated manufacturing. The region was developing a certain fascination with machines but most decidedly was not industrialized.

Three changes began to combine during the eighteenth century to accelerate manufacturing and ultimately generate the world's first industrial revolution. They affected much of western Europe, but particularly Britain, where the revolution first took shape.

New agricultural methods came into use in the late 1700s. Peasants in many parts of Europe, including Ireland, France, and Prussia, began to grow potatoes, a New World crop long regarded with suspicion. Potatoes offered several advantages over the grains Europeans had traditionally relied upon as staple food: Higher caloric value could be produced from smaller and sometimes less fertile plots of land, and for many decades potatoes were less subject to periodic diseases than were grains. Increasing adoption of the potato supported the beginnings of rapid population growth in Europe by the 1730s. Britain's population, for example, doubled between 1750 and 1800, and that of France rose by 50 percent. The potato also freed a percentage of rural labor for work in other areas, again because of its caloric yield from small plots. At roughly the same time, farmers in Holland began to develop new drainage systems by which swampland could be converted to agricultural use, and they introduced nitrogen-fixing crops that enabled them to keep fields in use every year rather than resting them every third year to regain chemical fertility. With less fallow land and more land in use overall, food production expanded, and this expansion also contributed to population growth and to the release of new workers for other potential work activities.

Although agricultural improvements took shape in various places, they received enthusiastic support in Britain, where aristocratic landlords were particularly interested in new and more rewarding production for market sales. Draining of marshes added cultivable land in eastern England. Innovators like "Turnip" Townshend spread the word about using nitrogen-fixing crops to increase production by eliminating fallow land. As in other parts of Europe, increased food supplies spurred British population growth and reduced the percentage of the labor force required in agriculture.

This was the context in which what some historians have called *protoindustrialization* began to intensify in several areas. Domestic manufacturing systems spread as more workers became available, and population growth and new consumer interests created new markets, particularly for textiles. Many rural workers began to farm only part time, taking orders for thread and cloth from urban merchants at other times. This capitalist system generated growing production. Though the workers involved used traditional methods based on manual labor and cooperation of the family in a household operation, they began to see themselves as different from peasants—more interested in urban fashions, for example, which created additional markets.

Another set of changes provided a context for new technologies. Massive strides in European science, in an already active commercial economy, encouraged attention to new devices in the manufacturing field. A host of scientific societies took shape that combined researchers with merchants and manufacturers and led to excited discussions about down-to-earth technological possibilities. Advances in chemistry helped trigger the discovery of new techniques for manufacturing and glazing pottery in eighteenth-century England. New scientific knowledge about the behavior of gases set a context for considering the possibility of harnessing steam to provide a moving force to replace unreliable water and wind as power sources. The first steam engine was invented by a French refugee in Holland in the late 1600s; several Dutch scientists discussed the prospect of propelling a boat by steam. Around 1700 the engine was improved in England by Thomas Newcomen, who applied it to drainage pumps for coal mines. A steam truck was invented in France in the 1760s, though it was never put to use. The engine was perfected in the 1760s by James Watt, a Glasgow craftsman who produced scientific instruments, and could be applied to industrial use. In a poem written in 1789, the English scientist Erasmus Darwin (grandfather of the evolution-theory biologist Charles) ecstatically praised the engine's possibilities:

> *Soon shall they arm, unconquer'd steam! afar*
> *Drag the slow barge, or drive the rapid carp;*
> *Or on wide-waving wings expanded bear*
> *The flying chariot through the fields of air.*
> *—Fair crews triumphant, leaning from above,*
> *Shall wave their handkerchiefs as they move;*
> *Or warrior bands alarm the gaping crowd,*
> *And armies shrink beneath the shadowy cloud.*

Along with changes in agricultural production and a stream of new inventions and attendant intellectual enthusiasm came additional shifts in England's domestic manufacturing system, initially beneath the surface. The nation was already a leader in world trade. It had a growing population by the 1730s, and the public was expressing interest in more fashionable clothing—an early manifestation of new consumer tastes. This setting prompted a handful of domestic producers to think about expanding their operations, in a gradual shift that proved to be the forerunner of a new organization of manufacturing labor. For example, the Halifax area in Yorkshire in the late seventeenth century was a significant center for the production of wool cloth by local artisans in the countryside who often combined their manufacturing with farming. Output from each worker was low, though the profits could provide some useful supplementary income. Even substantial farmers put their hand to the loom from time to time or used family members as workers. In the 1690s a few workers began buying more wool than they could handle themselves; they hired others to work the wool at home for them and, without abandoning their own labor at first, were on the route to becoming manufacturers. By the next generation, these same manufacturing families, a minority of the wool workers in the region overall, were beginning to separate themselves socially from their employed labor. They were no longer willing to share a beer; they were thinking of their workers as a class apart. One of them wrote in 1736, during a trade depression, "I have turned off laid off a great many of my makers and keep turning off more weekly." His "makers," clearly, had become disposable subordinates in the process of production, and a traditional manufacturing system was beginning to yield to a more structured hierarchy.

By the 1730s several of these strands of change were beginning to combine in England. Protoindustrialization meant that, although the total number of agricultural workers grew, even as aristocratic landlords consolidated their holdings and sponsored more efficient methods, the percentage of a rapidly growing population employed in agriculture declined. Market opportunities for manufacturing production rose, however, despite frequent slumps, through population growth, expanding international trade, and the growing appetite for consumer goods like fashionable clothing. As more and more workers and small businesses began expanding their operations by hiring wage workers, the profile of a new manufacturing middle class began gradually to emerge. Finally, new technology began to be developed for the sector that most obviously invited it: the domestic production system. In 1733 an English artisan, James Kay, invented the flying shuttle, a new kind of loom for weaving cloth that automatically moved thread horizontally through a frame when activated by a foot pedal. This machine was nothing fancy, and no new power was involved, but one worker with a child as assistant could now do the work of two adults. Inventions for automatically winding fiber to make thread followed in the 1760s. New opportunity and evolving attitudes on the part of the growing manufacturing class, plus the excitement surrounding technological change and the resultant encouragement to invention, were pushing the traditional production system well beyond its former bounds.

By the 1760s, then, several key ingredients of the industrial revolution had been assembled in England, after several decades of protoindustrial changes within the domestic manufacturing system. New entrepreneurs were ready to manipulate workers in novel ways. Inventions increased the number of industrial processes handled automatically. The manufacturing sector and its labor force were growing steadily. Then came a usable steam engine, which by the 1770s could be hooked up to some of the semiautomatic inventions already devised for manual textile workers. Because steam power was concentrated and could not be transmitted over long distances, workers had to be assembled near the engines to do their work; small factories had to replace household production sites. This final change, too, was developing rapidly in certain key sectors by the 1770s. Britain's industrial revolution was under way.

Britain Becomes the Workshop of the World

The initial explicit stages of the world's first industrial revolution—as opposed to the previous preparatory decades—involved a number of elements. Rapid innovation transformed several sectors of industry, with new technology and organization at the core of change. Without this innovation, the industrial revolution could not have been identified. At the same time, many branches of the economy were affected only slightly, and thus some overall measurements of industrialization remained modest. (It is for this reason that some scholars, failing to look at the longer-term picture, dislike the term *industrial revolution.*) Within the innovative sectors, intense misery pervaded the experience of many of the human beings involved; the industrial revolution was built on the backs of exploited labor. Finally, as the revolution caught on, it inevitably brought in its wake further change in both technology and business practices. Most of these developments occurred during decades when Britain nearly monopolized the new processes, winning a growing world role on the strength of its industrial lead.

The cotton industry commanded the central role in Britain's early industrialization. Cotton, as a fiber, had characteristics relatively easy to mechanize; it broke less often than wool and, particularly, linen. Further, cotton was a new product line in Europe, more open to innovation. It had been widely used in India, and an Asian market for cotton cloth already existed. In England, however, its novelty facilitated the introduction of new machines, though the raw fiber had to be imported. Workers were displaced indirectly by the rise of cotton because traditional linen production declined. The lack of a large established labor force in cotton obviated the need to prompt many traditional workers to change their ways directly, and this fact limited resistance. At the same time, cotton had great appeal as a product: It could be brightly colored for a population increasingly eager to make a statement through clothing, and it was easily washed, so appealed to people who were developing more stringent notions of personal cleanliness. Cotton was in demand, and this demand invited new techniques to produce the cloth in quantity.

By the 1730s a series of inventions began to shift cotton manufacturing increasingly toward a factory system. The flying shuttle, designed originally to improve hand weaving, was refined over another thirty years sufficiently in accuracy to make possible the application of nonhuman power. Edmund Cartwright patented a power loom in 1785; his description of his procedures revealed the new kind of thinking being applied to technical issues: "It struck me that as plain weaving can only be three movements which were to follow one another in succession, there would be little difficulty in producing them and repeating them." Indeed, mechanization involved isolating parts of the production process that

MAP 8.1 The Beginning of the Industrial Revolution: Great Britain, c. 1750–1820

could be accomplished through highly standardized, accurate motion and then applying to such motion equipment that could be linked to power sources. Weaving turned out to be among the more complicated stages to mechanize, and Cartwright's loom had to undergo substantial improvements before, by around 1800, it could be widely used.

More impressive developments occurred in the preparatory phases of making cotton. About 1764 James Hargreaves invented a spinning jenny device, which mechanically drew out and twisted the fibers into threads—though this advance, too, was initially applied to handwork, not to a new power source. Carding and combing machines, to ready the fiber prior to spinning, were developed at about the same time. Then, in 1769, Richard Arkwright developed the first water-powered spinning machine; it twisted and wound threads by means of flyers and bobbins operating continuously. These first machines were relevant only for the cheapest kind of thread, but other inventions by 1780 began to make possible the spinning of finer cotton yarns. These new devices also could be powered by steam engines as well as waterwheels. The basic principles of mechanized thread production have not changed to this day, though machines grew progressively larger, and a given worker can now tend a far greater number of spindles. Other inventions pertinent to the industrialization of cotton production included new bleaching and dying procedures (in the 1770s and 1780s) and roller printers for cloth designs, which replaced laborious block printing by hand—another new method that increased production a hundredfold while reducing workers' skill requirements.

Cotton production by the 1790s was advancing with extraordinary rapidity. New machines required a factory organization, for the power could not be transmitted widely. Workers had to be removed from their homes and clustered around the new machines, and cotton spinning was entirely concentrated in factories by the 1790s. Because mechanical weaving lagged, this initial industrialization spurred a massive expansion of domestic looms; the thread produced was distributed from huge warehouses in the new factory centers such as Manchester. Power weaving came into general use in the Manchester area only after 1806, then began the full conquest in cotton after 1815—to the immense distress of the hundreds of thousands of workers who had been drawn into the surrounding countryside to do the weaving. There were massive fortunes to be made in the industry. Robert Owen, a store assistant, began his Manchester factory in 1789 by borrowing £100, and by 1809 he was in a position to buy out his partners in his New Lanark Mills for £84,000 in cash—this in a country where only about 4 percent of the population earned more than £200 per year.

Sales of manufactured cotton goods soared, for with the new machines not only did output increase, but prices plummeted. Exports were essential, and by 1800 approximately four pieces of cotton cloth were sold abroad for every three disposed of at home. As late as 1840 cotton continued to provide about half the entire value of British exports. Continental Europe was a major market, but it consumed only about a third of Britain's export production in this field. Latin America was seized by British cotton exports after Spanish rule was cast off early in the nineteenth century. By 1820 the impoverished continent was buying a quarter as much cotton cloth from Britain as was Europe, and by 1840 the figure had risen to a full half. India and Southeast Asia were deindustrialized by a combination of British factory competition and colonial policy as machine products beat out hand labor; cotton imports from Britain rose by 1,500 percent between 1820 and 1840. Africa was another major market. Of the major nations, only China held out, until its economy was forced open in the early 1840s.

Until about 1840, Britain's industrial revolution consisted primarily of changes in the cotton industry, its massive results being expanding production and world outreach, but other developments were vital as well. Mechanization of wool spinning and weaving was well under way by 1800, impeded only by the higher cost and greater fragility of wool fiber. New machines and procedures were introduced into beer brewing; the big factories established included the great Guinness brewery in Dublin. Pottery manufacturing concentrated important developments in industrial chemistry during the late eighteenth century, and new methods reduced the work required in processes such as glazing and cutting. Several of these innovations created major health hazards for the workers involved—new grinding methods, for example, "hath proved very destructive to mankind, occasioned by the dust suckled into the body which … fixes so closely upon the lungs that nothing can remove it"—but productivity per worker expanded immensely, to the benefit of new pottery magnates such as Josiah Wedgwood. In the 1830s new printing presses were developed that could be powered by steam engines and thus greatly expanded production in such fields as daily newspapers. A few commercial bakeries also introduced important new methods.

The most striking mechanical strides outside the growing textile sectors occurred in metallurgy and mining. During the eighteenth century British manufacturers learned to produce coke from coal (by heating and concentrating it in special ovens) and to use coke instead of wood-derived charcoal for smelting iron ore. Coke production, in turn, depended on advances in furnace design and steam blasting (introduced by John Wilkinson in 1776). As coke supplies grew, furnace design for smelting and refining iron was also reconsidered; the result was larger furnaces and higher output per worker. Henry Cort's reverberatory furnace for refining iron (developed in 1784) saved fuel but above all increased productivity by 1,500 percent. Steam-powered machines to roll metal, replacing manual hammering, soon followed. The iron industry began to expand rapidly. Britain had produced 25,000 tons of pig iron in 1720; by 1796 the figure was 125,000 and by 1804 was 250,000 tons.

The growth of the iron industry had two further consequences. Coal mining surged to provide the fuel for iron smelting and for steam engines generally. Major advances in work methods at the coal face did not develop, though there were important improvements in timbering mine pits to allow deeper shafts. Transportation from the coal face did demand attention. Wooden and metal rails were laid down to facilitate carts of coal being pulled by horses or people; soon after 1800 experiments with steam-driven engines to pull the carts began. At the same time, the number of miners increased rapidly because this vital industry remained extremely labor-intensive.

At the other end of iron production, machine building expanded steadily. Inventions of new equipment, from spinning machines to the steam engine, did not always translate readily into production methods beyond the prototypes. Twelve years passed, for example, between Watt's construction of a working model engine (1765) and usable cylinders that could be widely manufactured. Before 1800 machine building was scattered in small shops and was performed with hand methods, and even after this date the industry long demanded highly skilled workers laboring with relatively little sophisticated equipment of their own. But attention in France and the new United States to the manufacturing of guns led to the development of precise patterns for designing machine parts, so that these parts could be interchangeably used on a given machine. Several machines were designed to bore and turn the machine pieces, and their industrial use gradually spread in Britain (and the United States and western Europe) during the early decades of the nineteenth century.

Headed by advancements in the cotton industry, Britain's early industrial revolution featured dramatic new methods that subsequently generated improved productivity and more standardized products in a host of industries. Heavy industry—mining and metallurgy—gained ground rapidly, though the importance of the labor force and the total product long lagged behind textiles. Vast numbers of new workers were drawn into factories and mines. Some of these people were relatively unskilled, for many of the new processes required only modest training compared with older methods, but some, as in machine building, applied extensive skills to new products. Developments were not uniform: Many production branches, as in the manufacturing of brass and other small metal goods, were scarcely touched, though they often expanded because of growing demand. Nor was progress steady: Great lags often intervened, as in mechanical weaving, between the initial devices and their widespread applicability. Britain's industrialization was a revolution, but it neither occurred overnight nor was tidily packaged.

The revolutionary quality, however, showed through in a host of ways. Urban growth was one of these. Cities of various sorts exploded in Britain in the late 1700s and early 1800s, the result of burgeoning banking operations, growing port activities, and so on. The biggest expansion, however, occurred in the factory centers as factories located near energy sources and a large labor force accumulated to facilitate factory operations. Manchester, Britain's cotton capital, grew from a modest town of 25,000 in 1772 to a metropolis of 367,232 by 1851. Leeds, Birmingham, and Sheffield, centers of textiles or metalwork, grew by 40 percent between 1821 and 1831 alone. Britain's industrialization revolutionized where many people lived by drawing work increasingly into the big-city context (and of course by making agriculture more efficient, thus less labor-intensive). During this period the majority of British families changed their residence and much of their framework of daily life as they shifted from reliance on agriculture to involvement with industry.

Industrialization Exacts a Price

The industrial revolution, even in its early phases, prompted major changes in business scale. Many operations started small; because initial textile machinery, in particular, was not costly, many small-scale innovations could draw on a wide array of available business talent. But there was obvious challenge. Traditional textile equipment for a home manufacturing operation cost a fraction of what was required to set up an early factory: By the 1780s British textile mills were valued at £3,000–£4,000, many times the £25 cost of a good hand loom. The first multistoried factory powered by steam, established in 1788, was valued at £13,000; its steam engine alone, large for the time at thirty horsepower, cost £1,500. Plants for metallurgy and mining operations were more expensive still.

Businesses did not immediately have to adopt radically new methods of capital formation and management systems, but the pressure to innovate was quite real. Many firms were established as partnerships because necessary capital was unavailable otherwise. Many factories, launched under the eye of an ever-present owner, had to generate a small bureaucracy when it became clear that directing the labor force, providing the necessary technical expertise, arranging for the purchase of raw materials, and selling the goods simply escaped the capacity of any one individual. Borrowing arrangements became steadily more elaborate, although abundant capital kept interest rates fairly low in early British industry. Family firms had to branch out to hire outsiders to participate in more specialized management structures. And although massive profits were possible—Robert Owen's achievement was replicated in a host of cases as a new class of wealthy factory owners began to emerge in the 1820s—the possibility of failure was very real as well. Sales recessions were frequent, particularly in industries like cotton that depended on exports. Poor harvests reduced income at home and cut deeply into industrial sales. Significant economic crises occurred at least once a decade; a particularly severe recession followed the end of the Napoleonic Wars in 1815. Workers suffered most in these catastrophes as unemployment soared, but many manufacturers collapsed financially as well.

The early industrial revolution in Britain was built on the backs of cheap labor driven mercilessly hard. In rural areas, the standard of living fell for many workers, who were pressed both by population growth and by competition from machine-made goods that cut into branches of domestic manufacturing. Many rural women, for example, lost their manufacturing income when spinning was mechanized. With less land available for small farmers, less supplementary employment, and competitive pressure on agricultural wages, stark misery spread in many agricultural districts. Although hand weavers enjoyed some real prosperity before 1800, when thread production soared but mechanized weaving had yet to take hold, their pay began to plummet thereafter. By 1811 wages were down one-third from their 1800 levels, and by 1832, when hand weaving in cotton was dying out in Britain, they had fallen by a full 60 percent. Industrialization was not entirely to blame for this collapse—population pressure and displacement of small farmers by aristocratic landlords played a role—but there can be no doubt of the massive hardships involved. Further, although the worst misery was centered in areas remote from the factories, the widespread deterioration also cut into the standard of living of industrial workers, who faced a growing amount of potential competition for jobs.

In the factories proper, however, wages in some sectors held up somewhat better, for new workers had to be drawn in. Mining wages, for example, seemingly improved in Britain's early industrial revolution. Skilled workers, needed to set up and maintain the new machines, also did well, often winning long-term contracts and other benefits. On the other hand, many employers, desperate for workers but desperate also to keep costs down to protect their expensive investments and allay their fears of business failure, looked for labor shortcuts. This search was the inspiration for hiring groups of orphans from London and other large towns, who were shipped in droves to the factory centers in return for employer provision of food and barracks housing. Extensive use of child and female labor was not in itself novel—families had always depended on work by all members to survive—but use of children and young women specifically because of the low wages they could be pressed to accept reflected the pressures of early industrial life and unquestionably constrained the nascent working class in the factories. To be sure, factory-produced goods such as clothing and utensils fell in price, but there were drawbacks, too: Urban housing often was costlier than its preindustrial rural counterpart, and food costs fluctuated. Historians of Britain's industrial revolution have debated the standard-of-living question for many decades without definitively agreeing about whether conditions grew worse or better. Certainly there was variety, and factory workers were not the worst-paid group in the British population. Certainly also, however, particularly before about 1819, there was widespread suffering in the factory cities, where few workers were able to afford much above a bare subsistence even as more of their employers grew fat from the fruits of the new industry.

Other pressures added to the burdens on the new factory workers. No regular provision for illness or old age cushioned industrial life, and factory workers, unlike many small farmers, had no plot of land to fall back on for at least a modest food supply if their strength began to fail. The frequent economic slumps often caused unemployment rates, even for skilled workers, to soar as high as 60 percent for several months or even a year, and food prices often went up in these periods. Not surprisingly, many workers, even those capable of improving their earnings, found industrial life extremely unpredictable, even nerve-wracking, and in the worst slumps, death rates rose in the factory centers. Furthermore, and again even for workers whose pay might have increased modestly, the industrial revolution cut into leisure time. The labor force was prodded to work harder than its preindustrial counterpart, and work hours inched up as employers sought to maximize use of the expensive machinery. Some textile factories drove their workers sixteen hours a day, Saturdays included. Traditional festival days, when rural workers had taken time off, came under attack as the new factories fined workers for unauthorized absences. Finally, factory jobs exposed many workers to new physical dangers: dust from textile fibers, accidents in the coal mines, and maimings by the fast-moving—usually unprotected—machinery.

The early industrial revolution depended on the need that growing numbers of workers had for jobs in order simply to survive. Necessity, not attraction, lay at the root of the formation of Britain's new factory labor force. Relatively low pay—declining pay in some circumstances—helped subsidize the investment in new machinery and supported the gains that motivated successful entrepreneurs, and increased work time contributed to growing output along with the machines themselves. And although the misery was worst in the early decades of industrialization—real wages and urban health conditions began to improve in the 1820s or at least in the 1830s—and although debate continues about exactly how bad things were, there is no doubt that desperately hard work and scant reward constituted key ingredients in the early industrialization process in Britain.

Not surprisingly, conditions of early manufacturing generated serious protest among many British workers, though labor organization was illegal and poverty limited the resources available for protracted struggle. Many workers struck or rioted against cuts in pay or high food costs. Beyond these specific efforts, a number of factory hands articulated a larger sense of the exploitation to which they were, in their judgment, subject and about the gap that had opened between them and the factory masters. A Manchester cotton spinner in 1818 condemned his employers for their "ostentatious display of elegant mansions, equipages, liveries, parks, hunters and hounds. … They are literally petty monarchs, absolute and despotic, in their own particular districts; and to support all this, their whole time is occupied in contriving how to get the greatest quantity of work turned off with the least expense." The spinner also excoriated the "terrible machines" that had so worsened the quality of work as compared with preindustrial life. Some workers did far more than talk. In a series of riots between 1810 and 1820 hand workers attacked and destroyed the textile equipment that threatened their jobs or at least their accustomed wages. These Luddite workers claimed inspiration from a mythical leader, Ned Ludd, whose office was supposedly in Sherwood Forest, and they pointed to a world of work in which skills would be valued, workers treated as equal producers rather than factory "hands," and machines outlawed. Their efforts failed, as did more ambitious unionization attempts in textiles and mining during the 1820s and early 1830s. But the resentment of the new working class that the factories had assembled could scarcely be denied. The industrial revolution created a new division between the directors of manufacturing, the owners, and the workers they sought to control. To many observers, this was one of the essential and deeply troubling features of the wider industrial revolution. A middle-class traveler to Manchester in 1842, W. Cooke Taylor, put it this way in a published travel account:

> As a stranger passes through the masses of human beings which have accumulated round the mills and print works … he cannot contemplate these "crowded hives" without feelings of anxiety and apprehensions almost amounting to dismay. The population, like the system to which it belongs, is NEW; but it is hourly increasing in breadth and strength. It is an aggregate of masses, our conceptions of which clothe themselves in terms that express something portentous and fearful … as of the slow rising and gradual swelling of an ocean which must, at some future and not distant time, bear all the elements of society aloft upon its bosom, and float them Heaven knows whither. There are mighty energies slumbering in these masses. … The manufacturing population is not new in its formation alone;

it is new in its habits of thought and action, which have been formed by the circumstances of its condition, with little instruction, and less guidance, from external sources.

Change Generates Change

By the 1820s, then, Britain's industrial revolution had introduced new technologies in cotton and other textiles, in pottery and metallurgy, and in aspects of coal mining. It had generated an unparalleled export surge that brought Britain's achievement home to peoples almost around the world. It had destroyed several traditional manufacturing sectors at home and abroad. It had introduced factory organization to many branches of production and had prompted a massive growth in British cities. It had created a dynamic new business class and an even more novel, as well as more numerous, working class. Even in a society already heavily commercial, with an important manufacturing sector, it had fundamentally altered the framework of social and economic life.

And the revolution would not stop. Innovations were not constant, but they recurred. Existing machines became more refined; the number of spindles on a cotton-spinning machine, for example, increased periodically, and the increase greatly heightened production per worker. The number of workers in major industries grew inexorably. So did the average size of factories and firms, their growth permitting greater specialization of labor and more bureaucratic management. These developments brought innovation in business practices and labor conditions beyond what the initial industrial revolution had required. A measure of the persistent change was output: In 1830 Britain produced about 24 million tons of coal, four-fifths of the world's total; by 1870 the figure was 110 million, still half of all the coal mined around the world. British pig iron production was 700,000 tons in 1830; thirty years later it had more than quintupled, to almost 4 million tons. Raw cotton imports rose sixfold in the twenty years after 1830; in this period also, the average productivity per worker doubled. All this meant steadily rising exports. By 1870 British exports exceeded those of France, Germany, and Italy combined, and they were three times the level of exports by the United States. Rising output boosted industrial profits, which provided additional capital for still further changes, and began to permit some definite if modest improvements in the standard of living of most workers even as income inequality continued to increase.

The ongoing industrial revolution in Britain involved more than expansion from an earlier base. It also meant radical new directions. A new breakthrough in metallurgy in 1856 brought changes greater in many ways than those previously created by the use of coke and coal. Henry Bessemer (along with inventors in other countries) worked on the problem of removing chemical impurities, in particular carbon, from raw iron (called pig iron). The conventional procedure demanded extremely labor-intensive operations, as highly skilled workers called puddlers stirred molten ore to remove the carbon. After repeated experimentation, Bessemer found that altered furnace design could accomplish the same results automatically; a blast of compressed air passed through the molten iron would extract the carbon. Not only were labor costs reduced, but the Bessemer converter made possible the construction of much larger blast furnaces, another huge productivity gain. Finally, the same procedures enabled industry to use the controlled reintroduction of carbon to make steel, a much tougher metal than iron but previously extremely expensive to manufacture. An industry already transformed was transformed anew, in a pattern that would be repeated often as the industrial revolution proceeded.

The most dramatic extension of industrialization in Britain after the initial decades occurred in the field of transportation. As output grew, pressure on transportation facilities inevitably increased: Goods had to be carried to market, raw materials to the places of manufacture. Improved roads and, especially, the spate of canal building helped, but inventors—aware from prior industrial experience that concerted experiments could produce dramatic results—looked for more genuine innovation. Initiatives with rail transport had already begun in the coal mines; the first steam engine for hauling coal out of the mines on tracks was introduced in 1804. In 1821 a group of inventors and entrepreneurs chartered a railway line between Darlington, a mining center, and the port of Stockton. Some of the wagons were pulled on rails by horses, but locomotives were also developed, under the guidance of George Stephenson. The first full-scale locomotive was unveiled in 1825, but its frequent breakdowns almost resulted in cancellation of any further experiments. An improved model featuring a larger boiler that could produce greater heat was tested in 1827 and put to regular use just a few months later. With this success established, a more ambitious rail line was opened in 1829 between the cotton port of Liver-pool and the great factory center in Manchester. A contest was set up for locomotive design, and one model attained a speed of twenty-eight miles per hour—an achievement marred, however, by a breakdown before the test was completed. More reliable models operated at about sixteen miles per hour, and this speed was sufficient to launch a spate of railway building in Britain and, soon, elsewhere.

Developed at about the same time were steam-driven ships (the first transatlantic steamship lines opened in 1838), and these and railroads plus faster communication via the newly invented telegraph, truly revolutionized the conveyance of goods, people, and information. More bulk could be transported over longer distances at greater speed than ever before. This result of industrialization also generated additional change. Labor recruitment could reach out more widely. Coal and iron (and soon steel) production had to expand simply to meet the demand generated by railroad construction and operation. The industrial revolution was beginning to feed itself, sprouting new branches to deal with the opportunities presented by prior developments. This same acceleration inevitably attracted attention elsewhere to the wonders of Britain's achievement. A growing number of countries judged the power of Britain's transformation not only in economic but also in military terms, and this dual interest was yet another spur to the ongoing momentum of the revolution.

CHAPTER NINE

New Causes

Why Did the Industrial Revolution Happen, and Why Did it Happen in Eighteenth-Century Britain?

Peter N. Stearns

Explaining the industrial revolution is a challenge to analysts of history. New kinds of debates have surfaced recently, particularly through attempts to take a more global approach. Identifying the factors that caused the industrial revolution is vital not simply as a historical exercise but as the basis for understanding the complexity of the challenges awaiting societies that tried to establish an industrial revolution even after Britain showed the way. The variety of developments that combined to create the first industrial revolution had somehow to be replicated, though not necessarily in identical fashion. This same daunting variety helps explain why a number of regions have not managed to launch full-scale industrialization to this day. Complex causes persist as a factor in world affairs.

Not surprisingly, historians have offered different emphases. Occasionally, industrialization is presented as flowing from a few dramatic inventions and from some new thinking about the economy, notably Adam Smith's market-oriented theories issued in 1776 that stressed the importance of vigorous economic competition free from government controls as a means of generating innovation and growing prosperity. Inventions were involved, of course—but why did they occur? And why did Britain produce more inventions than other countries (followed, in the formative decades of industrialization, by France and the United States)? New economic theories helped produce some policies favorable to industrialization, but these did not cause it; they came too late, and they affected too few people. Any explanation of the industrial revolution must account for new behaviors on the part of literally thousands of people: the entrepreneurs who gradually moved toward a factory system, the workers who staffed the factories, the investors who provided the capital, the consumers who eagerly accepted the machine-made products. A number of powerful factors had to combine to generate a change as substantial as even the early phases of industrialization.

For the industrial revolution to occur, considerable investment funds were required—the new machines were expensive, far costlier than any manufacturing equipment previously devised, even in the very small factories that characterized much early industry. Also needed was access to raw materials, including textile fibers, but particularly coal and iron, the sinews of the industrial revolution. Government interest in supporting economic innovation was a factor, and various kinds of specific government policies helped. Of major importance was an available labor force that did not have more agreeable employment options, for although some workers might be attracted to the industrial life because of high pay for their particular skills, the excitement of innovation, and greater independence from traditional family and community controls, most workers entered factories because they had little choice. Finally, industrialization, particularly in its first manifestation in Britain, required an aggressive, risk-taking entrepreneurial spirit that would drive businesses to venture into innovation. All these ingredients must be considered in connection with the causes of the industrial revolution. To be sure, recent reminders also affect analysis, reminders of how gradual the process was—how factory firms developed often as part of a very slow, multigenerational evolution from domestic manufacturing operations to a new willingness to organize and subordinate manufacturing labor. The industrial revolution need not be explained as a dramatic single eruption or a rapid, coordinated set of changes; early steps in industrialization help account for later ones, as the revolution rippled out from the minority of the population initially involved. Still, the challenge of explaining the process remains considerable.

Several basic factors were generally widespread in northwestern Europe by the eighteenth century; others were more particular to Britain. A large seam of coal ran from Britain through Belgium and northern France to the Ruhr valley in Germany, and the most intense early industrialization developed along this coal seam. Iron ore deposits also existed in western Europe, in some cases close to the coal sources. Without these raw materials—and especially coal as the energy source for smelting metal and powering the steam engine—early industrialization would have been impossible. Western Europe also had abundant wool and, through already established colonial trade, initial access to cotton (grown in the southern colonies of British North America and in parts of Asia).

The key resources, which had, of course, been sitting in the ground for many millennia, facilitated the industrial revolution by their presence, but they did not cause it. Far more important was the impact of the scientific revolution in western Europe during the seventeenth century. Few scientific discoveries directly affected early industrial technology, though the work on gases and chemicals was relevant, particularly to Watt's work on the steam engine; the fuller marriage of science and industry occurred only after the 1830s, when the industrial revolution was already well advanced. Science did, however, help persuade people that nature could be rationally understood and controlled. It promoted an outlook attuned to change and generated widespread new interest in technical experiments. Definitions of science, from the pens of such experimenters as Francis Bacon in England, had urged its application to material conditions. It was no accident, then, that a vast refocusing of Europe's intellectual orientation preceded the industrial revolution itself.

Europe's commercialization also helped set the context for the industrial revolution. Many Europeans were familiar with production for the market or were accustomed to buying some of the goods they needed rather than manufacturing every subsistence item locally. Habits of this sort were obviously essential to the industrial revolution, during which they were greatly extended. Like the scientific revolution, the expansion of commercial activities in the seventeenth century formed a vital precondition for industrialization. Through the domestic manufacturing system, direct links followed from commercial endeavors more generally. Further, during the eighteenth century Europe's increasing commercial system generated important changes in banking. England and several other countries established national banking systems, which facilitated nationwide marketing and thus expanded the opportunities for manufacturing and sales.

Commercial experience as a factor should not be overly stressed, however. Even in business-minded Great Britain, the new banks rarely lent money to industrial firms; they focused on merchant and real estate operations. Nor did many established merchants become involved in the early factories. Factories were regarded as risky and dirty, and respectable people, even in the business community, kept some distance. Early industrialists most commonly came from artisanal or manufacturing backgrounds, though the collaboration of individual merchants and landlords, particularly in the expensive operations of metallurgy, was vital. Commercial experience and commercial institutions prepared the industrial revolution, but some gaps remained to be filled before striving industrialists linked up with the existing commercial operations.

Another vital ingredient of Europe's industrial context—this one also taking shape before the industrial revolution but gaining ground steadily immediately before its advent—involved Europe's growing role in world trade. From the late fifteenth century onward, west European countries, ultimately headed by France, the Netherlands, and Britain, had won increasing control over international commerce. European ships and merchant companies dominated international trade, even in some cases in which exchanges did not directly involve Europe at all. Increasingly, a hierarchy emerged in the international economy, in which Europeans acquired minerals and agricultural goods from other areas (including their colonies in the Americas, India, and elsewhere) and in return sold manufactured products, including fine furniture, cloth, and metal goods such as guns. Because Europeans could price their goods to include the cost of processing, they were in general able to profit from the exchange. Not all parts of the world actively engaged in trade with western Europe at this point, but parts of eastern Europe (which sent grain, furs, and timber supplies), the Americas (precious metals, sugar, and tobacco), and India and Southeast Asia (spices, tea, and gold) added steadily to western Europe's wealth. The active slave trade that Europeans ran between Africa and the Americas was another source of profit.

Europe's role in preindustrial world trade set up the industrial revolution in several ways. Growing amounts of commercial experience developed through the trading companies, and new technologies relating to shipbuilding and warfare received impetus. Governments were encouraged to pay attention to the importance of fostering trade, though this attention at times led to heavy-handed efforts at control. Trade leadership helped stimulate a taste for new products. Growing interest in cotton cloth originated first from trade with India, particularly in Britain. The British government then sought (from the 1730s onward) to encourage cotton manufacturing at home and to prevent undesirable dependence on foreign manufacturing by banning cotton imports; this ban had the additional effect of reducing

India's economic vitality and opening India to British goods. At the same time, Britain used its holdings in India and particularly the southern colonies in North America to provide raw cotton for its new textile branch. Above all, foreign trade, including colonial trade, expanded the markets for European manufacturing and thus contributed directly to one of the obvious reasons to seek more productive technologies. Trade also provided capital through the growing wealth of many business and landowning groups. Thus, Europe's industrial revolution, which was to have such dramatic effects on the wider world, stemmed in great part from Europe's ability to draw disproportionately on world resources.

Three Approaches: Minimal, Western, and Global

Three approaches currently vie for attention in explaining the industrial revolution, though they overlap to some extent.

The first approach, and the most recent, urges that Europe, even including Britain, was not very different from other leading manufacturing centers like China and India; therefore, a causation scheme that relies heavily on European distinctiveness is off the mark. This view again follows from historians' growing realization that China and India benefited hugely from the world economy of the sixteenth and seventeenth centuries, earning huge profits in U.S. silver for their exports. Just like Europe, in broad outline, China had a strong merchant sector, widely sought manufactured exports, and much available labor. So why did Europe industrialize first? Simply because of its colonies, which provided cheap raw materials, new capital, and some additional spur to export manufacturing for colonial markets, plus the sheer accident that British coal mines, unlike the Chinese mines, flooded easily and so encouraged the invention and use of the steam engine to pump out water. It turned out that the engine had wider applicability as well.

This comparative explanation deserves consideration, particularly when the industrial revolution is regarded as a global event. It may seem somewhat barebones in accounting for such a huge economic change. It also does not explain China's slowness in copying Europe's new industrial lead, though other factors may enter here.

The second explanation is more familiar, and in emphasizing really distinctive Western qualities, it is almost a polar opposite of the minimalist approach. Even in this argument, Western distinctiveness no longer rests on some once-cherished staples, like Adam Smith's economic theories, which urged market competition rather than state regulation, or even a special entrepreneurial ethic, though these may still merit some consideration. Rather, in this view attention goes to governments eager to encourage economic growth as part of military competition, and thus willing to improve infrastructure (initially, roads and canals) and banking facilities while backing merchant activities as well. It stresses the surge of new consumerism that flowed through western Europe in the seventeenth and eighteenth centuries, which created new eagerness for goods like cheap but fashionable clothing and tableware. Stylish clothing, indeed, became so important that theft rates soared in the eighteenth century, a sure sign of a growing market for less expensive, but eye-catching, machine-made goods like colorful cotton cloth. The Western distinctiveness approach also credits the scientific revolution, not only in contributing knowledge that aided new inventions like Watt's improved steam engine, but in creating a wider approval of greater control of the environment and a wider expectation of progress in this world, rather than in heaven.

The final pattern of explanation places particular emphasis on Europe's position in the world as the basic source of the industrial revolution, but in contrast to the explanation by the minimalists it emphasizes the special importance of European commercial power and global exploitation. From world trade, including the slave trade, Europe gained new levels of capital essential to take risks on new inventions. From world trade, supplemented by an increasingly commercial domestic economy, Europeans developed a growing middle class, from which most of the new industrialists would emerge, and a taste for pleasurable goods that would feed the expanding consumer markets. From world trade, Europeans learned about the appeal of cotton cloth (from India) or porcelains (from China), which spurred efforts to generate factory substitutes back home. From world trade Europeans learned the profits to be made in selling processed goods globally, while seeking cheap raw materials in return. And if this imbalance could be enhanced by special measures, like British efforts to discourage Indian cotton production in favor of Britain's nascent industry, so much the better. The industrial revolution, in this model, emerged from the exploitative advantages Europe was already gaining in the world's markets, and of course it would extend the possibility of exploitation even further in the nineteenth century. The emphasis is on the global context of the industrial revolution and also on the special position Europe had already achieved in this context, which explains both industrialization and the West's long (though not permanent) leadership in the whole process.

All three approaches have analytical merit. They can, of course, be combined to some degree. But a certain amount of choice, particularly between seeing the industrial revolution as a global economic result from the outset and viewing it as the product of some special Western combination, is essential. The debate, in other words, stimulates a more precise assessment of historical factors, but it ultimately requires some reasoned prioritization.

Trigger: Why the Eighteenth Century?

All the factors pushing for the industrial revolution accelerated by the eighteenth century: The results of new science began to create a wider outlook; the Enlightenment, as an intellectual movement, brought new interest to technical progress and more discussion of the most effective economic policies; the growth of consumer expectations encouraged new markets; and Europe's world trade position improved steadily as well, particularly with new moves into India. The rapid expansion of domestic manufacturing gave some workers new spending money and growing urban contacts, which promoted new kinds of purchases and prepared an industrial labor force. Growing global trade helped build up domestic capital and provided further evidence of wider markets for manufactured goods.

Capping these developments, and arguably providing a final push, were the effects of a true population explosion, coming after several decades, in the seventeenth century, of demographic stagnation. Food was crucial. The lack of major agricultural changes in Europe between the late Middle Ages and the 1690s was ironic, given Europe's commercial advance. By the 1690s, this anomaly had begun to yield, the result being an agricultural basis for further economic change, via population growth. After long hesitations because the goods were not mentioned in the Bible, west Europeans began to grow calorie-rich New World crops, headed of course by the potato. Again, larger world history fed industrialization. Further, with the Dutch leading, new methods of draining and fertilizer expanded the available land and fertility. With more food came more people.

Rapid population growth resulted from new food supplies and other developments such as a temporary lull in major plagues. There was also a pause in the most devastating kinds of warfare between 1715 and 1792. Increased population pushed workers to seek new, even unpleasant, kinds of jobs, provided growing markets for inexpensive manufactured goods, and prodded even some prosperous families to seek economic innovation. An eastern French family, the Schlumbergers, was a case in point. In the 1760s the head of the family ran an artisan shop, producing cloth but displaying no particular business dynamism. He had twelve children; that all of them lived to adulthood was somewhat unusual but illustrative of the impact of population growth in a single-family context. Simply in order to provide for his brood in the accustomed respectable middle-class fashion, Schlumberger had to expand his textile operations, hiring domestic manufacturing workers and then tentatively introducing some powered equipment. His children, building on their father's example, became dynamic industrialists in the early nineteenth century, creating large textile and machine building factories and sponsoring the first local rail line. Population upheaval promoted economic dynamism in a number of ways and at various levels of the initial industrialization process in western Europe.

Britain as a Special Case

Finally, why was Britain, among the several areas of western Europe in which relevant changes had been taking shape, in the vanguard? Within the larger west European context, there were several special features in Britain. Population growth was extremely rapid in the eighteenth century. Its effects, in freeing the available labor from agriculture, were magnified by major agricultural changes. British landlords successfully pried land away from smallholding farmers through the government's Enclosure Acts. These required farmers to enclose their fields, usually by planting hedges, but the expense was beyond many small farmers, who had to sell out to the landlords. British agriculture became dominated by large estates, and although these employed many workers, they did not absorb a growing population as readily as peasant-dominated agriculture proved able to do elsewhere. Thus, there were hungry workers eager for new options. The enclosed estates, in turn, increased agricultural market production, providing food for growing cities.

British artisans were also unusual. Most urban artisans in western Europe belonged to guilds, which tried to protect members' working conditions by limiting new technology and preventing any employer from creating undue inequality or threatening wage rates by hiring too many workers. Guilds were ideal for a relatively stable economy, but they definitely inhibited both rapid labor mobility and changing techniques. Britain had once boasted a guild system, but it had virtually disappeared by the eighteenth century. The result was twofold: Employers had unusual freedom to bring new workers into established branches of production, and they were at liberty to tinker with new methods—perhaps the most important single source of Britain's lead in inventions.

Britain's extensive international trade provided capital and markets and also supplies of vital materials such as cotton. The British aristocracy was more favorable to commerce than its counterparts on the European continent; some British landlords directly participated in setting up new mines and manufacturing, and tolerance for commercial development was high. The British government favored economic change. Tariff regulations in the eighteenth century, such as the barriers to the importation of cotton cloth from India, spurred new industries. Other laws that discouraged the export of new machinery or designs impeded rapid imitation elsewhere of British gains. Laws made the formation of new companies relatively easy and officially banned combinations of workers—what we would call unions—and this ban, in turn, constrained protest. During the eighteenth century a number of local governments began to build better roads, and then a wave of canal building developed at the end of the century. The new infrastructure facilitated the movement of both raw materials and finished goods. At the same time, the British government did not attempt to regulate manufacturing extensively. Other European governments, though often eager to promote economic growth, tended to control manufacturing with regulations about product quality, techniques, and some working conditions. The British state was less interventionist. This was not always an advantage, as we shall see in other industrialization cases, but it may have served well in setting a favorable framework for the first industrial revolution.

Simple luck in terms of natural resources also aided Britain. It had excellent holdings in coal and iron, which were often located quite close together. The island nation had not only coastal waterways but good navigable rivers, which further facilitated the transport of the two materials that were so vital to early industrialization but were extremely heavy and costly to move over land. Britain was also running low on timber supplies by the early eighteenth century and had to search for alternative fuels, notably coal. This necessity, in turn, spurred industrial development, from the adaptation of the initial steam engine for mine pumping to the use of coal for smelting iron.

Finally, Britain apparently provided an optimal setting for producing individuals inclined to taking risks in business. Good market opportunities and an extensive preindustrial manufacturing system formed part of this framework. New ideas about science and material progress spread more rapidly in Britain than in most other European countries. A relatively small government meant limited chances for success by seeking bureaucratic jobs. Furthermore, Britain tolerated a number of Protestant religious minorities such as the Quakers, though this indulgence was incomplete: Protestants who were not members of the established Anglican church could not attend universities or gain government employment. This ambivalent situation encouraged members of these minorities, eager to demonstrate God's favor, to seek opportunities in business. Certainly the Protestant minorities produced a disproportionate number of early manufacturers, who were stimulated by a belief that disciplined work, frugality, and economic drive were pleasing in the sight of God, and who were eager to get ahead where the chances lay—through entrepreneurial initiative.

In sum, Britain concentrated many of the changes developing generally in western Europe and added an array of special factors ranging from flukes of nature to new forms of callous manipulation of agricultural labor. Quite possibly the more general shifts taking place

FIGURE 9.1 **In the 1800s, England's expanded and improved industries caused towns such as Sheffield, located in northern England, to grow in population and importance. Sheffield factories produced high-quality steel, silver-plated items, and other metal goods. (Courtesy of the Mansell Collection Limited. Reprinted by permission.)**

throughout Europe would have generated an industrial revolution elsewhere by the early nineteenth century; the uniqueness of the British combination should not be exaggerated. Nevertheless, the fact was that Britain came first and that its leadership can be explained.

For at least a half century the nation's effective monopoly on the industrial revolution was scarcely challenged. British industry enabled the country to hold up against the much larger population of France during the wars of the French Revolution and the Napoleonic era. By the 1830s Britain's industrial lead was so obvious, and its related need and ability to export cheap machine-made manufactured goods were so great, that the government changed its basic tariff policy. Britain became a pioneer in free trade, allowing imports of food and raw materials that helped keep prices (and wages) down while relying on manufacturing exports to balance the trade exchange and even to show a tidy national profit.

Britain was indeed pouring manufactured goods into the markets of the world. Machine-made textiles cut into customary production not only in Latin America but also in Germany. British iron products undersold traditional charcoal-smelted metal in France. Here, obviously, was a rude challenge. But here also was an opportunity. Britain's success in industrialization added another ingredient to the changes taking place in western Europe. Continental businesses and governments began to wake up to the possibility of copying British machine design and factory organization, realizing they must stir themselves lest they be engulfed in a British industrial tide. The industrial revolution began to spread.

For after Britain took the industrial lead, the whole question of causation takes on a different cast: The British model, and British success (including military success against Napoleon's forces), became causes in their own right for societies ready and able to recognize the message. Still, however, the analytical challenge is not over. For some societies imitated quickly, a fact suggesting that they had conditions very similar to those spurring industrialization in Britain or that they could supply alternative spurs. Other societies did not or could not follow up so readily, because they were defined by different economic, political, and cultural factors. In fact, the next industrial revolutions extended the phenomenon in the West alone; only later would some other societies follow suit (though often with impressive results), in a process that remains globally uneven to the present day.

Topic Six Questions

1. Explain the importance of the following innovations to British industrialization: the steam pump, which led to the Watt steam engine, and Henry Cort's reverberatory furnace.
2. Explain the changes in the cotton textile industry in the eighteenth century. Quantify the impact of these changes on British cotton exports.
3. Provide five benefits to British living standards due to industrialization.
4. Provide five negative consequences to the welfare of Britons during early industrialization.
5. Provide five detailed explanations as to why Britain industrialized first.

Topic Seven

The Second Industrial Revolution and the Growth of the World Economy

CHAPTER TEN

The Economic Development of Europe in the Nineteenth Century (IV)

The Revolution in Transport and Communications

Giovanni Luigi Fontana

Roads and Canals

Important technical discoveries that could be qualified as true inventions, and a combination of innovations that improved their performance revolutionized the ways in which goods, people and information travelled, over short and long distances. At the end of the eighteenth century, the speed of travel was still conditioned by the use of animal power or by navigation along rivers, canals and coasts. This limited the chances of extending productive activities and increasing exchanges. The railway, the steamship and telegraphy opened up a new era, as much in transport over land and sea as in communications. The new means of transport did not bring about the industrial revolution, which had begun before they appeared, but they had the effect of considerably speeding it up and continually expanding it. In 1815, it took forty hours to travel from Paris to Calais in a stagecoach; in 1914, a fast train took three hours and fifteen minutes. Heavy sailing ships, which were conditioned by wind directions and strengths, and sailed only when the captain thought fit, were replaced, in the second half of the nineteenth century, by regular steam services that transported people and valuable goods to different continents at much higher speeds. Thanks to telegraphy and a network of underwater cables, people in business and commerce could communicate almost in 'real time', from one hemisphere of the earth to the other. After the triumph of the train and the establishment of steamships, in the nineteenth and twentieth centuries, the automobile was to herald the revival of the high road, while in 1914 aviation was preparing to become more than just a sports feat.[1] Since it enabled the factors of production to be transferred, and the finished products to be distributed practically anywhere, transport was not only a commercial means of exchange, but itself also became part, and an important part, of the means of production.[2]

1 J. Heffer and W. Serman, *Il XIX secolo 1815–1914. Dalle rivoluzioni agli imperialismi*, p. 51.

2 C. Wilson, 'Transport as a factor in the history of economic development', in A. Vannini Marx (ed.), *Trasporti e sviluppo economico. Secoli XII–XVIII, Florence*, 1973, pp. 313–21.

Numerous connections can be established between the transformation of transport and economic development. The theory that the market was the driving factor and regulator of the economic system 'began to be developed just when the revolution in transport and communications was taking place, which in the middle decades of the nineteenth century, transformed the traditional relationship of man with space and the very dimensions of the planet'.[3] However, right from the very start of the industrial revolution, the changes taking place in the sector were being felt. Indeed, one of the main prerequisites of the British industrial revolution was the construction of a dense network of canals that made it possible to cut the cost of transporting raw materials and finished products by about three-quarters of the cost of transporting them overland. Until the 1840s the main investments were channelled into canals and the road network. In England the road network, with all its branches, reached even the remotest village. After the end of the seventeenth century, road maintenance was transferred from the parishes, which made use of the *corvée* system, to toll trusts. By the mid-eighteenth century, 3,400 miles of turnpike roads were in the care of trusts. Capital was private and the revenue from the local trusts was often insufficient to cover expenses. By the early nineteenth century only 6 per cent of the roads were in good condition. At any rate, 3,873 trusts managed 20,000 miles of turnpike roads in 1829 and in 1836 they reached their maximum extent of 22,000 miles, by which time the railways were beginning to compete with the roads and canals.

In many parts of Europe, only the major roads were kept in good condition, primarily to make it easier to move troops. The rest of the road system was given over to local authorities for their maintenance; but the local authorities had neither the financial resources nor the technical expertise required for keeping this up. France was the European country with the best network of communications. Finance came from public sources, and in the second half of the eighteenth century, although the network was particularly extensive, considerable progress was made in building new roads. Improvement in the road networks owed much to new systems of construction, such as those of the Corps des Ponts et Chaussées; this was set up in 1716 by the French to train engineers and manage road works, and was followed thirty years later by the Ecole of the same name. The Telford and McAdam techniques of construction also gradually spread all over Europe. In France, in the early nineteenth century, much of the 33,000 km network of trunk roads was started. The continual movement of troops made it necessary to build *routes impériales*, not only in France, but also in the north of Italy, Belgium and Germany.

Road building continued from 1815 to the middle of the century. Except in the northern states, Italy had to wait until unification before the road network was improved. Investment in road infrastructure came to a stop after the 1850s, and only when the automobile was invented did a new phase of investment guarantee the construction of a basic system for the

3 'cominciò ad essere elaborata proprio quando si compiva quella rivoluzione dei trasporti e delle comunicazioni che nei decenni centrali dell'Ottocento trasformò il tradizionale rapporto dell'uomo con lo spazio e le dimensioni stesso del pianeta'. C. Pavese, 'I trasporti e le comunicazioni', in P. Toninelli (ed.), *Lo sviluppo economico moderno*, p. 301.

mass transport of the twentieth century. The cost of overland transport decreased two to four times as a result of doubling the draught power of the horse: its performance increased even further with the construction of lighter carriages to replace the heavy coaches. With the advent of the railway, horse transport fell into disuse for long distances, while for short journeys it continued to be the main means until the early twentieth century.

Rivers and internal waterways had always been the most convenient, and least costly, route for trade, despite the difficulties of transport upstream, which was often very erratic and inconsistent. Barges took three to six days to go down the Rhine, from Strasbourg to Mainz, a distance of 220 km, but a month in the opposite direction. There was a great need for internal transport to be developed and modernized. On the one hand, this was because of the increase in maritime traffic, resulting from reduced transport costs and greater safety on the routes, and on the other hand, because of the increase in population, especially the urban population, that created a greater demand for inexpensive bulk goods. This demand could be met only by improving inland navigation. During the mercantilist period, great canals had been constructed in France, such as the one linking the Loire and the Seine, or the Languedoc canal that linked the Atlantic with the Mediterranean. They were also built in Spain, the Netherlands, Germany and Sweden, but especially in Britain, where river navigation was the natural complement not only to road, but also to coastal, transport. Between 1669 and 1749, more than 200 parliamentary measures were passed for improving internal communications, and over the next seventy years, £17 million were spent on building 2,000 miles of navigable waterways.[4] These were spontaneous initiatives promoted by local entrepreneurs. In Britain, during the first forty years of the nineteenth century, the construction of canals intensified. In continental Europe, canal construction was developed to a lesser degree than in Britain and the United States.

In 1812, the first European steamship, the *Comet*, made its appearance on the Clyde. By 1830, there were 315 British steamships with an overall capacity of 33,500 tons. British-built steamboats, with iron hulls to reduce the risk of fire, had already been at work on the Seine, the Rhône, the Loire and the Rhine for some time. To prevent the performance of the new boats from being affected by the seasonal variation in water level, impressive works to reconstruct the riverbanks were carried out, among which the most challenging project was to regulate the course of the Rhine. In France, especially in the thirty-five years between the fall of Napoleon and the Second Empire, the areas that were mainly involved were the industrial areas; new canals, such as the Saint-Quentin, built in 1810, were dug to link the coal-bearing regions to the urban markets, or to connect waterways carrying heavy traffic, like the Rhône–Rhine in 1834. Germany was behind with the building of canals, and 6,600 km of canal were built between 1873 and the First World War. The canals generally experienced growing competition from the railways, but the ultimate triumph of the railways was due not to any advantages in costs, but to better organization, to speed

4 *Ibid.*, p. 306.

and to the versatility of the service, except in a few areas like the Rhine valley, which had the advantage of an abundance of waterways. On the other hand, dry countries like Spain gained great advantages from the railway, and for all these reasons, no other innovation of the nineteenth century was so successful.

The Advent and Development of the Railways

The railway was the outcome of a combination of factors that had already existed before the nineteenth century: the rails used in mine galleries and ports, and to supplement canals in the British coal-bearing basins, trolleys and steam-powered machines. It became autonomous with the invention of the locomotive (1825), which was the most important invention in nineteenth century transport. After the introduction of the tubular boiler, the engineer George Stephenson (1781–1848) developed the Liverpool to Manchester line (1826–1829) in the heart of a great industrial area; it demonstrated the cost-effectiveness of the railway for the transport of both goods and passengers, with most of the technical problems being empirically solved at the same time. Subsequently, technical development followed two directions: seeking to achieve high speeds, and seeking to obtain the maximum energy to enable mass transport.

The first objective was achieved very rapidly and in 1835 a locomotive exceeded 100 kph. By the end of the century, journey speeds (excluding stops) had risen from 60 kph to 75 kph for French expresses, 40–55 kph for ordinary trains, while goods trains made do with a speed of 20–30 kph, which, however, was five to seven times faster than that of the horse-drawn wagon. In order to achieve the second objective, the weight and adhesion of locomotives was increased, the number of axles was doubled, and rolling stock, mounted on bogies, became longer. By 1865, a train could transport 200 tons and by 1900 as much as 2,500 tons.[5] Steel replaced iron and cast iron, and in the 1860s rail strength and wagon capacity increased. Continual refinements improved the performance of the railway. These included fuel economies made possible by compound boilers in 1876, and super-heating; better safety with the compressed air brake of 1868; gauge standardization and progress in management techniques. Natural obstacles were also surmounted: bridges, viaducts and tunnels enabled the railways to go across rivers, valleys and through mountains. In order to exploit traffic in northern Italy to their advantage, the German railways financed the boring of the St. Gotthard tunnel through the Alps (1872–1882), while their French competitors did likewise with the Simplon tunnel (1898–1906).

The expansion of the railways was exceptional: the 7,200 km that existed throughout the world in 1840 had risen to 925,000 km by 1906. Until then, the problem of having to finance projects on such a huge scale had never arisen, hence the diversity of solutions that were adopted, which ranged from private and public initiatives, to a combination of both.

5 J. Heffer and W. Serman, *Il XIX secolo 1815–1914*, p. 52.

At the beginning of the twentieth century, 70 per cent of the railway lines in the world belonged to private capitalist firms, the remaining 30 per cent to the state. However, by 1914 the capitalist model that regarded the railways as a wholly private concern and that predominated in the nineteenth century was to be found in only a few countries.[6] In Europe branch lines considerably reduced the profitability of investment, and thus at the start of the century, state ownership of the railways was preferred.

The railways reached their maximum density in the North Atlantic area. As Table 10.1 shows, it was in Great Britain that the railway system was conceived and adopted relatively quickly, in order to free traffic from the monopolistic exploitation of the canal owners. In 1835 alone, Parliament authorized investments of £15 million, more than had been spent on all the canals. This was a new, high-technology sector and it attracted investors. In England, it did not represent a factor for future economic development so much as an essential tool for sustaining the industrialization that was already under way. In short, the railways were a consequence of development, rather than a cause. There were thus no problems of finance or inadequacies in the mechanical and metallurgical industry to contend with. The British state could assume a marginal role in financing and constructing the network,

TABLE 10.1 **Construction cost of the railway network between 1830 and 1906**

Country	Cost (£ Millions)
United States	3,036
Great Britain	1,294
Germany	740
France	707
Russia	626
Habsburg Empire	468
India	266
Canada	262
Italy	205
Argentina	139
Australia	137
Belgium	87
Switzerland	59
Sweden	51

Source: J. Heffer and W. Serman, *Il XIX secolo. 1815–1914: dalle rivoluzioni agli imperialismi,* (ed.) S. Zaninelli, Milan, 1998, p. 54.

6 *Ibid.*, p. 55.

even though changes in the laws on capital companies (1825) enabled large enterprises to be set up with extensive share ownership. Similarly to what happened with the canals, the privately financed railways increased throughout the country without any co-ordination, until a special body was set up to co-ordinate the traffic in 1842.

In Britain, the railway spread to meet the demand for transport in a country that was already industrial. In the United States, which was second in the race to build railways, it spread to meet the demands of agriculture, which in its turn brought about rapid industrialization.[7] In short, instead of being a mere complement to the economic development already under way, as in Great Britain, in the United States, Belgium, France and Germany the construction of the railway network took on an important modernizing role. It motivated the engineering industry, stimulated *ad hoc* financing systems, and in the case of the United States—given the colossal size of the network—large-scale management systems; it heralded the subsequent development of the scientific organization of labour.

Belgium had always been one of the first to adopt British innovations, but being a country of limited size, the state took on the initiative of creating continental Europe's first network. The decision was also intended to underline the advantages of the country's newly won independence (1830), as was also the case with Italy later. Instead of the spontaneous development that took place in England, an organic system of transport was planned through state intervention, which provided the capital for its construction. The development of national ironworks and heavy engineering industries soon provided the materials to replace imports from Britain; between 1835 and 1842, 559 km of railway lines were built that linked the kingdom's wealthiest provinces together. The task of completing the secondary lines was left to private companies; these were initially British (900 km between 1845 and 1846) then Belgian, but they were successful only where the state could act as guarantor. The average cost of construction per mile (£16,500) was about half the British cost. In 1870, Belgium had about 3,000 km of railways (Table 10.2). Starting from this period, the state began buying back the private network at a low price, and by 1914 it owned 95 per cent of the total network. It could thus charge very low fares, and grant workers special season tickets, but it did not earn any great revenue. A similar model of development took place in Germany, and later in Russia.

Germany invested heavily in building and developing its railway network. The German states, and France, were the only other European areas involved in the pioneering stages of railway building (pre-1850). Around 1840, in the German areas, as well as in France, there were about 450 km each of lines in the mining districts and suburbs. Ten years later, Germany had 5,856 km of railway while France had only 2,915. In France the real take-off came during the Second Empire (1852), once the hostility of those advocating the completion of the canals had been overcome. In the German areas, steam navigation on

7 L. Girard, 'Trasporti', in H.J. Habakkuk and M. Postan (eds), *Storia economica Cambridge*, vol. VI, *La rivoluzione industriale e i suoi sviluppi*, Turin, 1974.

TABLE 10.2 **Extent of the railway network, 1840–1913 (km)**

Year	Great Britain	France	Belgium	Germany	Italy	Habsburg Empire	Russia	Europe	United States	World
1840	2,390	410	334	469	20	144	0	2,700	4,500	7,200
1850	9,757	2,915	854	5,856	620	1,357	501	23,100	14,400	37,600
1860	14,603	9,167	1,729	11,089	2,404	2,927	1,626	51,000	49,000	106,000
1870	20,000	15,544	2,897	18,876	6,429	6,112	10,731	101,300	85,400	205,200
1880	25,060	23,089	4,112	33,838	9,290	11,429	22,865	162,700	149,900	365,500
1890	27,820	33,280	4,526	42,869	13,629	15,523	30,595	208,000	249,700	566,900
1900	30,070	38,109	4,562	51,678	16,429	19,229	53,234	257,900	292,200	707,500
1910	32,184	40,484	4,679	61,209	18,090	22,642	66,581	321,600	358,400	925,300
1913	32,623	40,770	4,776	63,378	18,873	44,800	70,156	–	400,197	–

Source: Adapted from J. Heffer and W. Serman, Il XIX secolo. 1815–1914: *dalle rivoluzioni agli imperialismi*, (ed.) S. Zaninelli, Milan, 1998, p. 54; P. Toninelli, *Lo sviluppo economico moderno dalla rivoluzione industriale alla crisi energetica*, 1750–1973. Venice, 1996, p. 612; V. Zamagni. Dalla rivoluzione industriale all'integrazione europea, Bologna, 1999, p. 51.

the Rhine and the rivers west of the Elbe delayed the start of the railway, but in 1839 the Leipzig to Dresden line was opened, followed by lines transversely connecting the north-south navigable river valleys. By 1847, the Rhine and Berlin lines already reflected the supremacy of Prussia.

The construction of the German railway system did not follow a standard formula. It relied on government and private initiative, as well as on the heavy investment of foreign capital. Like the American railways, those in Germany were built on 'spartan' lines, with average costs of only £11,000 per mile, to which the lower cost of land also contributed. Locomotives initially came from the United States and Britain, but by 1843 domestic production already accounted for over half the demand. Initially governments avoided investing in railways, but since they could not fail to notice their military and political role, they took advantage of loans and bonds, in order to take control of a large number of companies. By 1860, the state was running 55 per cent of the Prussian network (see Table 10.1).[8]

In France before 1850, investment in the railway system was limited. Because it was impossible to finance it publicly in such a large country, the prevailing system was to grant temporary concessions to private industry, under state control. A law in 1842 provided for roles to be shared. The government would decide on the structure of the network, and assume responsibility for the purchase of land and infrastructure, including ballast, bridges, tunnels and stations; concessionary companies were responsible for the rolling stock, work force and organization of services under a system of contracts that were revised several times because of deficits in the running costs. British and French capital only gradually came to be invested in what seemed to be a sector too closely controlled by government policies and requirements. In 1848, France had only 1,800 km of railway, but by 1870 over

8 C. Pavese, *I trasporti e le comunicazioni*, p. 318.

15,000 km. In 1878, the state bought back 2,600 km, but by 1908 the whole western network was in deficit.

In the first half of the nineteenth century, in other countries, there was no lack of isolated initiatives; often the railway had been limited to connecting the capital with the sovereign's summer residence.

The twenty-year period between 1850 and 1870, which saw the construction of the European continental and North American networks, has been defined as the 'Golden Age of the railway'. In Europe 50,000 miles of new lines were built, compared with the 15,000 that had been operating in mid-century. The greatest development was in France, with 9,300 miles at an investment of 7 billion francs, thanks to capital being raised by the Crédit Mobilier, owned by the Pereire brothers. State guarantees to pay the interest on railway company bonds enabled it to catch up with Germany—in 1869 both had about 17,000 miles of track—and to rival Britain as regards quality of equipment and rolling stock. The lower availability of coal stimulated French engineers to adopt energy-saving solutions, such as double expansion locomotives, which placed their railways at the cutting edge in Europe.

In the Baltic area, in eastern and Mediterranean Europe, the railway era really started only after 1850. In Italy, the railway system was developed on the initiative of the government in the period after unification. Before unification, projects were very limited and mainly concentrated in the north of the country. The most important line was from Milan to Venice. The ruling class of the new kingdom of Italy saw the construction of a railway system as a fundamentally important condition for the consolidation of national unity, and the modernization of the country. However, because of the poor state of Italian industry, construction was achieved only by depending heavily on foreign countries for capital, as well as for fixed and rolling stock. Its meagre commercial success was moreover a heavy burden on the country's balance of payments.[9] In 1865, the network was privatized and concentrated in four mixed groups, with the intervention of foreign companies. The difficulties in this arrangement created a crisis in the system and, under the 1885 convention, led to a reorganization on French lines, whereby the national network was shared between three companies. From this period, better links with the iron and engineering sectors were created, which reduced the need for foreign help. The network continued to be extended; at the same time it created even greater disparity between the areas that were linked to it and those that were not. In 1905, the whole system was finally nationalized.[10] Other countries' experiences reflected their own particular political and financial circumstances. In the

9 G. Guderzo, 'A proposito dello sviluppo ferroviario in Italia dal 1850 al 1914. Aspetti geografici. economici e sociologici', *Bollettino della Società pavese di storia patria*, I–IV, 1972–1973, pp. 1–34.

10 V. Zamagni, 'Ferrovie e integrazione del mercato nazionale nell'Italia postunitaria', in *Studi in onore di G. Barbieri*, vol. III, Pisa, 1983, pp. 1635–49; S. Fenoaltea, 'Le costruzioni ferroviarie in Italia, 1861–1913', *Rivista di storia economica*, n.s., I, 1984, I, pp. 61–94; R. Lorenzetti (ed.), *La questione ferroviaria nella storia d'Italia. Problemi economici, sociali, politici e urbanistici*, Rome, 1989; A. Giuntini, *Contributo alla formazione di una bibliografia storica sulle ferrovie in Italia*, Milan, 1989.

Austro-Hungarian Empire, the state set up partnerships with foreign investors, while in Spain and Russia, foreign investment was seen as the best way to acquire new technologies.

The railways revolutionized the transport system: they caused the disappearance of the stagecoach, and limited traffic on the roads to the short hauls, and thus formed a complement to the railroads. The waterways were still used for heavy bulk goods, but no longer for transporting passengers and mail. The railways could reach areas that the waterways could not. In the last twenty years of the century—the third phase of railway building—the branch network in Europe was completed; the great international connections in Europe were created by means of the Alpine tunnels. Meanwhile transcontinental lines were also being built in North America, Asia and Latin America. By 1890, there were 208,000 km of track in Europe, compared with 51,000 km in 1860. The number of passengers had risen from 340 million to 1,750 million annually. In the United States there were 1,750 railway companies; thirty of them ran 66 per cent of the network of 167,000 miles, which exceeded the European network by 25 per cent.

Between 1883 and 1893, in the United States, the first coast-to-coast line was followed by another three, and by one in Canada. They were the main means of opening up the North American continent. The colonization of new territories, and the consolidation of anti-Chinese tsarist influence in Asia and the north Pacific, were made possible by over 6,000 km of the Trans-Siberian line (1891–1903). In the wave of European colonial, and imperial, expansion and with the support of British, French and German capital and technology, railways started to traverse Latin America, China, Africa and the Middle East. They were part of a whole network, which was connected to Europe by means of the ports. 'In the nineteenth-century collective imagination, when compared to the means of transport of seventy years earlier, the powerful and fast locomotives of the end of the century gave the measure of the break with the previous world.'[11]

Maritime Transport

The application of steel and iron, as well as technological improvements in the use of steam engines, also enabled great progress to be made in maritime transport. But the breakthrough for the steamship was more gradual than for the railways. The reason for this was not only the slow development of new technology for reducing fuel consumption and weight, but also competition from the sailing ships, which during the eighteenth century and the first half of the nineteenth, had greatly increased their speed and manoeuvrability. The four-masted clipper had evolved from the schooner, and was the pinnacle of sailing technology. It had a lower tonnage (3,000–5,000 tons) than other sailing ships, but it was faster, since it

11 'Nell'immaginario collettivo ottocentesco le potenti e veloci locomotive di fine secolo, raffrontate ai mezzi di trasporto di settant'anni prima, fornivano la misura della rottura con il mondo precedente'. C. Pavese, *I trasporti e le comunicazioni*, pp. 320–1.

could reach fifteen knots, 300 nautical miles a day, and thus was very useful over long distances. Between 1849 and 1875, it was used on the routes to India, the Pacific and Australia, without fear of competition from the steamship. By 1860, it was taking twelve to fourteen days to cross the Atlantic and about eighty from Liverpool to Melbourne, from Canton to New York and from San Francisco to New York. In 1869, the clipper was affected by the opening of the Suez Canal. This shortened journeys to India and Oceania, and changed the routes to the less windy inland seas. A number of sailing ships then started to adopt innovations that had been introduced on steamships: an iron hull and small steam engines to mechanize various operations such as the windlass, winch and capstan.

Until 1850, steam power brought progress to river rather than sea navigation. Initially, the steamship was in operation on the short sea routes. In 1818, the first sea connections were made on the Irish Sea and in 1821 between Dover and Calais. In the 1820s, they were started across the North Sea, the Baltic and the Mediterranean, with the transport of mail and passengers. From London to Calais it took twelve hours, and from Naples to Leghorn thirty-six. In 1838, the *Sirius*, a steamship with side paddle wheels and boilers working on distilled water, made the first crossing of the Atlantic entirely by steam. In 1840, the *Great Western* began regular mail steamer services, using mixed propulsion; in 1843, the *Great Britain* adopted the propeller, which required the use of gears to multiply the low number of revolutions of the engines.

In the middle of the century, the steamship still had sail rigging and resorted to mixed propulsion, to navigate in the event of engine failure. It was around 1860 that significant progress was made. Iron, and steel after 1879, was used to replace wood in the construction of the hulls, and reduced expenses for maintenance and wear. The propeller eventually replaced the paddle wheel. Double, and later triple, expansion compound engines (in 1869 and 1874 respectively) drastically reduced the working costs and the amount of coal that needed to be stored in the holds, while the amount of space for passengers and goods increased. Around 1880, auxiliary sails disappeared. Boilers with triple, and later quadruple, expansion led to greater cost-effectiveness, and enabled the tonnage and average speed of iron ships to be increased. Furthermore, steam was a labour-saving innovation, since crew numbers could be reduced.

In the 1890s, the tonnage of steamships ultimately surpassed that of sailing ships, but between 1860 and 1865 the sailing ships had a monopoly of traffic in passengers and emigrants to the United States, as well as the carriage of luxury goods. At the beginning of the twentieth century, steamships finally achieved supremacy. The first ones were built for the mixed transport of both goods and passengers, but later they became specialized. Merchant ships started to specialize even further, with vessels being dedicated to specific forms of transport, such as petroleum or frozen meat. In 1870, the first oil tankers connected the United States and Europe, and subsequently came to play an increasingly important role in international traffic.

Parallel to all these transformations, the maritime trade experienced unexpected rates of growth during the nineteenth century, initially with the construction of clippers, then of steamships. Predominance in shipbuilding, and sea power, remained a key element in British economic supremacy, at least until the First World War. In 1914, despite German and French competition, the merchant fleet was still one of the main sources of revenue for the United Kingdom. Whereas, at the end of the eighteenth century, Great Britain had a quarter of European shipbuilding capacity, a century later it was building more than half the ships in Europe. In 1875, the British had 1.9 million tons of steamships, against 4.2 million tons of sailing ships. In 1885, when the capacity of a single steamship equalled that of six sailing ships, Britain had 4 million tons of steamships, against 3.4 million tons of sailing ships. By 1890, the British had 5 million tons of steamships, which was 73 per cent of world tonnage; in Germany, 1.3 million tons of ships, out of 1.9 million tons, were of steel. Conversely, Norway, which like Canada and Italy had a large fleet of wooden ships, still had 1 million tons of sailing ships out of the total of 1.5 million tons.[12]

The new enterprises, based on the management of steamship lines, specialized in transport. Before the nineteenth century, there had been no regular ocean-going navigation service. In 1818, for the first time, American ship owners started a line with sailing ships setting sail from New York and Liverpool on fixed days, introducing a regular and punctual service that reduced uncertainty in the business field. This system was imitated by the steamship companies. They were subsidized by the government for postal services, and thus secured more profitable traffic.

Maritime navigation immobilized less capital than the railways, but it gave rise to significant investments in rebuilding ports and opening inter-oceanic canals. One of the most important projects of the whole nineteenth century was the opening of the Suez Canal, linking the Mediterranean with the Red Sea. 162 km long, and planned by Ferdinand de Lesseps, it was built between 1859 and 1869, after numerous technical, financial and diplomatic problems had been overcome. The duration of journeys between the countries of the North Atlantic, South East Asia and the Far East was considerably shortened. De Lesseps also planned a canal across the isthmus of Panama, but a combination of setbacks brought the enterprise (1881–1889) to a standstill. It was taken up again by the United States, with financial backing from the government, and finally completed in 1914.

The Economic Consequences

Means of transport can carry out a 'passive' function, namely the movement of goods and people, and an 'active' one, which is the promotion and multiplication of development.[13] By reducing costs, they free resources that can be channelled towards other

12 *Ibid.*, p. 326.

13 F.O. Voight, 'I compiti della moderna scienza dei trasporti', *Rivista internazionale di economia dei trasporti*, I, 1974, pp. 263 ff.

consumer products, and sustain economic growth.[14] The cost of transport can determine whether the movement of goods is hindered or boosted. One of the greatest economic outcomes of the transport revolution was the fall in maritime freight costs, and the steady reduction of railway tariffs. Lower freight costs came about because of increased competition; they seem to have been more a feature of the first half of the nineteenth century than the second, and therefore applied to sailing ships rather than steamships. But by 1910, freight tariffs were on average eight times lower than in 1820. Railway tariffs also decreased throughout the century. Lower transport costs made it much easier for people to travel; they greatly facilitated contacts and exchanges, as well as economic and social relations. The market for agricultural products could be opened up to a larger extent, and become more specialized. Manufacturing industries could obtain supplies of raw materials and essential intermediate goods more regularly and more cheaply, and could send their products everywhere. Cities could receive food produce, consumer goods and fuel more easily.

Economic geography was transformed. In the last twenty-five years of the nineteenth century, thanks to regular low-cost sea transport, the flow of American corn to Europe upset the cereal-producing economy of Europe. Marginal units of production, once protected by distance and geographical circumstances, were critically affected. Separate and exclusive economies increasingly lost the advantages deriving from their position. Furthermore, modern transport methods were an essential means not only for the rapid colonization of the American west, and the Argentinean pampas, but also for the opening up of Eurasian Siberia.

In general, the railways facilitated the integration of national and international markets, and the more rational allocation of economic resources. The construction of national railway networks triggered off a chain of transformations thanks to backward and forward linkages with other sectors of the economic system. Among the backward linkages was the mobilization of credit for financing investment. Since the railway sector was highly capital-intensive, it boosted forms of international co-operation between bankers and financiers; this was the case with the construction of the skeleton Italian railway system between 1860 and 1870, where English and French capital and technology predominated. The stock markets carried on a lively trade in railway bonds and shares, which were the principal shares of the time. During the Second Empire, the Paris market became the major centre for investment in the railways. Intense rivalry between the Pereire brothers and the Rothschilds over the financing of railway construction in the Mediterranean and Danube areas further enlivened the Paris market. In the face of competition from the financiers of Paris, Brussels and Vienna, London turned its attention to frontier countries, such as Australia, South Africa, India and Egypt, where the interests of the British Empire were considerable.

14 P.L. Spaggiari, *Trasporti, mobilità e sviluppo*, Parma, 1985; C. Pavese, *I trasporti e le comunicazioni*, p. 302.

Though to different degrees, and at different times, the railways played a driving role in economic development, since they involved a whole series of industries upstream in the production cycle. In particular, thanks to the multiplier effect of the investments, they propelled the construction industry, the iron and engineering industries (for infrastructure), and the services sector (for overall management). The forward linkages included market expansion, growth in the agricultural and food sectors, and the greater mobility of raw materials. But the labour market, company organization and the mechanization of office work also experienced far-reaching innovations thanks to the railways. Hundreds of thousands of people worked on building the national railway lines. They were the first great capitalist enterprises, with many delicate and complicated problems to solve; complex management techniques were developed, and the railways provided one of the earliest areas of employment for professional managers. The American railways were the first great enterprises with a multi-divisional structure, in which an articulated managerial hierarchy planned and co-ordinated the movement of trains; it also organized the traffic between the different operating units, and created a separation between company ownership and management. Innovative accounting techniques were adopted to deal with accounts relating to passengers, goods, fares, routes, timetables and cost effectiveness. By the end of the nineteenth century, new mechanical punch card systems were being used that were capable of rapidly processing enormous quantities of data.

The Telegraph and the Globalization of Information

Finally, the nineteenth century also saw important improvements in systems for spreading news and information. For over three centuries, the descendants of Francesco Tasso from Bergamo, who had run the postal services for the Venetian Republic and later the Habsburg Empire, had gradually extended the network to all the countries of the continent, by establishing themselves at the main courts of Europe. At the end of the eighteenth century, regular stagecoach services linked the main cities of Europe. In 1830, it took forty-five hours to get from London to Edinburgh at an average speed of 14 kph. French stagecoaches covered 200 km in a day, with 1.4 tons of goods and sixteen passengers and their luggage. In Prussia, it took forty hours to go from Berlin to Breslau, a distance of 300km.[15]

At that time, information travelled at the speed of horses. During the French Revolution (1792), the physicist Claude Chappe introduced the optic telegraph. By sending signals between positions that were visible to the eye, it was possible to send 8,464 words in code form; when visibility was good, a signal took twelve minutes to travel 300 km. Initially it was used for military purposes and by the police, but from 1830 its use was extended to business communications. Between 1830 and 1840, in Britain and France, the first lines

15 C. Pavese, *I trasporti e le comunicazioni*, p. 310.

serving the railways and the stock exchange were started, and later direct connections between the lines helped to spread a network of systems.

With the advent of fast transport systems like the railways, the information required for managing them needed to travel at even faster speeds. Several researchers devoted their energies to this, working independently. Cooke and Wheatstone developed discoveries that had been made earlier. The most original contribution, however, was made by Samuel Morse, an American, in 1835, who made a series of improvements to his telegraphic apparatus. His relay system sent back a signal automatically, by means of a code with a maximum of four impulses to distinguish each letter, which greatly extended its range and achieved high speeds of transmission. After 1843, different cities and continents were able to communicate with each other almost in 'real time', which meant hours and minutes rather than months and days, and once cables had been laid across the sea bed the world market was unified. British enterprises played a decisive role in laying the cables; in 1851 the first one was laid under the Channel, in 1866 cables crossed the North Atlantic, in 1872 they reached the Far East, and in 1874 Latin America. By 1902, when the two coasts either side of the Pacific were joined, the round-the-world network was complete. In 1914, 280,000 km out of the 516,000 km of underwater cables that had been laid down were controlled by British companies, both private and public. This was a powerful factor in confirming London, the capital of England, as the centre of the world market.

The effects of the symbiosis between telegraph and railway were thus extended to the financial market, and the 'railway mania' of 1840–1850 enormously extended the activities of the London stock exchange, giving rise to a dozen exchanges in the provinces that were linked to each other thanks to the telegraph'.[16] In the 1860s, in the main European countries, despatches from the stock exchange were far ahead of any others. The international telegraphic communication service called for measures to harmonize regulations and standardize technology, and was the first to do so, even preceding the railways and postal service. The first interconnections (Prussia–Austria, in 1849; France–Belgium in 1850) were followed in 1855 by the West European Telegraphic Union (between France, Belgium, Switzerland, the Kingdom of Sardinia and Spain). Ten years later, once the Morse code had been universally adopted in 1858, this led to the International Telegraphic Union, the first supranational administrative and technical organization. As regards the telegraph, in certain cases, finance first came from public sources and then passed into private hands (the United States) or vice versa. In Britain, in order to make up deficiencies and keep tariffs down the domestic network passed to the state; in Europe, it was the first case of the nationalization of a public service aimed at correcting distortions in the market.

Half a century after the appearance of the telegraph, the advent of the telephone, an invention of uncertain paternity, speeded up and intensified the spread of information even

16 'la railway mania degli anni 1840–1850 ampliò enormemente l'attività della Borsa di Londra facendo sorgere una dozzina di borse in provincia che comunicavano grazie al telegrafo'. *Ibid.*, p. 326.

further. Its appearance on the economic scene came about in 1877 because of the initiative of Bell. In 1879, the telephone transmitted 100 to 200 words a minute, instead of the fifteen to twenty of the telegraph, without any need for an operator. For the whole of the nineteenth century, it remained an eminently American innovation, limited to the world of business, 'since the usefulness of an apparatus within a network is based on the number and type of other users connected'.[17] Its use did not extend to private communication until the end of the century. By 1900 it served 6 per cent of households in the United States, but its main application was still limited to business. Finally, the way was paved for the invention of the radio and the creation of a system of mass communication by the first radio transmissions made by Guglielmo Marconi (1874–1937), in 1896.[18]

17 'perché un apparecchio in rete è utile in ragione del numero della tipologia degli altri utenti collegati'. *Ibid.*, p. 329.

18 These were sent from Poldhu, in Cornwall, England. (*Translator's note.*)

CHAPTER ELEVEN

The Economic Development of Europe in the Nineteenth Century (V)

International Exchanges and Monetary Systems

Giovanni Luigi Fontana

Europe and the World Economy

The network of international exchanges played a fundamental role in European economic development. By the start of the modern era, the European continent (particularly the Atlantic powers of Spain, Portugal, England and Holland) was at the centre of a dense network of international trade with the Americas, Asia and the coastal areas of Africa, and during the nineteenth century international trade experienced prodigious growth. With the revolution in transport, the entire world became a single market, where men, goods, capital and ideas became more mobile than they had ever been before. By 1913, the value of the international trade in goods was twenty-five times greater than it had been in 1820, and Europe dominated international exchange; more than three-fifths of world trade was carried out by eight nations. By far the greatest role was played by Great Britain, which in 1800 controlled 36 per cent of world trade, 27 per cent in 1840, and 23 per cent in 1873; even in 1914 it still controlled about 14 per cent. Until the 1880s, France was in second place, though a long way behind the leading country; however, at the beginning of the twentieth century, it was overtaken by Germany and the United States.

The development of exchange, which continued even during the protectionist period, but at a slower rate, led to an increasingly complex international economy, which remained firmly linked to the gold standard, because of the predominance of British trade and the stability of the pound sterling. During the nineteenth century, trade relations that already existed were further consolidated, while in other areas new links and balances were being formed. In the period between 1815 and the First World War, international trade and financial relations were intensified as a result of a number of factors which had a decisive influence.[1]

1 A.G. Kenwood and A.L. Lougheed, *The Growth of the International Economy, 1820–1990*, London and New York, 1992.

First, there was the technological progress that went with the British industrial revolution and the industrialization of the continent. The British cotton sector, for example, became totally dependent on imports of the raw material from Asia and the Americas, while, in the opposite direction, textile products, iron, steel, chemical and engineering products found new markets outside Europe. However, while on the one hand, technological innovation led to an increase in the international trade for low cost manufactured products, on the other, it led to production being imitated, with imported goods being replaced by goods produced domestically.

Second, there was a heavy increase in the natural resources used in manufacturing processes, and the flows of imports and exports within Europe, as well as to North America and the Third World areas increased considerably. Next, there was the revolution in transport and communications, which we have already analysed. In 1873, 27 million tons of goods were transported by steamship, but by 1898 this had increased to over 63 million tons. Commercial relations and political links were further consolidated by a series of projects like the Suez Canal (1869), the canal linking Rotterdam and the North Sea (1872), and the Panama Canal (1914), which also drastically reduced the cost of transporting goods to and from transoceanic destinations.

A further factor was the marked growth in world population. As we have already seen, the population of the planet rose from 900 million in 1800 to around 1.6 billion in 1900. European population growth led to unprecedented movements of people, which strengthened the economic, social and cultural links between different continents. There was greater mobility of labour than previously. Emigration caused salaries and incomes in the countries of emigration and immigration to converge.[2] Demand for consumer goods increased, as did the trade in products manufactured in Europe. The Old Continent increasingly came to depend for its food on produce from outside Europe. Imports of wheat are a case in point, and this will be discussed later in connection with European trade policies.

Finally there was the accumulation of capital. While England was largely self-sufficient as regards its supply of capital, the same could not be said of other European, or non-European, economies. The process of capital accumulation by the 'follower' countries was rapid, and large amounts of foreign investment were attracted by high growth performance.

The Triumph of Free Trade and the Development of International Trade

The development of international trade had been limited by high transport costs, by people's low purchasing power and by the poor variety of goods, but in the course of the nineteenth century it experienced an exceptional increase. Between 1820 and 1913, world exports

2 A.M. Taylor and J.G. Williamson, 'Convergence in the Age of Mass Migration', *European Review of Economic History*, 2, pp. 1977, 27–63; T.J. Hatton and J.G. Williamson, 'What drove the mass migrations from Europe in the late nineteenth century?', *Population and Development Review*, 1994, pp. 1–27.

increased thirty-three times,[3] and the period of free exchange between 1842 and 1873 was when the highest rate of growth was recorded. From the 1870s until the First World War, when protectionism increased, the volume of international trade continued to rise, but more slowly. Its impact on GDP was greater in smaller countries with more specialized products; in larger countries its impact was weaker. Furthermore trade became more multilateral. 'Countries did not need to balance exports and imports with each trading partner, because balance could be achieved in the aggregate, thus allowing greater flexibility in the use of world resources.'[4]

Fluctuations in trade are normally conjunctural, or related to the customs policies of different countries. Britain was the first country to break with the mercantilist tradition contested by the classical school, and by David Ricardo in particular. Nineteenth century liberal economic thought argued that after the natural barriers to trade and commerce between countries had been removed, it then became necessary to eliminate the artificial barriers, in other words the duties and prohibitions on imported and exported goods. International free trade allowed the principle of the specialization of labour to be extended, which increased the overall productivity of the international economic system and brought about a more efficient use of resources. It was also a powerful factor for modernization, since on the one hand, strategic raw materials and advanced technology could be imported, and on the other, manufactured products, even of inferior quality, could be exported to neighbouring areas, enabling the industries in the follower countries to become consolidated.

Economic change in the nineteenth century took place against a background of constant debate between free trade supporters, who rejected customs barriers, and protectionists, who argued in favour of the need for them, if only for a certain period. The advantages and disadvantages of protectionism have been one of the most debated and controversial issues among economists and economic historians ever since. There is, however, general agreement 'that excessive protectionism has only negative effects, while more modern theories of commercial strategy justify a moderate degree of temporary protection combined with stronger competitivity'.[5] The fact remains that no country, not even Great Britain, achieved industrial development where there was complete freedom of trade. The countries that were more favourable towards free trade were smaller ones like Holland and Denmark that gained greater benefits from international trade. During the nineteenth and twentieth centuries, the largest countries, like the United States and Russia, were also the most protectionist; like the newly unified Germany, they sought to promote the development

3 They were to increase a further sixteen times between 1913 and 1992.

4 'I paesi, cioè, non avevano bisogno di bilanciare esportazioni e importazioni con ogni singolo partner commerciale, perché le compensazioni si potevano effettuare sull'aggregato, permettendo in questo modo maggiore flessibilità di uso delle risorse mondiali.' V. Zamagni, *Dalla rivoluzione industriale all'integrazione europea*, Bologna, 1999, p. 117.

5 'sul fatto che un protezionismo troppo elevato ha effetti solo negativi, mentre le più moderne teorie del commercio strategico danno qualche giustificazione a una moderata protezione temporanea accompagnata da un rafforzamento delle capacità competitive'. *Ibid.*, p. 118.

of industrial sectors that were still in an embryonic state by focusing on the potential of the domestic market.

During the seventeenth and eighteenth centuries, most European countries, as we have seen, embraced mercantilist theories; trade relations with other states were based on a positive trade balance, and, for the economy to prosper, exports had to exceed imports. This meant that the state had to intervene to provide protection from the influx of foreign goods, and subsidize exports of national products. Fiscal motives went hand in hand with economic concerns, and in many European countries, customs and excise duties accounted for an important percentage of the total revenue from taxation.

In Britain during the second half of the eighteenth century, new ideas about the economic and commercial relations between states started to be formulated. The intellectual climate of the Enlightenment and the industrial revolution led to a general review of the trading policies that had hitherto been pursued. Three important works laid down the theoretical foundations of free trade: *The Wealth of Nations* by Adam Smith (1776), *On the Principles of Political Economy and Taxation* by David Ricardo (1819) and *Principles of Political Economy* by John Stuart Mill (1848). Adam Smith argued that the wealth of nations could be increased through the more efficient allocation of resources. Ricardo formulated the 'law of comparative costs', and demonstrated the advantages of specialization and the 'international division of labour', whose aim was to optimize resources. Another argument in common was that optimization could be achieved only by abolishing artificial barriers, since the 'invisible hand' of the market brought about the optimal allocation of factors and production.

However, in international competition the state only apparently adopted a stance of non-intervention, and the various governments attempted to achieve a 'natural equilibrium' of economies by means of trade agreements. Free trade was conceived and embraced particularly by strong economics, like that of Britain, while countries that were becoming industrialized adopted protectionism. During the upheavals of the French Revolution, the application of free trade theories met with considerable difficulties. Although the 1786 Eden Treaty between France and England, for the abolition of a number of customs duties, is considered the first step towards free trade, war expenses led to an increase in customs tariffs in line with mercantilist theories. Strong sectors, protected by these barriers, gained positions of privilege, which they were reluctant to lose when peace returned, and after 1815 protectionism increased once more. Manifestoes in support of protectionism included the *Report on the Subject of Manufactures* by the American Alexander Hamilton (1791) and *Das nationale System der politischen Oekonomie* by the German Friedrich List (1837). These writers questioned whether free trade could be adopted as an absolute principle; whether or not it was appropriate to apply protectionism had to be evaluated according to a country's level of economic development. List argued that free trade benefited countries that were already developed, while it prevented others from becoming industrialized. Thus the transition from an agricultural economy to a new industrial one could occur only with the aid of a protectionist system. These theories, which were also supported by the

American Henry Charles Carey (1793–1879), gained particular acceptance in the United States. On the New Continent protectionism continued to be applied in association with the political theories of Monroe. Protectionism was adopted by the United States during the Civil War, and until 1913 its industry was among the best protected from competition. In 1833, Germany adopted the Zollverein, a customs union that formed a type of common market, with customs duties between the German principalities being abolished in favour of a common tariff for foreign countries. The Zollverein was created under the auspices of Prussia, and initially linked twenty-five of the thirty-nine confederate states. In 1851–1852 the North Sea principalities became part of it, but Austria remained excluded. The customs unification of 'Little Germany' was the forerunner of the solution that was adopted in 1871 with political unification.

The fall in prices caused an increase in duties on specific products. Governments were preoccupied with lowering direct taxation, and thus tended towards raising customs duties on consumer goods. A typical case of this type of legislation was the Corn Laws; they were a complicated system of duties on imported corn that the British introduced during the Napoleonic Wars, when the price of corn had risen rapidly. In order to protect home producers, a duty system was imposed, with duties varying according to the home price of corn. This helped to protect the interests of the large landowners, who saw to it that prices were kept high. The economic and social costs fell on the less prosperous classes; but they also indirectly affected the industrial interests of the nation, through higher wages. The Corn Laws made it almost impossible to import cereals from abroad because of the imposition of customs duties, and led to increases in bread prices during the subsistence crises that were triggered off. Partial attempts to attenuate them, such as the sliding scale (1824–1826), made practically no impact on the protectionist system. In 1839 the Manchester industrialist Richard Cobden (1804–1865) formed the Anti-Corn Law League, and organized campaigns against the government for the repeal of the Corn Laws. Cobden argued how British industry depended on weather conditions that affected harvests; a poor harvest led to an increase in the price of bread, which brought about a decrease in the consumption of other products, and this resulted in unemployment, as well as a fall in British imports and exports. In dealing with the economic crisis of 1839–1842 and the Chartist revolt, Robert Peel (1789–1850) sided with the Manchester programme; in his government's budget of 1842, he reduced customs duties and reintroduced income tax. The 1846 subsistence crisis in Ireland led him to finally repeal the Corn Laws; it was a victory for industrial interests over protectionism, particularly of the agricultural classes. The Whigs continued to dismantle the mercantilist system until the ultimate triumph of free trade in 1860. The fact that Britain was at the peak of its economic power and political prestige led others to follow its example, and the first to do so was the France of Napoleon III.

Changes to the economic situation could come about only if the whole context of exchange regulations could be redefined, and the 1860 Cobden–Chevalier trade agreement between Great Britain and France is to be understood in this light. The agreement stipulated that Britain should remove all customs tariffs on imports of French goods, with the exception of wine and brandy, which were considered luxury goods; France was committed to reducing tariffs on British goods, and 30 per cent was to be the maximum rate that could be imposed. The significance of this agreement extended far beyond the two nations directly involved. It was an innovation that had exceptionally far-reaching consequences for the future of European trade relations. The so-called 'most favoured nation' clause meant that the effects of the agreement could be extended to other countries by only one of the two signatory nations. France, for example, negotiated a series of agreements with Belgium (1862), the *Zollverein* (1862), Italy (1864), Switzerland (1864), Spain (1865), Holland (1865), Scandinavia (1865) and Austria (1866). As a result of the most favoured nation clause, Great Britain came to enjoy the benefits of special privileges that France negotiated with the states with which it had signed a trade agreement. This meant that during the twenty years after 1860, free trade experienced a chain development that involved the majority of European nations.

Return to Protectionism

After the 1870s, in several countries there was a return to protectionism. To understand this change it is necessary to consider a number of factors that transformed the economic and political landscape of Europe in the last quarter of the century:

1. The achievement of considerable levels of industrial development led the entrepreneurial classes in several European countries to seek protection from increasing competition.
2. In the field of agriculture, imports of low-priced corn, especially from the United States and Russia, caused large landowners to advocate protectionism.
3. The economic crisis that affected the whole of Europe from 1873 made competition on the national and international markets considerably more difficult, and even many industrialists favoured a move towards protectionism.
4. The triumph of nationalism and imperialism changed the climate of international relations. The Austro-Prussian and Franco-Prussian Wars of 1866 and 1870 created a series of political conflicts that led to the First World War. In the complex interaction of politics and economics, there was an increasingly close connection between protectionism and policies of 'international prestige'.
5. Colonial enterprise led to a series of diplomatic clashes over the division of territory, especially in Africa. Territorial expansion outside Europe became a burden on the taxation systems of the majority of European nations.
6. With important nations abandoning free trade positions, chain reactions were created and led to a general drive towards protectionism.

All these factors breathed new life into protectionist interests that had never fully disappeared. After the 1870s, other European countries were led to adopt protectionism by the agricultural crisis that had developed because of competition from American and Russian grain; its arrival on the European markets was an effect of the increase in steamship navigation. The conditions were created for a coalition of interests between landowners, who were penalized by lower agricultural prices, and industrialists, who were affected by falls in consumption. This was the case in Germany, where tariffs on national products were adopted by Bismarck between 1879 and 1881; the decision was also dictated by political and fiscal advantages, and the system was developed, in a more moderate form, under Kaiser Wilhelm II (1888–1918). Trade agreements ensured the economic predominance of Germany over the agricultural countries of central and eastern Europe. Italy followed a similar route. In the pre-unification period, exports of agricultural raw materials and semi-finished products (especially silk) had been outweighed by imports of industrial manufactures, thus creating an adverse trade balance. Protectionism was applied in all the states, with the exceptions of the Grand Duchy of Tuscany, and the Kingdom of Sardinia from 1834.[6] The free trade position of the ruling class of the new Kingdom of Italy was closely linked with its foreign policy, as the 1863 Italo-French trade agreement showed. The transition to protectionism was gradual and not without difficulties; conflicts arose between ideologies, in international relations, and in differing interests in different sectors of the national economies. The post-unification ruling class in Italy held that some European countries should develop the primary sector, while others should maintain, or achieve, dominant positions in the secondary sector, in accordance with the theory of international specialization. Between 1861 and 1876, the historical right wing governments applied free trade policies; however, the new left wing government saw the need to accelerate industrialization through a more active role of the state with a 'semi-protectionist' policy, such as the 1878 customs tariff.[7] In 1887 came the turning point as regards tariffs (the *svolta tariffaria*),[8] though they were applied only in trade agreements with individual foreign countries. They were tenaciously supported by an agrarian-industrialist coalition led by the foremost industrialist of the day, the wool entrepreneur and senator Alessandro Rossi of Schio.[9] The Italian case is interesting because of its international repercussions. Hitherto France had been the trading partner of Italy *par excellence*, exporting industrial products and importing citrus fruits, silkworms and a range of fruit and vegetable produce. During the four years between 1888 and 1892, there was a 'tariff war' between France and Italy, during which tariffs were continually being raised. France did not stabilize its tariffs

6 L. Trezzi, 'I modi del coinvolgimento nello sviluppo economico europeo', in S. Zaninelli (ed.), *L'Ottocento economico italiano*, Bologna, 1993.

7 P. Pecorari, *Il protezionismo imperfetto. Luigi Luzzatti e la tariffa doganale del 1878*, Venice, 1989.

8 E. Del Vecchio, *La via italiana al protezionismo*, 5 vols, Rome, 1979–1980; A. Cardini, *Stato liberale e protezionismo in Italia*, Bologna, 1981.

9 Among others: S. Lanaro, 'Nazionalismo e ideologia del blocco corporativo-protezionista in Italia', *Ideologie*, 2, 1967; *id.*, 'Mercantilismo agrario e formazione del capitale nel pensiero di Alessandro Rossi', *Quaderni storici*, 5, 1971; L. Avagliano, *Alessandro Rossi e le origini dell'Italia industriale*, Naples, 1970; G. Are, *Alle origini dell'Italia industriale*, Naples, 1974; G. L. Fontana (ed.), *Schio e Alessandro Rossi. Imprenditorialità, politica, cultura e paesaggi sociali del secondo Ottocento*, 2 vols, Rome, 1985–1986.

until 1892, when the Tariffe Méline was applied. However, they were still lower than they had been in the first half of the century, since the most favoured nation clause set them at the lowest rate and eliminated any discrimination.

By 1914 the whole of Europe had returned to varying degrees of protectionism. The free trade group was reduced to the nations of north-western Europe with the most developed trade. Great Britain's economic interests worldwide enabled it to remain particularly open to free trade; the British economy thus became the pivot on which the whole economic system of international exchange turned.

Colonialism

The return to protectionism came at the same time as important political changes. Countries like Britain had considerable colonial experience; with its maritime development in the seventeenth and eighteenth centuries, Britain had created a series of areas of influence, free ports, and possessions, particularly in America and Asia. On the other hand, for France, the eighteenth century had marked the loss of its overseas possessions to Britain, and in the first decades of the nineteenth century Spain and Portugal had lost their colonies in South America. Meanwhile, industrialization in Europe brought about the need to expand markets for both finished products and raw materials, and Britain had started a new type of imperialism based on the occupation of vast areas of the globe. At the end of the nineteenth century, its empire stretched from Nigeria to South Africa, from India, Burma and Australia to Canada. Other European nations also set out on the same path; between 1830 and the end of the nineteenth century, France occupied part of Saharan Africa (initially Algeria, Tunisia, Morocco), equatorial Africa, Madagascar and Indochina. Since German interests were more focused on Europe, German colonialism was more restricted, and it was purely for political reasons that Bismarck launched into colonial enterprises. Belgian colonialism was also restricted, while Portuguese and Spanish colonialism was on the decline. Italian colonialism, with the occupation of Eritrea (1885), Somalia (1887–89) and later Libya (1912), was ultimately to fail.

Colonialism was a complex phenomenon and in the long term had many different aspects. From the economic point of view, which was not always uppermost, the colonies were markets for goods, capital and raw materials, and also as an outlet for growing populations, but these elements did not always equally apply to all the European colonies. There was as much difference in their political and economic links as there was in the types of colonies. Great Britain was the only European country that had close economic ties with its colonies. In 1854, about 55 per cent of British foreign investment was in continental Europe, in 1870 it was no more than 30 per cent, and in 1914 barely 8 per cent. On the other hand, in 1854, investments in the colonies and dominions, including India, accounted for no more than 20 per cent of total foreign investment, in 1870 it amounted to 45 per cent, and by 1914 as much as 65 per cent. These figures appear all the more astonishing in view of the fact that in the same period French investment in the colonies amounted to 4–9 per cent of all foreign investment. These figures perhaps substantiate the opinion that there was a connection between British 'economic decline' and over-commitment to typical products of the first industrial revolution. Since such products could be absorbed by colonial markets, Britain had less interest in converting to products that were typical of the second industrial revolution. In the long run, capital that could be used for important processes of technological innovation at home went to the colonies; but it also created a state of immobility in production because of its unsophisticated markets.[10]

The International Economy

With the expansion of European international trade, the international economic situation was taking shape. Taking 100 as the total volume of exports from European countries in 1913, in 1820 the index was barely 5, and in 1870 it was about 30. European trade thus witnessed unprecedented development both in developed countries and in those outside Europe. Table 11.1 shows Britain's clear supremacy throughout the nineteenth century. Although new powers like Germany and the United States had achieved considerable levels of industrialization by the end of the century (with Germany even surpassing Great Britain), the role of British trade still predominated. In 1914, Great Britain still controlled about 14 per cent of world trade. These were unparalleled results. Between 1840 and 1860, there was a threefold increase in the quantity of cotton traded worldwide, while that of sugar doubled in the thirty years between 1840 and 1870. Wool, cocoa, indigo, wood, corn, rubber, seed and even guano were at the centre of a dense network of worldwide trade.

Europe was at the centre of the world system, with about two-thirds of all exports and imports of raw materials and finished products (Tables 11.2 and 11.3). Table 11.2 shows how Great Britain accounted for a decreasing influx of raw materials, while Table 11.3 shows a decrease in the UK share of finished products. A new non-European producer, the United States, was becoming more and more important. However, the industrial role of the United States, which in the twentieth century was to be fundamental, was still not apparent; in 1880, around 80 per cent of its exports went to Europe, and in 1913 Europe still accounted for about 60 per cent of exports from the United States. Yet developments in America were being closely watched, and there were those who predicted its future role on the world scene.[11]

The system of international relations just described can be seen in terms of a 'core–periphery' model in which Europe at its centre firmly controlled the whole system, but saw most of its trade being carried on within its own boundaries. Indeed, it has been observed that the importance of the 'periphery' in the development of the 'core' of the system should not be overestimated. Between 1830 and 1910 (Table 11.4), about 80 per cent of the exports from European countries found buyers' markets within Europe itself. Although this percentage was considerably lower for Great Britain (about 40 per cent),

10 L.E. Davis and R.A. *Huttenback, Mammon and the Pursuit of Empire. The Economics of British Imperialism*, Cambridge, 1988.

11 E. Rossi, *Gli Stati Uniti e la concorrenza Americana*, Florence, 1884.

the fact remains that Europe was the centre of production and consumption regardless of economic events in other countries. In this case, it was the periphery that needed Europe, in order to start commercial and industrial development.

TABLE 11.1 Value of exports, 1820–1913 ($ million at 1913 prices)

Country	1820	1840	1860	1880	1900	1913	Exports as % of GDP in 1913
Great Britain	73	189	579	1,052	1,497	2,555	20.9
Germany	–	106	240	549	1,097	2,454	17.5
France	56	86	260	578	818	1,328	13.9
Italy	35	–	–	251	312	485	12.0
Belgium	16	29	87	224	386	717	50.9
Holland	–	–	–	166	267	413	38.2
United States	31	97	229	833	1,733	2,380	6.1
Japan	–	–	–	22	92	315	12.3

Source: adapted from A. Maddison, *Dynamic Forces in Capitalist Development. A Long-run Comparative View,* Oxford, 1991, pp. 311–15. 324–6.

TABLE 11.2 Distribution of world trade in raw materials, by continent, 1876–1913 (%)

	1876–1880		1896–1900		1913	
Area	Areas	Exports	Imports	Exports	Imports	Exports
Great Britain	30	3	26	4	19	6
Continental Europe	50	43	55	46	55	40
North America	7	16	8	19	11	17
Rest of World	13	38	10	32	14	37
World	100	100	100	100	100	100

Source: A.G. Kenwood and A.L. Lougheed, *The Growth of the International Economy,* 1820–1990. London and New York, 1992, p. 86.

TABLE 11.3 Distribution of world trade in finished products, by continent, 1876–1913 (%)

	1876–80		1896–1900		1913	
Area	Imports	Exports	Imports	Exports	Imports	Exports
Great Britain	9	38	10	31	8	25
Continental Europe	31	57	33	57	40	56
North America	8	4	10	7	12	11
Rest of World	52	1	47	5	40	8
World	100	100	100	100	100	100

Source: A.G. Kenwood and A.L. Lougheed, *The Growth of the International Economy,* 1820–1990, London and New York, 1992. p. 86.

TABLE 11.4 Changes in the structure of foreign trade (%)

Great Britain

	Raw Materials		Foodstuffs		Manufactures	
Years	Imports	Exports	Imports	Exports	Imports	Exports
1854 56	53.7	7.1	39.1	6.8	7.1	86.1
1890–92	40.2	14.1	43.0	4.9	16.8	80.9
1911–13	42.5	17.6	37.7	6.4	19.9	76.1

France (exports)

Years	Raw Materials	Agric. Products	Manufactures
1837–46	4.3	21.8	73.9
1867–76	10.0	38.0	52.0
1887–96	11.9	33.9	54.3
1907–13	14.6	27.4	58.1

Germany

	Raw Materials		Foodstuffs		Semi-Finished		Manufactures	
Years	Imports	Exports	Imports	Exports	Imports	Exports	Imports	Exports
1880–82	35.2	14.5	33.6	21.1	19.1	16.0	12.1	48.5
1890–92	36.6	15.8	37.0	14.6	16.5	15.6	10.0	54.0
1911–13	42.5	15.4	34.0	10.1	14.8	21.1	8.7	53.4

Italy

	Raw Materials		Foodstuffs		Semi-Finished		Manufactures	
Years	Imports	Exports	Imports	Exports	Imports	Exports	Imports	Exports
1881–83	12.7	12.7	20.6	32.5	29.5	29.5	15.4	15.4
1890–92	32.4	16.1	24.6	28.5	22.2	42.2	20.8	13.2
1911–13	37.2	14.3	19.7	29.3	19.9	24.9	23.2	31.5

United States

	Raw Materials		Foodstuffs		Semi-Finished		Manufactures	
Years	Imports	Exports	Imports	Exports	Imports	Exports	Imports	Exports
1821	5.5	60.8	10.9	3.9	7.3	9.8	56.4	5.9
1858–60	12.4	66.2	13.8	4.8	8.3	4.0	47.8	11.9
1890–92	23.1	36.1	18.4	17.9	14.9	5.3	26.6	15.0
1911–13	35.0	33.3	12.5	5.7	18.6	16.1	22.7	30.9

Japan (Exports)

Years	Primary Products	Light Industry	Heavy Industry
1874–80	47.1	45.3	7.6
1901–10	14.1	70.7	14.9

Source: P.A. Toninelli. (ed.) *Lo sviluppo economico moderno dalla rivoluzione industriale alla crisi energetica,* 1750–1973. Venice, 1997, pp. 620–1.

The growing European industrial powers created financial relations that appeared to be just as complex. Until 1850, as in the case of the construction of the railway system, the foreign investment of most European countries was on the continent itself, while in the second half of the century, capital was increasingly exported on a world scale. European industrialization had created wealth that was destined to find new uses. Great Britain, especially, had had trading and financial links with different trading partners, at least since the end of the seventeenth century, which led, on the one hand, to the investment of surplus capital abroad, and on the other to the refinement of various financial mechanisms for the efficient circulation and use of capital. The great expansion in international trade, with Great Britain as the uncontested leader, could not have taken place without the development of systems of financing.

The whole world market came to be regulated from London, which was the chief port and depot for raw materials and goods. Share and bond markets, foreign currency markets, central banks, private and commercial banks, brokers and other financial agents were the instruments of unprecedented financial expansion; at the heart of the system was the City. In the eighteenth century, about three-quarters of its operators, who were initially merchants and later merchant bankers, were already of foreign origin. London established its financial role with the nineteenth century, and with British industrial development, not only in Europe but also in the world. Bills of exchange were settled through the intermediation of merchant bankers; these were private bankers such as Baring, Rothschild, Schroeder, Hambro, Lazard and Peabody, who granted credit for short-term acceptance. The discount bankers intermediated between the banks holding credit and those seeking to place their assets. Neither Paris nor Berlin had such a specialized and well informed financial market. The supremacy of the pound sterling reinforced the efficiency of the London market; the quality of its services played a fundamental role in the equilibrium of the British balance of payments.

However, it was difficult to find a clear distinction between short and long-term transactions. Profits from trading activities might remain abroad in countries that were becoming industrialized as investments in the form of production activities, normally with higher returns than in the already industrialized countries; they could also be invested in the national debt, as for example in American government bonds. Such mechanisms help to explain the phenomenal growth of foreign investment during the nineteenth century. In 1855, foreign investment worldwide was £420 million; fifteen years later it had reached £1.3 billion, increasing to £4.7 billion in 1900; by 1914, it was £9.5 billion. On the eve of the First World War, Great Britain still accounted for 43 per cent of world investment, and was investing the equivalent of 7–9 per cent of its GDP overseas. Following some way behind was France, with 20 per cent, then Germany, with 13 per cent, and Belgium, Holland and Switzerland with 12 per cent. Foreign investment of the United States was still very modest, at only 7 per cent (Figure 11.1).[12]

---

12 See also C. H. Feinstein, P. Temin and G. Toniolo, *The European Economy between the Wars*, Oxford, 1998.

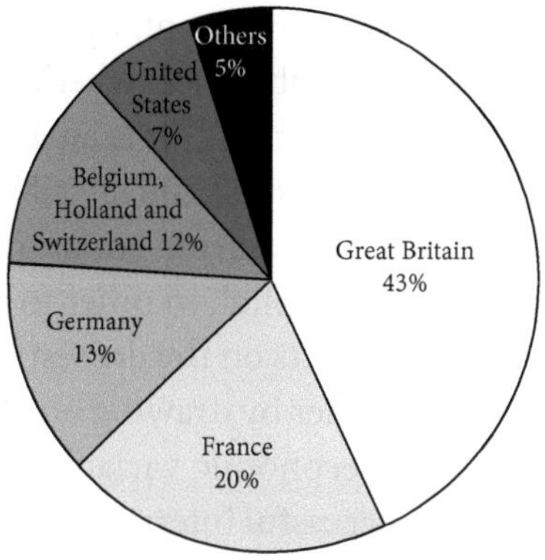

FIGURE 11.1 **Foreign Investment in 1914: Investor Countries.**

Source: R. Cameron, *A Concise Economic History of the World,* 3rd edn, Oxford, 1997, p. 311.

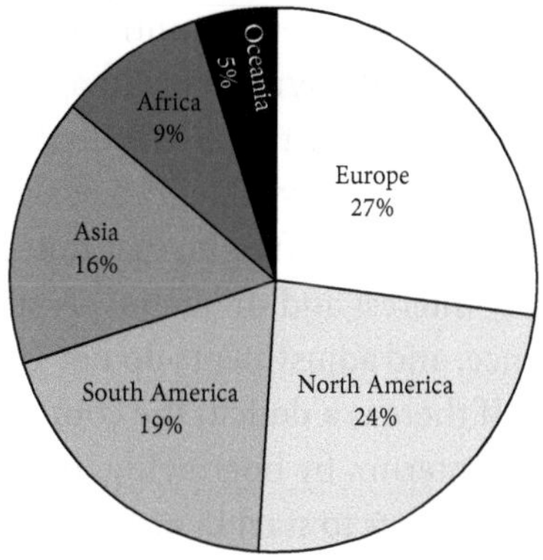

FIGURE 11.2 **Foreign investment in 1914: Recipient Areas.**

Source: R. Cameron, *A Concise Economic History of the World,* 3rd edn, Oxford, 1997, p. 311.

Europe was thus not only the world's greatest investor, but of all the continents it was also the greatest recipient of investments (Figure 11.2). Throughout the century, almost all the countries of Europe depended on investment from other European countries to a greater or lesser degree. In 1914, the Balkan countries of Russia and Turkey were the greatest recipients of capital in Europe; it came especially from France, Germany and Holland. For Russia, foreign capital was fundamental in the construction of the railway system, but also for financing the military and naval policies of the tsarist government. Foreign investment in Scandinavia was important for the renewal of its economies and the development of industrialization.

There were different reasons for the outflow of capital to non-European countries. Canada, Australia and New Zealand were seen as new centres for the development of European-style social and cultural models, but especially as models of production and consumption. Investment, particularly of British capital, in Latin America was channelled towards Argentina, Brazil and in part Mexico. On the Asian continent, China, Japan and especially India, at the time part of the British Empire, received substantial investments, while most foreign investment in Africa was concentrated in South Africa.

The Balance of Payments and the Gold Standard

With the aggressive expansion of international markets for goods, labour and finance, a true international economy took shape, and each country was forced to focus on its balance of payments account. This was the means whereby records of all payments made abroad could be matched against all payments received from abroad. Depending on their stage of development, countries had different types of balances of payment. By definition, the balance of payments is in a state of balance; if there is an imbalance, whether it is a surplus or a deficit, this is indicated in the balance on current account. It is an algebraic calculation of the visible trade balance (imports and exports of goods), the invisible trade balance (services, freight, insurance, tourism, banking), remittances from emigrants, and finally interest and dividends. A surplus is offset by exporting capital, in order to restore balance, and adjustments do not generally produce negative effects on the domestic economy. If there is a deficit, the country has to restore balance, either by drawing on reserves in the interim, by borrowing, or by intervening on internal economic variables. This is where one has to start in order to understand how the first successful international system of payments in history actually worked. First, the balance of payments of the predominant country, Great Britain, will be examined (Tables 11.5–6).

TABLE 11.5 International trade balance of Great Britain, 1816–1850 (£ million, period values)

Period	Imports	Exports	Import/Export Balance	Services	Capital	Overall Balance
1816–20	49.3	40.3	-9.0	14.5	1.7	7.2
1821–25	45.4	37.3	-8.1	14.2	4.2	10.3
1826–30	48.7	35.9	-12.8	10.6	4.6	2.4
1831–35	53.6	40.5	-13.1	14.1	5.4	6.4
1836–40	73.6	49.6	-24.0	18.6	8.0	2.6
1841–45	71.0	54.0	-17.0	15.4	7.5	5.9
1846–50	87.7	60.9	-26.8	22.0	9.5	4.7

Source: A.H. Imlah, *Economic Elements in the Pax Britannica. Studies in British Foreign Trade in the Nineteenth Century*, New York, 1969.

TABLE 11.6 Industrial income, investments and public expenditure, England and continental Europe, 1800–1910

	Income Produced by Industrial Sector (as % of GDP)		Investments (as % of National Expenditure)		State Expenditure (as % of Total Expenditure)	
Year	England	Europe	England	Europe	England	Europe
1800	19.8	22.0	7.9	12.6	15.3	7.4
1840	31.5	25.2	10.5	14.4	7.9	7.0
1870	33.5	31.3	8.5	17.2	4.8	6.3
1890	33.6	32.8	7.3	18.6	5.9	5.9
1910	31.8	34.4	7.0	19.5	8.2	5.7

Source: N.F.R. Crafts, 'La recente storia quantitativa della rivoluzione industriale', *Rivista di Storia Economica*, 3 (1989).

In the nineteenth century, the trade balance of the United Kingdom was constantly in deficit. Thus, the exportation of manufactures did not make it possible to accumulate capital that had been exported overseas. Emigrants transferred more capital abroad than they remitted to their families in Europe. Invisible services, such as revenue from the merchant fleet, banking, insurance and transport, enabled a surplus on the balance of trade in goods and services to be made (as in 1815–1835, 1855–1875, 1910–1914), as well as a decrease in the deficit (1835–1855, 1890– 1905), in the years when the export of goods was held back by protectionism or competition. The steady growth in foreign investments considerably increased the surplus of revenue from interest and dividends; it even sufficed to bring about a permanent surplus in the balance of payments. Thus during the nineteenth century, the British balance of payments was never in deficit.[13] This was one of the main strengths of the pound sterling, and it became the benchmark currency in the international monetary system. The 'gold standard', as it was known, was created in order to cope with the great increase in commercial and financial relations between different states. Where several different currencies were involved, an efficient currency exchange market needed to be created, and the solution was found in a monetary system that could provide a unit of account into which all the currencies could be converted.

During the nineteenth century, for internal exchanges there was a gradual move towards replacing metal money with banknotes. The use of gold and silver coins had meant that the nominal value of the coin was also a real value, and with the expansion of banking practices, the growing use of banknotes had caused a discrepancy between nominal and real value. Banknotes did not hold real value, but the bank that had issued them was committed to converting the nominal value into gold or silver. The issuing bank therefore had to hold a quantity of precious metal as a sufficient reserve to ensure convertibility of the paper money into precious metal at a fixed parity; this had to be kept equal to a specific amount of the reserve of precious metal, initially established by usage, and later by law. This link between precious metal and circulating paper money meant that, in order to increase the amount of money in circulation, new reserves had to be acquired; at the same time, if there was a decrease in precious metal the amount of circulating paper money had to be reduced. Since at any one time, the reserve of metal was not sufficient to convert all the banknotes in circulation, it was a fiduciary system, based on proper adherence to the rules of the game. If not, there could have been a rush on the banks to convert the notes; this would have led to the collapse of the system, and to a state of forced circulation of the banknotes. The system thus required strict discipline, in the issue of fiduciary money, as well as in the balance of payments. If a country was in deficit, and had to pay its deficit in gold, it needed to restrict growth, or decrease its money supply, so that internal prices would fall and demand would slow down. Imports would thus decrease, but exports could be increased, since they regained their competitiveness. In this way balance was restored

13 J. Heffer and W. Serman, *Il XIX secolo, 1815–1914. Dalle revoluzioni agli imperialismi*, ed. S. Zaninelli, Milan, 1998, pp. 65–6.

'automatically'. In a situation where there was a surplus on the balance of payments, the reverse happened. However, it could happen that countries with a surplus preferred to increase their reserves and not obey the rules of the game; in that case there was an increase in the amount of money in circulation, with the consequent 'sterilization' of gold. The whole burden of re-adjusting fell on the country with a deficit, sometimes forcing it to leave the gold standard and let its own currency fluctuate.

Observing that the system was thrown into crisis by wars and by the internal difficulties of individual countries, some scholars have argued that the gold standard was what made periods of great international stability possible, and not the gold standard that generated stability, even though that was one of its strengths.[14] Moreover, a fixed exchange system indissolubly links the monetary and fiscal policies of member countries to those of the leader country through the complex interplay of action and reaction, and if it is to function well, the entire international monetary system requires stable and secure leadership. The pound sterling was synonymous with stability, while the franc experienced two periods of forced circulation, between 1848 and 1850 and from 1870 to 1877, while the dollar fluctuated between 1862 and 1878. The nineteenth century showed remarkable monetary stability and the major currencies did not suffer any permanent loss of their purchasing power. However, it was the pound sterling that inspired unconditional confidence; nobody anywhere else had been able to secure such absolute convertibility. The only great market for international credit was the City, and bills of exchange could be transacted there at the best conditions possible. This is why, after 1880, states increasingly included foreign currency in their exchange reserves; this was essentially the pound sterling, which was preferred to gold, since it also guaranteed interest.

In the nineteenth century, the monetary base on which the exchange value of products was fixed was normally a precious metal. Some countries adopted bimetallism, using gold and silver; others adopted monometallism, either only silver or only gold. Until the 1870s, these systems meant that the world could be divided into three monetary zones. The first included countries that had adopted gold monometallism, and their systems were based solely on gold; of these countries Great Britain was the most important. In 1821, Parliament re-established the free convertibility of banknotes, which had been in forced circulation during the war against France; notes issued by the Bank of England were unlimited legal tender and until 1914 could be freely exchanged for gold. The second monetary zone was made up of countries using the silver standard, mainly countries lying on the shores of the Pacific and Indian Oceans. The third zone comprised the countries that had adopted bimetallism. Their system was based on gold and silver, and a ratio between the two metals was fixed by law; in France the ratio had been 1:15.5 since 1803. Bimetallism was inconvenient with regard to one aspect in particular: if there was variation in the price ratio between the two metals, the higher-priced metal had to be sold, and quantities of the lower priced

14 B. Eichengreen (ed.), *The Gold Standard in Theory and History*, London, 1985; V. Zamagni, *Dalla rivoluzione industriale*, pp. 124–6.

one bought until parity of price between the two metals was re-established. This was the aim of the Latin Monetary Union. The Union had been set up by France in the 1860s and 1870s, and apart from France, also involved Belgium, Switzerland, Italy (between 1865 and 1866) and later Spain, Serbia and Romania. But it was doomed to fail because of the influx of silver after the discovery of new deposits.

Great Britain, on the other hand, had preferred monometallism. In 1717 it had already been established that a golden guinea was worth 21*s*; in 1774, payments in silver coin had been limited to a maximum value of £25, and in 1816 to only £2. After 1821, when the Bank of England resumed conversion of banknotes into precious metal, gold effectively became a standard for the currency. Problems with using a system of bimetallism, and continual fluctuations in the value of silver, ultimately led to silver being excluded as a measure of account; since both gold and silver are also raw materials, their prices are determined by supply and demand. Until around 1870 there was no variation in either the mint ratio or the trading ratio, but then they started increasingly to diverge, to the disadvantage of silver. Between 1860 and 1890, the production of silver increased as normal in the United States and Mexico, while the production of gold, which had increased enormously after the discoveries in California (1848) and Australia (1851), slowly started to dwindle.

In 1873, the new country of Germany decided to put a new coin into circulation; this was the gold mark, and it replaced the silver thaler. The reason for the decision was compatibility with the pound sterling. However, this alignment of gold reserves created an imbalance in trade relations, and the bimetallism countries gradually adopted gold monometallism, so that they would not lose their gold reserves, or be swamped with silver, which was considered poor coin. This was the case of France and the Latin Monetary Union after 1876, and the United States in 1900; it came after long and vexed political debate. Very soon the majority of European and non-European nations adopted the gold standard following recommendations laid down at the Monetary Congress of Paris in 1876. When it became part of the gold system, Italy gained an acceptable level of monetary tranquillity, and it reinforced the basis for development at the end of the century; this was an important result after the monetary crisis that had hit the country in 1866. The negative results of the war against Austria had led the government to stop converting banknotes into precious metal, in order to meet unavoidable state expenditure.

At the start of the twentieth century, gold finally ousted silver, despite the fact that the production of silver was rapidly increasing, with the discovery of new mines after 1890 in the Transvaal, Australia, the Klondike and Siberia. The adoption of the gold standard was associated with British supremacy in international trade, and for the whole of the nineteenth century, because of British predominance in trade, international exchanges were based on the gold standard. Not only was it used for fixing the value of all currencies to gold, but it put British sterling at the centre of the system, and effectively made it a unit of international conversion.

Topic Seven Suggested Supplemental Readings:

Landes, David S. 1999. *The Wealth and Poverty of Nations*. New York, NY: W.W. Norton.

Topic Seven Questions

1 Explain the impact of steamships on economic development.
2 Explain the impact of railroads on economic development.
3 Explain the impact of telegraphs on economic development.
4 What were the Corn Laws? Why were they finally repealed? What were the major provisions of the Cobden-Chevalier (Anglo-France) Treaty?
5 Give five detailed reasons for European return to protectionism.
6 Describe and quantify the trade flows of the late nineteenth century. Describe and quantify the flows of international investments.
7 Explain the benefits and drawbacks of the international gold standard.

Topic Eight

The Stock Market Crash and the Great Depression

CHAPTER TWELVE

The Stock Market Boom and Crash of 1929 Revisited

Eugene N. White

In trying to explain the 1987 stock market crash, many analysts drew obvious but vague comparisons with the events of 1929. Newspapers published a chart, reproduced in Figure 12.1, showing the bull market of the 1920s superimposed on the 1980s. The degree of similarity between the two periods up to the crash was striking. Yet while analysts noted this close correspondence, they drew few inferences from it. Comparisons proved difficult because the crash of 1929 had received little scholarly attention since Galbraith's *The Great Crash 1929* (1954).

This paper will sort through many of the hypotheses offered to explain the 1929 boom and bust. Most of the factors cited by historians played trivial or insignificant roles. The central issue is whether fundamentals or a bubble drove the bull market upwards. An econometric resolution of this question is unlikely, for reasons that Flood and Hodrick explain in their contribution to this symposium. However, the qualitative evidence assembled in this paper favors the view that a bubble was present in the 1929 market.

The Conventional Wisdom

Galbraith's classic book still provides the most commonly accepted explanation of the 1929 boom and crash. He argues that a bubble in the stock market was formed during the rapid economic growth of the 1920s. Galbraith emphasizes the irrational element—the mania—that induced the public to invest in the bull market. The rise in the stock market, according to Galbraith's account (1954 and 1988, pp. xii–xiii), depended on "the vested interest in euphoria [that] leads men and women, individuals and institutions to believe that all will be better, that they are meant to be richer and to dismiss as intellectually deficient what is in conflict with that conviction." This eagerness to buy stocks was then fueled by an expansion of credit in the form of brokers' loans that encouraged investors to become dangerously leveraged.

Eugene N. White, "The Stock Market Boom and Crash of 1929 Revisited," *Journal of Economic Perspectives*, vol. 4, no. 2, pp. 67–83.

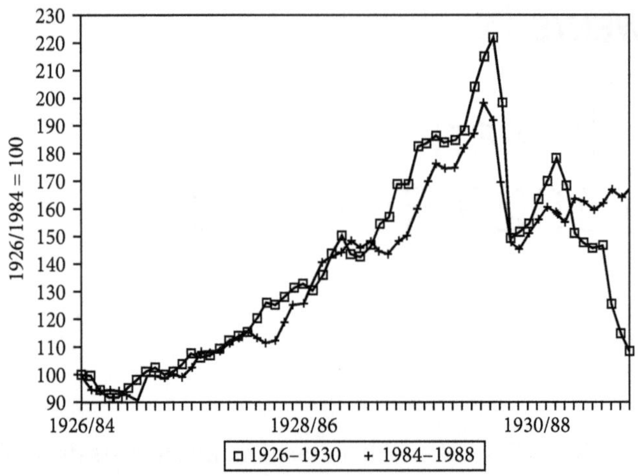

FIGURE 12.1 **Common Stock Indices**

Source: The index for the 1980s is Standard and Poor's 500. The data for the 1920s is found in the Board of Governors of the Federal Reserve System (1943).

Galbraith and other writers, like Kindleberger (1978), are vague about the causes of the halt in the market, believing that almost any event could have triggered irrational investors to sell. Instead, they focus on the inevitability of the bubble's collapse and suggest several factors that could have exploded public confidence and caused prices to plummet. The vertical price drops on Black Thursday, October 24, and Black Tuesday, October 29, forced margin calls and distress sales of stocks, prompting a further plunge in prices. When the stock ticker ran late, investors panicked and sold their holdings. In the following weeks and months, the market bounced downwards erratically, propelled by and perhaps propelling the depression.[1]

While Galbraith's book makes for compelling reading, there remain many unanswered questions. There is little discussion about how much fundamentals contributed to the bull market and what might have triggered the speculative mania. The argument about easy credit in the form of broker's loans seems strange at a time when the Federal Reserve was pursuing a tight money policy. Furthermore, little has been done to identify the precise role of external events in provoking the collapse. To address these questions, it is necessary to begin with a brief overview of the changes during the 1920s that set the stage for the stock market boom.

1 For the effects of the crash on the depression, see Friedman and Schwartz (1963, pp. 305–308, 334–342) and Romer (June 1988).

The New Economy and Stock Market of the 1920s

After World War I and a postwar recession, the stability and prosperity of the 1920s appeared extraordinary to contemporary observers. From 1922 to 1929, GNP grew at an annual rate of 4.7 percent and unemployment averaged 3.7 percent (U.S. Department of Commerce, 1975, Vol. I, p. 135 and 226). Part of this growth may be attributed to the emergence of large-scale commercial and industrial enterprises that took advantage of new continuous process technologies. Coordination by the emerging system of modern management, as described by Chandler (1977), produced more efficient vertically-integrated enterprises that captured economies of scale and scope.

The financial needs of these new enterprises altered the face of American capital markets. Regulations imposed on commercial banks in the nineteenth century severely limited their ability to provide large long-term loans, and firms turned to financing their investments out of retained earnings and bond and stock issues.[2] The market for industrial securities, which first emerged in the 1880s, came of age in the 1920s, as both old and new corporations issued equities to finance new plant and equipment.

Commercial banks did purchase more bonds, but they could not legally trade or acquire equities. To circumvent this restriction, they set up wholly-owned securities affiliates, which permitted them to enter all aspects of investment banking and the brokerage business. Peach (1941) found that the number of affiliates grew rapidly from 10 in 1922 to 114 in 1931. These affiliates attracted many new customers and became big distributors of stocks and bonds, enabling them to become underwriters. By 1930, commercial banks' security affiliates had obtained roughly half the bond originations. By moving into investment banking through their affiliates, commercial banks were thus able to continue servicing the needs of their corporate customers (White, 1986).

While the securities affiliates catered to a broader clientele than most traditional brokerage houses, many small investors might still have shied away from buying securities, lacking sufficient capital to purchase a diversified portfolio of stocks. This obstacle was eliminated by the investment trusts, which served the same function as mutual funds do today.[3] According to Carosso (1970), investment trusts grew from about 40 in 1921 to over 750 in 1929.

The growth of the securities market, assisted by the establishment of investment trusts and securities affiliates, allowed firms to substitute stocks and bonds for commercial bank loans. This development began well before the stock market boom, but the pace of change accelerated in the 1920s with the rapid growth of modern industrial enterprise. During this

2 National banks were prohibited from lending more than 10 percent of their capital and surplus to one customer. The effect of this regulation on banks' lending capacity was amplified by strict federal and state limits on branch banking that restricted banks' ability to grow.

3 Investment trusts were primarily institutions that sold securities to the public and used the proceeds to invest in stocks and bonds. There were two main types; management trusts where managers has discretion over the portfolio and fixed trusts where the portfolio could not be changed.

decade, banks found their traditional role as intermediaries sharply reduced.[4] In response, they sought to increase their fee income by offering new financial services, including trusts and insurance (White, 1984). Most importantly, they increased their role as brokers between the saving public and industry. Banks were familiar with their borrowers and conditioned to monitor their activities. However, many of the new investors they served lacked experience in buying stock and monitoring firms, thus creating a favorable condition for a bubble.[5]

Frederick Lewis Allen (1931) and Galbraith see the stock market bubble beginning in March 1928. This first upward tick is registered in the index of common stocks in Figure 12.1. In the months of April and May, this index increased 15 percent. In his influential account of the stock market, Allen dates the boom as beginning on Monday, March 5. In the aggregate indices, there is nothing extraordinary about this date. Allen's reason for selecting this day is the five point rise in General Motors' stock, which by the end of the week had increased 7 percent. Other stocks shared this excellent week, most notably RCA, which rose almost 14 percent.

Allen attributes the initial sharp rise in March to the purchases by big bullish speculators, but this increase can be justified by economic developments. The economy had been in a recession until late 1927. When business picked up, the stock market responded. General Motors was attractive because Ford (still a private company) had shut down to retool for the Model A. With its more advanced management and organization, GM was able to take advantage of this opportunity, increasing production and sales and seizing the leading position in the industry. Its management exuded confidence. At the end of the month, GM's president predicted its price would rise from 180 to 225, and he promised to return to stockholders 60 percent of earnings.[6]

The other stock that dominated the New York Exchange was RCA, the purveyor of a new technology. RCA's sales were growing by 50 percent each year. Its prospects, which looked excellent as the economy recovered, were reaffirmed by the release of the company's 1927 annual report in early March 1928. RCA stock was thus quite attractive, but not because it promised to pay high dividends like General Motors. The company had never paid a dividend, nor would it pay one for many years to come. The only reason to buy RCA in the short-run or even the medium-run was the belief that its business would continue to thrive and the price of its stock would increase in the hope of dividends in the distant future. Expectations of dividends from RCA had to be extremely diffuse.

Many other prominent companies that did not pay dividends caught the public's attention, too. These included Radio-Keith-Orpheum, the Aluminum Company of America, and the

4 Commercial loans as a percentage of total earning assets of national banks fell from 58 percent in 1920 to 37 percent in 1929 (Currie, 1931).

5 This appears to have happened in other asset market bubbles. A new group of less sophisticated investors also became active during the South Sea Bubble (Neal, 1990).

6 *Commercial and Financial Chronicle,* March 24, 1928, Vol. 126, p. 1988. Other automobile companies and suppliers ranked among the most heavily traded stocks and contributed to a lesser extent to the rise in the stock market indices.

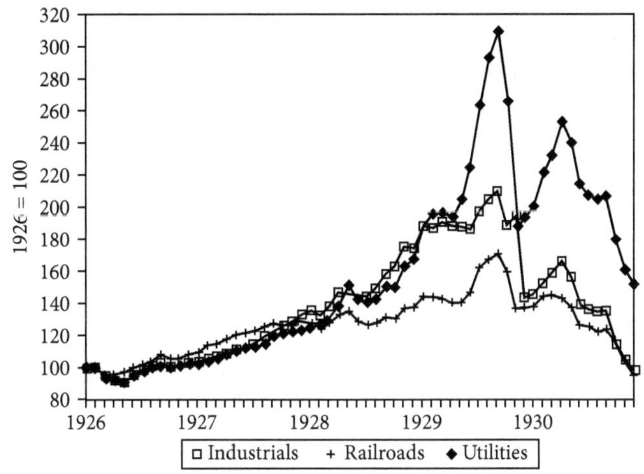

FIGURE 12.2 **Common Stock Indices**

Source: Board of Governors of the Federal Reserve System (1943).

United Aircraft and Transport Corporation.[7] Like RCA, these firms used new, developing technologies. The proportion of firms not paying dividends was also high among public utility holdings companies. These included the Commonwealth and Southern Corporation, Electric Bond and Share and the North American Company. The electric utility industry was undergoing a remarkable transformation in the 1920s where consolidation and expansion gave firms great economies of scale in production and transmission. This was another frontier industry with potentially high but uncertain returns.

The attraction of utilities' stocks is revealed in Figure 12.2 which shows indices for industrials, railroads, and public utilities. The boom in utilities far outstripped industrials, while the relatively stable, established railroads languished. Although previous writers have not concerned themselves with the prominence of public utilities and high-tech stocks, they were a central feature of the bull market.

The Role of Fundamentals in the Bull Market of the 1920s

Although most historians believe that the 1920s bull market was a bubble and concede only a small role for real factors, some contemporary observers attributed most of the market's rise to fundamentals. At the height of the market in August 1929, when many began to fear that there was excessive speculation, Charles Amos Dice (1929) of Ohio State University argued that the higher prices in the stock market were the product of economic fundamentals. Even after the crash in December 1929, Irving Fisher (1930) of Yale retained his conviction that the rise in stock prices was justified and wrote, "My own impression has

7 Wigmore (1985) offers a detailed description of the performance of individual firms and industries.

been and still is that the market went up principally because of sound, justified expectations of earnings, and only partly because of unreasoning and unintelligent mania for buying."

Both Dice and Fisher believed that earnings and dividends would continue to grow rapidly because of great economic improvements they saw in the economy. These changes—the systematic application of science to industry, the development of modern management techniques, and mergers that gained economies of scale and scope—are the same ones that economic historians have emphasized to explain growth in the '20s. Thus, although Galbraith ridiculed Dice and Fisher in the aftermath of the crash, their views cannot be dismissed lightly.

The convictions of Fisher and Dice have more recently found support in the work of Sirkin (1975). He believes that the high stock prices and high price-earnings ratios were a consequence of the expected rapid growth of earnings. Assuming that a price-earnings ratio of 15 would have been normal, Sirkin calculated that earnings would have had to grow at 9 percent for another 10 years in order for the peak P/E ratio of 20.4 to have been warranted. Since 9 percent was the average growth rate for 1925–1929, Sirkin concluded that there was no "speculative orgy."

The argument for a fundamental explanation of the stock market boom holds that the rise in stock prices would have been justified by continued economic growth if policy blunders by the Federal Reserve and the Congress had not plunged the economy into a depression. However, given the normal duration of business cycles, it seems unlikely that the boom could have been sustained that long. Furthermore, it is by no means evident that it was appropriate for the public simply to extrapolate from the growth rate of the past few years.

In analyzing the role of fundamentals, researchers have only had annual data, yet this hides some of the key developments of 1928–1929. Quarterly earnings are not available, but White (1989) created a new quarterly index of dividends for the firms in the Dow-Jones Index from 1922 to 1930. In Figure 12.3, this index and the Dow-Jones Industrial Index are graphed. This figure reveals the remarkable change that overtook the stock market. From 1922 to 1927 dividends and prices moved together, but while dividends continued to grow rather smoothly in 1928 and 1929, stock prices soared far above them.

The behavior of prices and dividends seems to imply that managers did not share the public's enthusiasm. Investors might have bid up stock prices based on an extrapolation of a few years' earnings growth, but managers did not increase dividends as quickly. The failure of dividends to keep pace with stock prices does not, however, necessarily imply the existence of a bubble, as it is generally believed that managers are hesitant to increase dividends unless they perceive a permanent rise in earnings. Yet, the available evidence suggests that many managers did not believe that their earnings would rise sufficiently fast to justify the prices of their stock.[8] Some executives were alarmed enough to warn the public. In 1928, A. P. Giannini, head of Bancitaly (the future Bank of America) stated that

8 Marsh and Merton (1987) have offered a model of the dividend behavior for the aggregate stock market. When White (1990) applied this model and forecast dividends for the 1929 boom, he found that the expected dividends differed little from the actual dividends, suggesting that stock prices should not have soared.

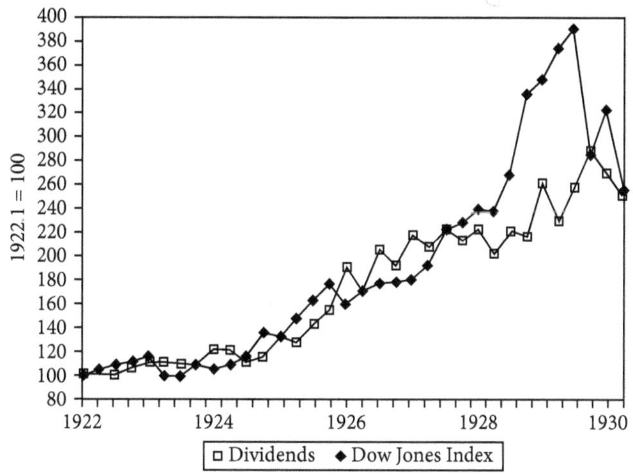

FIGURE 12.3 **Stock Price and Dividend Indices**

Source: White (1990) and Pierce (1986).

the high price of his bank's stock was unwarranted, prompting a sharp drop. Patterson (1965) has identified other companies where the management publicly stated that the stock was overvalued, notably Canadian Marconi and Brooklyn Edison.

A change in fundamentals may have initiated the boom, but fundamentals probably did not sustain it. The continued disappointment of unrealized dividends and public statements of some managers did not slow the rise in stock prices. This leaves the greater part of the boom to be explained. One favored candidate is easy credit.

Credit and the Stock Market Boom

Many economic historians believe that the expansion of brokers' loans helped to create the bubble.[9] Kindleberger argues that stock market credit was a key element in generating the mania. Galbraith sees the ability to purchase stock on margin as a great speculative lure. A buyer needed only to provide a fraction of the required funds, borrow the rest and enjoy the full capital gain less the interest on the borrowed funds. Even Irving Fisher believed that ability to borrow money encouraged "unwise speculation."

It is easy to understand the presumption that a credit expansion fueled the stock market boom by looking at Figure 12.4. This graphs an index of the New York Stock Exchange's

9 When an investor bought stock on margin, his broker usually paid the difference by contracting a broker's loan from a bank that was collateralized by the stock. Call loans were the most important type of brokers' loans. These loans had a daily call option and floating interest rate. Of lesser importance were time loans that had a fixed maturity and interest rate.

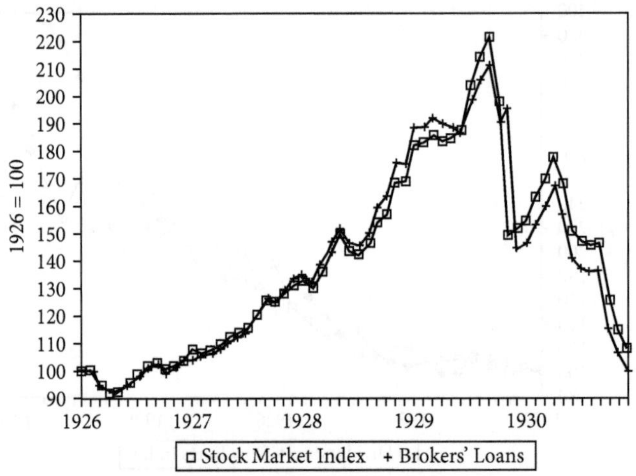

FIGURE 12.4 **Stock Prices and Brokers' Loans**

Source: Board of Governors of the Federal Reserve system (1943) and the New York Stock Exchange *Year Book* (1931).

brokers' loans and an index of stock prices. These two indices are almost indistinguishable, especially for the period of the boom. While this coincidence may seem convincing, it is hard to understand how credit to buy stock could have been easy when credit in general was tight in the second half of the 1920s. The Federal Reserve pursued a contractionary policy beginning in January 1928, with open market sales and a rise in the discount rate from 3½ to 5 percent. By Hamilton's (1987) measurement, money was tight during the whole course of the boom. In 1928 and 1929, high-powered money and the consumer price index fell and Ml grew only slightly in 1929.

The Federal Reserve's tight money policy during these years was a consequence of its fears about the flow of credit to the stock market. The Federal Reserve had always been concerned about excessive credit for speculation. Its founders were influenced by the real bills doctrine and had hoped the new central bank's discounting activities would channel credit away from "speculative" and towards "productive" activities.[10] Although there was general agreement on this issue, the stock market boom created a severe split over policy.

The Federal Reserve Board believed that "direct pressure" could be used to rechannel credit away from speculation. To curb stock market speculation, the Board wanted member banks making loans on securities to be denied access to the discount window. The Federal Reserve Bank of New York contended that the Federal Reserve could not refuse to discount otherwise eligible assets for its individual members and that it was impossible to control credit selectively. It argued that speculation could only be reduced by raising the discount

10 The real bills doctrine asserted that banks should invest primarily in short-term commercial bills that represented actual production. The Federal Reserve Act attempted, in part, to implement this doctrine by limiting the types of assets that were eligible for discounting at the Federal Reserve banks. See West (1977).

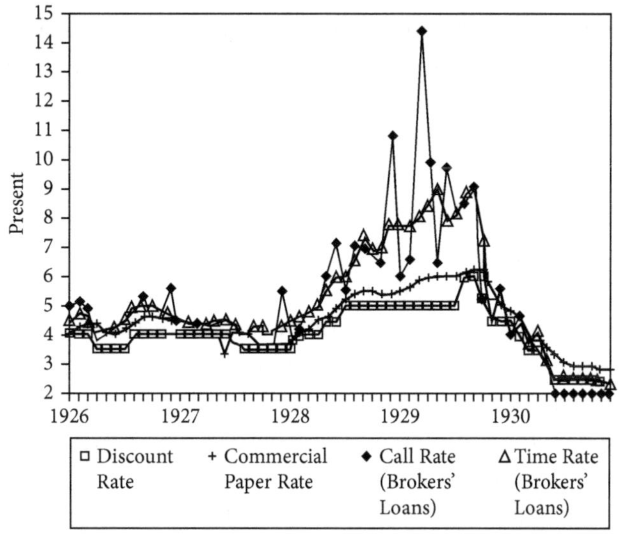

FIGURE 12.5 **Interest Rates**

Source: Board of Governors of the Federal Reserve System (1943).

rate. Between February 1929 and August 1929, the directors of the Federal Reserve Bank of New York frequently voted to raise the discount rate, only to be turned down by the Board, which reaffirmed its policy of direct pressure.

Looking at the rapid growth of brokers' loans in 1929, the Federal Reserve Board was understandably frustrated and angry, but it was not because its member banks failed to comply. Loans to brokers by New York member banks on their own account reached a peak at the end of December 1927, and then declined. Loans made by these banks on account for out-of-town banks also grew slowly during the boom. The rapid growth occurred in loans from private investors, corporations and foreign banks in Europe and Japan, which quickly substituted for bank loans.

Historians acknowledge this flexibility of credit, and Kindleberger identifies the rising supply of brokers' loans from non-bank sources as responsible for fueling the boom. This interpretation, however, ignores the rise in the interest rates on brokers' loans. Figure 12.5 shows the movements in the discount rate, the commercial paper rate and the two rates for brokers' loans. After moving together with the other two rates for 1926 and 1927, the call and time rates increased sharply. Although the differentials were not constant for the whole boom, they remained very large, suggesting that it was the rising tide of speculation that demanded funds, not any independent creation of credit.[11]

11 A simple econometric model of the market for brokers' loans (White, 1990) finds no evidence for a supply-side shift that could have fueled speculation.

The interest rate differentials also suggest that lenders no longer regarded brokers' loans as very safe and insisted on a substantial premium. This is buttressed by Smiley and Keehn's (1988) finding that margin requirements began to rise sharply in October 1928, soon reaching historic levels. While borrowers may have been quite sanguine about the rise in the market, lenders did not completely share their optimism.

Brokers' loans did not contribute to the stock market boom. Instead, the demand for credit to buy stock pulled funds into the market, forcing a major reallocation of credit in the money and capital markets.[12] As the call rate rose, there was a sharp decline in commercial paper. In September 1927, $600 million in commercial paper was outstanding. By September 1929, according to the Board of Governors of the Federal Reserve's *Banking and Monetary Statistics* (1943, pp. 465–466), it had declined to $265 million. Ivan Wright (1929) discovered that commercial banks provided more loans and discounts to firms that had previously relied on the commercial paper market. These firms' former lenders moved into the call market from which banks had been discouraged by the Federal Reserve. The growth in the new issues of domestic stock increased dramatically, while issues of domestic bonds and notes declined from $3183 million in 1927 to $2078 million in 1929 and foreign securities fell even more from $1338 million to $673 million. This evidence reaffirms the independent character of the stock market bubble, whose demand for funds and new issues forced major changes in other financial markets.

Testing for A Bubble in the Stock Market

If loans to buy stock were not cheap and the role of earnings and dividends was restricted, the surge in stock prices requires an alternative explanation. The surviving candidate is that a bubble appeared in the stock market. Although a large literature has explored the existence of bubbles in financial markets, the econometric identification of bubbles is elusive.[13] A large literature has explored existence of bubbles in financial markets. The models consider the possibility that the price of a stock may not reflect simply its market fundamentals—that is, the expected present value of all future dividends—but may also include some bubble element. Flood and Hodrick provide an exposition of the basic model in this journal. As they and Hamilton (1986) have pointed out, the problem with bubble tests is that they specify a set of market fundamentals and then ascribe any leftover price movements to a bubble. Thus, one may perceive a bubble only because the model was not correctly specified.

12 The stock market boom also had a powerful effect on the demand for money, via the demand for transactions balances to buy stocks. Field (1984) has shown that this caused money markets to tighten further as the boom progressed, misleading the Federal Reserve as to the actual effect of its policies.

13 See Diba and Grossman (1988), Campbell and Shiller (1988) and the related literature on stock market volatility, including Shiller (1981), Mankiw, Romer and Shapiro (1985), and Kleidon (1986).

In addition to this problem, these empirical tests have relied on annual data for stock prices and dividends. Annual data may be sufficient to detect long-term bubbles, but they will not pick up the 1928–1929 boom and bust. Furthermore, the data employed is all aggregate. As Figure 12.2 showed, not all stocks were caught up in a wave of speculation. Railroad stocks were excluded from the boom, while utilities were the favorites of speculators. Fisher's equally weighted stock price index (1966) reached its peak in February 1929, indicating that the majority of stocks on the New York Exchange did not fully participate in the boom. Thus, aggregate annual data may not capture a possible bubble in 1928–1929, even if the model is correctly specified.

Although dividend data for this period is almost exclusively annual, price data is more abundant. Using the daily and monthly Dow Jones Industrials index, Santoni (1987) and Santoni and Dwyer (1989) have performed runs tests and Box-Pierce tests on the estimated autocorrelations for the period of the boom. They found that prices followed a random walk and that there was no evidence for the market feeding on itself; however, as Blanchard and Watson (1982) and Shiller and Perron (1985) have shown, the power of these tests can be very low.

While it may be currently impossible to determine econometrically whether a bubble was present in the 1928–1929 stock market, considerable qualitative evidence suggests that the necessary conditions were present. Blanchard and Watson (1982) posit that bubbles are likely to appear when fundamentals become difficult to assess. Although they believe that bubbles are unlikely in blue chip stocks, the stock market of the 1920s had characteristics favorable to the emergence of bubbles. Fundamentals became difficult to judge because of major changes in industry. In automobiles, there was an abrupt shift from the dominance of the proprietary Ford Motor Co. to the more modern General Motors. While investors had every reason to expect earnings to grow, they lacked the means to evaluate easily the future path of dividends. RCA was also a highly successful firm in a new industry whose technology was rapidly changing. Not only were RCA's prospects uncertain but the absence of any dividend record left investors with little to judge fundamentals. Other high-tech firms and utilities, with no history of dividends and possibly brilliant futures, became favorites in the boom even though their fundamentals were difficult to assess.

The overall sophistication of investors was weakened by the influx of new people into the market. Since the turn of the century, the demands of industrial finance and regulation had reduced the role of commercial banks and increased the need to sell stock to the general public. Even before the boom began, many people who had never bought stock before entered the market. One identifiable group of new investors was women (McMullen, 1930), whom brokers catered to with special programs and even their own rooms to watch the ticker tape. Women's magazines carried articles on how to buy stocks, including John Raskob's famous interview (Crowther, 1929) entitled "Everybody Ought to be Rich." While these changes are not easy to quantify, they do provide qualitative evidence on the existence of conditions that enhanced the likelihood of a bubble appearing in the stock market.

The speculative urge that had propelled the market upwards began to falter in the autumn of 1929. The decline and then sudden plunge of the market has been well-chronicled, but the number and variety of explanations for the crash have left its causes unclear.

Causes of the Crash

The students of 1929 have had a tendency to minimize the importance of any single factor precipitating the crash. They treat the demise of the bull market as an endogenous collapse of expectations. Galbraith and Kindleberger argue that the stock market was inherently unstable and anything could have shattered the public's confidence. Yet something did convince investors that their expectations of future price increases were no longer justified. Contemporary pundits offered many explanations, including the excessive issues of new stock, decisions by government regulators, the Smoot-Hawley tariff, foreign stock markets, and declining brokers' loans. This section considers each of these and finds them to be minor or irrelevant factors in the crash. Instead, the downturn in the business cycle, made more severe by tight credit, prompted a revision in expectations.

The rising stock market made it attractive for companies to issue new stock. In 1927, $1474 million of new preferred and common shares were issued. By 1929, this reached $5924 million, with over $1 billion of shares issued in September. As in other bubbles, where speculation began with a nearly fixed supply of an asset, rapid price rises called forth significant additions to the supply. Fred I. Kent (Fisher, 1930, pp. 48–49) suggested that the issue of new securities overwhelmed the market. But while these increases were large, they were modest in comparison to the total supply. The value of the stocks listed on the New York exchange alone was $89.7 billion on September 1. In response to this increment in supply, prices might have sagged but not collapsed. New stock issues were, at most, a small contributing factor to the crash.

Utilities were among the high-flying stocks of 1929. Some pundits claimed that Massachusetts' refusal on October 11 to allow Boston Edison to split its stock sent a threatening signal to the market. Regulators denied the request on the grounds that it would encourage further speculation, and they began a rate inquiry. If the crash began in the utilities because of this announcement, there was no sign of anticipation or reaction in the Dow Jones indices. The index for utilities and the index for industrials dropped by the same proportion, under 1 percent on that day. While the regulatory decision was upsetting to the Boston Edison stockholders, it must be considered an irrelevant factor in the crash.

In most explanations of the Great Depression, the passage of the Smoot-Hawley tariff is regarded as a key factor in disrupting the international economy. Fisher (1930) believed that anticipation of the tariff contributed to the crash, while Jude Wanniski (1978) gives the tariff sole responsibility for the market's collapse. If the tariff was a key factor, it should have especially hurt the export industries through decreased foreign demand by the operation of the foreign trade multipliers and foreign tariff retaliation. Nontradeables and

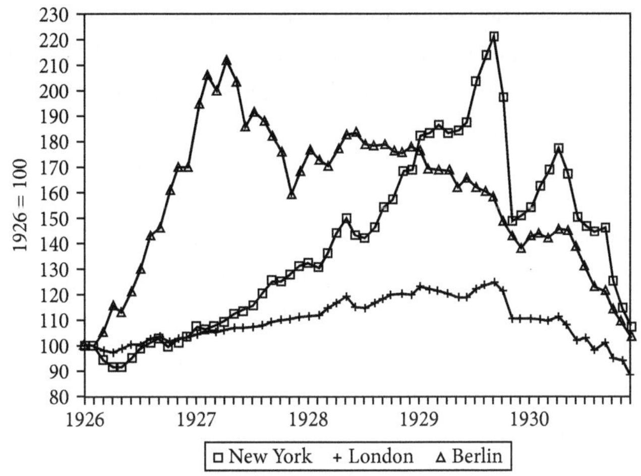

FIGURE 12.6 **European Stock Exchanges**

Source: Board of Governors of the Federal Reserve System (1943), *The Bankers' Magazine* (June 1931), and the *Federal Reserve Bulletin* (May 1931).

import-competing industries would not have sustained the same injury and might have benefited. After identifying industries as exporters, import-competing or nontradeables, White (1990) finds that the stocks of all groups declined approximately the same percentage at the time when the tariffs passage was assured. There is thus no evidence to support of the view that the Smoot-Hawley tariff significantly contributed to the crash.[14]

The failure in Great Britain of the business and financial empire of Clarence Hatry on September 20, 1929, has been cited by Galbraith, Patterson, and Fisher as an important shock to first the London and then the New York market. Fisher based his argument on his own stock price indices that showed London prices fall sharply and in advance of New York's. However, this drop does not square with the broad monthly index published by The Bankers' Magazine (1931). This index is depicted in Figure 12.6 along with indices for the New York and Berlin exchanges. By October 18, after Hatry and before the Wall Street plunge, the index had fallen 2.8 percent. This is far less than the drop Fisher found and hardly alarming, given larger earlier declines. Furthermore, American Railway stocks accounted for almost half of the 2.8 percent fall. The London market simply reacted to the New York market.

14 The assumption that the Smoot-Hawley tariff played a key role in beginning the Great Depression has recently been challenged by Eichengreen (1986). He finds that the direct and feedback effects of the tariff on the American economy were small and its stimulus to new foreign tariffs was slight. Eichengreen believes that the only way in which the tariff contributed to the depression was by increasing the American balance of payments surplus, thereby putting additional strain on other countries' ability to adjust under the gold standard. His work suggests that the market had even less reason to consider the passage of the Smoot-Hawley tariff singularly bad news.

In comparison to the worldwide bull markets of the 1980s, foreign stock markets in the 1920s often moved independently of New York, as seen in Figure 12.6. There was no boom in the Berlin market, which began falling in early 1928. The German decline stemmed partly from the reduction in post-World War I American lending, as investors turned their sights on New York, and partly from the tight monetary policies of the Reichsbank. The weak stock prices in European markets before October 1929 were more a consequence of the stock market boom than a cause of its demise. The Federal Reserve's tight monetary policy forced Great Britain and Germany to raise their discount rates to counter short-term capital's attraction to New York's high interest rates (Clarke, 1967). For months, the New York Fed had wanted a higher discount rate to tame the stock market. Finally the Board allowed it to raise its discount rate from 5 percent to 6 percent on August 9. As Hamilton (1987) has shown, falling prices made real rates much higher in 1929. Responding to a deterioration in their balance of payments, the British increased their bank rate again in September.

This general rise in interest rates did not have any immediately observable effects on brokers' loans. Weekly reports of brokers' loans show that they peaked on October 9 at $3941 million and then fell to $3823 million on October 23. This decline was not a signal of some catastrophe, as there had been larger temporary drops before. As in the months during the boom, brokers' loans responded rather than drove the stock market's decline.

The inadequacy of these explanations leads back to the question whether any abrupt change in dividends or earnings might have set off the crash. The aggregate figures give no hint of new developments. The quarterly dividends of the Dow-Jones industrials show healthy increases in late 1929, rising 12.8 percent in the third quarter and 11.6 percent in the fourth. The first drop of 6.3 percent appears only in the initial quarter of 1930.

However, there was evidence of an oncoming recession. In the absence of any quarterly earnings, the Federal Reserve's index of industrial production may be used as a proxy. This first dropped in July 1929.[15] In August and September, some of the Federal Reserve's other indices began to fall. This mixed news and rising real interest rates, at home and abroad, spelled an incipient recession; and it was all that was necessary to cause stockholders to revise their expectations.

The market drifted downwards in early October. As the volume of trading rose, brokerage firms were swamped, margin calls became more frequent and the ticker began to run behind. When prompt reporting of prices became impossible, investors lost track of their position. Panic selling began on Black Thursday and Black Tuesday. The vertical price drops forced margin calls on impaired accounts and led many others to liquidate their holdings. Although the frenzied selling occasionally abated, the market could not be talked up by bankers or by big investors' purchases of stock.

A more widespread financial crisis threatened as out-of-town banks and other lenders withdrew their loans to brokers. New York city banks stepped into the breach and quickly increased their loans. They were encouraged by the Federal Reserve Bank of New York,

15 The peak of the business cycle has been dated from August 1929. The decline in all the Federal Reserve's indices came only when the October figures were published after the crash.

which made open market purchases and let its members know that they could borrow freely at the discount window. The direct financial effects of the crash were thus confined to the stock market. The New York Fed's prompt action ensured that there were no panic increases in money market rates and no threat to the banks from defaults on security loans.

This intelligent policy was the doing of the New York Fed; and, as Friedman and Schwartz (1963) have chronicled, the Board disapproved and censured New York. In spite of the recession, the Board maintained its tight money policy. The continued decline in the stock market after October 1929 in Figure 12.1 reflects the economy's policy-aggravated slide into depression. This contrasts the market's recovery in 1988 when no recession was in the making and the Board recognized the importance of monetary ease.

Conclusion

The technological and structural changes in industry in the 1920s promised higher earnings and dividends. While these developments created a stock market boom, they also made fundamentals more difficult to evaluate, thus setting the stage for a bubble. The October panic can be traced to early signs of a recession that made the dissonance between dividends and stock prices clear. When panic selling began, intervention by the Federal Reserve Bank of New York prevented a collapse of the financial system. This response was appropriate, but the same cannot be said for earlier attempts to halt the market. Instead of allowing the stock market bubble to expand and burst of its own accord, the Federal Reserve's policies helped to push the economy further into a recession. Fear of a new speculative fever led the Federal Reserve Board to oppose easier monetary policy after the crash; hence, the tentative revival of the economy in 1930 was not assisted.

Although economists are generally skeptical about policy makers' ability to learn from history, the Federal Reserve did not make the same mistakes in 1987. In the months prior to the crash, the Fed was not preoccupied with speculation. When the collapse came, it followed the example of the New York Fed in 1929 and prevented a spillover to the banking system. Afterwards, it refocused its attention on general economic conditions. Spectacular as the crash of 1987 was, there was no reason for it to precipitate a second Great Depression.

References

Allen, Frederick Lewis, *Only Yesterday, An Informal History of the Nineteen-Twenties.* New York: Harper and Row, 1931.

The Bankers' Magazine, London, 1929–1931.

Blanchard, Olivier J., and Mark W. Watson, "Bubbles, Rational Expectations, and Financial Markets." In Wachtel, Paul, ed., *Crises in the Economic and Financial Structure.* Lexington: D. C. Heath and Co., 1982, pp. 295–316.

Board of Governors of the Federal Reserve System, *Banking and Monetary Statistics.* Washington, D.C.: U.S. Government Printing Office, 1943.

Campbell, John Y., and Robert J. Shiller, "Stock Prices, Earnings and Expected Dividends," *Journal of Finance,* July 1988, *43,* 661–676.

Carosso, Vincent P., *Investment Banking in America, A History.* Cambridge: Harvard University Press, 1970.

Chandler, Alfred D., Jr., *The Visible Hand: The Managerial Revolution in American Business.* Cambridge: Harvard University Press, 1977.

Clarke, Stephen V. O., *Central Bank Cooperation, 1924–1931.* New York: Federal Reserve Bank of New York, 1967.

Commercial and Financial Chronicle, New York, 1928 and 1929.

Currie, Lauchlin, "The Decline of the Commercial Loan," *Quarterly Journal of Economics,* August 1931, *45,* 698–709.

Crowther, Samuel, "Everybody Ought to be Rich," *Ladies' Home Journal,* August 1929.

Diba, Behzad T., and Herschel I. Grossman, "Explosive Rational Bubbles in Stock Prices?" *American Economic Review,* June 1988, *78* , 520–530.

Dice, Charles Amos, *Hew Levels in the Stock Market.* New York: McGraw-Hill, 1929.

Eichengreen, Barry, "The Political Economy of the Smoot-Hawley Tariff," NBER Working Paper, August 1986.

Federal Reserve Bulletin, May 1931.

Field, Alexander J., "Asset Exchanges and the Transactions Demand for Money," *American Economic Review,* March 1984, 71, 43–59.

Fisher, Irving, *The Stock Market Crash—and After.* New York: Macmillan, 1930.

Fishes, Lawrence, "Some New Stock-Market Indexes," *Journal of Business,* 1966, *39,* 191–225.

Friedman, Milton, and Anna J. Schwartz, *A Monetary History of the United States, 1867–1960.* Princeton: Princeton University Press, 1963.

Galbraith, John Kenneth, *The Great Crash 1929.* Boston: Houghton Mifflin Company, 1954 and 1988.

Hamilton, James D., "Monetary Factors in the Great Depression," *Journal of Monetary Economics,* 1987, *19,* 145–169.

Hamilton, James D., "On Testing for Self-Fulfilling Speculative Price Bubbles," *International Economic Review,* October 1986, *27,* 545–552.

Kindleberger, Charles P., *Manias, Panics and Crashes: A History of Financial Crises.* New York: Basic Books, 1978.

Kleidon, Allan W., "Variance Bounds Tests and Stock Price Valuation Models," *Journal of Political Economy,* October 1986, *94,* 953–1001.

Mankiw, N. Gregory, David Romer, and Matthew D. Shapiro, "An Unbiased Reexamination of Stock Market Volatility," *Journal of Finance, July* 1985, *9,* 677–689.

Marsh, Terry A., and Robert C. Merton, " Dividend Behavior for the Aggregate Stock Market," *Journal of Business,* 1987, *60,* 1–40.

McMullen, Frances D., "Women and the Ticker Tape—A Year after the Crash," *The Women's Journal,* November 1930.

Neal, Larry D., "How the South Sea Bubble Was Blown Up and Burst." In White, Eugene N., ed., *Crises and Panics: The Lessons of History.* Homewood: Dow Jones-Irwin, 1990.

New York Stock Exchange, *Year Book,* 1930–1931, New York, 1931.

Patterson, Robert T., *The Great Boom and Panic, 1921–1929.* Chicago: Henry Regnery Company, 1965.

Peach, W. Nelson, *The Security Affiliates of National Banks.* Baltimore: Johns Hopkins Press, 1941.

Pierce, Phyllis, ed., *The Dow Jones Averages, 1885–1985.* Homewood: Dow Jones-Irwin, 1986.

Romer, Christina, "The Great Crash and the Onset of the Great Depression," NBER Working Paper, June 1988.

Santoni, Gary, "The Great Bull Markets 1924–1929 and 1982–1987: Speculative Bubbles or Economic Fundamentals?" *Federal Reserve Bank of St. Louis Review,* November 1987, *69,* 16–29.

Santoni, Gary, and Gerald P. Dwyer, Jr., "Bubbles vs Fundamentals: New Evidence from the Great Bull Markets." In White, Eugene N., ed., *Crises and Panics: The Lessons of History.* Homewood: Dow Jones/Irwin, 1989.

Shiller, Robert J., "Do Stock Prices Move Too Much to be Justified by Subsequent Changes in Dividends?" *American Economic Review,* June 1981, *71,* 421–436.

Shiller, Robert J., and Pierre Perron, "Testing the Random Walk Hypothesis: Power versus Frequency of Observation," *Economic Letters,* 1985, *18,* 381–386.

Sirkin, Gerald, "The Stock Market of 1929 Revisited: A Note," *Business History Review,* Summer 1975, *44,* 223–31.

Smiley, Gene, and Richard H. Keehn, " Margin Purchases, Brokers' Loans and the Bull Market of the Twenties," *Business and Economic History,* 1988, *17,* 129–142.

U.S. Department of Commerce, *Historical Statistics of the United States, Colonial Times to 1970,* Washington, D.C.: U.S. Government Printing Office, 1975.

Wanniski, Jude, *The Way the World Works.* New York: Basic Books, 1978.

West, Robert Craig, *Banking Reform and the Federal Reserve, 1863–1923.* Ithaca: Cornell University Press, 1977.

Wigmore, Barrie A., *The Crash and Its Aftermath.* Westport: Greenwood Press, 1985.

White, Eugene N., "Banking Innovation in the 1920s: The Growth of National Banks' Financial Services," *Business and Economic History,* 1984, *13,* 92–104.

White, Eugene N., "Before the Glass-Steagall Act: An Analysis of the Investment Banking Activities of National Banks," *Explorations in Economic History,* January 1986, *23,* 33–55.

White, Eugene N., "When the Ticker Ran Late: The Stock Market Boom and Crash of 1929." In White, Eugene N., ed., *Crises and Panics: The Lessons of History.* Homewood: Dow Jones/Irwin, 1990.

Wright, Ivan, "Loans to Brokers and Dealers for Account of Others," *Journal of Business,* April 1929, *2,* 117–36.

CHAPTER THIRTEEN

The Nation in Depression

Christina D. Romer

The economic cataclysm of the 1930s was an international phenomenon experienced by countries in all parts of the globe. Countries as diverse as the United States, Germany, Chile, and Japan all experienced significant depressions in the 1930s. Thus, the title of Charles Kindleberger's classic book *The World in Depression* (1973) captures an important feature of the Great Depression. These international aspects, especially the importance of the gold standard in causing the downturn and transmitting depression from one country to another, have been emphasized in recent years in excellent books by Peter Temin (1989) and Barry Eichengreen (1992). These books have rightly received widespread attention and have successfully changed the focus of much analysis of the Great Depression from the United States to the world economy.

While such a change from American provincialism is surely healthy and warranted, adopting an international perspective on the Great Depression risks losing sight of the many ways in which the U.S. depression differed in timing and severity from depressions elsewhere. More important, it may obscure the many uniquely American causes of America's Great Depression.

This paper examines the ways in which the U.S. experience during the 1930s resembled that of other countries in some regards, and fundamentally differed in other aspects. I also evaluate the evidence on the causes of the Great Depression in the United States and the sources of the eventual recovery. I suggest that the path of American output and unemployment before 1931 can be explained quite well with only domestic factors. Even after 1931, international factors affected American economic conditions mainly through their impact on American policy decisions. In many ways the broad conclusion of this paper is summarized well in another classic book on the interwar era. In *Economic Survey, 1919–1939,* Arthur Lewis states (1949, p. 52):

> It is clear that the centre of the depression was the United States of America, in the sense that most of what happened elsewhere has to be explained in terms of the American contraction, while that contraction is hardly explicable in any but internal terms.

Comparative National Experiences

The experiences of various countries during the 1930s is a well-worked topic.[1] This section uses annual data on industrial production for 24 countries to illustrate many salient features of the individual national experiences. I focus on industrial production because this series is often the most accurately measured national indicator of macroeconomic health.[2] Furthermore, many other series that one might think are more representative of a business cycle, such as the unemployment rate or real GNP, are very highly correlated with industrial production.

The Great Depression started in most countries at around the same time. This can be seen in Figure 13.1, which shows industrial production in five major countries between 1927 and 1937. In annual data, the peak in industrial production occurred in 1929 for 13 of the 22 countries for which a peak can be identified.[3] Seven countries peaked in 1930 and two peaked in 1931. The only country to peak in 1928 was Poland, which was a fairly minor industrial country.[4] The countries in which production peaked in 1929 include most of the major industrial producers, such as the United States, Canada, Germany, Japan, and the United Kingdom. France and Sweden were the largest industrial countries to peak in 1930.

Based just on industrial production, there is little in the timing of the onset of the Great Depression to set the United States apart from the 12 other countries tied for first place. If one wanted to argue that the United States was in some sense earlier than the others, the series to analyze would be some indicator of building activity. Construction was the first sector to weaken in the United States and it weakened sooner here than elsewhere. Of the 11 countries for which the League of Nations provides data on building permits or some other indicator of building plans, only the United States and Belgium peaked in 1928.[5] Planned construction did not turn down in countries such as Germany, France, and the United Kingdom until 1929 or later.

1 In addition to Kindleberger (1973) and Lewis (1949), Eichengreen (1992) and Eichengreen and Sachs (1985) point out crucial similarities and differences in the experience of various countries during the Great Depression.

2 The industrial production data reported by the League of Nations were typically compiled by government agencies in the individual countries. As a result, the quality of the series differs substantially from one country to another. The American series, which is from the Board of Governors of the Federal Reserve System, is among the more comprehensive and reliable national indexes.

3 No peak or trough can be identified for the Soviet Union, because it grew continuously through the Great Depression, or for South Africa, because the data for 1931 and 1932 are missing.

4 In the League of Nations index of world industrial production, Poland gets a weight of 2.1 percent, while the United States gets a weight of 31.1 percent. The weights assigned to the other countries in the top five are: Germany, 17.5 percent; United Kingdom, 12.9 percent; France, 10.1 percent; and Japan, 5.9 percent (League of Nations, 1932, p. 47).

5 The building activity data are from the League of Nations (1936, Appendix II, Table 3, pp. 154–155). In this comparison I only include countries for which the data reflect permits or some other indicator of planned, rather than completed, construction.

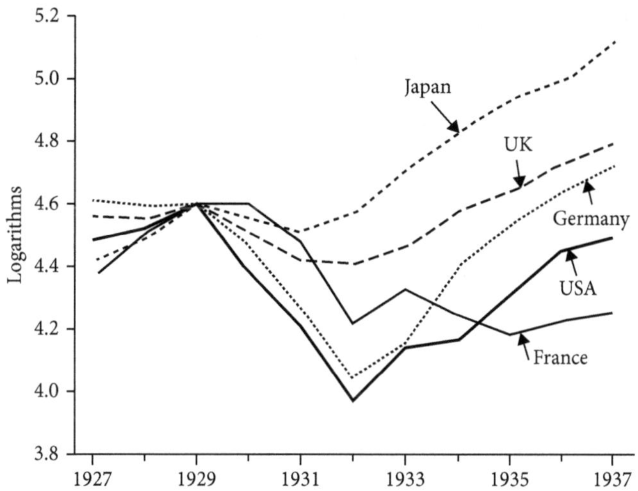

FIGURE 13.1 **Annual Industrial Production in Five Countries, 1927–1937**

Sources: The data on industrial production for 24 countries are from the League of Nations (1936, Appendix II, Table 2, p. 142 and 1938, Table 1, p. 44).

While the early downturn in construction is one way in which the onset of the Depression in the United States differed from other countries, more important differences involve the immediate severity of the Great Depression in the United States and the peculiar composition of the decline in American output. For most countries, the first year of the Great Depression was a fairly ordinary bad year. Table 13.1 shows the distribution of the percentage fall in industrial production between 1929 and 1930. The median decline in output for the 15 countries experiencing a decline was just over 9 percent. Industrial production in the United States, in contrast, declined 21 percent in the first year of the Depression. Thus, the Depression was "great" in the United States sooner than elsewhere.

Another feature of the American experience in 1930 was that the initial fall in industrial production was more concentrated in consumer goods and less concentrated in investment goods than in many other countries. For example, the ratio of the percentage fall in the production of investment goods to the percentage fall in the production of consumption goods was just over two for the United States, but close to three for Canada and over four for Germany.[6] In the United Kingdom, however, the decline in industrial production in 1930 was even more skewed toward consumption goods than in the United States.

6 These composite indexes of the production of investment goods and current consumption goods are from the League of Nations (1938, Appendix III, Table 2, pp. 124–25). This comparison quite likely understates the peculiarity of the behavior of American consumption in 1930 because the consumption series indexes include mainly nondurables, while an unusually large fraction of the initial decline in consumption in the United States was in durable goods.

TABLE 13.1 **Distribution of the Percentage Change in Industrial Production**

A. 1930

Percentage Change	Countries
5.1 to 10%	Denmark, South Africa, New Zealand
0.0 to 5%	Chile, France, Greece, Norway, Sweden
-0.1 to -5%	Estonia, Romania
-5.1 to -10%	Finland, Hungary, Italy, Japan, Netherlands, UK
-10.1 to -15%	Belgium, Czechoslovakia, Germany
-15.1 to -20%	Austria, Canada, Poland
-20.1 to -25%	USA

B. Peak to Trough

Percentage Change	Countries
-0.1 to -10%	Greece, Japan, New Zealand
-10.1 to -20%	Denmark, Romania, Sweden, UK
-20.1 to -30%	Chile, Estonia, Finland, Hungary, Norway
-30.1 to -40%	Belgium, France, Italy
-40.1 to -50%	Austria, Netherlands
-50.1 to -60%	Canada, Czechoslovakia, Germany
-60.1 to -70%	Poland, USA

C. 1933

Percentage Change	Countries
15.1 to 20%	USA
10.1 to 15%	Denmark, Finland, France, Germany, Japan, Netherlands, Romania
5.1 to 10%	Chile, Greece, Hungary, Italy, UK
0.0 to 5%	Austria, Belgium, Canada, Estonia, New Zealand, Norway, Poland, Sweden
-0.1 to -5%	
-5.1 to -10%	Czechoslovakia

Sources and Notes: The data on industrial production for 24 countries are from the League of Nations (1936, Appendix II, Table 2, p. 142 and 1938, Table 1, p. 44). The data for 1925 to 1929 are converted to a 1929 base to be consistent with later data. The Soviet Union is excluded from all parts because it did not experience any fall in output during the 1930s. South Africa is excluded from Parts B and C because the data for 1931 and 1932 are missing.

As the Great Depression dragged on through 1931 and 1932, nearly all countries experienced a significant depression. However, there was again substantial variation in the peak to trough amplitude across the countries for which the League of Nations collected industrial production data.[7] In this contest the United States was a clear loser, with a peak to trough fall in industrial production of 62 percent. Only Poland also experienced a fall

7 The peaks and troughs refer to the actual highs and lows in the annual data on industrial production. For most countries there was no ambiguity in these dates because there was a single high followed by a single low. However, for France, the observations for 1929 and 1930 were the same and there was an intervening peak in 1932 before the absolute trough in 1935; 1930 and 1935 were chosen as the turning points. For Romania, there was a local peak in 1929 and a local trough in 1930 before the absolute extremes in 1931 and 1932; 1931 and 1932 were chosen as the turning points.

in production of this magnitude. The experiences of all of the countries are shown in Part B of Table 13.1. As can be seen, Canada, Czechoslovakia, and Germany experienced peak to trough declines in output approaching that of the United States. On the other hand, several major industrial countries, including the United Kingdom, Japan, and Sweden, experienced remarkably mild downturns. For example, the peak to trough decline in industrial production in the United Kingdom was less than a third as large as that in the United States. France had a reasonably large peak to trough fall in production of just over 40 percent, but between the peak in 1929 and the absolute trough in 1935 there was a significant recovery in 1933.

The timing of the trough in industrial production, on which the preceding amplitudes are based, is remarkably similar across countries. Of the 22 countries for which a trough can be identified, 15 reached their lowest point in 1932. Figure 13.1, which shows industrial production in the five largest industrial producers, shows that the United States, Germany, and the United Kingdom are among the countries that have a trough in 1932. Japan, along with Chile, Finland, New Zealand, and Norway, hit bottom earlier, in 1931. Czechoslovakian industrial production reached its lowest point in 1933 and French industrial production, as just mentioned, did not reach its absolute minimum until 1935. Production in all of the remaining countries reached its lowest level in 1932.

Based on these turning points, there is no evidence that the United States was particularly unusual in the duration of the declining phase of the Depression; most of the industrial world turned around at roughly the same time. The United States was somewhat unusual, however, in the strength of the initial recovery. As can be seen in Part C of Table 13.1, industrial production in 1933 grew faster in the United States than in any other nation, though France, Germany, and Japan were all close behind. U.S. growth slowed noticeably in 1934, but then surged again in 1935 and 1936.

The composition of the growth of industrial production during the early recovery in the United States was also somewhat different from that of many other countries. While the initial downturn had been skewed toward a fall in the production of consumer goods, the initial upturn in the United States was skewed toward an increase in the production of investment goods. According to League of Nations statistics, the output of investment goods in the United States rose 42 percent in 1933, while the output of consumer goods rose 10 percent, a ratio of more than four to one. In Japan and the United Kingdom, in contrast, production of investment goods rose only about twice as fast as production of consumption goods, and in France production of investment goods grew less rapidly than production of consumption goods. Germany had a composition of production growth that was similar to that of the United States.

While various countries began their recoveries at roughly the same time, there was much variation in when each economy was (in some sense) fully recovered. A crude measure of the date of recovery is simply the year in which industrial production reached its pre-Depression peak. This occurred in 1932 for New Zealand; 1933 for Japan, Greece, and Romania; 1934 for Chile, Denmark, Finland, and Sweden; 1935 for Estonia, Hungary, Norway and the

United Kingdom; 1936 for Germany; and 1937 for Canada, Austria, and Italy. The United States, Belgium, Czechoslovakia, France, the Netherlands, and Poland did not recover before the end of the sample in 1937.[8] This comparison suggests that the United States was not only among the first countries to slip into depression, but also among the last to recover.

Causes of the American Depression

Documenting the timing and severity of the Great Depression in the United States and abroad is more straightforward than explaining what caused the national and international collapse. Not surprisingly, an experience as devastating and complex as the Great Depression has many different causes. Fortunately, the source of the Great Depression is a topic that has generated a vast literature and many fruitful conclusions. This section argues that the path of output and employment in the United States in the 1930s is, contrary to common perception, very well understood. I also suggest that, at least up until the start of the third year of the American Depression, domestic factors were the prime cause of the drastic decline in American output.

Framework

At the broadest conceptual level, the Great Depression in the United States can be analyzed quite well with the simple aggregate supply-aggregate demand model familiar to introductory economics students. Between 1929 and 1933, a series of shocks caused aggregate demand to decline repeatedly in the United States. These declines in aggregate demand moved the economy down along an upward-sloping aggregate supply curve. The net result was both progressively worsening unemployment and deflation.

There is substantial disagreement among scholars about why and when the U.S. aggregate supply curve became upward sloping, though nearly all agree that wages and prices were far from perfectly flexible in the 1920s and 1930s. Some studies of price flexibility conclude that wages and prices have been sticky since the turn of the twentieth century, implying that the only thing unique about the Great Depression was the size of the shocks (Allen, 1992; Schultze, 1981; Gordon, 1980). Other studies, using different data and different specifications, find that wages and prices did not become less flexible until around the time of the Great Depression (Sachs, 1980; Mitchell, 1985; O'Brien, 1989). For example, O'Brien argues that nominal wages became particularly rigid in 1929 and 1930 because firms were mistakenly convinced that maintaining wages would be good for business. He suggests that this belief had its origins in the bankruptcies of the early 1920s and President Hoover's oratory. Other factors often cited as explanations for increased rigidity after World War I are the rise of internal labor markets, which replaced day-to-day wage agreements with

8 The League of Nations data are not kept on the same basis after 1937. Using the modern Federal Reserve Board index of industrial production (the League's American statistics are based on an early version of this index), industrial production in the United States returned to its 1929 level in 1937, but then fell again in 1938.

set pay scales, and the increasing size and market power of American corporations, which broke the lockstep relationship between costs and prices.[9]

There is also substantial disagreement about whether more wage and price flexibility would have prevented aggregate demand movements from having the large real effects that they had in the 1930s. In the conventional textbook model a fall in wages and prices raises real balances, lowers interest rates, and thus stimulates investment. The rise in investment serves to counteract at least some of the fall in demand. Tobin (1975) and De Long and Summers (1986) suggest that this traditional model is too simplistic because it ignores the effect of deflation on expectations. Since the expected real interest rate is what matters for investment decisions, deflation, which generates expectations of further deflation, could in fact depress aggregate demand further by raising real rates. Proponents of the debt-deflation hypothesis, first enunciated in the context of the Great Depression by Irving Fisher (1933), add that unanticipated deflation, by raising the real value of existing debt, raises the risk of default and depresses the economy by limiting credit availability.

Despite this debate on the role of deflation, the fact that prices and wages were not perfectly flexible in the 1920s and 1930s means that movements in aggregate demand had real effects. Thus, the discussion about the causes of the Great Depression in the United States has rightly focused on the source of the collapse in aggregate demand in the late 1920s and early 1930s. The evidence suggests that domestic spending shocks related to the stock market crash were crucial in the first year of the Depression, while monetary shocks were important in later years. The later monetary shocks were partly the result of slavish adherence to the gold standard and partly due to the peculiarities of American financial institutions and policies.

The Start of Recession

The U.S. economy was clearly cooling off in the summer of 1929, as shown by the monthly data on U.S. industrial production in Figure 13.2. Seasonally-adjusted industrial production peaked in July 1929 and declined slowly between July and October 1929 (falling 3 percent over three months). The source of this slowdown is almost surely the tightening of Federal Reserve policy in 1928. Hamilton (1987) shows that the Federal Reserve began contractionary open market sales of securities in January 1928. This policy did not result in a drastic decline in the money supply because banks greatly increased their borrowing at the discount window. According to Hamilton (p. 149), banks undertook this heavy borrowing because the boom on the stock market led to enough of an increase in the demand for loans that "banks found it profitable to replace unborrowed reserves with borrowed reserves despite the sharply higher cost of doing so."

The interaction of the open market sales and the increased demand for money and brokers' loans caused by the stock market boom (documented by Field, 1984) led to a significant

9 Jacoby (1985) discusses the rise of internal labor markets and Alfred Chandler (1977) documents the fundamental change in the structure of American business around World War I.

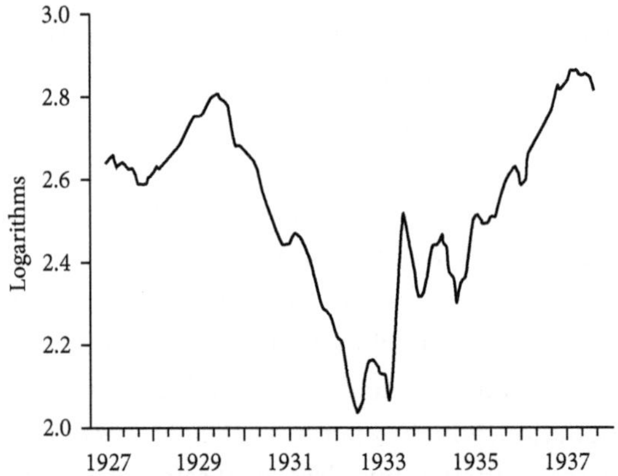

FIGURE 13.2 **Monthly Industrial Production in the United States, 1927–1937**

Sources and Notes: The industrial production series is from the U.S. Board of Governors of the Federal Reserve System (1986, Table A.5, p. 171). This series is on a 1977 base and is seasonally adjusted.

increase in both nominal and real interest rates. Figure 13.3 shows that the nominal commercial paper rate rose from 4.0 percent in the fourth quarter of 1927 to 5.5 percent in the fourth quarter of 1928. The realized real interest rate—calculated by subtracting the change in the producer price index over the following quarter (at an annual rate) from the commercial paper interest rate—rose even more steeply, from 5.6 percent in the fourth quarter of 1927 to 9.5 percent in the fourth quarter of 1928. Regression estimates of the expected real interest rate (that is the nominal rate less expected inflation), which are given in Figure 13.3, also show a substantial rise in real short-term rates.[10]

This rise in interest rates is enough to explain why the economy was slipping into a recession in the middle of 1929. The industries that started to decline first were those that were typically thought to be interest-sensitive. For example, as discussed previously, building permits for new construction in the United States peaked in 1928 and then declined 21 percent between 1928 and 1929. New automobile registrations peaked in November 1928, rebounded slightly in the spring of 1929, and peaked for the last time in July 1929.[11]

The monetary explanation for the onset of recession in the United States is more plausible than alternative explanations that stress the fact, evident in Figure 13.1, that Germany and the United Kingdom experienced a minor recession in 1928 before rebounding

10 These estimates are derived from a regression of realized real interest rates on current and lagged values of the growth rate of industrial production, the inflation rate, the nominal commercial paper rate, the growth rate of M1 relative to normal, and quarterly dummy variables. Under the assumption of rational expectations, the fitted values of the regression provide estimates of expected real interest rates. See Romer (1992) for a complete description of this estimation.

11 The automobile registration data are from Standard Statistics (1930, p. 182). I seasonally adjust this series by regressing the logarithm of registrations on eleven monthly dummy variables, a constant, and a linear trend.

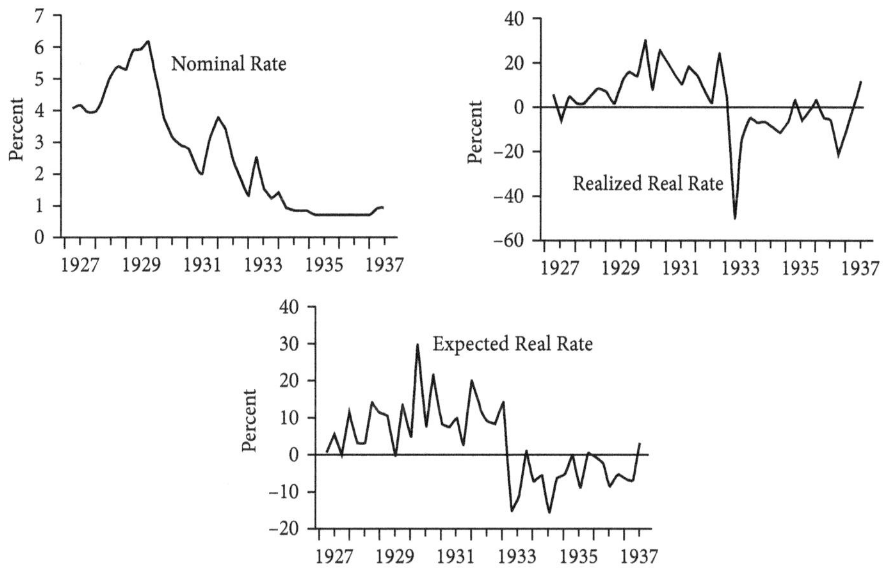

FIGURE 13.3 **Quarterly Commercial Paper Rates in the United States, 1927–1937**

Sources and Notes: The nominal commercial paper rate data are from the U.S. Board of Governors of the Federal Reserve System (1943, pp. 448-451, and 1976, p. 674). The data cover four- to six-month prime commercial paper and are not seasonally adjusted. The realized real interest rate series is calculated by subtracting the change in the producer price index over the following quarter (at an annual rate) from the nominal commercial paper rate. The producer price index is from the Bureau of Labor Statistics (1986). In this calculation neither series has been seasonally adjusted. The expected real commercial paper rate series is from Romer (1992, Figure 4).

somewhat in 1929. Such a recession abroad could have affected the U.S. economy by depressing our exports. However, American exports continued to rise between 1928 and 1929, suggesting that this effect was not present. Furthermore, at their highest, U.S. real exports in the mid-1920s were only a little over 6 percent of real GNP.[12] Therefore, even a large fall in American exports would have been unlikely to depress the U.S. economy greatly.

The likely importance of monetary tightness in mid-1929 suggests that a domestic policy decision was the cause of the onset of the recession that eventually became the Great Depression. However, this policy decision could certainly have had international roots. Hamilton (1987) and Temin (1989) both suggest that the change in Federal Reserve policy came at least partly in response to an outflow of U.S. gold to France because of an undervaluation of the French franc. Thus, adherence to the gold standard was to some degree responsible for the change in monetary policy. As Hamilton notes, however, protection of the gold standard could not have been the only motivation of the Federal

12 The series on real exports is constructed by ratio splicing the index of the quantity of total U.S. domestic exports from the Bureau of the Census (1975, Series U225, pp. 891–92) onto real exports in 1982 dollars from the Bureau of Economic Analysis (1986, Table 1.2, p. 6) in 1929. Real GNP in 1982 dollars is constructed by ratio splicing the Kendrick real GNP series (1961, Table A-IIa, p. 294) onto the BEA series in 1929.

Reserve because the monetary stringency continued even after gold inflows began in 1929. Hamilton's (p. 148) view is that "the major factor influencing monetary policy during 1928–1929 was surely the stock market." This view is echoed by Friedman and Schwartz (1963, p. 290), Temin (1989, pp. 22–23), and Eichengreen (1992, p. 217). By all these accounts, the Federal Reserve hoped to stem the stock market boom by raising interest rates.

While adherence to the gold standard was probably not the main factor behind the change in U.S. monetary policy in 1928, it was a crucial factor in determining the response of other countries. Eichengreen (1992) suggests that because the gold stocks of most European countries were already low by the mid-1920s, the increase in the U.S. interest rates, which drew gold to the United States, forced many countries to tighten their monetary policies along with the United States. Thus, the roughly contemporaneous cooling off of most of the world economy can be understood as a feedback effect from U.S. monetary policy aimed at stemming the American stock market boom.

The Onset of the Great Depression

The recession that started in the United States in the summer of 1929 became suddenly worse following the stock market crash in October 1929. Between October and December 1929, industrial production declined nearly 10 percent, and by the end of 1930 the Great Depression had started in earnest in the United States. Indeed, the decline in output during the first 18 months of the Depression was almost as large as in most previous and subsequent recessions in their entirety. For example, the fall in industrial production from the peak in July 1929 to December 1930 was 37 percent, while the peak to trough decline for the recession of 1921 was 40 percent and for that of 1938 was 39 percent. As discussed above, this was not true of most other countries; the rest of the world experienced much milder drops in industrial output in the first year of the Great Depression.

The source of this sharp decline is almost surely not contractionary monetary policy. The monetary contraction in 1928, though significant, was not large by historical standards. For example, while the nominal commercial paper rate rose 1½ percentage points between 1927 and 1928 (fourth quarter to fourth quarter), it rose nearly three percentage points between 1919 and 1920. Realized real rates, which rose just under four percentage points between 1927 and 1928, rose an unbelievable 140 percentage points between 1919 and 1920 because of an enormous drop in producer prices. Furthermore, immediately following the stock market crash, the Federal Reserve Bank of New York bought large amounts of government bonds, thus increasing the stock of high-powered money. Both nominal and real interest rates fell substantially between the fourth quarter of 1929 and the first quarter of 1930; for example, the nominal commercial paper rate fell from 6.25 percent to 4.88 percent over this interval and the regression estimates of the expected real commercial paper rate given in Figure 13.3 fell 9.1 percentage points. Real rates surged up again in the second quarter of 1930, but are not consistently high until after

TABLE 13.2 **Decomposition of the Change in GNP in the United States in Recessions**

		Fraction of the Change in GNP Accounted for by:				
Year	Percentage Change in GNP	Consumption	Inventory Investment	Fixed Investment	Net Exports	Government Purchases
1904	-1.3	−0.76	0.66	0.83	0.26	0.01
1908	-8.6	0.56	0.24	0.35	-0.05	-0.10
1914	-7.9	0.12	0.23	0.63	0.09	-0.08
1917	-2.4	0.66	0.74	0.74	0.26	-1.40
1920	-1.1	-2.92	-1.71	-0.68	1.44	4.88
1921	-2.4	-1.95	2.56	0.51	0.43	-0.56
1930	-9.3	0.46	0.24	0.38	0.02	-0.10
1931	-6.2	0.38	0.03	0.62	0.06	-0.09
1932	-15.8	0.50	0.20	0.26	0.01	0.04
1933	-3.0	0.66	0.04	0.19	0.09	0.03
1938	-5.5	0.22	0.94	0.38	-0.26	-0.28

Sources and Notes: The data on real GNP and its components are from Kendrick (1961, Table A-IIa, pp. 293–295). The table shows the decomposition of the change in GNP for all years between 1900 and 1942 in which GNP declined. The rows may not sum to one because of rounding.

the banking panic in October 1930. Thus, it is hard to see how monetary conditions, working through conventional channels, could have caused the nasty turn that the depression took in late 1929.

The onset of the Great Depression in the United States following the stock market crash was led by a collapse in domestic consumption spending. As discussed above, consumer spending played a larger role in the fall in output in the United States between 1929 and 1930 than in many other countries. Temin (1976) points out that consumer spending in the United States declined much more in 1930 than in either 1921 or 1938, the two other significant interwar recessions. Table 13.2 shows the composition of the decline in real GNP in the United States in every year in which GNP fell between 1900 and 1942. While Temin's comparison of 1930 to 1921 and 1938 clearly overstates the peculiarity of 1930, it is certainly true that consumption accounted for a much larger fraction of the decline in real GNP in 1930 than in most previous or subsequent recessions. Indeed, the only years of GNP decline outside the Depression when consumption was nearly as important were 1917, when the United States was participating in World War I, and 1908, another year of substantial stock market volatility.

Table 13.2 also re-emphasizes how unimportant net exports were to the onset of the Great Depression in the United States. The fall in net exports in 1930 accounted for just 2 percent of the total decline in real GNP. This is much smaller than the contribution of net exports in the three recessions just before the Great Depression.[13] This suggests that the international downturn had little feedback effect on the U.S. economy through American exports.

The most likely source of the precipitous drop in American consumption following the stock market crash in 1929 is the crash itself. In a previous paper, I showed that the stock market crash in October 1929 and the subsequent gyrations of stock prices through the middle of 1930 generated tremendous uncertainty about future income; the stock price movements did not necessarily make consumers and investors pessimistic about the future, only highly uncertain (Romer, 1990). This uncertainty is clearly reflected in the forecasts made by contemporary analysts. Not only was there more variation across forecasts of future income immediately following the Great Crash, but the analysts expressed great uncertainty about their forecasts and speculated that consumers and businessmen felt the same way.

The effect of this uncertainty was that consumers and producers immediately cut their spending on irreversible durable goods as they waited for additional information about the future. This effect is seen most clearly in the fact that department store sales and automobile registrations declined precipitously in November and December 1929, while grocery store sales and ten-cent store sales actually rose; this is exactly what one would expect if consumers were shying away from irreversible goods but had not substantially changed their point estimates of future income. The role of the stock market crash in causing the decline in consumer purchases of durable goods is also seen in regressions of the output of consumer durables on total output, lagged output, wealth, and stock market volatility (Romer, 1990, p. 610). The coefficients from such regressions suggest that stock market volatility has a significant negative effect on the output of consumer durables and that the tremendous rise in volatility in late 1929 and early 1930 can more than account for all of the fall in the production of consumer durables in 1930.[14] In addition to its effect through uncertainty, the stock market crash may also have depressed consumer spending by decreasing wealth (Temin, 1976) and by shifting households' balance sheets toward illiquidity (Mishkin, 1978).

This discussion suggests that both the initial recession in the United States in the summer of 1929 and the acceleration of the decline in late 1929 and 1930 are ultimately attributable to the stock market boom and bust of the late 1920s. The stock market boom is the prime explanation for why the Federal Reserve was pursuing tight monetary policy starting in

---

13 This result also holds if one examines exports rather than net exports. Real exports accounted for just under 10 percent of the decline in real GNP in 1930. In 1914 they accounted for 11 percent of the fall in GNP; in 1917 they accounted for 51 percent; and in 1921 they accounted for 53 percent.

14 Only part of the rise in volatility in late 1929 and early 1930 was due to the Great Crash itself. The repeated surging and plummeting of stock prices between November 1929 and June 1930 also increased volatility tremendously. In Romer (1990) I show that overall stock price volatility was much higher in 1929 and 1930 than it was following the stock market correction in October 1987. This difference in volatility is large enough to explain why the real effects were so much smaller in 1988 than in 1930.

1928. The stock market crash is the prime source for the collapse in durable goods purchases starting in November 1929. Pointing to the stock market, of course, only pushes back the mystery one level. However, the research discussed by White (1990) suggests that the boom and bust of stock prices can best be described as a bubble that burst. Since bubbles are, almost by definition, inexplicable events, the stock price swing is legitimately viewed as an exogenous shock. Furthermore, since the stock market boom and crash were, to a first approximation, a uniquely American phenomenon, the onset of the Great Depression in the United States had uniquely American roots.

The Worsening of the Great Depression

If the American Great Depression was severe by late 1930, over the next two years it became horrific. As Figure 13.2 shows, after recovering slightly at the start of 1931, industrial production in the United States tumbled steadily from April 1931 until July 1932. Over this 15-month period, industrial production declined nearly 43 percent; by July 1932, the index of industrial production stood at less than half of its peak value in July 1929. Unemployment increased at a rate one would expect given the fall in output; by 1932, the unemployment rate stood at over 24 percent. Prices also behaved as one would expect if the fall in output were caused by a decline in aggregate demand: the producer price index declined by slightly over 40 percent between July 1929 and July 1932.

The source of the continued decline in production in the United States was almost surely a series of banking panics. Beginning with a first minor wave of panics in the fall of 1930, Friedman and Schwartz (1963) document four waves of banking panics in the United States. The second wave occurred in the spring of 1931, the third in the fall of 1931, following Britain's abandonment of the gold standard, and the fourth in the winter of 1933, around the time of Roosevelt's inauguration. Over the four years from 1930 to 1933, more than 9000 banks suspended operations and depositors and stockholders lost roughly $2.5 billion (Friedman and Schwartz, 1963, p. 351), the equivalent of 2.4 percent of nominal GNP in 1929.

The impact of these banking failures took many forms. First, the bank failures had a direct impact on the money supply. As depositors became nervous about the safety of banks, the ratio of deposits to currency fell dramatically. This greatly reduced the money multiplier, with the implication that a given stock of high-powered money could then support a much smaller total money supply. Because the Federal Reserve did nothing to increase the stock of high-powered money, the money supply declined sharply.[15] For example, Ml (currency plus demand deposits) declined 28 percent between July 1929 and July 1932. The realized real interest rates given in Figure 13.3 show that real rates were very high in 1931 and 1932. This is what one would expect if the monetary contraction generated substantial deflation and nominal rates were bounded by zero. Regression estimates of the expected real rate also

15 Indeed, in October 1931 the Federal Reserve deliberately raised the discount rate and as a consequence lowered the money supply substantially further.

averaged over 10 percent in these two years. Such high real interest rates are no doubt part of the reason that fixed investment plummeted during this phase of the Great Depression.

The banking panics almost surely also affected the economy in ways unrelated to interest rates. For example, Temin (1976) finds that pessimism had replaced uncertainty among consumers and businessmen by the end of 1930. The financial upheaval surely contributed to this pessimism and is likely to have further depressed consumer spending and investment. The financial panics also disrupted the intermediation function of banks. Bernanke (1983) points out that banks are an important source of funds for small businesses that cannot issue stocks or bonds. When a particular bank fails, all of the long-term relationships and information about local small borrowers accumulated by the bank are lost. It becomes more expensive for another bank to loan to one of the failed bank's customers, because it has to learn all over again which firms are prudent and which are unreliable. Bernanke finds that this rise in the "cost of credit intermediation" caused by bank failures was important in 1931 and 1932 and explains much of the deepening of the Great Depression in the United States during this time. The disruption of intermediation presumably worked through credit rationing of small borrowers and the related decline in investment.

Having argued that the banking crises of 1931 and later were a crucial cause of the deepening and sustaining of the Great Depression in the United States, the obvious questions are what caused the financial panics and why did the Federal Reserve do so little to contain them. The cause of Federal Reserve inaction is the easier of the two questions to answer. Friedman and Schwartz stress ineptitude and fear as the main culprits (1963, pp. 371, 407–19). They believe that certainly up through October 1930, the Federal Reserve could have stepped in with expansionary open market operations which would have raised output and put banks on a firmer footing. In particular, they argue that the U.S. gold supply was such that the Federal Reserve could have pursued a unilateral expansionary monetary policy without running into a serious constraint from the gold standard. The Federal Reserve failed to act, Friedman and Schwartz argue, because of a fear that monetary expansion would reignite speculation on the stock market, and because a power vacuum on the Board of Governors led to deadlock and indecision.

After mid-1931, it is harder to make the argument that the Federal Reserve was unconstrained by the gold standard. When Britain abandoned the gold standard in September 1931, the United States experienced a serious outflow of gold because there was widespread speculation that the U.S. would be forced to devalue soon as well. Eichengreen argues that in this situation the Federal Reserve had no choice but to raise interest rates in hopes of stemming the gold drain (1992, pp. 293–98). Friedman and Schwartz disagree, arguing that the Federal Reserve was in a very strong position to withstand the gold outflow because of its still large gold reserves and its legal power to suspend gold reserve requirements if they should become binding (1963, p. 396). At the very least, Friedman and Schwartz suggest, the Federal Reserve could have been more willing to discount bills brought to them by member banks at the higher interest rate than they actually were, thereby allowing banks experiencing runs to get much needed cash.

Whatever one's view of the pressure that the gold standard ultimately put on the Federal Reserve's ability to respond to the financial panics in 1931, there is little doubt that the Federal Reserve could have done something to stop the first wave of panics in late 1930. If one believes that the panics built on one another through the effect on income and the effect on expectations, then a different decision by the Federal Reserve in the fall of 1930 might have prevented the later panics that so decimated the U.S. financial system. In this case, one would have to say that American policy mistakes in 1930 played a crucial role in determining the course of output not just in 1930, but in later years as well.

Uniquely American factors are also important for explaining why the United States was so prone to financial panics in the first place. Bernanke and James (1991) point out that many countries in the world experienced financial crises in the 1930s. However, the source of the financial fragility in the United States was quite different from that of other countries. For example, the organization of American banking, with its emphasis on small, undiversified banks, made the American financial system particularly susceptible to local shocks and unable to withstand runs. More important, the great expansion of agricultural lending during World War I left the American farm sector unusually heavily in debt. When deflation started in 1930, farmers were the first to default, and this sent undiversified rural banks into failure (Chandler, 1970, pp. 53–66). The unique conjunction of undiversified banking and a particularly large increase in agricultural indebtedness in the 1920s made the financial panics in the United States both more severe and more persistent than in other countries. Again, the American problems of 1931 and 1932 stem from peculiarly American roots.

Sources of the American Recovery

In the spring of 1932, the Federal Reserve adopted a noticeably expansionary monetary policy, largely under the threat from Congress that if it did nothing the legislature would intervene. The behavior of expected real interest rates shown in Figure 13.3 and the path of industrial production shown in Figure 13.2 suggest that this monetary expansion lowered real interest rates and generated a noticeable recovery in real output in the United States. Industrial production rose 12 percent in the four months between July and November of 1932. However, this monetary expansion ceased when Congress adjourned in July and the Federal Reserve was able to return to its policy of caution. In early 1933, the final wave of banking panics pushed the economy back into depression. Only in April 1933 did the American recovery begin in earnest.

The recovery of the United States from the Great Depression has been alternatively described as very fast and very slow. It was very rapid in the sense that the growth rate of real output was very large in the years between 1933 and 1937 and after 1938. Monthly industrial production increased by 79 percent between the trough in March 1933 and the peak in July 1937. As shown in Table 13.1, annual industrial production in 1933 actually increased faster in the United States than in any other country. This expansion was not limited to industrial output. Real GNP grew at an average rate of nearly 10 percent per year in the four years between 1933 and 1937, and again in the three years between the recession of 1938 and the outbreak of World War II in the United States in December 1941.

The recovery was nevertheless slow in the sense that the fall in output in the United States was so severe that, despite these impressive growth rates, real GNP did not return to its pre-Depression level until 1937 and its pre-Depression growth path until around 1942. This fact leads to the frequently heard statement that the American Depression did not end until the outbreak of World War II.

The war, however, was not the main source of the American recovery, at least not in the way that is typically thought. In another paper, I find that the U.S. economy began recovering in 1933 primarily because of huge increases in the money supply (Romer, 1992). Soon after taking office, Roosevelt, using emergency powers granted to him by the Congress, allowed the dollar to depreciate substantially. A new lower price for the dollar was fixed by law in January 1934. This devaluation greatly increased the nominal value of existing American gold stocks. The Treasury could have ignored the increase in the nominal value of its gold reserves and left the money supply unchanged. Instead, the Treasury issued gold certificates equal to the amount of the increase in gold reserves and deposited them at the Federal Reserve. As the government spent the money, these gold certificates were converted into Federal Reserve notes, which are a component of the monetary base. As a result, high-powered money in the United States increased 12 percent between April 1933 and April 1934.

Devaluation also brought with it a large inflow of monetary gold from abroad as foreigners traded gold for the now less expensive dollars. After 1934, gold continued to flow to the United States because of political unrest in Europe. Hitler's increasing belligerence caused Europeans to want to invest in American assets, which required that they buy dollars with gold. The Treasury could have sterilized this gold inflow by borrowing the dollars to trade for the gold. Instead, the Treasury paid for the gold with deposits at the Federal Reserve, and then replenished its account by issuing gold certificates. As a result, high-powered money increased another 40 percent between April 1934 and April 1937.

This increase in high-powered money led to an increase in Ml of almost the same amount: Ml increased 49 percent between April 1933 and April 1937. That Ml did not increase by more than the base is evidence that the money supply was growing during the mid-1930s because of policy decisions and political events in Europe, rather than because of endogenous changes in the money multiplier caused by the recovery itself. Temin and Wigmore (1990) argue that, even before the money supply actually increased, devaluation helped to spur recovery by signalling the switch to a more expansionary monetary regime. They suggest that devaluation immediately stimulated purchases of farm equipment and other capital goods by generating expectations of future monetary ease, inflation, and real economic growth.

After 1934 the huge increases in the American money supply had exactly the effect on the U.S. economy that a traditional aggregate supply-aggregate demand model would lead one to predict. Figure 13.3 shows that real interest rates plummeted in response to the gold inflows. This came about because nominal rates fell slightly and actual and expected inflation rose substantially (the producer price index rose at over 8 percent per year between January 1933 and January 1937). This fall in real interest rates was followed fairly quickly by a recovery of interest-sensitive spending, such as construction spending and consumer purchases of durable goods. This effect can be seen in the fact that the American recovery, more than in other countries, was led by a surge in the output of investment goods. One piece of evidence that suggests a causal link between the fall in interest rates and the surge in particular types of spending in the United States is the fact that American consumer spending on durable goods turned around before consumer spending on services. This indicates that some factor that affected only durables purchases, such as a fall in interest rates, was initiating the recovery.[16]

That increases in the money supply generated the recovery suggests that movements in aggregate demand were as important for ending the Great Depression in the United States as they were for causing it. However, there is an obvious question about whether the increase in the U.S. money supply during the recovery should be considered an accident caused by international developments or the predictable result of conscious American policy. The right interpretation, I believe, is a mixture of both. The political upheaval in Europe that caused gold to flow to the United States was clearly an international shock. Indeed, there is a very real sense in which the tension leading up to the outbreak of World War II in Europe did help to end the American Depression by causing the U.S. money stock to grow.

On the other hand, Johnson (1939) shows that the Roosevelt administration consciously chose to devalue and not to sterilize the subsequent gold inflows, precisely because it wanted to increase the money supply and cause inflation. In this way, the international gold flows may simply have provided a convenient way for the executive branch to bypass the overly cautious Federal Reserve. In the absence of such gold flows, Roosevelt and the Congress would quite possibly have used the threat of amending the Federal Reserve's operating procedures to force the Federal Reserve to increase the money supply. However, devaluation was clearly important in any case, because no country could pursue a wildly expansionary monetary policy for a sustained period and still maintain a fixed exchange rate. Thus, as argued by Eichengreen and Sachs (1985), the decision to abandon the old gold parity was a crucial precondition for recovery.

Conclusion

The American Depression was unique in many ways. While many countries experienced a depression at roughly the same time as the United States, the onset of decline and the

16 The monetary expansion and the concurrent restructuring of the banking system could also have stimulated construction and investment through increased credit availability.

subsequent rebound were much more extreme in the United States than elsewhere. The overall depth of the Great Depression was also larger in the United States than in any country other than Poland. Finally, the American Depression was initiated by a fall in consumption and ended by a rise in investment to a degree that was quite different from the experience of many other industrial countries.

The picture that I have painted of the American Great Depression is one that stresses the importance of national, rather than international, aggregate demand shocks; the experience of the United States during the 1930s differed in important ways from that of other countries because the American experience had many uniquely American roots. The United States slipped into recession in mid-1929 because of tight domestic monetary policy aimed at stemming speculation on the U.S. stock market. The Great Depression started in earnest when the stock market crash in the United States caused consumers and firms to become nervous and therefore to stop buying irreversible durable goods. The American Depression worsened when banking panics swept undiversified and overextended rural banks and the Federal Reserve failed to intervene. Finally, the American Depression ended when the Roosevelt administration chose to increase the money supply tremendously after 1933.

Most of these shocks contain an international element, in one way or another. The tight monetary policy of 1928 was partly aimed at stopping a gold outflow. The Federal Reserve was less able to respond to financial panics in 1931 because expansionary monetary policy would have led to a serious loss of gold. Increasing the money supply after 1933 was very simple because capital flight from Europe brought billions of dollars worth of gold to the United States. Although these international complications were present, they were not decisive. At each stage of the Great Depression, it was ultimately American shocks and American policy decisions that determined the path of American output and employment.

References

Allen, Steven G., "Changes in the Cyclical Sensitivity of Wages in the United States, 1891–1987," *American Economic Review,* March 1992, *82,* 122–40.

Bernanke, Ben, "Nonmonetary Effects of the Financial Crisis in the Propagation of the Great Depression," *American Economic Review,* June 1983, *73:3,* 257–76.

Bernanke, Ben, and Harold James, "The Gold Standard, Deflation, and Financial Crisis in the Great Depression: An International Comparison." In Hubbard, R. Glenn, ed., *Financial Markets and Financial Crises.* Chicago: University of Chicago Press for NBER, 1991, 33–68.

Chandler, Alfred D., *The Visible Hand: The Managerial Revolution in American Business.* Cambridge: The Belknap Press of Harvard University Press, 1977.

Chandler, Lester V., *America's Greatest Depression, 1929-1941.* New York: Harper and Row, 1970.

De Long, J. Bradford, and Lawrence H. Summers, "Is Increased Price Flexibility Stabilizing?" *American Economic Review,* December 1986, *76:5,* 1031–44.

Eichengreen, Barry, *Golden Fetters: The Gold Standard and the Great Depression, 1919-1939.* New York: Oxford University Press, 1992.

Eichengreen, Barry, and Jeffrey D. Sachs, "Exchange Rates and Economic Recovery in the 1930s," *Journal of Economic History,* December 1985, *45,* 925–46.

Field, Alexander, "Asset Exchanges and the Transactions Demand for Money, 1919–1929," *American Economic Review,* March 1984, *74:1,* 43–59.

Fisher, Irving, "The Debt-Deflation Theory of Great Depressions," *Econometrica,* October 1933, *1, 337–57.*

Friedman, Milton, and Anna J. Schwartz, *A Monetary History of the United States, 1867–1960.* Princeton: Princeton University Press for NBER, 1963.

Gorden, Robert J., "A Consistent Characterization of a Near-Century of Price Behavior," *American Economic Review Papers and Proceedings,* May 1980, *70,* 243–49.

Hamilton, James D., "Monetary Factors in the Great Depression," *Journal of Monetary Economics,* March 1987, *19,* 145–69.

Jacoby, Sanford, *Employing Bureaucracy: Managers, Unions, and the Transformation of Work in American Industry, 1900-1945.* New York: Columbia University Press, 1985.

Johnson, G. Griffith, *The Treasury and Monetary Policy, 1933–1938.* Cambridge: Harvard University Press, 1939.

Kendrick, John W., *Productivity Trends in the United States.* Princeton: Princeton University Press for NBER, 1961.

Kindleberger, Charles, *The World in Depression.* Berkeley: University of California Press, 1973.

League of Nations, *Review of World Production, 1925–1931.* Geneva, 1932.

League of Nations, *World Production and Prices,* 1935/36 and 1937/38. Geneva, 1936 and 1938.

Lewis, William Arthur, *Economic Survey, 1919–1939.* London: George Allen and Unwin, 1949.

Mishkin, Frederic S., "The Household Balance Sheet and the Great Depression," *Journal of Economic History,* December 1978, *38,* 918–37.

Mitchell, Daniel J. B., "Wage Flexibility: Then and Now," *Industrial Relations,* Spring 1985, *24,* 266–79.

O'Brien, Anthony Patrick, "A Behavioral Explanation for Nominal Wage Rigidity During the Great Depression," *Quarterly Journal of Economics,* November 1989, *104,* 719–35.

Romer, Christina D., "The Great Crash and the Onset of the Great Depression," *Quarterly Journal of Economics,* August 1990, *105,* 597–624.

Romer, Christina D., "What Ended the Great Depression?" *Journal of Economic History,* December 1992, *52,* 757–84.

Sachs, Jeffrey, "The Changing Cyclical Behavior of Wages and Prices, 1890-1976," *American Economic Review,* March 1980, *70:1,* 78–90.

Schultze, Charles L., "Some Macro Foundations for Micro Theory," *Brookings Papers on Economic Activity,* 1981:*2,* 521–76.

Standard Statistics Co., *Standard Statistical Bulletin,* 1930-31 Base Book Issue. New York: Standard Statistics Co., 1930.

Temin, Peter, *Did Monetary Forces Cause the Great Depression?* New York: W. W. Norton, 1976.

Temin, Peter, *Lessons from the Great Depression.* Cambridge: M.I.T. Press, 1989.

Temin, Peter, and Barrie A. Wigmore, "The End of One Big Deflation," *Explorations in Economic History,* October 1990, *27,* 483–502.

Tobin, James, "Keynesian Models of Recession and Depression," *American Economic Review Papers and Proceedings,* May 1975, *65,* 195–202.

U.S. Board of Governors of the Federal Reserve System, *Banking and Monetary Statistics.* Washington, D.C., 1943 and 1976.

U.S. Board of Governors of the Federal Reserve System, *Industrial Production,* 1986 Edition. Washington, D.C., 1986.

U.S. Bureau of Economic Analysis, *National Income and Product Accounts of the United States, 1929–1982.* Washington, D.C., 1986.

U.S. Bureau of Labor Statistics, *Historical Data on the Producer Price Index.* Microfiche. Washington, D.C. 1986.

U.S. Bureau of the Census, *Historical Statistics of the United States, Colonial Times to 1970.* Washington, D.C., 1975.

White, Eugene N., "The Stock Market Boom and Crash of 1929 Revisited," *Journal of Economic Perspectives,* Spring 1990, *4:2,* 67–83.

Topic Eight Questions

1. According to Eugene White, what was the role of fundamentals in the boom market of the 1920s? What was the role of a bubble?
2. Why does Christina Romer title her reading "The Nation in Depression?" In what ways was the Great Depression in the United States different than in the rest of the world?
3. Describe the changes to each of the components of GNP during the 1930s: consumption, investments, net exports, and government purchases.

Printed by Libri Plureos GmbH in Hamburg, Germany

9 781516 546107